D0821489

THE
WHOLE
OF
THEIR
LIVES

THE WHOLE
OF
THEIR LIVES

Communism in America—A Personal History
and
Intimate Portrayal of its Leaders

BY
BENJAMIN GITLOW
WITH A FOREWORD BY
MAX EASTMAN

Biography Index Reprint Series

BOOKS FOR LIBRARIES PRESS
FREEPORT, NEW YORK

INTERNATIONAL STANDARD BOOK NUMBER:
0-8369-8094-8

LIBRARY OF CONGRESS CATALOG CARD NUMBER:
78-179726

PRINTED IN THE UNITED STATES OF AMERICA
BY
NEW WORLD BOOK MANUFACTURING CO., INC.
HALLANDALE, FLORIDA 33009

TO MY WIFE—BADANA

The labor involved in this work would
have been impossible without her devotion and loyalty, especially in the dark
and fearful years of adversity, when it
required many sacrifices on her part, and
courage too, to stand together with me
against the hostile stream.

CONTENTS

FOREWORD

By Max Eastman

I have known Ben Gitlow for thirty-five years. He is a heroic figure to me, and to others who know intimately what he went through. His moral force is of the kind we need desperately in these days.

Our civilization is in peril because so many eager and uncritical minds, beguiled by the communist ideal, instead of being trained in virtue, are trained to renounce all moral standards in the service of their ideal. Those consecrating themselves to communism must not only cast out truth, mercy, justice, and personal honor, but undergo a sickening discipline in lies, cruelty, crime, and self-abasement. They must endorse such "Leninist" maxims as these:

"We do not believe in external principles of morality . . . Communist morality is identical with the fight to strengthen the dictatorship of the proletariat."

"We must be ready to employ trickery, deceit, lawbreaking, withholding and concealing truth."

"We can and must write . . . in a language which sows among the masses hate, revulsion, scorn and the like toward those of differing opinion."

This doctrine of immorality on principle, invented by Marx, brought into focus by Lenin, and carried into limitless action by Stalin, is playing a major role in the disintegration of our Graeco-Christian civilization. Many who go in for communism in a mood of high-minded revolt against lesser evils come to a point where they realize this fact and apprehend its consequences with horror. But by that time they are consecrated; they are fixed firm. Their whole life-pattern—daily bread and daily nutriment of esteem—is conditioned upon their staying firm. They lack the force of character, the clarity of mind, the self-reliance, the pure and sheer daring, to back out and be called a renegade.

That is what Ben Gitlow did. He was no literary sympathizer changing his view on the sidelines. He was the most devoted communist in the United States—his devotion proven, at least, by the severest test—and he backed out from the inmost positions of power.

From infancy Gitlow had breathed in the idea that if a workers' state took over the industries and operated them without paying profits to capital, there would be no more poverty or injustice in the world. His father, driven out of Russia by the Czar's police, earned his living in a shirt factory in New York, but worked in a little socialist print shop on the side. His mother too was a worker—a mirthful and much loved worker—for socialism. Ben was a regular American boy, good at baseball, better at the shot-put, still better at football, and continually elected president of his class. But he read more highbrow books than the other boys, and he joined the Socialist Party at sixteen as a mere matter of course.

After completing three years of high school, he took jobs in factories and department stores in order to help his brother through medical college. His real career, however, was in the Socialist Party as orator and organizer. He became the first president of the first department store workers union in America, losing a good job in the process. And by the time the Bolshevik Revolution occurred in Russia he was a socialist member from the Bronx of the New York State Legislature.

He believed that the day which he had awaited almost from the cradle was about to dawn. His socialism had always been of the militant type, more concerned with labor action than the pious dreams of the reformists. And his first thought now was to join the "left wingers" in organizing an American Communist Party. His lifelong conviction and cool courage gave him a leading role in this hazardous undertaking—gave him the prickly distinction, also, of being the first man arrested in the United States for advocating communism.

His trial occurred in 1919 in the midst of the famous "red raids" of Attorney General Palmer. Clarence Darrow undertook to get him off by hushing the implications of the subversive things he had said. But Gitlow would have nothing to do with that. He was a revolutionist, and he insisted that Darrow defend him on the sole ground of the "right of revolution." It was a day of joy for the extreme reds when Gitlow stood up to receive sentence. Instead of mitigating his crime, he redoubled it by denouncing the United States Government as a "capitalist dictatorship," calling for its overthrow, and demanding the inauguration in its place of a "dictatorship of the proletariat." For this act of daring, he received from the court the maximum sentence of five to ten years at hard labor, and from his party comrades the crown of perfect martyrdom. No other communist career in the United States opened so brilliantly or contained such promise. The Moscow Soviet elected him an honorary member, and the Soviet government tried to secure his release by offering an arrested American, known to history as Kirkpatrick, in exchange.

After serving three years in Sing Sing Prison, Gitlow was pardoned by the "capitalist dictatorship"—pardoned, to be slightly more exact, by Governor Al Smith—and went back to his task of organizing the dictatorship of the proletariat. In the succeeding years he occupied every important post in the American Communist Party: editor-in-chief of its paper, member of its Political Committee, member of its Secretariat of Three, General Secretary of the Party, director of its strike and trade union policy, secret leader of the Passaic textile workers strike, the biggest communist strike in our history, and twice the communist candidate for Vice President. He made his first trip to Moscow in 1927 at the special request of the Kremlin. An extended conversation with Stalin on the problems of the American movement ensured him the highest advancement. He became a member of the executive committee both of the Red Trade Union International and the Communist International, and within the latter was elected to the Praesidium, the inside ruling group of the world communist movement.

He was, in short, a top communist leader, and every road to prestige and power in the life he had chosen was open before him. He had only to stifle a growing doubt in his mind as to whether this power that tasted so sweet was really leading to the liberation of the proletariat—as to whether, indeed, a party dictatorship could ever lead to the liberation of anybody. He had accepted Lenin's one-party system as a temporary expedient because Russia, while laying the foundations of socialism, was surrounded by a hostile world. No one foresaw that Stalin would one day announce in the same breath the "complete victory of socialism" and the permanence of the one-party system. But Gitlow at least had premonitions. From the first he found it hard to believe that this overbearing military discipline of the members of a small party was the *one and only* road to the millennium. Life seemed to him too complex, the world "much too large," as he says, for this single and simple solution of a problem involving the whole of mankind.

In the minds of most strong leaders the social ideal and the power with which they hope to achieve it become blended inextricably. And power, being the more primitive object of desire, has the stronger hold on their wills. When loyalty to both becomes impossible, it is the ideal that goes overboard, not the struggle for power. That is how champions of the people become tyrants over them. That is how "dictatorship of the proletariat" becomes dictatorship of a party over the proletariat, dictatorship of a politburo over the party, dictatorship of a man over the politburo. This march of events was completed when Ben Gitlow attended a meeting of the Praesidium of the Communist International in Moscow, May 1929.

Stalin was then just clenching his control of the Russian Communist Party by eliminating his last rival, Bukharin, and was preparing to extend his sway to the remote corners of the Comintern. The American party was the only one in the world which sent up a delegation resolved to defend its right to independent judgment. Gitlow and Lovestone were the leaders of this party, elected by an immense majority over a faction led by William Z. Foster. To break their wills, Stalin had his henchmen introduce into the Praesidium an "Address to the American Party," in which their leadership was denounced in the immoderate language customary among Bolsheviks: they were "Right deviators," "unprincipled opportunists," "gross intriguers," "slanderers of the Russian Communist Party," etc. etc. This, it was proposed, Gitlow should vote for and the whole delegation should sign. Instead, the American delegates prepared a unanimous "Declaration" rejecting it on grounds of conscience and conviction. That was a new and distinctly American note in the history of the Comintern, and it brought Stalin in person to the Praesidium. His words were brusque, rude, and abusive. They do not appear so in the official record, but the substance of what he said is there:

"You are, of course, familiar with the Declaration. Comrade Gitlow read it here during the course of his speech. The fundamental feature of this Declaration is that it proclaims the thesis of *non-submission* to the decisions of the Praesidium of the Executive Committee of the Communist International. That means that the extreme factionalism of the leaders of the majority has driven them into the path of insubordination, and hence of warfare against the Comintern . . .

"And now the question arises: do the members of the American delegation, as communists, as Leninists, consider themselves entitled not to submit to the decision of the Executive Committee of the Comintern on the American question?"

To obtain an answer to this question Stalin proposed that the Praesidium take an immediate vote on the Address to the American Party. This put straight up to Gitlow the question of moral principle. If he voted yes, he would confess himself a false leader and brand himself with the epithets quoted above. His "confession" would be in the hands of the dictator, his submission absolute and irrevocable. We have seen this done a thousand times; it is the method by which the solidarity of the communist parties is maintained. Though the fact is little known, even Trotsky at one time "confessed his mistakes" and "capitulated" at the demand of the party heads.

The Address to the American Party was adopted unanimously except for one vote. That was Gitlow's.

The American delegation was present, and Stalin's next move was to demand that each one stand up and declare personally whether or not he would abide by the decision of the Praesidium of the Executive Committee of the Communist International. He was out to conquer America, and to conquer these leaders of the American party was the first step. Gitlow has described what happened.*

"One by one the members of our delegation took the floor and stated that they adhered to the Declaration which we had submitted. I believe that never before had the Red Hall of the Comintern witnessed such a dramatic closing . . . Bedacht was pacing up and down in the rear. He turned to me. His face was pale and covered with a cold sweat. 'Comrade Gitlow! It is now a decision! The whole situation is changed! We must accept! I will accept!' I looked at him with disgust. I turned to Lovestone and told him about Bedacht . . . Then Lovestone rose to speak. He ended with the declaration that he stood by the statement of our delegation. I was to speak last, after Lovestone . . . I stated that I could not accept the demand put upon me to discredit myself before the American working class, for I would not only be discrediting myself and the leadership of the Party, but the Party itself which gave rise to such a leadership. I spoke slowly and calmly. Yet my whole being was aflame with the deepest emotions, for I was taking a stand that would cut, perhaps forever, the

* In his book, *I Confess*, copyright 1939. E. P. Dutton Co., N. Y.

knot that tied me to the communist movement, the movement I helped to build in the United States, the movement for which I had gone to prison. I had given all of my time and efforts to the movement, never seeking position, honor, or reward, because I believed that communism paved the way to economic betterment and freedom never before enjoyed by the individual. But in what Stalin was proposing I recognized the seeds of a despotism that would be more ugly, more brutal than the despotism of the Czars. I spoke out. 'Not only do I vote against the decision, but when I return to the United States, I will fight against it!' As I said this, I looked straight at Stalin. It left the crowd aghast for a moment. Then a long drawn-out whistle arose from the crowd, as if it wanted to say, 'Whew, did you hear that?'

"Stalin rushed to the platform. I had never seen him so angry before. His reserve was gone, and the low, slow delivery supposedly characteristic of the man, a delivery which he affected, was gone. He burst into a tirade against us."

Again the rough talk is omitted from the official record, but the essence of Stalin's speech, so far as concerns the great question at issue, is contained in these words:

"Apparently the comrades do not fully realize that to defend one's convictions when the decision had not yet been taken is one thing, and to submit to the will of the Comintern after the decision has been taken is another . . . True Bolshevik courage does not consist in placing one's individual will above the will of the Comintern. True courage consists in being strong enough to master and overcome oneself and subordinate one's will to the will of the collective, the will of the higher party body . . . And this is true not only in respect to individual parties and their central committees; it is particularly true in respect to the Comintern and its directing organs, which unite all parties of communists throughout the world . . . They talk of their conscience and convictions . . . But what is to be done if the conscience and conviction of the Praesidium conflict with the conscience and conviction of individual members of the American delegation? What is to be done if the American delegation received only one vote for their declaration, the vote of Comrade Gitlow, while the remaining members of the Praesidium unanimously declared themselves against the declaration?"

A very simple thing, of course, was done. The American delegates, with the exception of Max Bedacht, were promptly demoted

from their posts in the party. Comrade Gitlow was dropped from
the Praesidium and from the Executive Committees of the Profintern
and the Comintern, and by the time he got home he was expelled
from the American Party. From being a high official in a power-
structure supposedly on its way to take over the world, he became
an obscure, penniless, professionless and well-nigh friendless person,
walking the streets of New York looking for a job.

This was no surprise to him. He knew what he was doing to
himself when he defied Stalin. The act was deliberate—as deliberate
as his defiance of the United States government had been. In both
cases it was a matter of standing up for his convictions.

I think the second defiance required a higher kind of courage—
it certainly required more intellectual force—than the first. There was
no joy of the fanatic in it, no glory of the leader, no martyr's halo,
no gang support, no place in other minds, no future for himself—
nothing but obscurity, poverty, solitude, and the stigma of a renegade.

No, it was not "Bolshevik courage"—the courage to subordinate
oneself to a gang that is doing what one does not believe should be
done. In that Stalin was right. And I think the contrast between
these two kinds of courage, or rather between the two conceptions of
morality lying behind them, is quite as momentous to mankind as the
contrast between the two economic systems prevailing in Russia and
the United States.

In substituting for the old heaven beyond the clouds a new
paradise called "classless society" to be attained right here on earth,
Marx supplied a faith and goal-of-sacrifice to many doubt-bewildered
minds. But in declaring civil war, and the morals of civil war, to be
the road to this new paradise, he set these minds free from the restraints that make any decent society possible. He drew a dividing
line between ideal aspiration and right conduct. He turned the best
men into the worst. It is for the sake of a world in which men shall
live together in truth, love, justice, freedom, and loving-kindness that
the communists actually *teach* hate, lies, treacheries, tortures, slanders,
self-abasements, murders—massacres if need be. These are the sanc-
tified roads to the goal. Humanity has never been, nor can conceiv-
ably be, confronted with a menace more fateful than this.

That is why it is so important that Ben Gitlow's non-bolshevik
courage be understood and appreciated. While waiting in Moscow for
a visa, uncertain when, or indeed whether, he would get home, he
wrote to his wife:

"Regardless of what happened or may happen, as far as I am concerned, I made a clean, principled fight. I have not lost my self-respect; that is important. I can look everyone square in the face . . . If I had been unprincipled, I could have risen to the zenith of power and place. Now I have lost whatever place I had."

In making his principled fight against the pressure of this debased religion and its church, the monolithic party, Ben Gitlow was defending not only democracy, but civilization itself against totalitarian degeneration.

THE
WHOLE
OF
THEIR
LIVES

"We must train men and women who will devote to the revolution, not merely their spare evenings, but the *whole of their lives.*"

VLADIMIR ILYITCH ULIANOV—LENIN

From LENIN ON ORGANIZATION, page 44, paragraph 7. Daily Worker Publishing Co., 1926.

Lenin first wrote the above quotation in the Social Democratic newspaper *Iskra,* No. 1, in 1900.

CHAPTER ONE

THE ROMANTIC PERIOD

WHEN Lenin in 1917 addressed the people of Petrograd from the balcony of the palace of the dancer, the beautiful Kshesinskaia, the courtesan of Tsar Nicholas II, the people listened to him with mixed feelings, many with expressions of hostility. They did not recognize mighty Russia's destiny in the little fellow dressed in baggy pants who addressed them. They were puzzled when he warned:

> "Here in the palace of the former imperial ballerina are coming in streams the Russian delegates from the factories, with the gray, scarred and lousy messengers from the trenches, and from here new, prophetic words will spread over the land."

But Lenin knew what he was saying. He foresaw how his prophetic words would spread from Russia throughout the world. Indeed in a few short months what Lenin said from the ballerina's balcony swept like a prairie fire over the earth, reaching every nook and corner of the United States where radicals congregated. From New York to San Francisco, from Duluth to New Orleans, in mines and mills, on the corners of skid rows, in hobo jungles, beer halls, labor temples, at union meetings, among the denizens of Greenwich Village and Chicago's Dill Pickle Club, in squalid tenements and sumptuous apartments, socialists, anarchists, wobblies, liberals, intellectuals of the left, workers, aristocrats and bohunks of every shade and color, from light pink and yellow to deepest red, huddled together and in heated discussions weighed the significance of what came from the lips of Russia's red messiah.

Great is the power of words and of ideology over man. The American radicals succumbed to Lenin's words. They repeated them over and over again as if they were learning a new vocabulary—the vocabulary of revolution. Lenin's words were fine-sounding words;

3

words of hate that called for action, that inflamed emotions. Overnight the American radicals became ardent converts of Lenin. They hit the revolutionary trail with gusto. Their exaltation developed in them a fanaticism so extreme, so cocksure that no one dared question the infallibility of what Lenin said. From him the American radicals got what they were looking for—a guide to action—the short cut to revolution.

Out of this fanaticism the American communist movement was born—a movement which turned the American radicals who joined it into intolerant zealots. American radicals discarded their idealism, their devotion to humanity, for the rituals of communist bigotry. In less than two years communism succeeded in tearing down the old structure of American radicalism by firmly establishing the communist hegemony over the radical scene.

The radicals, who became communists, went through a personal metamorphosis so complete that they were mentally and morally changed into different human beings. The men and women who took the road to communism became the voluntary victims of a conditioning process which subjugated the will of the individual to the will of the organization. Converts had to prostrate themselves before the supreme revolutionary authority of the communist organization. Honest idealists became knaves. Men abandoned families, on party orders, to live with women communists. Patriotic soldiers became traitors and spies.

Dreamers and visionaries, the timid souls among the radicals, were transformed into machiavellian political tricksters and hardened conspirators. Men and women imbued with a compassionate tenderness for others became sadistic gangsters. Intellectuals deserted the truth to become communist artists in uniform, prostituting their abilities in order to serve the party line and pollute the cultural life of America.

Chicanery, intrigue, conceit, tricks of the sycophants and double-dealers—the black attributes of Satan and his fallen angels—constitute the stock in trade of the communists not only in dealing with their enemies but also in their relations with each other and with their friends. The fact that the communists are caught in the mesh of their own Mephistophelian system explains why the history of American communism is, in addition to its other aspects, a story of personalities and events taken from the handbook of crime.

The story of American communism begins with the outbreak of the Bolshevik Revolution in November, 1917. Prior to the emergence of communism on the American scene, native radicalism was a powerful influence in American life. In 1916 Eugene V. Debs, Socialist candidate for president of the United States, polled one million votes. The vote indicated that the Socialist party, counting women who did not have the franchise, unnaturalized foreigners and young people, had a following of over two million persons.

The I.W.W. (Industrial Workers of the World), a militant, radical, trade union organization, had grown into a significant aggregation of western lumber workers, metal miners, fishery and migratory workers, and also had considerable influence among textile and factory workers on the eastern seaboard.

The anarchists, with the fiery Emma Goldman and the intrepid Alexander Berkman at their head, constituted the third important section of American radicalism.

In the conservative trade unions of the American Federation of Labor progressivism began to make itself felt. The progressive trade unionists set themselves high ideals, were honest and did much to improve the conditions of the workers and to reform the trade unions.

To these main streams of American radicalism must be added the militant section of the women's suffrage movement whose leaders and members worked together with the radicals to batter down the opposition to women's suffrage. In the same category were the members of Margaret Sanger's birth control movement who went to prison for their beliefs and engaged in hunger strikes to force the authorities to release them.

Radical influences were especially strong among the foreign born. The Jews, Germans, Italians, Slavs and Irish made up a considerable proportion of the radical elements.

A conservative estimate of the numerical strength of American radicalism which made up the left when the communists struck out for power, places its number around the 3,000,000 mark. In 1917 American radicalism was predominantly American in its outlook and honest in its ideals. Thoroughly democratic, the American radicals worked for the betterment of mankind. Humanitarian to the core, American radicalism rested on the bedrock of individual liberty and recognition of the rights of man.

Lenin's young colts soon changed all this. They beat the communist tom toms. They fought and yelled at all meetings at which radicals congregated. With passion and venom they hurled about newly learned revolutionary phrases and slogans. Loudly they proclaimed that the American revolution was imminent. Overwhelmed by the rapid succession of revolutionary events in Europe which seemed to herald the doom of the capitalist world, and cowed by the bombardment of communist oratory, the American radicals fell prey to an ideology which was the antithesis of what they believed.

The communists aimed their "big berthas" at the Socialist party, the largest and most important section of American radicalism. They drew their inspiration from Lenin, who in his letter to the "American Working Class" in 1918 characterized the socialists with whom he disagreed as ". . . this scum of international socialism, these lackeys of bourgeois morality who think along these lines." Lenin's American stalwarts went after the "scum" in earnest. In less than a year's time the communists had gained an overwhelming and decisive majority of the Socialist party's 100,000 members. In less than two years' time they had wrecked the Socialist party so completely that the Socialists have never been able fully to reconstitute themselves as a party and a political force.

While the American communists were barnstorming the radicals, the Russian Bolsheviks, with a few handpicked delegates from European countries who were in Russia at the time, organized the Third, the Communist International—the Comintern. The American communists, even though they could not agree among themselves and had organized two communist parties which opposed each other, pledged their loyalty to the Comintern and joined the organization. John Reed rushed to Moscow to represent the Communist Labor party, to be followed soon afterwards by Louis C. Fraina, the representative of the Communist party of America.

Hell-bent for revolution the communists smashed everything in the radical movement which stood in their way. Institutions which it had taken the radical idealists years of self-sacrifice to maintain fell before the savage onslaught of the hammer and sickle. Mounting the shambles the communists unfurled the red flag and raised their clenched fists in defiance of American capitalism and the government. But eliminating those in the radical movement who opposed them did not bring the revolution. The final victory—the revolution—which was to drop the United States into their laps did not materialize.

Revolution Around the Corner

To the American radicals, who in 1917 aligned themselves with the Communists, the Russian Bolshevik Revolution was part of a world picture, a piece in a jig-saw puzzle that fitted into place and gave a clue to what the picture would be like when all the parts were finally pieced together. The seizure of power by the Bolsheviks was a signal that the die had been cast—that the era of decisive revolutionary struggles for control of the world was on. Without delay they set out to do in the United States what the Bolsheviks had done in Russia. Thus an event in a country thousands of miles away from the United States set the stage for the opéra bouffe which followed in America.

At the start the American communists operated as if the revolution was already on. They had the will to revolution and were intent on imposing their will upon the country. The communists, wherever they found themselves, independent of each other, took the initiative. They organized revolutionary committees, formed regiments of red guards, set up workers and soldiers councils and injected themselves into strike situations for the purpose of turning the strikes into political and revolutionary channels. They actually fomented general strikes and took over the affairs of cities in the United States and Canada. They published newspapers in all important industrial areas and distributed manifestoes by the millions calling upon the American workers to revolt.

Wildly enthusiastic crowds attended the hundreds of communist mass meetings which took place every week throughout the country. Money poured into communist coffers by the hundreds of thousands of dollars. As the war chests filled up the comrades became more bold and confident, and the leaders discussed schemes for crushing the United States government.

Two months after Tzar Nicholas II was deposed, at an anti-conscription meeting in New York Emma Goldman shouted:

"Follow Russia's lead!"

Pandemonium broke loose as the crowd in a wild frenzy started a demonstration. Fraina followed Goldman, declaring that the Russian revolution was not just a political revolution but a social revolution. He called attention to the Soviets of Workers, Soldiers and Sailors of Petrograd and predicted that similar soviets would soon rule Europe and the industrial centers of capitalist America. He predicted that the masses in the United States through their soviets would take matters into their own hands to end conscription, to end war and to bring about the downfall of all capitalist government. He ended by shouting: "Long live the Soviets! Long live the revolution!" A thunderous roar of approval burst from the wildly cheering crowd.

A manifesto distributed at the meeting asked: "Why don't you do the same things here that your brother workers are doing in Russia?"

From March, 1917, to June of the same year the revolutionary radicals who spearheaded the communist movement made every minute and every hour count. Anti-draft plots spread throughout the nation and into the schools and colleges. The movement, though branded pacifist, was distinctly anti-capitalist and revolutionary.

Alarmed, the country took special measures to counteract the movement. In New York the police prepared for an armed conflict. At a conference held in Madison Square Garden on the night of May 31, under the auspices of the First American Conference for Democracy and Peace Terms, the police, expecting trouble, displayed their new equipment for the suppression of revolutionary mobs. New York's finest patrolled the streets around the Garden with rifles and tommy guns. Police squads placed their machine guns at the strategic points from which they could mow down the crowds gathering to enter the conference. Powerful searchlights flooded the dark streets, and police on horseback with drawn revolvers raced up and down the street approaches to the Garden. In spite of all this display of suppressive power, the young radicals ran in and out of the surging mass of humanity, defied the police and distributed the banned anti-conscription and revolutionary manifestoes. The police succeeded in rounding up only five of their number, who cursed their captors and warned them that when the revolution came their heads would be rolling in the gutters.

Inside the Garden, every inch of space packed to capacity, a cheering, howling mass of humanity unanimously adopted a resolution calling for the immediate formation of a "People's Council" similar to the Council of Workers Soldiers and Sailors of Russia. Fifteen thousand inspired radicals voted for a resolution that called for revolution. They did not worry about the display of police power around the Garden. Meeting that power and even more power would come later when the American people backed the resolution with action—with bullets.

Another memorable meeting took place on the eve of registration for the draft at Hunts Point Palace, the Bronx. Ten minutes after the doors were opened every available space in the hall was occupied. Over three thousand persons jammed a hall that normally accommodated two thousand. And still the crowd kept streaming in from all directions. Police estimated that when the meeting started at 8 o'clock more than fifteen thousand persons were solidly massed on the street in front of the hall and another fifteen thousand in adjacent streets. New York had never before seen such a demonstration. The police had all they could do to control the crowds. A greater concentration of police suppressive power was in evidence than on the night of the Madison Square Garden meeting. A gauntlet of police, home guards and militia, each man belted with bullets and displaying a loaded revolver, lined both sides of the wide stairs leading to the hall.

The crowd outside was tense and excited. A little incident might create the spark to set off a mass explosion of bloody consequences. Powerful searchlights flooded the crowds. New York's plain-clothes detectives, assisted by men from patriotic agencies, mixed with the crowds in search of radicals armed with weapons.

Inside the hall one felt the nervous tension of the occasion. Alexander Berkman and Emma Goldman, reflecting the temper of the radical movement, exhorted the crowd with revolutionary appeals for action which landed them in prison and caused their deportation to Soviet Russia. Every mention of Soviet Russia, every mention of the impending Bolshevik revolution in the United States, received thunderous salvos of applause. Meetings of this type took place in the large cities and industrial centers from coast to coast, everywhere attended by large enthusiastic crowds who listened starry-eyed to bombastic revolutionary speeches and applauded appeals for the overthrow of the predatory capitalist government of the United States.

Out of this radical revolutionary fermentation the communists emerged as an organized, disciplined force. The organizations of the anarchists, the socialists, the pacifists, the I.W.W., were broken up and reduced to impotency. The communists survived to grow into a dynamic force with which the American people must contend.

Revolution in a Vacuum

The hotbed of American communism was in New York City, the intellectual and political center of the movement. Here the conflicting ambitions and intrigues of the communist leaders kept the movement in a perpetual state of agitation.

Like every important period in history the romantic period of communism produced the man that best typified the period—the great Yogi, the man who aimed to be the American Lenin, Louis C. Fraina.

Fraina started his revolutionary career as a disciple of Daniel DeLeon, the founder of the Socialist Labor party. His bushy hair, thin, emaciated face, delicate fingers and deep, sonorous voice were well known at the Socialist forums he frequented, where he tried to impress the audience during discussion periods with his profound knowledge of Marxism. He joined the Socialist party prior to the outbreak of the Russian revolution and became the leader of a Marxian faction that sought to transform it from a reformist to a revolutionary party.

Fraina's radical phrases fell on deaf ears. His bid for leadership in the Socialist party went unanswered. But history played into his hands. The Bolshevik Revolution brought Fraina into the spotlight as the exponent, the interpreter of bolshevism. The radicals wildly acclaimed him. Over-night the long-haired nuisance became a power in the Socialist party, a power that threatened the leadership of Morris Hillquit and the "Old Guard."

The Russian Federation of the Socialist party came out in favor of bolshevism and organized the Slavic Federations of the Socialist party into a powerful Pan-Slavic bloc. The moving spirits in the bloc declared that they were the official representatives of the Bolshevik government. They went much further and insisted that the American revolutionary movement must submit to their direction and dictation. They claimed that because they were Russians they were entitled, in the United States, to a priority on bolshevism.

Since Fraina supported this view the leaders of the Pan-Slavic bloc took him into their fold, and thereby acquired an English voice. The Letts of Boston, members of the Slavic bloc, engaged Fraina in 1918 to edit the *Revolutionary Age*, a weekly newspaper which explained to the membership of the Socialist party what bolshevism was. This assignment in journalism established Fraina as an authority on bolshevism and the recognized ideological exponent of the Communist ‖faction in the Socialist party.

Fraina's bosses, the Boston Letts, played a prominent role in the history of American communism and in the Soviet government's secret service organization. Their large building in Roxbury, Massachusetts, housed, among the many enterprises the Letts ran successfully, a large printing plant and a hall which seated 1200 persons. The Letts built up their organization by sheer guts and sacrifice. They were a hard-headed lot of uncompromising revolutionists, many of whom had seen active service with the famous bands of Lettish terrorists in the 1905 Russian revolution. Besides providing Soviet Russia with secret couriers, OGPU agents and international propagandists, the Boston Letts supplied the two men who, at different periods, were in charge of the illegal apparatus of the Communist party of the United States—the apparatus through which the American Communists carried on espionage, forged passports, distributed counterfeit money, judged the loyalty of other communists and punished enemies of the movement. The Letts had able executives and two-fisted men who could kill without blinking an eyelash. Most of them were idealists who did what they did out of devotion to the cause in which they believed.

Fraina, established in his Roxbury editorial office, like a man who awaited the call of destiny, worked feverishly trying to jam into seconds the labor of hours. He pounded the keys of his typewriter. He attended numerous organization meetings and conferences. He ran up and down the eastern seaboard making inflammatory speeches. Fraina did his job well. He made the radicals conscious of bolshevism, popularized Bolshevik slogans, interpreted the writings of Lenin, Trotsky, Bukharin, Radek, Zinoviev and the rest of the intellectual giants of bolshevism.

Comrade Jeanette Pearl, Fraina's faithful and devoted wife, an indefatigable worker, helped him in his whirl of activities. She did not assume his name, for to do so would be to submit to the capitalist institution of marriage, an unpardonable sin for a communist. Jeanette worshipped her comrade. She preferred to be hidden in his shadow so long as she could do the big and little things for him. She was his private secretary, his menial, his errand boy, his hausfrau, shared his bed and took his abuse.

Comrade Pearl did not go to Boston. Fraina had his duties to perform in Boston and she his interests to look after in New York. She usually met him on week-ends when he visited New York. For Comrade Pearl these week-ends spent with Fraina proved miserable. As the weeks passed he became more bitingly caustic in his attitude to her. The gossiping tongues at communist headquarters on Twenty-ninth Street talked in whispers about the cute little Irish girl that Fraina had in Boston. Jeanette felt instinctively that the tales were true, but she set personal feelings aside and continued to worship her red god.

Around that time the communists of Boston held a revolutionary demonstration. They paraded behind a large red flag, the display of which was banned by a city ordinance. Fraina led the demonstration arm in arm with his little Irish girl. Behind them marched Sidis, famous as an infant prodigy who won Harvard honors in mathematics in his teens. Directly in back of the youthful, jubilant genius marched a column of heavily armed men commanded by the powerful Lett, Jurgis, whose six feet of muscle and brawn stooped slightly forward like a gorilla.

The human dynamo Jurgis did not know fear. During World War I he had worked as a ship-fitter in the Hog Island shipyards. Marching into socialist headquarters he had addressed the organizer in charge.

"Comrade, I want literature, good revolutionary stuff."

"What do you want it for?"

"I want to distribute it in the shipyard tomorrow."

"But you will be arrested."

"Who me? Never Jurgis. The first cop that comes near me I'll flatten. Come on, give me five hundred pieces."

Jurgis took the bundle of leaflets with him into the yard wrapped in a pair of overalls. When the shifts changed, in broad daylight, he began to distribute them, skipping in and out among the workers in order to avoid the guards. When they caught up with him he swung his powerful arms left and right. The guards staggered under the sledgehammer blows and Jurgis, excited and laughing like a little boy, escaped.

In 1919 Jurgis went to Soviet Russia without money in his pockets and without passports. He boarded a freighter in Boston Harbor, made contact with the crew and was off. He saw Lenin and received a dangerous assignment requiring him to go to the Baltic countries, then hotbeds of anti-Soviet activity, to establish communist cells among the counter-revolutionists, to set up machinery for the distribution of Bolshevik propaganda, to build up an organization of trusted secret couriers among the seamen, and to carry out acts of sabotage.

Jurgis's band in the Boston demonstration were armed with brass knuckles, short lengths of pipe, blackjacks and knives. They were under orders from Jurgis to fall upon the police should they attempt to interfere with the parade. The communists were determined to capture the streets. The inevitable happened. Boston's blue coats met the parade head on. They ordered the marchers to stop and a number of them made a rush for the red flag. Jurgis let fly with his fists—a policeman went down. Jurgis gave the signal to attack by roaring, "Down with the police!" His red guards went into action. The police belabored the demonstrators with their clubs. Fraina's Irish girl scratched the faces of the police with her nails. Sidis, bleeding profusely, went down in a heap under the blows of policemen's clubs. Fraina, the revolutionary hero, beat a hurried retreat.

Fraina and his little Irish girl fled to New York to avoid arrest. The news of what happened in Boston reached communist circles in New York before Fraina. At communist headquarters on West Twenty-ninth Street, Fraina became the center of an admiring, noisy circle. Next to him, flushed with excitement, stood the Irish girl, and on the crowd's rim stood Jeanette. She kept staring at the girl who clung closely to Fraina's side. Everyone expected her to blow up but instead she waited silently and patiently for an opportunity to speak to Fraina. Jeanette served two gods—the Communist party and Fraina. All through her life she remained loyal to both. The Irish vixen soon afterwards left the communist movement. The realism and danger of communism did not appeal to her romanticism. Instead she sought satisfaction for her adventurous spirit in the realm of make-believe, in the field of fiction, where she became a writer and an authority on the short-story.

Jeanette continued to turn the pages of real life. Her devotion to a movement and to a man who failed that movement transformed her into a tragic figure who carried on her communist duties like a ghost. Fraina's downfall came rapidly. He was tried in 1920 by a special committee consisting of the leaders of the Communist party on serious charges brought against him by Santeri Nourteva, the brilliant Finnish aide to Ludwig C. K. Martens, first Soviet ambassador to the United States. Nourteva accused Fraina of being an agent provocateur and a spy in the pay of the Department of Justice. At the trial a Russian, Dr. Nosovitsky, a chum of Fraina's and a highly trusted member of the Communist party, defended Fraina and was responsible for his exoneration. Soon afterwards it turned out that Dr. Nosovitsky himself was an anti-Soviet adventurer. Nosovitsky wielded a strange influence over Fraina, the nature of which often came up for discussion in top communist circles. Every one in the Central Committee knew that Fraina acted as if his life and career depended on the mysterious doctor, who got from him everything he wanted to know about the movement, even the most confidential matters. Ugly rumors spread in party ranks about Nosovitsky's power over the frail Fraina, but they were never substantiated.

Soon afterwards Fraina went to Moscow at the express invitation of Lenin. No other man in America was similarly singled out. No other American had been received, as Fraina was, by the top circles of the Bolshevik hierarchy. Lenin and Trotsky personally took him into their fold. He so won the confidence of Zinoviev, the first president of the Comintern, that he became one of Zinoviev's powerful and dreaded inner circle that dominated Comintern affairs. The way in which Fraina was welcomed in Moscow, the powerful contacts and friends he acquired, made certain the realization of his ambition to return to the United States as the recognized leader of American communism.

But when the crowning glory of communist leadership was his, Fraina threw it away to the four winds. How explain this about a man who was a bundle of pompous vanity and egotism? Perhaps the way the Comintern leaders behaved in 1920 influenced him. At a time when the Russian people were living on the barest necessities and barefoot Russian soldiers dressed in rags were defending Bolshevik power, the Comintern leaders were living lavishly, without restraints on the advantages which power brought them. Perhaps the cynicism of curly-headed, near-sighted Radek and the vanity and foppishness of the shrill feminine-voiced Zinoviev undermined his faith in the idealism of the movement. It is likely that as part of the small clique which ruled the Comintern he observed on what a flimsy basis principles rested; that promises were quickly broken; that idealism rested upon a foundation of lies and double dealing became the accepted conduct of those in power. Fraina did not realize that he was being molded according to a pattern. Like most of the men and women who joined the communist movement he was unaware of the changes in moral attitude which he had undergone. He was in no position to grasp the significance of the human equation in communism, the dominant power of the movement over the mind and being of the individual.

When Fraina came back to the United States no one suspected that in the immediate future he would become the center of an international scandal. On his return he reported to the Central Executive Committee of the underground Communist party on the grandiose plans which the Comintern had worked out for Mexico, Central and South America—plans which linked the countries involved with the Communist party of the United States in an over-all plan to foment revolutions in Mexico and other countries as a step towards the seizure of the American continents for communism.

Fraina informed the American communist leaders that Moscow had formed a small committee consisting of himself, Carl E. Johnson, alias Scott, one of the Boston Letts who operated as a Chekist spy and Comintern agent, and Sen Katayama, a Japanese communist who worked as a cook in New York. The Comintern endowed the committee with full power to carry out the plan. After preliminary details were worked out at meetings in New York, Fraina went to Germany to receive last-minute instructions from the Comintern and the money set aside to subsidize the plan. The sum Fraina received ran into six figures—the exact amount has been shrouded in mystery—but some of the men in the top leadership of the American Communist party at that time swore that it amounted to $386,000.

For poverty-stricken revolutionists who had to worry where their next meal was coming from, the fund entrusted to Fraina represented a staggering sum of money. And he did not return to the United States on the day he was expected. He lingered on in Germany and other European countries, squandering large sums of money in extravagant living, and then dropped out of sight altogether. Scott dispatched Soviet spies to Mexico to search for Fraina. When they caught up with him in Mexico City they demanded an accounting of the funds entrusted to him by the Comintern. They got little satisfaction. What transpired at the Mexican conferences was never officially reported. Unofficially, however, the air was surcharged with ugly rumors about money scandals involving not only Fraina but also Scott and other prominent communist officials. Officially, Scott reported to the Central Executive Committee of the underground Communist party of the United States that Fraina had disappeared with the Comintern's money and confidential instructions and could not be found.

Fraina, in Mexico, avoided communist circles. The Mexican communists who were to get a large slice of the money vowed that if they ever caught him they would kill him. But for reasons unknown to the American and Mexican communists the Comintern did not want Fraina's life. He spent many years in Mexico, living a life of ease on the large and luxurious hacienda of a wealthy Mexican senorita.

When Fraina prepared to return to the United States he evidently communicated with Comrade Jeanette, still a loyal and devoted Communist party member. She prepared, for submission to the proper party authorities, a lengthy brief in which she tried to exonerate Fraina. She appeared before party committees and held conferences with communist leaders, begging that Fraina be taken back into the Party, on probation, as a rank-and-filer. She bombarded the Comintern with communications and appeals on Fraina's behalf, and demanded over and over again that the Party allow her to go to Moscow to present Fraina's case to the Comintern. The Party stubbornly refused. As late as 1930 she carried on negotiations with Comintern Reps and with OGPU agents for Fraina's readmission into the Communist party. All her efforts proved futile. Fraina did the next-best thing. In 1933 he joined the communist opposition group of his old crony in the communist underground, Jay Lovestone. While a member of the Lovestone group Fraina went through a metamorphosis in his ideological conceptions and rejected totally the so-called theoretical and scientific bases of Marxism and communism. Jeanette thereby lost her man, for she remained loyal to the Communist party to the very end, the devoted communist always in step with the party line.

A Sacrifice on the Altar of Communism—John Reed

Great souls are tossed about by the storm of events during epoch-making crises. John Reed was such a soul. Yearning for the meaning and the rhythm of life he became involved, as a result of war and the Russian Revolution, in an inner conflict between the demands of history and those of his artistic soul. Reed the artist was forced to do what he was not fitted to do. Before he could have a full view of the beautiful horizon, the Russian Revolution caught him up in overpowering arms and crushed him. Feeling with his heart, unable abstractly to accept the logic surrounding man's social relations, Reed succumbed to the inhuman conceptions of the Marxists at the helm of the Soviets. His attempts at rationalization, at trying to square his conscience with the realities of bolshevism, caused him acute mental anguish. A man who radiated the will to live in the end failed to summon that will on his own behalf.

Reed, like Fraina, was an outstanding figure in the beginnings of American communism. Fraina was the ideological brain, the Marxian iceberg of dialectical abstractions. A living movement could not enthuse around Fraina alone. John Reed supplied American communism with the heart and soul.

But Reed, the soul of American communism, did not have the patience to read the dry, laborious works of Karl Marx. American communism's great hero was in reality never a Marxist, never a communist. His moral and spiritual antecedents, the values he placed on freedom and individual liberty, ran counter to everything communism stood for.

Reed went to Russia as a reporter during the Revolution accompanied by his charming and beautiful wife, Louise Bryant, also a journalist. He reached Petrograd just before the Bolsheviks took over. What Reed saw on his arrival in Russia he had witnessed on a smaller scale in Mexico. He had seen it in the war-torn Balkans, and had made its acquaintance in the muddy trenches of the World War—human flesh in agony, striving desperately to liberate itself, to win for itself a durable peace and security. But in Russia Reed witnessed it for the first time on a gigantic scale, a volcanic social eruption involving an enslaved nation of millions in revolt.

The stirring events of the historic drama unfolding before his eyes made a deep impression on Reed. He mistook the upsurge of the masses for bolshevism. To Reed, who loved the militant fighting spirit of the singing wobblies, who idealized the solidarity of labor, who went to prison for helping the striking silk weavers of Paterson, the Bolshevik Revolution was the realization of his dreams, of his hopes for a socialist utopia, the grand finale of a social system he abhorred, which divided mankind into rich and poor—the exploiting and the exploited.

Eager for action in the great cause, Reed joined the Bolsheviks and became an important collaborator in their foreign propaganda department, turning out the propaganda the Bolsheviks hoped would cause the soldiers in the trenches to revolt. Reed, the Bolshevik propagandist, used his journalistic skill in an attempt to incite a world revolution. He also acted as the number-one public relations counselor of the Bolsheviks, sending out dispatches written for the purpose of presenting the Bolsheviks in a favorable light to the rest of the world.

Reed was swept off his feet by the unfolding drama of a mighty revolution which he felt was destined to change the course of history. Busy getting visual impressions, he had no time to ponder the pros and cons of bolshevism. What he saw the great Russian mass do he liked, and he accepted bolshevism without reflecting on what was going on behind the scenes. Reed took his impressions of the moment for substance; the will to absolute power of a handful of extremists headed by Lenin for the will of the people hungry for bread and freedom.

The Revolution did not mature Reed into a revolutionary politician. Circumstances over which he had no control, however, were to turn his activities upon his return to the United States into political channels. A lovable American, an individualist imbued with the rebellious spirit of the Pacific frontier, he became the prisoner of a movement that advocated the suppression of liberty and held individualism in contempt. He became the tool of an ideology he did not understand, supporting a philosophy of government and action which, upon his return to the Mecca of Communism, was to turn his stomach and break his spirit.

John Reed, courageous, adventurous spirit, never ran away from a fight. When word reached him in Petrograd during the early days of 1919 that *The Masses* edited by Max Eastman had been suppressed and that Eastman and his associate editors including Reed had been indicted for sedition because of their opposition to American participation in the World War, Reed made up his mind forthwith to return to the States and face trial.

Taking Lenin and Trotsky into his confidence, he informed them of his decision to return to America to stand trial and of his intention to utilize his time back home for the Bolshevik cause. The Bolshevik leaders were no fools. They appreciated the importance to Soviet Russia of getting the right publicity in the proper places, especially in the United States. Trotsky had been in America. He knew what tremendous power the American press wielded. Lenin too had long ago recognized the power of the press. Reed sought the picturesque, the adventurous course. He asked to be made a revolutionary courier. He wanted to brave the hostile frontiers, his bags and pockets stuffed with revolutionary contraband. The Bolshevik leaders elected otherwise. They decided on a course that would dramatize Reed's return to his native land. Lenin ruled that Reed be appointed to a diplomatic post. He argued that Reed traveling as a Soviet diplomat would enjoy a degree of diplomatic immunity that would safeguard his return to the United States; moreover, he could take the material he had collected for a book on the Bolsheviks' rise to power and other material and confidential papers and instructions which the Bolsheviks wanted smuggled into the States. The shrewd Lenin recognized that in appointing Reed to a diplomatic post the Bolsheviks were making a gesture of solidarity to the radical elements in the United States.

But when Lenin discovered how displeased the United States government was over the appointment of Reed to the post of Soviet Consul-general at New York, he beat a hasty retreat, concluding that he had made a serious mistake in identifying the Soviet government with the reds in America. Reed's appointment was withdrawn as hurriedly as it was made, the Soviet Foreign Office issuing a dispatch to that effect before he arrived in New York harbor.

The reaction of the American government to Reed's appointment to a diplomatic post settled for Lenin a serious question of policy. The top Bolshevik circles decided that hereafter the subversive activities of the Soviet government against other states should be conducted through agencies ostensibly not identified with the Soviet state apparatus. This important decision broke the ground for the organization of the Communist International and numerous other agencies and organizations dedicated to the overthrow of capitalist states and to world revolution.

The All-Russian Soviet of Petrograd gave Reed a farewell reception. Speaking before the Soviet, that predicted that his arrest in the United States would parallel the Karl Liebknecht case in Germany since he too would be arrested for opposing the war and conscription. Albert Rhys Williams, an American journalist who had just started his career as a Soviet apologist, directed his speech at the American trade union movement. He called upon the American workers to support the Bolsheviks and to follow the ideals of the Soviet government. Boris Reinstein predicted that the world revolution soon would sweep over the world and that the proletariat of the United States would play an important role in it. It was not by accident that three men, all from the United States, made speeches which were sent out as press dispatches to the States. These speeches, emanating from the All-Russian Soviet, embodied Lenin's three-fold plan for America. Reed's arrest was to dramatize and intensify American opposition to the war. Labor was to follow the advice of Williams and go communist. Reinstein's speech was directed to the American communists not to lose time in organizing for the world revolution.

Reed did not grasp the significance of his send-off. Lenin's shrewd tactics towards the United States, tactics which Stalin uses in the execution of his foreign policy, involved the advocacy of conflicting measures diametrically opposed to each other. On the one hand Lenin threatened America with the bolshevization of American labor and world revolution, while on the other hand he offered the country the olive branch of domestic tranquillity and good profits to be gained by recognizing the Soviet government and doing business with the Bolsheviks. Lenin did not, however, sacrifice communist principles by such complicated and involved tactics, for he sought material gains for bolshevism from two opposite ends: material assistance from the capitalist government through an understanding, and revolutionary allies from labor for the impending struggle for the mastery of the world.

As a Bolshevik courier Reed outdid himself. Though the United States Customs held him up for over eight hours in New York harbor Reed smuggled into the country the material he had collected for his book, the material Lenin and Trotsky entrusted him with, and a load of revolutionary propaganda and contraband. The authorities had taken every precaution and they were puzzled. They did not know that Reed made friends with members of the crew, was helped by I.W.W. seamen and got direct aid from James Larkin, who put his Irish rebel network in New York harbor at Reed's disposal.

Reed faced two Americas on his return. One feared him and violently opposed his new ideas. The other, radical America, welcomed him as a hero and applauded his every word. Penniless, with just one suit to his name, a threadbare gray tweed norfolk, Reed became a familiar figure at radical meetings where his appearance always evoked a wild uproar of cheering and applause. He had a mission to perform regardless of the cost to himself in energy and health. Bolshevik Russia's red missionary worked tirelessly and fought valiantly to get his message across to the people. The newspapers, the magazines, the publishing houses which controlled the mediums which suited Reed best, whose doors had always been wide open to him, now slammed those doors shut in his face. Reed was a boycotted man, deprived of his means of a livelihood.

After a long day of conferences, mass meetings, organizational duties and hours at the typewriter, John Reed would drag his tired feet to One Patchin Place and climb wearily up the three flights of stairs to the dingy, dirty apartment on the top floor. One Patchin Place, a small structure of red brick, in front of which a scrawny ailanthus grew, was nestled in a quaint alley, a Greenwich Village landmark.

Strewn all over Reed's living-room were newspapers, pamphlets, letters, torn envelopes, manuscripts and books. Ashes obscured the base of the little wood-burning fireplace. Heaps of dust covered newspapers, and printed matter lay piled high in utter confusion on the large flat-top desk. Its drawers were open, each packed with printed rubbish and paper. On a little table stood a dirty, smudged enameled coffee pot, an ash tray full of cigarette butts, and a couple of unwashed cups and saucers. The cot against the wall of the small room directly across from the fireplace was always mussed, with a few pillows scattered on its untidy surface.

Reed on entering the apartment usually threw himself upon a large stuffed chair, pressed his temples between the palms of his hands, stretched out his legs in their full length, and sat motionless for a few minutes. One hardly knew whether he was relaxing or thinking. Then he would get up from the chair with a jump, grab some newspapers from the desk, and toss them into the fireplace. Lighting the papers, he hurled kindling wood and large chunks of coal after them. Throwing off his jacket he picked up the coffee pot, rinsed it superficially, filled it with water and coffee and set it to boil on a greasy, black castiron two-burner gas stove. Lighting a cigarette he would sit down and talk. And when he talked, he rambled over the universe, never confining himself for a long time to one subject. He talked about his experiences as a reporter in Germany during the war, about Mexico, about the West, about his family tree and about anything else that came into his mind.

Then devoting twenty hours a day to making America Bolshevik-conscious, Reed seldom brought up the subject of communism. His life's interests seemed elsewhere for he rambled along about books, plays, the drama, about himself and literary critics. Frank Harris frightened him. When Reed came across the critic on the street, he became apprehensive and quickened his steps to avoid meeting a literary monster who made his blood curdle.

Closest to his poetic soul were the wobblies who rode the rods, the singing hobos, the lumberjacks, the quiet, solemn-faced Finns, the squareheads and their leader, the sentimental one-eyed big Bill Haywood. He never forgot the silk weavers of Paterson and their strike, in which he participated and which landed him in jail. Indelibly impressed on his mind was the I.W.W. pageant of that strike staged in New York's old Madison Square Garden. He took a boyish pride in the fact that he wrote and helped put on what he considered the most impressive dramatic event ever witnessed.

Reed despised the political socialists even though he considered himself a socialist. There were too many smug doctors, dentists and lawyers among them to suit him. "All the Socialist party needs," he once said, "is a few undertakers to bury us."

The coffee ready, Reed poured himself one cup after another and chain-smoked cigarettes. "I like this place," he remarked, now thoroughly relaxed, "the building hidden away in an alley, in the center of the metropolis and the heart-soothing fireplace when the coals burn and the blue flames shimmer in the soft red glow of the embers." The musty old hole on the third floor of One Patchin Place was Reed's paradise. Louise tidied it a little when she was in town. Usually she sat perched up on the couch, her shoulders against the wall, a miniature of well-shaped daintiness and charm, with large dreamy eyes that looked straight at you. Jack seldom talked about Louise, but Louise always talked about Jack. They had been to Russia together. Louise, too, was favorably impressed by the Bolsheviks but did not accept them completely as Jack had done. She did everything she could to help gain American recognition for the Soviets even though she was positive that bolshevism was not good for America.

Before a Congressional committee Louise admitted that she had been permitted to leave Russia as a courier for the Soviets. She was asked:

"Do you advocate a Soviet for this country."

"No," replied Louise.

"Do you approve a Soviet government for this country?"

"No, I don't think it will work."

"Do you believe in a Soviet government for Russia?"

"It's none of my business. It's their affair and all I ask is that they be allowed to settle it themselves."

"Are you a capitalist or a proletarian?"

"I am poor. I suppose I am a proletarian."

The congressmen were taken aback by her manner. How, they

wondered, could such a pretty and likable American girl be the wife of such a flaming red as John Reed?

To Reed's close friends in the movement she opened up her heart and bared her worries about Jack. She often remarked: "John knows what he is doing. It's too bad that what he can do best, his writing, must suffer. I know what a great personal sacrifice that means to him. I hope that in later years he will not be sorry." She was deeply pained when the poet who wanted to write a truly great and moving drama, put on the cloak of a communist politician and discarded the cloak of the artist.

The Connolly Club, just off Broadway on Twenty-ninth Street, housed communist headquarters and the editorial offices of the *Revolutionary Age*, edited by Fraina, and the *Voice of Labor* edited by Reed. The comrades gathered at the Connolly Club to get information, to play pool, to eat ham and eggs made the way Jim Larkin wanted them made and to enjoy coffee or Irish tea with cookies.

Reed kept his door ajar to catch the drift of the conversation. Often he would jump off his chair, join the crowd and engage in a spirited discussion; he liked to start heated arguments even though he did not stay around to finish them. Once when the place quieted down Reed rushed into the room and asked excitedly, "Comrades, what do you think about the materialistic conception of history and economic determinism? Which is right?" The question set off a discussion, for there was always a comrade in the room who prided himself on being a Marxian student. Such comrades were Reed's meat. Now he quoted Marx verbatim by pages, referring to page number and chapter. The student of Marx looked at Reed with puzzled contempt, shouted to be heard above the banter of words, demanded that Reed produce Volume I of Marx to prove his contentions. To which Reed quickly replied with a smile, "Sorry, comrade, I did not comprehend the extent of your ignorance on the subject. I did not refer to Volume I containing the elementary postulates of Marx. I referred to Volume III which contains Marx's final and basic philosophical conclusions,"—backing up his retort with numerous verbatim quotes and references all manufactured in Reed's imagination. The heated argument on, the Marxian student stumped, Reed returned to his office flushed, excited as a young colt. Hitching up his pants he sat down at the typewriter and pounded away on the keys.

In his serious moments Reed sometimes discussed the kind of a communist movement he believed in. He wanted a rank and file movement, backed up by an independent militant revolutionary trade union organization like the I.W.W. He had no use for a movement dominated by politicians.

"Ben," said Reed, "we've got to have a movement with guts, whose members will hoof it over the country and concentrate wherever they are needed. We must build a disciplined movement but not one bossed by politicians."

Unaware that his position differed from that of the Bolsheviks, he thought he could build a Bolshevik organization by simple frank discussion without political pressure and regimentation, thus displaying his ignorance of the essence of Bolshevik organization. He had been too busy watching the stirring events of the Bolshevik Revolution and had no time left to study the form of Bolshevik organization and how it works. When he did learn how ignorant he had been it was too late.

As the editor of what he termed a rank-and-file labor paper, he concentrated on securing articles from workers in the shops. He buttonholed workers, talked to them about their experiences and prodded them into writing articles. When the articles reached Reed, scrawled in long-hand, written poorly and ungrammatically, he re-wrote them into finished masterpieces. Then he went around boasting what excellent articles the workers from the shops were writing for his paper.

Reed looked upon the Bolshevik Revolution as a great step in the liberation of mankind from poverty and oppression. He failed to grasp the basic relations of bolshevism to the individual. He accepted the Bolshevik theory of government and approved measures which he would have fought had his own government used them. Reed recognized that the Soviet government was a dictatorship but fell into the error of considering the Soviets synonymous with the people. In one of his speeches he said: "The Soviet government is not a democracy. It's a dictatorship of the proletariat by the force of arms to protect the rights of the people. And who are the people? Why, the Soviets!"

Essentially an artist, Reed refused to reduce life to the mechanistic theoretical equations of the Marxists. His heart beat in unison with the heartbeats and aspirations of humanity and he saw and felt with compassion the suffering of the humble and lowly of the earth.

In Croton-on-the-Hudson Reed owned a modest cottage situated on the side of a slope overlooking an expanding scene of green beauty which fell away to the Hudson, a silver thread below the purple hills.

Once there, the fog of worry, the expression of fatigue lifted from his brow. His eyes brightened and laughter came to his face. For one who visited the place for the first time Reed's delight in this pastoral retreat revealed him in his true light. With deference and reverence he approached the shed, a distance below the cottage, hidden in the trees and shrubbery. "This shed," remarked Reed, "is my workshop, my sanctuary. Within its walls I meditate in a world of my own and write."

Before entering the cottage Reed looked southward. "In that direction is Sing Sing Prison. When the siren's howl disturbs the stillness of the night you know that a prisoner has escaped. I've heard the warning a number of times. Each time I went out on the road hoping to meet the poor devil in order to hide him from his pursuers." So spoke the man who hated prisons and jailors. Yet he gave three years of his life, all that was left of his promising career, to an organization which sought in the name of socialism and freedom to turn the world into a prison for all mankind.

By the time the first anniversary of the Bolshevik Revolution rolled around, six months after he had arrived from Russia, Reed showed, by his weary, bloodshot eyes and the fatigue lines on his face, the terrific pace at which he was going. He delivered speeches without being paid for them. He wrote for the revolutionary press. Some weeks he received $20.00, and then followed weeks in which he was not paid at all. He often had to borrow a dime or a quarter for coffee and a doughnut.

Reed did not like Fraina. Fraina was what Reed was not. He was vain, graspingly ambitious, spoke a Marxian gibberish that sounded like Greek to Americans, fouled his politics and lacked principles. Reed welcomed the chance to become the editor-in-chief of a communist paper of his own when the left wing of the Socialist party decided to publish *The Communist*. He would get out a real paper, a lively, fighting weekly in tabloid form, not loaded down with Fraina's Marxian verbiage. Aimed against the right wing bosses of the Socialist party Reed's paper proved more effective than Fraina's. The right wing socialists felt Reed's sting and immediately got out a paper called *The Socialist* to counteract *The Communist*. Reed welcomed the new antagonist for he now had a concrete object against which to aim his guns.

In revolutionary politics the personal ambitions of the leaders play an important role. The altruistic souls motivated by high ideals and principles are common in the rank-and-file and rare in its leadership. The struggle for power in the communist organization proceeds as bitterly as it does at royal courts. The leaders who promise the masses a paradise on earth, free from greed and corruption, are no amateurs in political horsetrading and trickery. It does not take them long to develop the astuteness of machine bosses such as Tweed and to adopt the political practices of a Tammany Hall.

Reed was no politician. Circumstances, the accident of place and time pushed him to the top of the American communist movement. He never sought personal power. But the communist leaders around him were different. They had not, like Reed, seen bolshevism in action but they understood it better and came more completely under its influence. The American communist leaders recognized in bolshevism essentially a movement for power. To them bolshevism meant a realistic approach to the problems of the capture of power by whatever means possible, whether it involved a trade union, a small branch of the Socialist party, a Communist party or a government. Leadership they interpreted as the assumption of power or the securing of positions from which to wield power. It was therefore not difficult for them to make the obtaining of personal power the first and predominant principle to which all other matters were subsidiary. Out of this leadership concept developed the ethics, or more correctly the negation of ethics, which rest on the premise that power is in itself the essence of morality.

To the consternation of Reed the American communist leaders played the game according to the rules laid down by Lenin and not according to the preconceived notions of Reed. Lenin was above all a shrewd practical political boss who cynically advised his inner circle that if they wanted to play politics they must be prepared to play dirty.

Reed soon learned that communist leaders may, with impunity, break one day the solemn pledge they made the day before. The communists held a national conference in New York City in 1919 for the purpose of perfecting a national organization with which to capture the Socialist party at its convention to take place in Chicago in August. Delegates were elected by the communist factions within the Socialist party with that specific understanding. A few days before the conference opened the leaders of the Russian bloc of Slavic Federations of the Socialist party projected the demand for the immediate formation of a Communist party, which naturally they would dominate.

Reed fought the proposal. At the conference Reed's point of view prevailed. Being outnumbered by the Americans the Russian-Slavic bloc bolted the conference. They hurled invective at the Americans, insisting that the Slavs were the only genuine Bolsheviks and that the Americans would have to accept their direction and leadership.

Reed enjoyed a Pyrrhic victory. For at the same time that Fraina, Ruthenberg, Lovestone, Ferguson and the other top American leaders of the communist movement were supporting him they were carrying on secret negotiations with the Russians for the purpose of double-crossing him—bargaining with the Russians over the price they were to be paid for their duplicity.

The conference elected a national council which included all the leaders who had supported Reed's position. Reed thought the issue settled, only to discover when the National Council met that the majority of the council had double-crossed him and capitulated to the Russians. Ferguson, speaking at the council meeting, said, "Comrades, the Russians made the Revolution, we did not. They know how; we do not. I for one trust the Russians and will follow them." Thus spoke the Executive Secretary, the boss of the National Council of the Left Wing, the man holding the most important communist post in America.

Ferguson was later sent to Sing Sing Prison. He appealed his case and won. In prison he got a belly-full of what was in store for communist leaders. He left the movement on his release from prison, got himself readmitted to the Chicago Bar and settled down as a successful bourgeois professional.

Reed found himself out on a limb. The National Council proceeded to do the direct opposite of what the conference which had elected them had instructed them to do. This shocked Reed, who believed in personal integrity; he fought back by taking the matter to the membership. Reed then discovered what many communist leaders have discovered since: that the applause of communist masses does not indicate the influence and power which a communist leader has in a communist organization. Believing in the righteousness of his cause and the correctness of his position, he fought on and presented his case at a membership meeting of Local Bronx of the Left Wing, one of the City's largest communist sections, where Jay Lovestone opposed him in a bitter, acrimonious debate. Lovestone, in true Bolshevik style, referred to Reed as "the so-called proletarian who lives on a sumptuous estate in Westchester, where the idle rich live."

Lovestone, immaculately dressed, knew that Reed, who still wore his old, threadbare norfolk, would, when the meeting was over, most likely have to borrow a quarter to pay for a cup of coffee and a sandwich. Yet the knowledge did not prevent him from dragging Reed through the mire as a member of the country's landed gentry.

When arguments failed and it looked like a Reed majority Lovestone and his Russian followers counted the votes and voted Reed down by a majority of one. Overjoyed at his victory over Reed, Lovestone rushed to Reed like a young pup and offered him his hand. Reed told him to go to hell and left the hall.

The reports indicated that though Reed was beaten in New York he had mustered enough legitimate delegates, elected from the state organizations of the Socialist party, to carry the national convention of the Socialist party for a communist program. Reed, Larkin and I went into a huddle and decided to participate at the Chicago convention of the Socialist party. We raised the money quickly from our supporters. Reed and I left together for Chicago.

Reed had a hectic time in Chicago. The general staff of the Russian-Slavic bloc now felt they had the upper hand. They presented Reed's committee with an ultimatum in which they offered to accept the rank-and-file delegates but insisted that some of the leaders had to be excluded from the Bolshevik movement for their defiance of the true Bolshevik course. They were willing to accept Reed on the grounds that he was young and would learn how to be a good Bolshevik. Reed turned thumbs down on the proposal, declaring his course required no defense, and concluded by saying: "I am willing to accept the proposal of unity but not on the basis of submission to the Russians and the purging of Gitlow and others who made the fight with me."

Though the communist marauders of the Socialist party failed to agree on matters of control, that did not prevent Reed from joining them in carrying out Lenin's orders to smash the Socialist party. They fell upon their mother organization and tore it apart limb from limb. What was left has been wrecked by successive splits, all of them engineered by the communists—the last one coming in 1932 when Norman Thomas and his militants raised the banner of pseudo-bolshevism. The mighty party of socialist reform had to give up its name. The membership fell below the 5000 mark.

The convention came to an end with the organization of the Communist Labor party. Reed had been elected its representative to the Congress of the Communist International. At the first meeting of the newly elected Central Executive Committee, Reed explained why it was advisable for him to leave for Moscow immediately. "Comrades," argued Reed, "we are in the unfortunate position of having two communist parties in the United States. One we control. The other the Russian-Slavic bloc controls. That Communist party will survive which gets the endorsement of the Bolsheviks. It is therefore most important that I get to Moscow before Fraina does. I propose that I leave for Moscow as soon as arrangements for my departure can be made."

Back in New York, Reed went into a huddle with Larkin and worked out with him the necessary arrangements for his trip. Dressed as a seaman in coarse trousers and a flannel multicolored shirt, a cap cocked rakishly on his head, false seaman's papers in his pockets, a two-weeks' stubble on his chin, Reed bade his intimate friends goodbye. In the company of a couple of Irish dockers he went to make his ship, scrambled aboard a Swedish freighter in the darkness of the night, and was off on his mission.

For a well-known revolutionist traveling on forged papers to get into Soviet Russia, surrounded by a hostile world, was no easy task. It took Reed almost three months to reach his goal. He arrived in Moscow in the winter of 1919 and lost no time in reporting to the Executive Committee of the Communist International. He presented the case of his party, the Communist Labor Party, and asked for its immediate recognition. But Zinoviev, the chairman of the Comintern, was in no hurry. He ordered Reed to submit a written report in which were to be included opinions on the economic and political developments in the United States. Reed had time not only to draw up a lengthy report but also to take an extensive trip through Soviet Russia.

Upon his return to Moscow the Comintern Executive informed Reed that their decision called for the unification of the two communist parties of the United States into one communist organization. Reed accepted the decision for unification. But on hearing that he had been indicted by the Chicago Grand Jury, together with the other members of the Central Executive Committee of the Communist Labor party, he insisted that he be permitted to return immediately to his native land even if arrest meant long imprisonment. Zinoviev opposed his return and requested that he remain in Russia. The same tack was followed by the other Bolshevik leaders and the Comintern Executive.

Zinoviev placed many obstacles in his way in order to prevent his immediate departure. Two attempts to leave Russia were foiled at the border. Reed, puzzled, tried to understand what had happened. Each time he blamed himself and concluded that he was slipping in his technique of crossing hostile borders. Never did he suspect that perhaps Zinoviev and the Comintern shared some of the responsibility for his failure. He did not stop to question why the proficient Comintern apparatus for smuggling persons and revolutionary propaganda and contraband out of Russia had fallen down in his case.

Reed did not give up hope. He got his bearings, took greater precautions and tried again. The third attempt through Finland ended disastrously. He was arrested, his person loaded with revolutionary contraband, confidential instructions, letters, and almost one million Finnish marks to be converted into American dollars for financing communist activities in the United States. His trip in the bunker of a Finnish freighter bound for Sweden had ended at Abo, where he was taken off the ship on a raw March day and lodged in a cold, foul, unventilated dungeon of the Abo police station. With one of his kidneys removed, Reed could not go on living indefinitely in a chilly, wet cell on a fare of dry salt herring.

Efforts to secure a passport for him from the United States failed. When the Finnish government gave representatives of the American government access to his papers Reed concluded the jig was up. He knew the papers were loaded with dynamite against him. Included were letters to Soviet secret agents in America, instructions to American communists on how to prepare the continent for a revolution, special propaganda material and instructions and decisions from the Comintern to the American communists. This revolutionary contraband plus the large sum of money Reed carried out of Russia compromised him too much. To expect a passport from the government he conspired to overthrow was sheer folly; so he did the next-best thing.

Reed withdrew his request for a passport and asked to be returned to Soviet Russia. Released in June, the American pilgrim returned to the Red Mecca, a wreck of his former self—emaciated, his cheekbones sticking out prominently, his face and body covered with festering sores, gums blue and swollen, teeth discolored and eyes sunk deep in his forehead.

Back in Moscow, the city Reed had left in high spirits, the American Bolshevik slowly began to catch up with himself. As the dark veil lifted he caught a glimpse of the colors in their true light. The towers of the Kremlin spread dark shadows from which Reed recoiled. Reed brooded over the fact that he had been betrayed in Finland by a Russian communist sailor, selected by Zinoviev from the trusted personnel of the Comintern's Cheka to act as Reed's companion and protector. The incident threw light on his two other unsuccessful attempts to get out of Russia.

On July 2, 1920, the second Congress of the Communist International opened. Reed had recovered sufficiently to attend. The opening session took place in Petrograd amid great fanfare. The gigantic parade which preceded the opening, the tribute paid to the revolutionists who had fallen in the battle for freedom and socialism, revived in Reed some of his old-time spirit. But the glamour wore off when the Congress, sitting in Moscow, got down to serious business. Reed found himself in opposition to the Bolshevik leaders and the Congress majority. The more they flattered him, the more they played on his revolutionary responsibilities in an effort to get him to change his mind, the more uncomfortable Reed became.

Fraina had arrived before the Congress opened. He fawned before the seats of the mighty and became an intimate of Zinoviev. The feminine-appearing Zinoviev wielded great power. To cross swords with him, as Reed did, took courage, for Zinoviev, a bitter-ender, never forgot.

Reed called upon the Congress to make English an official language. Zinoviev beat down his proposal. In the crown room of the Kremlin Reed fought before the mighty Bolshevik leaders to have the Congress give more serious consideration to what he wanted to propose on the trade union question. Again Reed went down in defeat. He could not make a dent in the combination against him.

Karl Radek delivered the report on the trade union question. Reed had opposed the official position at meetings of the sub-committee. Radek, of Polish-Jewish origin, served as Zinoviev's errand boy and constituted the third member of the powerful trio consisting of Zinoviev, Kamenev and Radek. Unmercifully he lashed out against Reed, putting words into Reed's mouth that he had never uttered. Reed was up against a master juggler of words, a man whose pen and tongue were vitriolic. Radek as a journalist prided himself on his ability to write on two opposing sides of the same subject for the purpose of presenting the one which suited the occasion. As a political journalist he had no equal throughout Russia.

Fraina, unlike Reed, fell into the swing of things. He was under instructions from his own organization in America to take the same position on the trade union question that Reed had. All the communists in the United States were of the opinion that the American Federation of Labor had to be smashed. Lenin had a private talk with Reed on the question. Lenin informed the American that though he agreed with him that the reactionary leadership of the A F of L must be destroyed he was not in favor of smashing the organization.

The Comintern Congress megaphoned Lenin's view. Fraina conspired with Zinoviev to dispose of Reed's opposition. The Congress elected a special committee to study the question further. Lenin's appointment to the committee indicated its importance. Reed, a member of the committee, fought stubbornly for his position. Lenin opposed him. When the committee presented its final draft of policy to the Congress, turning down Reed's proposals, the Congress by an overwhelming majority supported Lenin.

Reed took his defeat badly, not because he lost, but because of the methods employed against him. He was, however, too popular, too well-known throughout Europe and America, to be ignored in the election of members to the Executive Committee of the Comintern. But the election to the Executive did not appease Reed. He continued, in the Executive, to fight Zinoviev and Radek on the trade union question.

The Congress over, Lenin's strategy became clear: The Soviet government pushed for peace with the capitalist powers in order to develop trade and secure economic assistance; the Comintern worked for the building up of a strong international communist movement committed to the fomenting of class warfare and revolution in strict conformity to the policy of the Commissariat of Foreign Affairs. Lenin's policy called for working with the capitalist powers with one hand and undermining them with the other. In addition, Lenin developed a pincers movement against the capitalist world, one arm of the pincers movement called for the organization of a communist revolution on the European continent, to begin in Germany; the other arm provided for the breaking up of the British Empire by financing and organizing nationalist revolutionary movements for independence in the British colonies. Lenin figured that success of the revolutionary pincers movement would give the Bolsheviks the undisputed control of the world.

In carrying out Lenin's policy the Politburo of the Communist party of the Soviet Union directed the Comintern to arouse the Mohammedan masses of the Near East against the British. In conformity the Comintern called a Congress of Oriental Nations at Baku as the first step in a plan to set the Near East aflame against Britain. The Comintern Executive ordered Reed to attend the Congress as a representative of the American proletariat. Reed personally appealed to Zinoviev to be spared the long and arduous trip to Baku. He explained that he needed a rest badly and had not fully recovered his health since his release from Abo prison. Zinoviev insisted that Reed was the only American who could fill the Baku assignment. Speaking in German he laid the law down to Reed as follows: "Die Komintern hat ein Beschluss gemacht. Gehorchen sie." (The Comintern has made a decision. Obey.) Reed was still a well-disciplined communist. Though weak and spiritually troubled he joined the junket.

Radek had charge of the special train which left Moscow loaded with nondescript delegates corralled from all parts of the world, many of them adventurers who represented nobody but themselves. The "Near East Revolution Limited" pulled out of Moscow bound for Baku with a sick, disappointed American revolutionist aboard. . . .

Louise in New York got worried about Reed's condition and, fearing the worst, disguised herself as a sailor, secured seaman's papers and got a job aboard a ship. Alone, passing as a man, roughing it with the crew, she made the perilous journey in order to be near the man she knew needed her badly. When she arrived in Moscow Reed had already gone to Baku. On his return Louise was struck by the deterioration in his appearance. The color was gone from his face. He looked sick and ill at ease. The happy-go-lucky American boy she knew had been replaced by a subdued, tired young man. In September Reed fell ill. He complained of severe headaches and loss of strength. Louise took care of him until he died. During this time he told her what was bothering him, and later when she visited me in Sing Sing, she repeated much of it. I will give the story of his last days in her own words as they were impressed upon my memory.

Louise Bryant's Story

"Jack died because of a great personal disillusionment. He was no longer sure of his bearings. He entertained grave doubts concerning the course he had taken. The cause for which he was prepared to give up his life did not measure up to his expectations. Ever since his return to Soviet Russia from Finland, from his horrible experiences in Abo prison, an inner conflict raged within him—between what he believed in and what he saw and experienced—that played havoc with his peace of mind.

"You would not have recognized poor Jack. The confinement in Finland, the salt fish diet, were in themselves bad enough. But when you consider that for weeks he had been kept in solitary confinement, completely cut off from the outside world, you can begin to understand what that meant to a man as alive and active as Jack. Yet it was nothing compared to the hours Jack spent trying to figure out why Zinoviev had such little regard for the safety of a comrade bound on an important mission as to attach to him a man who on the first opportunity betrayed him to the police. Left alone in prison, as you well know, even little happenings assume large proportions. But what Jack was thinking about, the thoughts he grappled with, were no small matters. They loomed large and threatening in his mind.

"A very sick man returned to Russia. As soon as he gained sufficient strength to resume his duties he threw himself into the work of the Comintern. But his new experiences added to his demoralization. The cheap politics, the way in which the Russians dominated and bossed Comintern affairs and the disregard for principles went against his grain. He still thought he believed in communism but was beginning to feel that what was taking place in Russia differed from the ideal state of Socialism in which he believed. A very much confused man, he stuck to his ideals and resented what the Comintern and the Russian leaders were doing.

"The Baku conference turned out to be his most distressing experience. Though the Russian people were suffering badly from the lack of bare necessities and starvation was rampant, the delegates enroute to Baku were lavishly supplied with rich food and liquor, including rare wines and champagne. Reed saw no excuse for flaunting such extravagance in the faces of the poverty-stricken masses. When he complained Radek and Zinoviev laughed at him.

"On the way the train picked up delegates dressed in various, oriental garments, tough-looking wild men, who guzzled vodka by the tumblerful, most of them unaware of the purposes for which the conference was called. As soon as the train entered the Caucasus Radek outdid himself in providing suitable entertainment for the delegates. Old Mohammedan women boarded the train followed by beautiful Caucasian girls. Some of the girls were barely fourteen years old. The old women disrobed the girls before the delegates. The nude beauties stood before the gaping eyes of those who called themselves communists, who were prepared to tear down the rotten structure of capitalist society in order to build a new, a better world. What followed turned out to be an orgy of drunken lasciviousness in which Radek was the central figure. It thoroughly sickened and disgusted Jack who was, as you know, no prude. But he strongly resented the barter of human flesh. He told me that there were many fine Russian girls who went along to act as secretaries and stenographers. Had any of these chosen to engage in sexual intercourse with the delegates, it would have been perfectly all right with him, but he objected to the use of prostitution by the leaders of the Comintern on the strictly capitalist basis of buying and paying for the commodity.

"The Baku Conference did much to open Reed's eyes. He witnessed a conference in which Kurd, Caucasian and oriental chiefs, gangster leaders, smugglers and adventurers mingled with European communists and communists from the United States, to shout approval of all the prearranged motions and resolutions worked out by the Politburo of the Communist party of Soviet Russia. Radek and Zinoviev did most of the engineering of the conference and most of the talking. Delegates were shoved up on the platform from all countries to greet the conference in their native tongues. But it did not matter to Zinoviev and Radek what they said or didn't say. The wires carried only Radek's manufactured version of what they said. Often the versions of what was said at the conference sent out to Germany, Britain and the United States differed from what was sent out to the Russian people.

"Jack had sharp verbal encounters with Zinoviev and Radek. He warned them not to garble his speeches. Radek laughed at him. Told him not to be naïve. Zinoviev, his vanity hurt by Jack's persistent opposition, warned him that a revolution must be carried on with the material one has on hand. 'A Bolshevik,' he said angrily, 'is a hard realist, one not moved by cheap maudlin sentiments; neither is he concerned whether what he does conforms to bourgeois ideas about justice and morality.'

"Jack noticed how power and the lust for power affected the Bolshevik leaders. After his return from Baku I spent a lot of time with him talking about his experiences and disappointments. He was

terribly afraid of having made a serious mistake in his interpretation
of an historical event for which he would be held accountable before
the judgment of history. He lacked confidence in himself; was not
sure of the ground on which he stood. He blamed himself for becoming a politician; he was not cut out for one. Perhaps Zinoviev and
Radek were right and he was wrong. They were, after all, revolutionary politicians who had been hardened by years of activity and strife.

"I tried to argue with him; to bolster up his morale. 'Pull yourself
together, Jack,' I pleaded. 'When you get back to the States you can do
the things you set your heart on doing.' But he kept looking at me
through his saddened eyes and ended up by saying, 'Honey, it's no use.'

"When Jack first complained of being ill he did not take it
seriously. I did not like his looks. He said it was nothing to worry
about. He became progressively worse. The physicians assigned to his
case spent days trying to determine the nature of his illness. Jack lay
on his cot racked with fever. What disturbed me most was that he
just wasn't interested in getting better. I pleaded with him, for his own
sake, not to give up. He didn't respond.

"The stupid doctors finally decided Jack had typhus. His condition by that time was so bad that they ordered him removed to a
hospital. I begged to be left with him. What I saw on my visits to the
hospital alarmed me. He did not receive the care he should have been
given. I knew he needed me desperately. Only when delirium set in was
I allowed to be at his side. I spent horrible days and nights with him,
days and nights I can never forget. He raved and he cried. He spoke
constantly of being caught in a trap. They were terrifying words
coming from Jack. You know the rest. He died three days later, Ben.

"It is my strongest conviction," concluded Louise, wiping away
her tears, "he died because he did not want to live."

John Reed died on Sunday, September 17, 1920. A great funeral
procession was arranged, flowery eulogies were given, and Reed was
finally buried in the Kremlin Wall as the first great American Communist hero, and today to the uninitiate he is still that. But what is
not generally known is that the Comintern breathed a collective sigh
of relief rather than sorrow when Reed died.

The Irish Contingent

The American communist movement owes a great deal to the Irish and the Irish-American radicals. The Irish escaped the handicaps of the other foreign-born elements in the movement. Accepted as Americans, they considered themselves natives and acted accordingly. The Irish communist contingent consisted of a small number of individuals. In leadership, however, they commanded a position relatively out of proportion to their numbers. From the Irish contingent the communists got organizers, writers, editors, speakers, trade union leaders and valuable contacts with important elements in other trade unions. The Irish constituted a virile, aggressive element which boasted of revolutionary traditions and was proud of the achievements of the Irish revolutionists.

The Irish looked up to James Connolly as the Lenin of the Irish radicals. Before the ill-fated Easter Rebellion in 1916 which cost him his life, Connolly had been to America and lectured before branches and forums of the Socialist party. He studied the works of Marx and applied his special brand of Irish Marxism to the Irish revolutionary cause for independence. He left behind him in the United States a resolute band of Irish socialists with whom he maintained intimate contacts while preparing to strike the blow for Irish freedom.

The outstanding Irish personality in the American communist movement owes his downfall more to an anachronism of time and place than to the strange mixture of traits in his character which set him apart from other men. Jim Larkin typified in his habits, in the bombastic harangue of his oratory, in his unflinching courage and mule-like stubbornness, a mass leader whose very appearance before the populace won their sympathy and acclaim. Standing over six feet tall, his large, prominent nose setting off sharp features, eyes that in anger sparkled fire, Larkin stood out in any crowd.

Larkin was the dynamic figure who welded Irish labor into a militant trade union organization. In founding Liberty Hall in Dublin he established the storm center of the Irish Revolution. In Liberty Hall were housed the headquarters of the Irish Transport and General Workers Union which played a notable part in the war for Irish freedom. There its National Executive met under Larkin's leadership and plotted the strikes for economic and political purposes which rocked Ireland and disturbed the complacency of the British lion. Larkin's union, the counterpart of the one big union idea, was a semi-political trade union organization with revolutionary tendencies and socialist sympathies. It constituted the largest labor union organization in the country, numbering over 150,000 members drawn from all important industries and services. Larkin's union was both anti-British and anti-war, but not pacifist, for it employed the most violent methods against the British. In 1918 the union called a general strike against conscription and forced the British government to abandon the conscription of Irishmen. Larkin's union included dockers, seamen, women workers, laborers, intellectuals, factory workers, clerical workers and agricultural workers; it operated cooperative restaurants and tailoring establishments. Virtually every section of Irish labor was under its influence. The British government fought Larkin and his organization. Many of its members and leaders paid with imprisonment and death.

James Connolly was closely associated with Larkin. The two men complemented each other. The first was a scholar and revolutionary leader like Lenin; the other a revolutionary trade unionist and mass figure, all heart and passion, like William D. Haywood of the I.W.W. Larkin, in spite of his egotism, looked up to Connolly, served under him and respected his opinions.

The decision of Connolly that Larkin should proceed to the United States to secure arms for an Irish uprising against Great Britain was the unmaking of Larkin, for it resulted in uprooting him from Irish soil. Transplanting him to the soil of another country was like transplanting a tree to a soil and environment in which it could not grow.

Larkin, the Irish patriot, found no contradictions between Catholicism, to which he devoutly adhered, and the materialistic conceptions of Marxism which dominated his political thinking and program. At his first meeting in New York, at New Star Casino, he shocked a socialist audience by unbuttoning his shirt and producing a golden cross. Holding the cross before him he shouted at the audience, the large majority of whom were not Irish, and decidedly atheistic, "There is no antagonism between the cross and socialism. A man can pray to Jesus and be a better militant socialist for it. There is no conflict between the religion of the Catholic Church and Marxism. I stand by the cross and Marx. I belong to the Catholic Church. In Ireland that is not held against a socialist. I defy any man to challenge my standing as a socialist and a revolutionist."

Directly in back of quaint Patchin Place, where Reed lived, is situated a little alley which is entered from Sixth Avenue. The alley actually serves as a courtyard for a few dilapidated red brick tenements hugging each other closely. On the ground floor of one of these tenements, in a dark ugly flat, Larkin established his headquarters and lived in utter disregard of cleanliness. Papers, pamphlets, books, rubbish, left-over food bits and dirty tea cups cluttered the place. Here, sprawled over a large stuffed chair, the towering man held court. On the small gas stove tea was usually brewing, a dark concoction which Larkin drank by the bucketful. Here came emissaries from the four corners of the British Empire to report to the founder and commander of the Irish Citizens Army. His was an informal court. The haughty Larkin did not insist on ceremony but he did insist upon dominating the scene. He did not lack the human touch for he was a rough, congenial, witty gentleman who laughed loud and boisterously.

Reports were given to him verbally, never in written form. In a like manner he gave orders to men who stood before him in great awe and respect, men who navigated the seven seas, who faced death and meted it out too. Here came smugglers who knew how to circumvent the British Navy, saboteurs who cooperated with the German Imperial Government for considerations beneficial to the Irish cause, Irish-American labor leaders and longshoremen who reported on allied munitions waiting shipment to Europe. Larkin in his arms transactions often called in Ludwig Lore, editor of the German language socialist daily newspaper the *Volkszeitung,* who acted as the link between Fritz Von Papen, Military Attaché of the German Embassy and the Irish. That collaboration had a part in a great catastrophe.

The Black Tom Explosion

In the early morning hours of July 30, 1916, a terrific munitions blast shook an area around New York harbor for a distance of ninety miles. The harbor and its environs were bombarded by the explosion of big shells for over twenty-four hours. Shipping in the busy harbor was imperiled and crippled. Black Tom, a New Jersey peninsula which sticks its nose into New York Bay towards the Statue of Liberty, on the morning of the explosion was lined up with freight cars loaded with munitions destined for France. In addition, its twenty-four huge warehouses were stored with goods valued at more than $25,000,000. To its docks were tied barges loaded with shells and high explosives. Fifty employees of the Lehigh Valley Railroad watched this vast store of munitions and goods at midnight, July 29.

The origin of the greatest munitions explosion in all history is shrouded in mystery. Mystery surrounds the explosion of Johnson barge No. 24 which backed into the end of the north pier just before midnight where the fire at the end of the pier was supposed to have started. No satisfactory answer has been given why a barge loaded with high explosives was backed into a burning pier. Some witnesses said the fire started on the Johnson barge; others insisted it started on the pier, and still others claimed it started among the freight cars. All, however, were agreed the fire started at midnight; yet the Jersey City Fire Department did not get the alarm until after the fire had been blazing for forty minutes. When the apparatus arrived the flames were out of control, the heat so terrific that the firemen were unable to approach near enough to check the conflagration.

Also connected with the explosion is the weird tale of the captain of the tugboat *Geneva,* who shortly before two o'clock saw the flames shoot out of Johnson barge No. 24. He claimed he came around to the end of the pier to tow the barge to safety, knowing that it was a floating arsenal. When he got to the pier, so his story goes, he found another barge burning. Hooking hausers to both, he hauled the burning barges out into the harbor. He got out only a short distance when the second barge was blown to pieces in a great explosion which shook buildings 15 miles away. He thereupon cut loose barge No. 24 and sped out into the harbor to safety. Barge 24 floated up against the Jersey Central pier, from which it had been towed before, and from that barge alone a bombardment continued for hours.

The force of the first Black Tom blast threw burning freight cars high into the air and fires immediately consumed the freight yards. When the fire reached a row of cars loaded with dynamite an explosion shook the environs and ripped a huge crater in Black Tom which filled with water and formed a lake. Five warehouses were pulverized; the others burned. Ellis Island suffered damage. The known dead reached six and the injured over thirty-five. The small loss of life was miraculous for an explosion of such proportions. Every window in

Jersey City was shattered. Miraculous too was the fact that New York City, within the range of the exploding heavy shells, suffered no serious damage or loss of life beyond the shattering of windows in the downtown area.

The plotters of the Black Tom explosion were disappointed in the result. They counted on a large loss of human life to launch a campaign to stop the shipment of munitions to England and France. Such a campaign was actually started. The German-Americans, the Irish Republicans and the radicals united in calling for an embargo on all munitions shipments to the Allies.

Captain Von Papen's scheming brain knitted the sabotage organization together. Included were German agents, bankers who supplied the cash, a motley crew of American swindlers and adventurers, Irish revolutionists, conversative pro-Irish labor leaders and German-American socialists. The work of this crew was linked up with revolutionary activities in Mexico and other Latin-American countries and was tied in with the anti-war peace propaganda which the radicals were conducting and which had at the time assumed large proportions.

The Black Tom explosions followed on the heels of the arrest and conviction of Sir Roger Casement after he had been landed from a German U-boat on the Irish coast. A German tramp steamer loaded with arms for the Irish revolutionists, which followed the U-boat, was blown to bits by the British Navy. To cap the events which incensed Larkin was the crushing of the Easter Rebellion in Dublin and the killing of his friend and co-worker James Connolly.

Without the aid of the Irish revolutionists and their connections on the waterfront, without the link which the German-American socialists established between them and Von Papen, the Black Tom catastrophe never would have taken place. The Irish network using Lore and his aides passed on the information. The saboteurs did the rest.

Even after the war was over and as late as the year 1919, Lore maintained connections with the Germans and rendered assistance thereby, through Larkin, to the Irish revolutionists. Larkin and Lore were no adventurers. They were sincere revolutionary socialists. Whatever they did was not from monetary but from idealistic considerations. Larkin during the time he was in the United States could have easily amassed a fortune and lived like a prince. The opposite was true. Though he had power and influence over thousands of Irishmen who obeyed his beck and call, he was always penniless, lived under the most frugal circumstances, and never concerned himself about his appearance and personal well-being.

Larkin was not ashamed of what he did for the Irish revolution. He opposed the war because he was a socialist and an Irishman opposed to Britain. He harbored no illusions on how the Irish were to win their freedom from the British. He advocated in the struggle for freedom the employment of every agency of force and violence. And he openly proclaimed that he was engaged in the procurement of arms for the Irish revolutionists with which to fight the British.

Larkin was an unusual organizer. He never gave one the impression that he was doing things. One never saw Larkin sitting at a desk, talking to a secretary, dictating letters or concerning himself with office details. More likely you would see him bent over a stove, frying bacon and eggs in a greasy pan. Yet he made the contacts he needed; got ladies in high places to carry out dangerous missions for him; had the powerful Irish-American labor union circles back him up, and controlled the activities of an army of Irish rebels who worked as seamen on British, American and neutral vessels. All served him loyally and kept him well informed. These seamen together with dockers on the eastern seaboard fitted into a combination worked out by Von Papen that caused havoc with American munition shipments destined for the war.

The Black Tom explosion, far from being an accident, was part of a well-prepared plan, depending upon the utilization of many forces which operated independently and in ignorance of each other. The report, a year later, of Colonel Beverley W. Dunn bears out this contention, for it concluded that the Black Tom disaster was the work of incendiaries and that the evidence in the explosion pointed to plotters.

Larkin, the Communist

Larkin must be considered one of the founders of the American communist movement, for he, Reed and I formed the big three who defied the Russian-Slavic bloc in seeking to organize a truly American Communist party. It was no accident that Larkin's Connolly Club on West Twenty-ninth Street became the national organization center for the communist movement and housed its first national headquarters.

Larkin, a typical rebel, had no use for conventions and laws when they interfered with his political objectives. His tactics and policies sprang from Irish experiences rather than from what the conditions in the United States demanded. Like every other Irishman, Larkin considered himself more American than most Americans. In this he was badly mistaken for he never fully understood the United States.

Larkin's famous Connolly Club included Jews, Russians, Poles, Americans, one Canadian, an Englishman and a number of Irish socialists. What Larkin did was to seize the headquarters of the Socialist Party branch to which he belonged and convert it into the club. At its opening session in March, 1918, he flayed the reformists in the Socialist party and called upon its members to transform their party into a Bolshevik—a Communist—party.

Larkin refused to take orders but never tired of giving orders which he expected others to carry out explicitly. This characteristic he displayed during his trial in 1920 for criminal anarchy. The Lusk Committee arrested Larkin at his home on the night the committee made a city-wide raid on all communist headquarters in New York. Over 2000 communists were seized and taken to the large auditorium at police headquarters for questioning by the Lusk Committee and its investigators. Larkin was brought in late in the evening. Swaggering, he greeted the comrades with a wave of the hand and a laugh. Sitting down in the rear of the hall, he amused himself by poking fun at the police. Most of those questioned were released. About sixty were held over. Larkin and I were the last called up. We were not questioned or searched like the rest but instead were taken down to the basement and thrown into a cell. Shortly afterward Larkin was tried and sentenced to 5-10 years in Sing Sing.

When Larkin was released from prison and deported to Ireland, the returning hero proved to be a stranger to the Irish people. In Dublin great crowds greeted their returning leader with impressive demonstrations of enthusiasm. They had no way of judging the deterioration which had taken place in the man as a result of his long absence from his country and his people, and because of his affirmation of the communist cause.

The Communist International placed great hopes in Larkin. The Comintern had its own plans for exploiting his popularity. One of the first things Litvinov did when he was appointed ambassador to Great Britain was to make a special visit to Dublin to demonstrate the solidarity of the Soviet government with the cause of Irish freedom.

He was wildly acclaimed. But the Comintern made its plans for Ireland without Larkin and was therefore in for surprises.

When Larkin finally did get to Russia, he did not go to receive orders, he went to negotiate. The Comintern patiently tried to maneuver him into a position in which he would be forced to act as its tool. Larkin balked and kicked the traces. Negotiations with him came to nought. Without breaking ties with him, the Comintern proceeded cautiously to work in Ireland, through Irish communists who were amenable to Moscow domination. These were instructed to work behind Larkin's back, to utilize whatever value remained in exploiting his reputation. The Irish communists were under instructions to break away from the Larkin myth as soon as the time proved propitious. Moscow, in addition, sent secret, confidential information and instructions to the Communist parties of the United States and of Great Britain apprising them of Larkin's relations with the Comintern. Steps were taken to tear down the man and destroy him as a leader.

The weakness of the communist movement in Ireland prevented the Comintern from carrying out its campaign against Larkin. When he died in 1947, the Comintern, ignoring its position on the man, revived the "Larkin myth" and claimed him as its own. The Communist party of the United States, that of Great Britain and that of Ireland, paid tribute to Larkin, the great Irish communist and labor leader, ignoring the fact that he had broken with the communist movement and that they had been secretly doing everything possible to undermine his reputation and influence.

Larkin, in spite of his many faults and idiosyncrasies, will be remembered as the man who built Ireland's labor movement and inspired the Irish laboring masses with hope and a will for freedom. For having the courage to cast aside the international communist movement he helped organize, he will be remembered among the great who hated injustice and loved liberty.

The Tragedy of the One-Eyed Monster

How a great American labor leader became the pawn in a scheme which led him, of his own volition, into a trap from which he never escaped, gives an insight into the diabolical machinations of the communist mind.

The story begins in Moscow in July, 1920, when the Red Trade Union International was organized. The Comintern's new policy, which was being fought by Reed and the I.W.W. among others, was to bore from within the conservative trade unions rather than to smash them.

In order to browbeat the opposition into submission to the new trade union line, Lenin, in spite of the pressing demands of the government upon his time, wrote a special pamphlet for this purpose, under the title, "Left Communism, An Infantile Disorder." Four chapters out of ten are devoted to the history of Russian communism from the year of its birth in 1913 up to the time the pamphlet was written. Strictly Russian experiences are used for the foundation of communist policies and tactics to be applied in other countries.

Lenin struck out against the opposition with all the power and prestige of his position. His pamphlet, first published in 1920 and immediately translated and printed in every important language, took the place of the Bible among the communists and is universally used by them, even at the present day, in training communists in the fundamental principles of communist tactics and strategy.

After the July, 1920, organization of the Red Trade Union International, trusted Chekists, loaded down with money, were sent out of Moscow to the four corners of the earth to line up support for the Profintern and to bring delegates by hook or crook to its first Congress to be held in Moscow in the summer of 1921.

The man selected for the American hemisphere for this important job, Carl E. Johnson, originally hailed from the famous communist Letts of Roxbury, Mass. He and his wife, early in 1919, made the journey to Soviet Russia. The Bolsheviks enrolled them in the Cheka to work as spies and secret agents of the Comintern in other countries. Johnson was a handsome man, almost six feet tall. He was a good dresser and spoke excellent English with a pleasant foreign accent. His keen judgment and intelligence, his ability in negotiations, his capacity under all circumstances to keep a poker face made him an outstanding Chekist and later a key figure in the international affairs of the OGPU. Dressed in a suit tailored to perfection he looked more like an energetic, progressive businessman than a shabby representative of the proletariat.

His wife cut an unusual figure. Shorter than he, she was plump and had an olive-drab, oily, round face in which narrow slits disclosed sharp penetrating eyes. She spoke only when necessary—sharply and with biting sarcasm. She too was Lettish and active in the Roxbury Lettish club. Dressed in a kimono she would be mistaken for Chinese anywhere. Husband and wife complemented each other and composed a team used by the Soviet government's secret service in the most difficult and dangerous situations in practically every important country in the Americas, Europe, and the Orient.

Johnson, alias Scott, arrived in the United States in 1920 with over a quarter of a million dollars in his pockets. His main tasks included: one, to organize support and obtain delegates for the Profintern Congress from the countries of North and South America; two, to organize communist parties in Canada and Mexico; three, in collaboration with the Communist party of the United States to secure a notable delegation from the country to the Profintern Congress; four, to lay the foundations for a campaign for the capture of the A F of L by the communists; and five, to get Haywood to go to Soviet Russia. Quite a ticket to give one man!

Soon after his arrival he organized the Communist party of Canada and laid the ground work for the organization of the Communist party of Mexico. Scott also organized the machinery for the smuggling of diamonds and jewelry into the United States from Soviet Russia, duty free, for the purpose of subsidizing communist activities. Scott also tied up A. I. Heller with the underground apparatus of the Comintern responsible for the transfer of monies from Soviet Russia to the communists. He put Julius Heiman, respectable and successful businessman, a secret member of the Communist party, in charge of receiving the diamonds and jewelry and then converting them into good American dollars.

From the day Scott landed in the United States up to the present time, the science of duplicity worked out by Lenin, backed up with Moscow gold and an army of spies and Comintern and Profintern secret agents, has been the official, the basic line of strategy of the American communists.

Before Scott's departure for the United States, he received instructions which stressed the importance of undermining the influence of the I.W.W. in the American communist movement. The Comintern leaders told Scott that since the I.W.W. was an anarcho-syndicalist organization opposed by the Comintern, the strong ideological and sentimental ties between Haywood's organization and the communists had to be broken just as effectively as the Comintern had rejected Reed's trade union proposals. The Comintern leaders discussed with

Scott the person of William D. Haywood, the one-eyed leader of the I.W.W., and what steps should be taken to get him out of the way in the United States. A decision was reached: Scott must leave no stone unturned to get Haywood to leave the United States as a delegate to the Profintern Congress. The Comintern figured that with Haywood out of the way the task of dealing with the I.W.W. would be an easy one.

When Scott met Haywood he was out on bail. Depressed by the prospects of returning to prison, there to spend the rest of his life behind prison bars, Haywood fell an easy prey to Scott's well-laid plans. Scott brought Haywood tidings about the organization in Moscow of a new International of Revolutionary Unions. "The I.W.W.," he pleaded, "must not stay out of the new organization." He painted a glowing picture of the tremendous revolutionary progress being made in Europe and Asia. He asked Haywood not to desert the I.W.W. at such a critical and decisive turn in the world's history by going to prison. He presented him with example upon example of how the Russian revolutionists acted in similar situations, and pointed out that Lenin, Trotsky, Bukharin, Zinoviev and every other leader of the revolution who was in a position to do so, defied Tsarist laws and courts, became fugitives from justice, holding that active service in the cause of the workers and revolution outweighed every other consideration, including the submission to bourgeois legality.

Scott promised Haywood that not a single man or woman who had contributed money to provide the heavy bail set in his case would lose a single penny when he forfeited his bail by fleeing to Russia. He gave Haywood his word of honor, plus the guarantee, the official "pochat," of the Soviet government in this respect.

Haywood's flight to Moscow marked the disappearance from the American scene of the last of the pre-Bolshevik radicals—men and women such as Debs, Max Eastman, Reed, Goldman, Berkman and others, who had strong convictions and a moral sense of right and wrong, champions of the people who stood by their principles regardless of the personal sacrifices involved, and who refused to accept blindly the dictates of Moscow.

Everything was done to give Haywood an impressive welcome when he arrived in Russia. At the border Red Army bands played for him, and workers delegations and shouting, enthusiastic crowds with red flags and flying banners surrounded him. At every stop enroute to Moscow the same demonstrations of welcome greeted the overjoyed

American. He arrived in Moscow just as the delegates came pouring into the city from all parts of the world to attend the First Congress of the Profintern.

A. Losovsky, now head of the Foreign Information Department of the Soviet government, had charge of the Congress. Losovsky, a member of the Mensheviks at the outbreak of the Bolshevik Revolution, hated the Lenin gang. As soon as he was sure which way the wind blew, he deserted his friends and jumped on the Bolshevik bandwagon. A craftier, more cunning, more unprincipled charlatan would be hard to find anywhere. His soft delicate fingers were those of the intellectual, not of the manual laborer. Before Stalin put him in the foreign office he claimed proletarian origin as a cap-maker. Right after his appointment as assistant to Foreign Minister Molotov he changed his biography to read that he was a steel-worker.

Losovsky, appointed president of the Profintern, took Haywood in hand. A sumptuous room was set aside for him at the Comintern's Lux Hotel on the Tverskaya, Moscow's main street leading to the Red Square. He was provided with secretaries, a string of interpreters and guides, all Chekists under instructions to be with the American night and day, never to leave him alone. They injected him with doctored information that molded his opinions. He was dined and wined and flattered like a royal prince. What the excited and pleased American from the wide open spaces of the West did not know was that he was virtually a prisoner of the political police who dogged his steps and spied on him night and day.

Haywood enjoyed the honor accorded him, and appreciated the fact that the Bolsheviks gave him the center of the stage at the Profintern Congress. The Profintern Congress took place at a time when the Bolsheviks were riding roughshod over the Left-Socialist and Anarchist elements which had previously supported them but were now in opposition. The leaders of Russian unions who dared to call strikes for strictly economic demands, who had the courage to ask for increased wages to meet the rising costs of living, were arrested and thrown into prison. The workers who went out on strike got the same rough treatment. The Executive Board of the Printers Union sat in prison because it gave a reception to members of the British Labor Delegation; anarchists, social revolutionists, syndicalists, discontented workers and peasants were herded into prisons and detention camps like so many cattle. Emma Goldman and Alexander Berkman, having been deported by the United States, were in Moscow. They carried on a campaign among the delegates to the Congress for the liberation of political prisoners who had started a hunger strike in protest against the injustice of their imprisonment and the intolerable conditions under which they were forced to live. In addition, the Russian people were hungry and a severe famine threatened.

Meeting under these unfavorable conditions, the Bolsheviks took no chances and surrounded the Profintern Congress with an army of Chekists. Lenin repeatedly had to be called away from his state duties to quiet the fears of foreign delegates aroused over the reports they heard about what was going on in Russia. Losovsky manipulated the delicate situation skillfully, preventing outbursts of protest at the sessions of the Congress. Nevertheless, the well-greased Congress machinery ran into a hitch as it neared its concluding session. Acting upon Lenin's orders and the orders of the Politburo of the Russian Communist party, Bukharin delivered a scathing denunciation of the anarchists and the anarcho-syndicalists, calling them a gang of bandits and hooligans, traitors and counter-revolutionists who fought against the proletarian revolution and thought nothing of murdering communists.

In spite of Losovsky's attempt to steamroller the conference and prevent the delegates from answering Bukharin's speech, the Congress was forced to listen to the protests of the anarcho-syndicalist delegates of France against the brutal treatment of the Russian anarchists and the nefarious methods employed to discredit them.

The American delegates at the Congress, including Haywood and the heads of the Syndicalist League of North America, Comrades Earl Browder and William Z. Foster, said nothing. Why did Haywood, who always championed the right of free speech, who worked with and collaborated with the anarcho-syndicalists in the United States and internationally, suddenly turn mute? It was not his character to hide behind the cowardice of silence. Haywood hesitated and held his tongue, for he did not want to take a position or say anything that might be interpreted as support of counter-revolution. It took Emma Goldman and Alexander Berkman a long time to break with the Bolsheviks. Haywood could not be expected, so soon after his arrival in Russia, to see the truth and to break with the men who had freed him from a life behind prison bars and had welcomed him as a hero and a comrade.

But Big Bill Haywood learned soon enough how he was trapped, and realized he could do nothing about it.

After the Profintern Congress adjourned, Losovsky no longer had any use for the one-eyed monster from Uncle Sam's country. Haywood, reduced to a circus performer for display before groups of Russian workers, was kept busy traveling throughout Soviet Russia, always in the company of Cheka secretaries and interpreters, making speeches in English before gaping Russian workers who did not understand what he said. The Cheka interpreters translated Haywood's remarks into Russian which Haywood did not understand. Thus mutual ignorance divided Haywood from the Russian workers.

Losovsky deliberately kept him away from sessions of the Executive of the Profintern whenever important matters were up for consideration. Haywood stayed on in Russia with nothing of importance to do. He became morose and embittered, not with the world but with himself. He learned too, that all was not rosy in the Soviet paradise. Left to himself he reviewed his folly. Scott, when he returned to Russia, did not bother to see him. Haywood knew he had been a fool, a confounded fool. Return to his native land? That was impossible. He had disgraced himself and deceived his friends. He had violated the confidence they had put in him: he had been dishonest. For Scott's promise that his bail-bond would be made good by the Soviet government was never lived up to.

Soon Haywood was moved from his sumptuous quarters in the Lux to the more modest quarters reserved for the clerks and stenographers working in the Comintern. The Comintern supplied him with a wife, a simple woman, a houseworker of peasant origin who spoke only Russian. She attended to his wants and he took what she gave him. For the Russian woman, the bargain provided her with better quarters, with ample rations and the security which goes to one who complies with communist orders.

Haywood, the man of action, now lived a lonely life within the four walls of a small room, isolated from his friends and the world. The glamour of touring the proletarian hinterland and making speeches to stupid Russians who stared at the *Amerikanski* freak was over for him.

Those who occasionally visited him were American communists and American communists who paraded as liberals in order to direct and influence the army of liberals and intellectuals being drawn into the Communist party orbit. With them Haywood always talked about his I.W.W. He refused to believe the stories they told him about the collapse and deterioration of the organization he loved. It became obvious, as the conversation progressed, that the worth of bolshevism no longer impressed him and that he had returned to the philosophy of his youth, the idea of the one big union.

Haywood loathed the Soviet system, for he was essentially an individualist who cherished liberty and freedom of action. The dictatorship of the proletariat denied both to the individual. He realized that he had run away from one prison into another, one from which he could not flee, the prison this time being a vast country in which the human lives of millions counted for nothing.

In 1927 Haywood reached the conclusion that he had not much longer to live. The sharp pains in his chest came from his heart. He decided the time had come for him to write his autobiography and presented the proposal to the Comintern. But Haywood could not write the book himself. He had to tell his story to some one who could then compile what he said in book form.

Fortunately, without the consent of the Comintern, he secured the services of a former member of the I.W.W. who was sojourning in Russia. The book finished, Haywood turned it over to the Comintern for publication.

The Comintern publishing department held the manuscript for many months without publishing it. After Haywood died the manuscript was turned over to Alexander Trachtenberg, representative of the Comintern Publishing Department in the United States, for final revision and publication. He changed and revised the book to conform to the Party line, had the Party okay his revisions, and then had it published by International Publishers. Haywood was in no position to object to post-mortem editorial changes.

Haywood spent his last days in a narrow private room in the Kremlin Hospital, a room just large enough to accommodate the hospital bed on which he lay. The Bolshevik chiefs upon whose invitation he had come to Moscow were conspicuous by their absence. I visited him after his Russian wife pleaded with me that Haywood was very sick and was asking to see me.

"Do you know, Ben, I am awfully glad you came," said Haywood with some agitation.

"Calm yourself, Bill," I said.

"I'm not excited. I feel like a fool lying here, doing nothing, just because those damn Russian doctors think I am going to die. But let's forget about my illness. Let's talk about the States."

He lay there quietly for a moment and then, in a voice tense with emotion, he said, "Ben, listen. I am speaking calmly. I don't know what you are planning. I don't know what the Comintern and the Profintern are doing but I can tell you this: don't leave your country. Russia may be all right for the Russians but it is no place for an American. Look to America for freedom and hope."

The doctor came in and motioned that the visit must be ended.

Haywood looked out of his one eye intently as if he were trying to see into eternity. Clasping my outstretched hand, his own trembling, he said in a low, tremulous voice, "It's good-bye this time. Good luck and remember me to America."

A few days later Bill Haywood was dead.

CHAPTER TWO

THE COMMUNISTS TAKE TO THE CELLARS

THE idea of organizing a Communist party was first raised in the latter part of June, 1919. By September, 1919, less than four months later, in Chicago, a communist movement with far flung international connections made its appearance on the American scene. Approximately 75,000 men and women were enrolled as dues-paying members. Surrounding the 75,000 Communist party members were nearly 1,000,000 sympathizers who came from practically every radical and liberal group in the country. The communist "enfant terrible" was no premature baby. He was indeed a Gargantuan giant at his birth.

The delegates to the conventions at which the communist movement was officially launched, as soon as the conventions adjourned, rose to their feet and lustily sang the Moscow version of the *Internationale*. When the last phrase, "The International Soviets shall be the human race," rang out amid thunderous applause, the delegates grabbed up their portfolios crammed full of revolutionary dynamite and rushed out of the Windy City in all directions to various parts of the country, hell-bent for revolution.

Before the week passed, national, state and city offices were opened and functioning. Newspapers and magazines published in English and in twenty-three foreign languages made their appearance. Communist propaganda by the ton was printed and distributed. Speakers and organizers covered the country. The communist baby not only yelled for revolution, he also diligently got on the job to build the organization for sovietizing America.

What the communists of 1919 lacked in political experience they made up for in other ways. They were alert and quick to learn from experience. They had courage too, and were not afraid to tackle situations, without adequate preparation, in which they faced danger and formidable opponents. The communists challenged the labor unions

53

and their officials. They injected themselves into strike situations, attacking the strike leaders and calling upon the workers to turn their strikes into political struggles for power. They openly defied the United States government and violated its laws. Every leaflet, every newspaper, every communist magazine bristled with revolutionary slogans calling upon the American proletariat to take up arms and overthrow the capitalist government of Wall Street. The communists backed up their revolutionary romanticism with an inexhaustible store of energy—energy of dynamic power generated by the fires of fanaticism.

Had the communists then had the time to benefit by their mistakes, had they had an opportunity to learn and understand more about the country in which they operated, they would in a short time have become the balance of power. From the moment representatives of the American communists arrived in Moscow to arrange for the affiliation of the movement with the Communist International, from that moment on the American Communist party became a branch office of Moscow. Moscow made the decisions governing the actions of the American communists. The Russians laid down the Communist party line. The Comintern played the tune, the American communists danced accordingly.

The American anti-communist opposition acted quickly. It did not give the American communists the time they badly needed to consolidate and perfect their organization. The opponents of communism were greatly alarmed and not without reason. Communist revolution had swept over one-sixth of the globe. The red flag of communism made its appearance on the European continent. Germany, Italy, Austria, Hungary and Bulgaria looked like the countries next to be mowed down by the sickle and hammered into submission to a Red dictatorship. Strikes, rebellions and mutinies were the order of the day. In staid, conservative England, with the closest ties to the United States, industrial unrest rocked the country. In London, Liverpool and elsewhere, the British bobbies were organizing themselves into unions and opposing the very authority of the government they, as civil servants, had to defend. The strike of the Liverpool police proved one of the bloodiest affairs in the history of British labor. Troops had to be called out. Widespread looting took place. Pitched battles between the mobs and the troops resulted in many deaths. The British Navy dispatched three large warships to guard the port in order to prevent the destruction of the docks and shipping facilities. Evidence indicated that the British communists were attempting to turn the discontent and industrial disorder following the end of the war into revolutionary political channels and that Lenin and his associates were pumping money into England's Red movement to help them do this.

Immediately following the organization of the Communist party, industrial warfare broke out in the U. S. involving every major industry. Serious race riots took place with great loss of life. The communists injected themselves into the strike situations, even though they had at the time no important roots in the unions. They issued manifestoes to the strikers calling upon them to seize the struck industries and to take up arms against their government. During the strike of the motormen and conductors of the Brooklyn Rapid Transit Company, the communists called upon the workers to take up arms and immediately organize Soviets. In addition to all these disquieting factors, the influence of Europe on the American labor scene was being definitely felt. Following the British lead, municipal and civil service workers seriously began trade union organization. The police formed policemen's unions affiliated with the American Federation of Labor.

The dramatic break came when the policemen of Boston went out on strike on September 9, 1919, just one week after the Communist parties had been launched. An outstanding figure in the policemen's union of Boston, a policeman of Irish extraction, was a close sympathizer of the Communist party and collaborated with the communists in the conduct of the strike.

The situation in Liverpool was repeated in Boston. Crowds surged through the streets of the city smashing store windows and looting. Lawlessness gripped Boston. Doors were bolted and padlocked. Store windows were heavily boarded up. Boston looked like a city in a state of siege. Troops were called out. Machine guns were used on the mobs. Cavalry dashed through the streets breaking up the crowds. People were killed and the hospitals filled with wounded. For four days Boston was a stricken, terrorized city.

The communists were active in the strike. Some of the most violent episodes of the strike took place in Roxbury where the communist Letts were concentrated. Emissaries from the Boston communists were hurriedly dispatched to New York to report on the situation to communist leaders and to get advice and orders on how to proceed. Communist organizers were rushed to Boston. Rank-and-file members who were foot-loose were directed to go to Boston to help the local comrades intensify the strike violence, to work for the calling of a general strike, and to politicalize the strike by directing it against the government.

The State and Federal authorities took no chances. Governor Coolidge depended not only on the National Guard but also on the promise of the United States government that the War and Navy Departments were prepared to step into the situation whenever that became necessary. Washington forced Gompers to take a hand in the situation in order to counteract communist pressure for a general strike. He killed the idea for a general strike just in time to prevent the Central Trades from voting on the proposition.

The strike smashed, Boston returned to normal. But the country was frightened. A sinister force had succeeded in undermining the citadel of law and order, the police. Something had to be done.

From fear and panic came a demand for action against labor and against the Reds. The reaction soon crystallized into a definite policy. The communists challenged the government. The government accepted the challenge and proceeded to act. Secretary of War Baker in his address before the Ohio Federation of Women's Clubs, on October 15, 1919, threw down the gauntlet to the communists in the following words:

"In our country, since the armistice, there has been a growing agitation and unrest manifesting itself sometimes in race riots and mob disorder, but for the most part evidenced by widespread industrial controversies. Our newspapers are daily filled with accounts of violent agitation by so-called Bolshevists and radicals counseling violence and urging action in behalf of what they call revolution . . . In the meantime the timid may take heart. Sometime ago I telegraphed every State in the Union that in the event of any civil disorder which he found himself unable to control by reason of the demobilization of the National Guard, the governor should communicate directly with the commanding general of the department in which his state lies, and I correspondingly telegraphed to every department commander to respond instantly with the aid of Federal troops to any call from the governor who found himself unable with the means at his disposal to suppress disorder and to enforce the local laws . . . We have an army of tried soldiers, of true Americans . . . They will respond instantly to the call of any governor to suppress riots and disorder in any part of the country. They are not partisans in any dispute except one and that is the dispute between those who want order and those who try to create disorder in America."

September 2, 1919, the communist movement was officially launched. September 9 the Boston Police strike began. September 22, the nation-wide Steel strike led by William Z. Foster started. At the end of October the soft-coal miners under the leadership of John L. Lewis staged a nation-wide Coal strike stretching from the Appalachian coal range to the Pacific in defiance of a government order not to strike. Alexander Howatt, President of the Kansas miners,—he later joined the Communist party—defied the courts and the government by declaring: "We'll call their bluff. The strike can't be stopped."

On November 5, the preliminary skirmishes in the coming smashing counter-blow against the communists took place. The communists were taken off guard and were totally unaware of what was in store for them even though the opening gun was fired directly at them. A heavily armed squadron of the New York police commanded by a sergeant of the Bomb Squad swooped down on the headquarters of the Russian branch of the Communist party during a meeting. Using the clubs freely and brutally they broke up the gathering and arrested four Russian communists on charges of criminal anarchy. Thousands of manifestoes printed in English calling upon the workers to come to Rutgers Square to celebrate the second anniversary of the Bolshevist Revolution were confiscated. The manifestoes called for a nation-wide general strike on November 8 and for the overthrow of the government by armed force and the seizure of power by the proletarians.

The Rutgers Square demonstration from where the revolution was to start did not materialize. Mayor William F. Hylan informed the Communist party that he had banned the demonstration. The communists defied him by declaring they would go ahead with their plans. Hylan refused to be bluffed and backed up his words with police action. The police, armed to the teeth, massed around the square under orders to deal ruthlessly with the communists should they attempt to hold a demonstration.

After much bickering, in which the communist leaders threw ugly words at each other, the Rutgers Square revolution was called off.

The national leaders with bowed heads and red faces went to Guffanti's Restaurant on Seventh Avenue to drown their shame in dago red and spaghetti.

The Communist Labor party wing of the communist movement decided to hold mass meetings in halls to celebrate the anniversary of the Bolshevik Revolution and refused to cooperate in the Rutgers Square affair. The meeting held in the Brownsville section of New York City gave a fair picture of the temper of the Communist Labor party. The hall was packed with screaming, cheering, enthusiastic communists. Dr. Morris Zucker, the Brownsville dentist, shouted: "We are here tonight to celebrate the second anniversary of the Russian Soviet Socialist Republic and the birth of a new revolutionary movement here. The day is soon coming when the proletariat will be able to meet the capitalist class bayonet for bayonet and machine gun for machine gun. The government that will send armed men to the coal regions to deal with strikers is on its last legs."

Other speakers who addressed the meeting were Ludwig Lore, James Larkin and the author. Larkin and i had no inkling that the next day we would be caught in the net prepared for us by the government. Also seated on the platform, and one of the meeting's chief speakers, was Ludwig C. K. A. Martens, first Soviet Ambassador to the United States, who delivered a speech in favor of world revolution. Martens, though Soviet Ambassador, was a secret member of the Communist Labor party and supported it liberally with embassy funds.

The Lusk Committee formed by the New York State Legislature to investigate subversive activities subpoenaed Martens to appear before it for interrogation. He refused and was arrested. Once before the committee, he proved an affable and informative witness.

Martens, a fair complexioned man of medium height, born of German parents in Russia, looked like a German. After his discharge from the German army, in which he served for two years, he met Lenin in Switzerland in 1901 and an intimate friendship followed. Martens came to the United States in 1916 as a German, not a Russian subject. During the war he failed to register as an enemy alien. He claimed that one month before the United States entered the war, that is, in March, 1917, he applied by mail for Soviet citizenship. No copies of letters or documents to substantiate his claim were presented. The fact that the Soviet government did not come into being until seven months later, on November 7, 1917, did not bother Martens in the least.

Though not recognized by the United States, Martens maintained an embassy at 110 West Fortieth Street, New York City. His staff, with a few rare exceptions, was made up of members of the American communist movement. That Martens had ample funds with which to operate, his own admissions prove, though he did not give the entire story of his financial dealings. He admitted under oath that he received a minimum of $30.000 monthly from Europe, or a yearly total of at least $360,000. He failed to disclose that he received additional funds in the form of loans to the Soviet government from rich Russian-American pro-Bolshevik businessmen which amounted to close to a million dollars and that he acted as custodian of special monies brought by couriers from Russia, earmarked for explicit communist activities in North and South America.

Martens in his frank testimony indicated that the Bolsheviks were more interested in world revolution than they were in the niceties of diplomacy. The hypocrisy and duplicity of present-day Soviet diplomacy was lacking in his testimony. He appeared on the stand first as a Bolshevik, a protagonist of world revolution, and second, as the Ambassador of a power seeking American recognition.

He stated without the quiver of an eyelash that he was in the United States to aid the spread of world-wide revolution. Archibald E. Stevenson, the counsel for the committee, put the question to him: "Isn't it a fact that in stating its wishes to overthrow the capitalist system, the Soviet government wishes to overthrow all capitalist governments?"

Martens nonchalantly answered: "It is their wish to change from the capitalist to the socialist system."

"How do they expect this change to come about?"

"The change may come by purely pacific means or it may come through a bitter struggle. They (the Soviets) do not care how it comes."

"Whether it comes by terror or by diplomacy?"

Martens smiled. "It is a matter for the working class."

"Isn't it a fact that the Soviet issues propaganda advising the propriety of overthrowing capitalist governments in other countries?"

Martens replied, "Yes, as a means of defense."

The committee did not realize that in that answer the unrecognized Soviet Ambassador to the United States had laid down the basic line of Soviet diplomacy which has been adhered to under all exigencies. Though the basic line may be hidden in the complex relations which the Soviet government maintains with other governments, though the line may appear to be totally obscured by the skillful maneuvers of the Soviet Foreign Office, what is characterized as realism in the conduct of Bolshevik foreign affairs hinges on the basic line of Soviet foreign policy stated so succinctly by Martens back in 1919. In order to understand this basic line of Soviet diplomacy one must grasp the full implications of what Martens said when he stated that Soviet propaganda for the overthrow of capitalist governments was a means of defense. Defense in the Bolshevik mind connotes a much broader meaning. To the Bolshevik, defense means a matter of survival. From the days of Lenin, the master-mind of communism, to the supreme ruler, Stalin, the survival of Soviet power and communism is held impossible unless capitalism with its political and social structure is destroyed. It explains why the theory of world revolution has never been abandoned and why the Soviet government at great expense and effort maintains and supports communist parties in other countries.

The first serious blow to stagger the communists came on November 7, 1919, when the communists throughout the country were celebrating the second anniversary of the Bolshevik Revolution. The Department of Justice on a nation-wide scale swooped down upon the foreign-born elements who belonged to the Communist party and on the Russian anarchists, who, at the time, supported the Bolshevik cause. Aided by local police, an army of deputies drawn from private detective agencies, using a caravan of army trucks, raided communist and radical headquarters in New York, Chicago, Detroit, Philadelphia, St. Louis; in Jackson, Michigan, Newark, New Haven, Hartford and other cities.

Before the communists had time to get their bearings as to what happened to them on November 7, the New York State Lusk Committee, the next day, on the night of November 8, carried out simultaneously seventy-one raids against communists and their organizations in New York City where the greatest numerical concentration of the movement was to be found. Close to two thousand men and women were thrown into patrol wagons and hurried to police headquarters on Centre Street. The raids proceeded all night long. Lists of those to be arrested included every known communist leader. Those who escaped the dragnet were visited in their homes and, if found, were promptly seized. The raiders smashed and wrecked communist property and headquarters. Money boxes were pried open and the cash stolen. Printed material, books, pictures and banners were confiscated. In all, the authorities confiscated twenty-five tons of material. The top communist leaders who were in New York were arrested, as were practically all the secondary leaders.

Before the week was up, headquarters were cleaned and reopened and communist activity went on as before. The communists lost no time in starting a defense campaign on behalf of the victims of the raids. Thousands of dollars flowed into defense headquarters. The communists utilized the attacks to whip up sympathy for themselves among the American people and thereby won many new friends among liberal and progressive forces who opposed the brutal, suppressive, and unconstitutional methods used in the raids.

The wave of suppression against the communists had receded. The communist leaders thought the worst was over. But by January of the following year, the anti-communist wave broke upon the communists with such force that the organization was left in a complete shambles.

The January raids were well prepared by the Department of Justice. Attorney General Palmer put private detective William J. Flynn in charge of the anti-red crusade, a man he claimed was the greatest anarchist expert in the United States, one who knew all the men of that class and could pretty nearly call them all by name. A special file in the Justice Department indexed 200,000 communists. Palmer's plan called specifically for raids on the headquarters, meeting places and homes of communists, to take place simultaneously on the same day, and at the same time from the Atlantic seaboard to the Pacific coast. Local and state law enforcement agencies were enlisted in the crusade.

In Boston the five hundred arrested were shackled and chained hand and foot and marched through the streets. The conditions on Deer Island where the prisoners were confined and held incommunicado were chaotic and brutal. One of the captives, unable to stand the strain, plunged headlong from the fifth floor to the corridor below and dashed his brains out.

In New York over 3,000 communists were rounded up. The raids were conducted with romantic wild west bravado, the detectives shouting war whoops as they rushed into buildings with drawn revolvers and swinging clubs.

In Philadelphia those arrested were subjected to a third degree inquisition in which were used the worst physical force methods and torture known to the police.

In all the large cities, east, north, west and south, the story was the same. The raids were thorough, efficient, spectacular and effective. The few communists who escaped the night of horrors were completely dazed. For the communists who remained, to build something out of the wreckage seemed an almost impossible task. Before the communists had time to check their losses, they received another severe jolt when the State of Illinois indicted all the national communist officials for violation of the state sedition act.

The Comintern rushed to the assistance of the American communists, supplying them with organizational help and funds with which to rebuild the Party. But the Party failed to make headway. The communists, with few exceptions, just stayed away from meetings and refused to take part in communist activities. The communists believed that the situation in the United States was similar to that in Tsarist Russia when liberal and radical parties were forced to function illegally as underground organizations. The communist leaders yielded to this sentiment and took to the cellars. There was nothing left for the Communist party to do but transform itself into an underground organization.

Lenin, in dealing with the art of conspiracy, held that a revolutionary movement can use the severe blows delivered against it to its own advantage. Lenin considered defeats temporary setbacks in the march towards victory. He maintained that a lost strike need not necessarily be considered a defeat for the workers if the communists are able to exploit the situation created by the lost strike to arouse in the workers a rebellious attitude against their government. Lenin admonished the communists not to shrink from fomenting disorders and bloodshed, even if by doing so the strike were lost, provided the violent tactics serve communist political ends. Communists have followed Lenin's strategy in strikes, demonstrations, political campaigns and in armed uprisings repeatedly.

Though the Palmer raids almost wrecked the Communist party, indirectly they helped the cause of American communism immensely. How explain such a paradox when the communists lost as a result of the raids nearly 60,000 dues-paying members?

The raids helped the Communist party separate the wheat from the chaff. The communists who did not have the courage to withstand the dangers accompanying membership in the Communist party went to the side lines. The 16,000 Communist party members who remained in the two communist parties, after the raids, voluntarily undertook the perils of Communist party membership. They constituted the men and women who were willing to put up with the rigors of communist life, its regimentation and strict discipline. They put their personal lives at the disposal of the party, the party to do with them whatever was thought fit and proper. The small communist residue of the 1920's formed an intransigent, fanatical body of zealots—the human element that went into the building of a monolithic organization, an organization of one will and mind.

What happened to the 60,000 members who disappeared from the membership rolls? Did they lose faith in the movement and cease to be communists? Did they succumb to the anti-communist hysteria and turn anti-communist? Not at all. Out of this number, a few, an insignificant number, were lost to the movement. The overwhelming majority of them remained staunch communist sympathizers, devoted slaves to communist ideology and generous supporters of the movement. They made up a dependable layer between the Communist party membership and the large army of sympathizers and fellow travelers, who, in 1920, numbered over 600,000.

Operating through this secondary communist mass, the underground Communist party, in spite of the smallness of its dues-paying membership, was nevertheless a large and powerful organization. Because of this phenomenon, the Communist party maintained its hegemony over the American radical scene. *To judge the influence and potentialities of a Communist party by the size of its membership is to make a serious blunder, for the communist organization extends far beyond the limitations of its dues-paying members.*

Absolute, dictatorial powers were lodged in the Central Executive Committee and its powerful sub-committee, the political committee. These two committees met in secret. Special trusted couriers directed the members of these two committees to the meeting places, which were changed with each sitting. Once the meeting of a committee started, the doors were bolted and no one was allowed to leave the room until the session adjourned. All party members, including the party leaders, adopted aliases or, as the communists preferred to call them, party names.

The meetings of the Central Executive Committee and its subcommittees were generally held in private homes, in studios of communist artists, in dingy halls in the East Side ghettos of New York and in the offices of communist newspapers and printing plants. To the meetings of the Central Executive Committee came Cheka agents, couriers from Moscow and communist emissaries from European and Latin-American countries. These meetings, as will be shown, were more than just political gatherings discussing American political problems.

The underground headquarters of the Communist party were secret haunts known only to a few trusted communists and the leaders put in charge of the headquarters. Once the decision was made the underground organization rapidly took form. In less than a month's time the communist underground ringed the country. Secret national, district, state, local, city and neighborhood headquarters were established. In underground printing plants, dependable union printers blurred the union label number and printed tons of communist propaganda and material. Secret distribution centers were established where the literature was received and then distributed by courier to specified comrades for distribution to the public. The U. S. mail and the Express companies were also used for this purpose, the communists camouflaging the material thus shipped. A communist paper when mailed was wrapped in a copy of the New York *Times* or the *Christian Science Monitor* and given a fictitious return address.

How was the underground organized? Not along democratic lines. The Central Executive Committee, consisting of a handful of the Party's top national leaders, selected the state and district leadership; the state and district leadership, only with the approval of the national leadership, appointed the city and local leadership who in turn, with the approval of the state and district leadership, appointed the leadership of the neighborhoods and sections. The rank-and-file was organized into cells of five to ten known to each other only by their aliases or party names.

The communist underground quickly developed into a complex conspiratorial organization which acted as the official agency in the United States of the Soviet government. The underground had built up intricate machinery which fitted into one gigantic whole and was wired to the Moscow switchboard which controlled the machine's operations.

Americans will find it difficult to understand the communist organization. It is necessary that they should, for the plan of operations which had its beginnings in 1921 is still in force. The present-day operations are, however, more diversified and complex, and the machine is more skillfully run. Its workings are hidden by a multitude of apparently independent, non-communist organizations which employ clever devices of subterfuge to camouflage the real objectives of the communist power-house.

An examination of the minutes of the communist underground for the year 1922 will throw light on the ramifications and diversity of activities of the organization. It will show how the Soviet government built up its American fifth column by taking full advantage of the freedoms prevailing in the United States.

The underground Communist party acted as a consular agency for the Soviet government, for it had the authority to pass on applications of Americans who desired to visit Soviet Russia and to decide who should or should not be allowed to enter the country. Sometimes the Soviet government overruled the decisions of the Communist party in this respect. Generally, however, they were scrupulously followed.

Communist party credentials, stamped in red on a narrow ribbon of white silk, two inches wide by three inches long, carrying the official seal of the party, the hammer and sickle, and signed by the Secretary of the Communist party of the United States, served as the best passport to Soviet Russia. When presented at the border the holder received official attention immediately, and special considerations and privileges. The holder of such an American Communist party passport passed through the customs without interrogation and he was immediately provided with the best of reserved accommodations for his trip to Moscow.

It was not easy to get a Communist party passport to the Soviet paradise. The Party had to be satisfied that the visit to Russia was essential and would prove beneficial either to Russia or to the communist movement.

Besides acting on visas and passports the underground Communist party advised the Soviet government on its purchases in the United States. Communist party members served as advisors to Soviet purchasing agents and committees and also as industrial espionage operatives. The Cheka, later to be known as the GPU, the OGPU and NKVD, always maintained connections with the Communist party, the party serving as an important vehicle in its espionage activities in the United States, Canada, Mexico and the countries of

South America. The Communist party of the United States is proud of the spies it has supplied to the Soviet government out of its own ranks.

Whenever the Soviet government set up offices in the United States, trading offices like the Amtorg, consular offices, diplomatic offices, secret espionage headquarters, shipping agencies and organizations for the promotion of better trade relations and American-Soviet friendship, the American Communist party was not only informed and consulted about it, but also cooperated in the establishment of them by supplying, from the party ranks and from trusted fellow travelers, the workers needed to carry on their activities.

The American Communist party is also part of an international organization serving the interests of one of the world's great powers. The Party serves that power slavishly, as the American link in an international conspiracy which has for its objective Soviet world supremacy. *The job of the Communist party of the United States is to so undermine the foundations upon which American democracy rests that the United States government can be overthrown and the country made a vassal of the Soviet state. The American Communist party is not bound by principles in carrying out its end of the conspiracy; nor does it respect American traditions or the laws of the country.*

It is governed by an inner circle of compact, highly trained professional revolutionists. These form a sort of elite guard of privileged people, carefully selected, for they are destined to become the future rulers of America should the communists gain power. They are shrewd enough to recognize that on the purely communist issues they cannot mobilize millions of people for action. The communists have learned from history that once they can get the people to support their slogans and issues they can seize power even if the communists represent an insignificant minority. Lenin demonstrated that when he raised the slogan of "Peace, Bread and Freedom," the Russian people who knew nothing about communism fell for the slogan, and Lenin with his insignificant band of 45,000 communists in a country of 165,000,000 was able thereby to utilize the crisis resulting from war, hunger and defeat to grab the reins of power.

Never before in the world's history has there been such an organization as the Communist party. The Party is everything at one and the same time. It is the driving center of hundreds of organizations functioning under assumed, misleading names and for all kinds of purposes. It is a trade union center and an organizer of unions. It is the center of many relief organizations which in the past have collected millions of dollars under false pretenses for communist purposes. It is a large and successful insurance society. It is an educational center which functions under high-sounding names, running many schools in which tens of thousands of students are matriculated. It runs student organizations, parent and teacher organizations, and organizations of the arts, sciences and professions. It maintains a military organization. It organizes and sends out expeditionary forces. It runs youth organizations, women's organizations and veterans' organizations. It has organized and controls thousands of purely local organizations. It operates as a cultural organization holding down positions of great power and influence in the movies, the radio, the theatre, in book and magazine publishing fields. It operates unions of civil service workers and government employees and officials. It is a social and political termite penetrating and boring into every field and activity. It organizes the foreign-born in the United States for its own purposes. It seeks to divide the Negro population from the white population and to organize the Negroes as the fighting revolutionary vanguard of the communists. The Communist party is the center of many Negro organizations, organized by communists and operating under false colors. Wherever the United States has influence, there the Communist party has set up special organizations whose purpose is to break down American prestige. It has also formed special committees and organizations to oppose American policies in Latin America, in China, in Africa, in Japan and wherever American interests may interfere with the interests of communist Russia.

To keep track of this marvelous machine is well nigh impossible. Yet in the communist organization nothing is left to chance. Everything is under control. The high command is in constant session, reviewing the work and activities of these numerous diversified organizations. To do this the Communist party organization is departmentalized and the departments broken down into subdivisions. Each department is headed by one or more of its outstanding national leaders, the more important departments going to the leaders who are members of the political committee and the secretariat. National Party headquarters is like a huge switchboard connected by direct wires to all the departments. It is the brain and nerve center of the movement.

The Communist party in its functions is actually a government, a Quisling government, operating within the framework of the legally constituted government. Hitler had his Quislings but they were just individuals, rank amateurs. The communist Quislings have international cohesion with a great world power and super organization.

When the Communist party was an infant, in 1921 and 1922, the pattern of communist organization was already clearly defined. The minutes of the Central Executive Committee held July 26, 1922, in the home of the author at 46 Greenwich Avenue, New York City, throws the spotlight on Moscow's relations with the communist underground when the American communists were not yet out of their swaddling clothes. Attending were important personalities in the communist movement here and abroad. Present were: Bedacht under the name of Marshall, Browder as Ward, Minor as Ballister, Katterfeld as Carr, Lovestone as Wheat, Boris Reinstein—Buffalo socialist who went to Russia at the outbreak of the Russian Revolution and became a Soviet citizen—under the name of Davidson, Professor Walecski as Brooks and Joseph Pogany as Lang. Reinstein, a confidant of Lenin on American affairs, had just arrived from Moscow as the official representative to the Communist party of the Red Trade Union International. Professor Walecski, a Pole and a mathematician of note, came from Moscow as the plenipotentiary of the Comintern with decisive powers over the American Communist party. Pogany, renowned as a powerful figure in the short-lived Hungarian Communist Revolution, an associate of Bela Kun and an agent of the Comintern, was sent by the Comintern to work with and direct the affairs of the American communist movement. Scott, the Chekist, also was present, as were Nat Kaplan, titular head of the underground communist youth, using the name of Ganly, and Rose Pastor Stokes as Sascha. Kaplan up to the present time uses the alias of Ganly and as Ganly headed an important local in Detroit of the C I O Automobile Workers Union.

Earl Browder acted as chairman of the meeting. He introduced Walecski who dealt with the decisions made in Moscow to unite all the American communists into one Communist party. "We need unity, the American communists must unite and give up their factional struggles because the Comintern has given the American communists important tasks to perform. We must build a powerful opposition in the unions to prepare the grounds for the communists taking over the unions. The tactic of the United Front must be energetically pursued in order to win the masses away from their reactionary and reformist leaders. The American comrades must take the initiative in helping to build up the communist movement in Mexico and throughout South America if we are to succeed in undermining American imperialism. The communist underground organization must be maintained under all circumstances and at the same time we must transform the Workers party, the legal expressions of the American communists, into a powerful party which must be converted into an open communist party as soon as conditions in the United States will permit."

Walecski left no doubts that Moscow had its hands on the strings which manipulated the affairs of the American communists.

Foster delivered the report on what was being done to undermine Gomper's regime in the A F of L in preparation for an assault by the communists on the unions. Browder supplemented Foster's report.

On the insistence of the Professor, the agenda for the convention of the American Communist party to be held the following month was thrown into the wastebasket and a committee, headed by him, was chosen to draw up a new one.

Again, close study of the communist underground from 1920 to 1922 will reveal that the organizational forms under which the communists operated and the methods they employed are the accepted forms of communist activity today. However, today's methods are more subtle, more involved, the intrigues more circumspect, and their diplomatic duplicity is woven in such Mephistophelian threads that it is difficult to put one's finger on the origin of the infamy for which the Communist party is directly responsible.

Minor, more than any other communist, comprehended the paradoxical, ethical concepts of Lenin. Minor, the tall American from the South, the artist whose cartoons assumed vigorous expression and portrayed ideas graphically and boldly in black and white, grasped the content of Lenin's moral system, a system which justified every violation of the moral code, including the commission of the most heinous crimes, providing revolutionary objectives were benefited. Minor was duly impressed by Lenin's system of political and human relations based on the denial of human rights in the interests of what, Lenin stressed, were the historical necessities of the exploited millions —necessities which Lenin shrewdly expounded in terms of socialist idealism and utopian promises to the masses—necessities, if a better world were to come sometime in the distant future.

Robert Minor, Lenin's Disciple

Robert Minor's role in the American Communist movement is an amazing story of intrigue and drama.

From the Bolshevik standpoint, Robert Minor is the most important figure in American communism for he has done more than any other American communist, living or dead, to transform the American communist movement into a real Bolshevik movement. Reed, who brought the tidings of bolshevism to America, did not understand the basic foundations of bolshevism or its intrinsic values. In its service he gave his heart and his enthusiasm. Disillusioned, he found himself alone with his doubts, without direction or purpose in life. He gave up the ship because he had neither the energy nor the will to break the shackles which kept his mind in bondage.

Minor was not that kind of man. Endowed with the artist's keen sense of proportion, intellectual and extremely emotional, he was at the same time dispassionate and calculating in his politics. He first went to Russia in 1918, via San Francisco and the Pacific, as a correspondent for the New York *World,* the Philadelphia *Public Ledger* and Max Eastman's *Liberator.* He spent over nine months with the Bolsheviks.

Lenin took him into his confidence and spent hours talking with the American. Trotsky, who had been in America, discussed American problems with him. Energetic and aggressive, Minor lost no time in making contacts with the top Soviet leaders who were worth knowing.

In the nine months Minor spent in Soviet Russia what happened to the artist who saw objects in their proper perspective? What happened to the philosophical anarchist who sought the truth? What strange gyrations took place in the mind of the American-born genius? How did a man imbued with the passionate romanticism of the South, with a sense of chivalry and fair play, forget so soon his lofty ideals of justice and liberty? In the story of Minor, essentially sincere in his motives, whose principles were founded on honest convictions, is to be found the key to the riddle of the Bolshevik mind.

Minor, in the early years of American communism, was the only communist in the United States not confounded by the paradoxical, ethical concepts of Lenin. The ideas which Minor absorbed from Lenin remained inside the man. Dark mysterious shadows enveloped his soul as the new ideas transformed the individual. A revolutionary politician emerged.

Five months after Minor had left Moscow, the American newspapers reported that the American newspaper correspondent and cartoonist who had mysteriously disappeared from his Paris hotel room had been found in the custody of American military authorities. No reason was given for Minor's detention. Mystery shrouded his case. Yet before the American people knew what the case was about, Hugh C. Wallace, the American Ambassador to France, had already interested himself in the case and predicted Minor's early release. The House of Representatives at the same time began an investigation of the circumstances surrounding his disappearance. Minor loomed as an international figure in international politics for, besides having had a long interview with Lenin, he had also had a long private interview with Colonel House, Wilson's right-hand man of the American Peace Delegation at Paris.

Not until June 14, 1919, did the United States learn that Minor was being held in an American military prison at Coblenz charged with being a Bolshevik agent engaged in circulating propaganda among the troops of the Army of Occupation for the purpose of undermining their morale and loyalty. Though these were serious charges Colonel House requested Minor's immediate release. General Liggett, head of the American Army of Occupation, refused the request. Minor had influence in powerful U. S. government circles. When arrested he carried credentials from the American Peace Commission entitling him to all the privileges enjoyed by correspondents covering the peace conference. He had passports and special government passes entitling him to travel in Germany, Russia, Holland, England, France and other countries. He had in his possession passes obtained from General Harris, the head of the American Mission at Berlin, giving him extraordinary privileges. Minor traveled freely from France into Germany, from Germany into Russia, like an important dignitary. He covered the Ruhr districts during the outbreak of revolutionary strikes in that area and kept in close touch with Lenin and Trotsky concerning their progress.

Minor, facing a military trial, possible conviction for treason, and death by a firing squad, showed little concern over his arrest and refused to talk. In July Minor learned that he was accused of being a Bolshevik agent and was held for treason. His father, an influential Democratic politician and Federal Court Judge in Texas, in alarm wired his son from San Antonio not to spare any expense in arranging for his defense. The case suddenly assumed such international and domestic importance that it was taken out of the hands of the American Army of Occupation and turned over to the American General Headquarters.

When arrested, Minor had a taste of what solitary confinement in a military prison is like, but not for very long. Pressure behind the scenes caused his transfer to a large room of his own with all hotel conveniences and more besides. The army assigned an orderly to him who took care of his personal wants. He received excellent food and plenty of it. His comforts were looked after with great concern. This unusual pampering of a prisoner charged with being a traitor indicated that powerful influences were at work on Minor's behalf. American newspaper circles were astounded to what extent men of high official standing in the government were busy trying to quash the case.

Orders were received to postpone the trial even though the American Paris Embassy hinted that the proceedings might have a sensational outcome. Rumors about what was going to happen to Minor kept piling up until suddenly, out of the clear blue sky, orders came from General Pershing himself that Minor be forthwith released. When Minor was put aboard a train for Paris, a free man, P. H. Williams, head of the intelligence section of the American Army, crammed the evidence against Minor into a briefcase and left for the United States to present the evidence to his government. To date no satisfactory answer has ever been given as to why Minor was released.

Minor was in charge of the manufacture and distribution of propaganda material for the communist "Spartacus" armed uprising in Germany, having received that assignment directly from Moscow. He wrote pamphlets which charged that the bankers were keeping the American soldiers on the Rhine. A special appeal written by him for distribution among the soldiers was signed by the Communist party of Germany. Addressing a meeting of German communists in Berlin Minor declared: "The time is ripe to spread the doctrines of Lenin and Trotsky among the American soldiers." Minor's propaganda was drawn up for the purpose of creating unrest, dissatisfaction, defection, and revolt by weakening the fighting efficiency and morale of the occupation forces.

The Minor technique to undermine the morale of an army, once the enemy has been defeated, was used effectively once more by the American Communist party in World War II in developing a movement among the American soldiers calling for their speedy demobilization and return home. The communists, inspired by Moscow's interests in Europe and Asia, came near wrecking the morale of the American fighting forces abroad by inducing hundreds of thousands of loyal, patriotic soldiers to demonstrate and strike against their officers, and to defy discipline. It brought about the disorganization and premature demobilization of the American Army and did incalculable harm in undermining the prestige of our government abroad.

Minor arrived in Germany from Russia in February, 1919, after he had succeeded in obtaining a personal interview with Lenin for publication in the American press. The facts here presented concerning Minor's career, following his return from Russia, may challenge expert psychologists but will be understandable once the mechanics of the twisted thinking of the communist mind is adequately appraised.

Upon his arrival in Germany, Minor wrote three articles on Soviet Russia which were featured by Pulitzer's New York *World* as highly significant. The first one appeared on February 4, 1919, with the following introduction by Arno Dosch-Fleurot, the World's European staff correspondent:

"Robert Minor, whose interview with Lenin, the Bolshevik leader, follows, furnishes the most important contribution that has been made to contemporary Russian history. In two more cabled articles he will explain what occurred in the Russian Revolution in the last few months. *These cables will show that Minor is no Bolshevist.* Texas-born of Virginia blood, *he is so aggressively democratic that some would call him an anarchist.*

"Because he thought there had been a miscarriage of justice he gave a year of his life to save Thomas J. Mooney from hanging in San Francisco. Then he went to Russia, when he thought the Bolsheviki were giving the perfect liberty that he craved.

"After being through the terror he came to Berlin disillusioned and embittered."

According to Dosch-Fleurot who personally interviewed Minor when he came out of Russia, the aggressively democratic Texan came out of the communist paradise a disillusioned, embittered man.

Nevertheless, immediately after the publication of his articles in the *World*, we find Minor acting as a Bolshevik agent, engaging in treasonable activities against his own country and trying to foment communist revolution in Germany and throughout Europe. Explain then how the bitter anti-Bolshevik could at the same time be such a trusted Bolshevik agent and propagandist!

Minor was not crazy at the time, nor was he an irresponsible, stupid chameleon who changed his colors in different surroundings and climates. He was no uneducated proletarian easily swayed by slogans and demagogy. A keen, well-trained and analytical mind guided his conduct.

Minor's articles in the *World* and his interview with Lenin prove that during his nine months' sojourn in Russia he got a good insight into the Bolshevik regime. He saw through the tinsel of the revolutionary show, which the Bolsheviks had put on, to the substance of the revolution. Minor's articles were eye-openers. His criticism of bolshevism then holds good today, twenty-seven years later, when Stalin, not Lenin, is the supreme ruler. Minor wrote:

"This time Lenin knew he was giving an interview and he appreciated the effect it might have on the outside world."

He continued: "I did not agree with Lenin's idea of what he was building but said nothing." Nevertheless Minor, who wrote he did not agree with what Lenin was building, at the same time was trying to carry out Lenin's blue print for Germany and the rest of Europe. One Minorian paradox follows another as Minor goes on to explain: "Lenin could not afford to tell the whole truth about the entrance of the non-Bolsheviki into the government, for he must maintain the intransigent front. The main fact in the new situation is that the so-called nationalization of Russian industry has put insurgent industry back into the hands of the business class who disguise their activities by giving orders under the magic title of 'People's Commissars.'"

But it did not matter to Minor whether Lenin could afford to tell the whole truth or not, or to put it inversely, it did not matter to Minor whether he was telling the whole truth or not, for even as Minor was writing those words he was preparing to carry out Lenin's instructions.

Continued Minor, in words which cannot now be erased, for they are a matter of record: "I said to Lenin, I was going to Germany, and his interest quickened."

"You will arrive in time for the second revolution," (Germany's coming communist revolution—author's explanation) he said. "If you get a chance, give my regards to Dr. Liebknecht, Rosa Luxemburg and Clara Zetkind."

Thus Minor announced to the world that Lenin expected a communist revolution to break out in Germany when Minor arrived there; he did not hesitate to ask Minor to give his regards to the outstanding persons who were expected by the Bolsheviks to lead that revolution. And Minor continued:

"As Lenin talked, he kept hitching his chair nearer to mine until his knees touched mine and his finger waved under my nose. I really felt submerged by his personality which seemed to fill the room."

Here we have a confession that Minor really felt submerged by Lenin's personality. But it did not stop him from writing the following words—words which would have merited death for a man writing them inside Soviet Russia:

"The interview was in the Kremlin, ancient seat of the Tsars. As I came away, two smart limousines drew up and deposited several well-dressed men of the business type. This class had been lying very low only a few months ago. They are the type the Bolshevik creed denounces as 'Bloodthirsty minions of predatory capital.'

"There is a difference now. The business types ride in fine automobiles as before, live in fine mansions and are again managing the old industries, *with more authority than ever before.* Now they are 'people's commissaries'—servants of the proletariat—and the iron discipline of the army under red flags has been developed in order to protect them against all annoyance. A rose smells as sweetly to them under any other name."

And the man who wrote such annihilating criticism of Bolshevik rule was given a most important and confidential mission in Germany by Lenin himself, and in addition, upon his arrival back home in the United States, was co-opted upon Moscow's orders into the highest and most trusted committees of the Communist party.

But Minor had much more to criticize. Of the Red Army, lauded by the communists the world over as the armed advance guard of world revolution, he wrote: "It looks to me as if there is more of an army about it than there is anything Red, but it is called Red because that is the popular color."

He debunked the popular estimation of bolshevism in the following words: "They (the Russian people) have not yet discovered that if bolshevism means the peasants taking the land and the workmen taking the factories, Russia is now the one place where there is no bolshevism."

Minor, the Bolshevik agent, dropped one anti-Bolshevik gem after another as he continued: "The bolshevism of discipline has features that should make those who died for the October Revolution and put Lenin into power turn in their graves." The Bolshevik Minor who risked being shot as a traitor for carrying on seditious communist propaganda among American troops would have us believe he did so on behalf of a system he described as follows:

"The dazzling opportunities of military promotion in the un-crowded field is too much for young Russians of all kinds to resist. Lenin's officers are young—young as Napoleon's were. I heard some one say: 'Will these officers make a counter-revolution?' The reply I would not fully endorse, but it has significance. 'No, because a counter-revolution has already been made.'"

Upon his release from the Coblenz military prison Minor returned to the United States. At a private meeting with anarchists Minor reported to his flock that what he had written against bolshevism was true in substance. He verified the reports that the Bolsheviks were exterminating the anarchists. He spoke in a manner that gave every one the impression that he himself, because of what he had seen of bolshevism in action, was opposed to communism as a system of government and a social philosophy.

It has been shown that Minor in February, 1919, wrote articles against bolshevism, and from February, 1919, until June, 1919, when he was arrested by American military authorities, acted as a Bolshevik agent and propagandist who tried to foment a Bolshevik revolution in Germany; who tried to get the American troops to revolt and who met with French communists and plotted with them how to win the French labor movement for bolshevism. Yet when he returned to his own country at the end of June, 1919, he privately repeated to his friends the charges he made in his articles to the *World*. But he did not confine his opinions in America to the spoken word. He wrote articles presenting a serious critique of bolshevism and its political structure. These words of his add to the Minor enigma:

"The anarchist song still faintly echoes down the Volga and the Don and the Dnieper, and in Moscow and in Petrograd workshops, and a note or two of it may still creep into Lenin's state affairs; but he very soon began suppressing the anarchists and building the police force."

Parading in America as an anarchist, Minor continued to write "that in arrogating all power to the iron central authority, sapping the power of the once locally autonomous soviets, the Bolshevik leaders had destroyed the revolution and the only hope of real communism in Russia."

Minor went much further by stating:

". . . the course of compromise, which began as early as the Brest-Litovsk treaty had led inevitably to the eradication of the original form of locally autonomous soviets and to the crystallizing of a police bureaucracy, to military conscription, to the extinction of press freedom, to the repression of parties more revolutionary than the Bolsheviks, and into alliances with the bourgeoisie of their own and foreign countries."

To Minor, then, communism in Russia stood for a militaristic police state which suppressed freedom and human rights. A truer definition of the communist dictatorship as it exists up to the present time cannot be given. Yet this intellectual acrobat, capable of such dazzling twists and turns, in the next few months performed a breathtaking somersault. He wrote in the *Liberator* a scathing and vitriolic attack on anarchism, defending the suppression of the anarchists by the Bolsheviks, using all the lies and demagogy which the Bolsheviks had manufactured in their campaign against the anarchists and other radical and progressive oppositions to them. Minor now, publicly for the first time, took on the appearance of a full-fledged communist.

Forgetting everything derogatory he had ever said before about the Russian Army and about Bolsheviks and democracy, Minor, before a gathering of 2000 who packed the Central Opera House in New York, shouted as he waved his long arms in the air to give emphasis to what he was saying: "The Russian Army is the most powerful in Europe and the only one not subjected to disintegration. The Bolsheviks have established the most complete democracy the world has ever known. Long Live the Soviets!"

It becomes necessary to harmonize all these contradictions, to discover the logic in Minor's mental gymnastics in order to fathom the mystery of the Bolshevik mind.

Was Minor a radical, intellectual weathervane who turned in the direction of the winds from the left striking him at a given time, as a weather-cock does to the pressure of the wind? The tall, muscular Minor definitely had a mind of his own, plus a will backed up by an intense ambition for power and personal glory. Was the Texas-born

American intellectually dishonest? How could he advocate and attack one and the same thing at the identical time? The answer to this psychological riddle is not a simple one. To answer it simply is to declare that according to the evidence presented, Minor was an intellectual charlatan. But Minor is a communist, a Bolshevik, and has been a good one ever since his first visit to Russia. In fact he holds the distinction of being the first American communist to really grasp what the philosophy and methodology of bolshevism was all about, at a time when the other Americans who pretended to be communists were in a romantic fog. How then could a good Bolshevik, one thoroughly cognizant of its ideology and program, give expression to such violent anti-Bolshevik sentiments? For as a Bolshevik Minor was basically honest to himself and to the demands of the supreme communist authority. He was rendering at that particular time service to the cause, a service which he was selected and privileged to carry out.

The question was once asked in the Comintern, "What makes a good communist?" Speaking on behalf of the Politburo of the Russian Communist party and as President of the Comintern Zinoviev answered: "A good communist is a comrade who loyally carries out a decision of his party, regardless of what that decision asks him to do, and even though at the time he does not see the logic for the decision and disagrees with it."

When Minor left Russia in February 1919, after his interview with Lenin, the Bolsheviks stood at the crossroads. The direction in which the pendulum of history would swing would determine the course of their future policy, internally as well as externally. Should the pendulum swing to the left and a communist revolution sweep over Germany, which Lenin and the other Bolshevik leaders strongly hoped for, then the revolutionary struggle for the mastery of the globe would have to be intensified and brought to a decisive conclusion. Should the attempt at German communist revolution be defeated, causing the pendulum to swing to the right, the Bolsheviks would have to make a temporary retreat and come to some *modus vivendi* with the Western world. The desperate plight of the Russian people made it impossible for the Bolsheviks to keep going much longer just on revolutionary slogans and promises. But since the Bolsheviks were unable to determine which way the pendulum was going to swing they could not come to a decision on where to put the emphasis of their policy—on extending revolutionary activities for world revolution or on making a truce with the capitalist world. Lenin hedged on both these policies and adopted a complicated program which momentarily satisfied both urges. Lenin's program left the Bolsheviks free to follow either one direction or the other, or both, should the historical impasse clear up.

Minor, the American, fitted ideally into Lenin's plans. The timing, so important in launching a campaign for political objectives, was just right. Minor was leaving Moscow at the historical hour of dead center. A push in one direction or the other would determine the course of history. Lenin decided to try to push it towards the extreme left by fomenting the German revolution as the first step in a world-wide global conflagration. But, like a good general, Lenin did not cut himself off from retreat should he fail. He had too much at stake in Russia not to attempt to soften the attitude of the capitalist world, especially the United States, towards Soviet Russia, for Russia needed badly the manufactured goods, food and raw materials which America had in abundance.

Lenin knew that the world would be interested in what he had to say to Minor, a newspaper correspondent representing a powerful American newspaper. He was alert to the fact that the people of the United States would be duly impressed if Minor, in reporting the interview, adopted an anti-Bolshevik line which would create a favorable impression of the Bolsheviks in American government and business circles.

In his writings, spoken words and actions, Minor reflected the complex cross-currents of Bolshevik policy. Lenin had just announced that the Bolsheviks were ready to recognize Tsarist Russia's pre-war debts which they had originally repudiated. This bid to the capitalist profit incentive Minor followed up by showing that the Russians, far from being revolutionists, were, in fact, the opposite—it was they who had brought the world-disturbing social revolution to an end. As per agreement with Lenin he went on to prove that the businessmen were coming back into their own and had behind them the backing of a trained military force with which to enforce labor discipline. Part of Minor's thesis was to call attention to the fact that the Bolsheviks were not anarchists as most Americans believed. Minor's appeal to the American people was obvious: Why not recognize the kinship between the forces of law and order in the United States and the Bolsheviks in their common opposition to anarchism and the radical forces of disorder, accept the olive branch offered by Lenin, get back the money loaned to the Tsar and do business with the Bolsheviks?

He spoke at conferences with anarchists as an outraged anarchist who had lost all respect for the Bolsheviki. But when the American government and business circles did not bite at the bait Lenin offered them, Minor suddenly dropped his camouflage and the communist-Bolshevik appeared in true aspect. Suddenly, like a bolt out of clear blue sky, Minor issued a blast against the anarchists—backing up the bloody regime of suppression against them. It was no longer an anti-Bolshevik Minor that paraded up and down the country but a rabid Bolshevik who called for the violent destruction of American capitalism by setting up in place of the democracy of the United States, a proletarian dictatorship, a Soviet, a Bolshevik government.

But the incongruities of Minor's conduct are not answered by calling Minor dishonest. The Bolshevik Minor was honest to himself as a communist and to the movement which he served. A communist has no conscience, for he views life objectively, in line with the party program. Abstract spiritual factors, above the banality of man, play no role in a communist's life. A communist recognizes only material existence in the limited narrow sense, and therefore is not bothered by moral prerequisites, his conduct being bound solely by that which is embodied in the decisions of the Communist party majority.

Since party decisions are temporal matters, changing with time and modified by existing conditions, the true communist is not only inconsistent from time to time but also often adopts a position which is directly the opposite of what he vehemently advocated previously. The renunciation of religion, the ostracizing of God as having no place in the mind of the true communist, does not mean that God is thrown out of the Bolshevik window, for in Communist Russia, the Greek Catholic Church as a Soviet State Church has been revived. The Moslem priesthood and rituals are supported and in the capitalist countries a host of influential fellow travelers in all religious denominations, ministers, priests, rabbis and laymen, constitute a backdrop shield for atheistic communism. But that is only half the story. In the place of the spiritual, the eternal God, the communists have installed a God dressed in red robes and wielding the scepter of the hammer and sickle—the God of Power. The communist God is above morality and law. It recognizes as good, as honest, as justifiable, as commendable, conduct and actions, no matter how reprehensible, which enhance communist power. Power is the one basic principle—the religion of communism.

To tear down the moral structure of civilization became the all-absorbing ambition of Minor's life. He tried to impress on the minds of the American communists why they should not abide by bourgeois morals, that obedience to the accepted ethical code was not a proletarian necessity. Minor often spoke on this theme.

In a debate with the Socialist, James O'Neal, in 1921, answering an argument by O'Neal on the inconsistency of Fraina's advocacy of freedom of speech, Minor stated: "Fraina advocated the right of free speech until he learned from Moscow that that was a petty bourgeois thing to ask." Minor continued, facing O'Neal and sneering at him: "Let me set you right. If a man is a moralist of a theological type he will do things which he thinks are idealistic. But if he is a modern materialistic revolutionary *he will do the things not that are metaphysically moral but the things that work,* and he will take a position on free speech when it is the bourgeois dictatorship that is on top, and he will take a position against free speech for the bourgeoisie when it is the workers who are on top."

As he finished he shook his fist threateningly in the face of the dumbfounded O'Neal and the crowd went wild with applause.

Minor rejected the idea that a communist can be a religiously moral person who will do the things which he thinks are right. Minor stressed the antithesis of idealism and communism. True communists cannot be idealists. A communist, according to Minor, is a revolutionary materialist who will not do the things which are moral but only the things which will work in the interest of the movement to which he belongs. The communists will fight for freedom of speech in the United States because they do not rule the country. But once they get power the communists will never grant the right of free speech to others.

Minor contended that the communists would do whatever would work even if it violated the moral concepts and laws established by centuries of experience and the ages-long struggle for justice in human relationships. Minor was fully conscious of what he was preaching, for in his efforts to develop a Bolshevik mentality in the American communists, he wrote: "Honesty is a bourgeois virtue." From this it logically followed that to lie, to be dishonest was a communist virtue. The diabolical ethical code was not Minor's invention. It was, and still is, the code of bolshevism. Getting the American communists to reject the ethical concepts of civilization constituted the central point in the campaign for the bolshevization of the American communists.

Minor drove the soul out of the communists and in its place substituted objectivity. The leaders understood the implication of the word; the simpletons who make up the majority of the rank-and-file did not. Following Minor's lead the officials of the Communist party admonished the party members to drive sentiment out of their hearts in order to be guided in their actions by what the movement demanded of them. Human conduct, the comrades were told, must not be based on ethical or religious abstractions but on concrete tangible objectives. The leaders kept pounding into the heads of their followers that communist loyalty consisted not in loyalty to one's wife, family, children or one's country but to the organization to which the communist belonged—The Party. They pictured the Communist party as the final, the highest form of the collected will of the toiling masses who compose the working class. Hence they claimed everything the Party willed was justified, that the Party could do no wrong. Hammered home was the idea that communist morality consisted in completely subordinating oneself to the Party. Thus were the men and women of the Communist party transformed into beings devoid of all spiritual idealism, without a sense of right or wrong, to be used as the communist machine saw fit.

Bob Minor, native American, Texas-born of Virginian blood, from a family rooted in the American way of life and steeped in the lore and traditions of the country, can look with satisfaction at the success of his handiwork as Lenin's American disciple; a worthy teacher, for his conduct set the example for his students to follow.

The Communist Underground At Work

The communists in the underground fought against the common enemy, the capitalist government, but fought more furiously among themselves. The leaders formed factions to win the favor of Moscow in order to get control of the party organization for themselves. The stakes were high: large and rich institutions, close to fifty newspapers and magazines, real estate valued in the millions of dollars, control of unions and their treasuries, control of relief and defense organizations with access to the hundreds of thousands of dollars which they collected, the right to over five thousand paid jobs, supervision of North and South American continental affairs for the Comintern, ties with the GPU and Soviet government agencies and receipts of huge subsidies from Moscow in the form of money, cable drafts for money, diamonds, jewelry, gold, handicrafts, books, pictures and shiploads of printed propaganda.

The leaders of the communist factions traveled continually to and from Moscow and kept the wires to Moscow hot with cables informing the Comintern in detail of everything that transpired in the communist underground. Yet, in spite of all the factional warfare and confusion which reigned in the underground, constructive work went on, for in this period the foundations of the communist movement were laid and the shape of things to come took on form. The pattern then worked out, elaborated upon, is the pattern which is used today.

Moscow played an active and decisive part in the consolidation of the American communist forces and in putting the Communist party on its feet. In the person of Scott, the GPU agent, the Comintern had a specialist on revolutionary organization par excellence. Scott headed a special committee directly responsible to the Comintern which had authority over the communist organization not only in the United States but also in Canada and Mexico and throughout South America. With him on the Committee were Sen Katayama, the Japanese Communist, and Fraina. Katayama soon left for Moscow where he became a prominent member of the Comintern's inner circle. Fraina's role in squandering this committee's money has already been dealt with. But Scott had other funds, estimated at the time to top a quarter of a million dollars, money supplied by Moscow, to be spent in Canada, Mexico, the United States and Latin America.

The underground Communist party did not confine itself to the cellars for long. It soon came out into the open, in a camouflaged dress, under the name of the American Labor Alliance. Though the American Labor Alliance claimed it was a progressive labor organization, independent of the Communist party, its finances were supplied by the Communist party, its leading officials were Communist party leaders and its affairs were conducted by the Executive Committee of the underground Communist party. Unable to put into the field a ticket of its own, the American Labor Alliance called upon the American people to boycott the elections. That was in November, 1920. A year later the communists with the consent of the Comintern dumped the American Labor Alliance into the garbage can and launched, in December, 1921, a legal radical party called the Workers Party. This party like its predecessor was just a cloak for the communist underground. In communist circles the underground was known as the number one organization and the Workers Party as the number two organization. Number one ran everything. Number two served as a shield for its public activities.

Communist Rackets

The underground Communist party ran a number of organizations directly related to the Soviet Union. Only a few will be dealt with, for the others and those subsequently formed continue now to be operated along the same lines.

The Technical Aid Society for Soviet Russia was formed presumably to train men and women for constructive work in Soviet Russia. Its work was conducted primarily in the Russian language. It organized artels and cooperatives on specific lines such as laundry cooperatives, tailors cooperatives, metal workers cooperatives, etc. Those who joined paid for their training and supplied the money with which to buy machines, tools, supplies and whatever else the cooperative needed in order to set up an establishment in Russia and keep it going. They supplied not only the working capital but also the money for the transportation of their families and equipment to Soviet Russia. Out of these transactions the Society made a substantial profit.

The Technical Aid Society also constituted an agency which gathered technical information and bought machinery for Russian enterprises. The Society functioned too as a consular and shipping agency for the Soviets. In addition the Technical Aid Society engaged in other activities which were not publicized, and about which the United States government did not become suspicious.

Through the Technical Aid Society's shipping facilities many Comintern agents and OGPU spies were brought illegally into the country. These, supplied with the Society's Soviet passports, traveled freely all over the United States, Canada and South America. The Technical Aid Society also engaged in industrial espionage for the Soviet government. Many of the industrial secrets which the communists stole from the files of the places in which they worked were turned over to the Technical Aid Society for transmission to Russia.

The Communist party had full authority over the affairs of the Society. All its officials, secretaries, teachers, organizers and paid people were Communist party members. Officials took money out of its treasury and turned it over to the Communist party whenever the Party ordered them to do so.

The Technical Aid Society also performed political functions. The Society had great influence among the Slavs because the Technical Aid Society was empowered by the Soviet government to issue passports to Slavs who wished to return to Russia. From the passport and visa business large sums of money were collected, most of which found their way into the coffers of the Party. The Technical Aid Society in order to stimulate the desire among the Slavs to aid in Russian reconstruction and to go to Russia carried on a campaign on behalf of the Communist party through mass meetings, through study groups, in its official publications and through printed propaganda. The Russians who wanted to go home were told they had to learn what communism was and that it was advisable for them to join the Party.

The individuals who gave up their life's savings to go to Russia found out after they had gone to Russia and when it was too late that they had made a serious mistake. The poor dupes who fell for the sweet propaganda and went to Mecca to enjoy Socialism soon besieged the representatives of the American Communist party in Moscow with requests that they be permitted to return to the United States, never giving their disappointment as the reason—for to do so meant prison or worse—but always claiming that they had special personal considerations which made a trip back to the States necessary. Few of the requests were granted.

The Communist party organized the Friends of Soviet Russia to collect funds for the relief of the victims of the great Russian famine of 1921. The communists who held the official and leading positions in the organization got their jobs through the Communist party. The communist underground selected them all, including the editors of the official journal, *Soviet Russia Today*. A certified public accountant selected by the Communist party did the accounting of the books in order to hide how the Communist party stole hundreds of thousands of dollars donated by a generous public for famine relief.

Not only did the Communist party give out and control the jobs of the Friends of Soviet Russia, it also made all the important policy and administrative decisions for the organization. The jobholders who opposed party decisions and refused to carry them out either had to submit to Communist party discipline or were forthwith removed from their jobs.

The Friends of Soviet Russia served as an important vehicle

in which the communist underground carried on its semi-legal and public activities on a grand scale. In the Friends of Soviet Russia the Communist party had a splended pro-Soviet propaganda agency, composed of national, state and local sections. There were trade union divisions, professional groupings, women's divisions, youth divisions and groups organized along religious lines. The staff was padded with the names of Communist party organizers who were paid their salaries and expenses by the relief society but who devoted all their time to the work of the Communist party. A considerable number of the Party's national officials were put on the relief organization's payroll. The Communist party repeatedly made decisions directing the officers of the relief organization to turn over large sums from the organization's funds to the Communist party treasury. The Central Executive Committee authorized the local organizations of the communist underground to rifle the contents of a percentage of the collection boxes during tag days in their territories. The relief racket proved a good paying proposition for the Party, a racket depending on the idealistic, humanitarian appeal of saving Russian men, women and children from the horrors of starvation.

The racket did not originate with the American communists. What the American communists did was part of an international scheme hatched by the Bolshevik leaders of the Comintern. The Russians realized that what the national sections of the Comintern could raise would be a drop in the bucket compared to the needs of the famine-stricken Russians who were dying by the millions. To save millions of lives, relief, on a gigantic scale, had to be obtained from a government which had the resources, the foods, the medicines, the supplies and the necessary transport and organization to get it to the Russian people. Only the United States was able to cope with such a humanitarian life-saving task. Herbert Hoover undertook the job and carried it out splendidly in spite of the mistrust and interference of Russia's communist rulers. Instead of being thankful for the job Hoover did in rescuing Russian humanity, the communist rulers were resentful and retaliated by vilifying the man. The communist campaign in the United States against Hoover had its inception in Russia and was inspired by direct orders from the Comintern to the Communist party. For actual relief the Bolsheviks depended upon the help supplied by the Hoover Relief Mission. The Comintern therefore decided that the relief organizations dominated by the communists should be tied together into an international relief organization. The communist international relief set-up opened a central bureau in Paris. To this bureau were sent all relief monies collected by the communist relief organizations, not squandered in the home countries. The Paris bureau issued receipts for the same to prove that the monies were legitimately handled. Afterwards the monies received by the Paris bureau were allocated to the communist parties in Europe and America to help finance communist activities. The bulk of the money received in Paris came from the American "Friends of Soviet Russia." Often the exchange of funds for receipts between the Paris office and the National Office of the Friends of Soviet Russia took the form of correspondence and bookkeeping transactions, for no actual money was sent for the receipts received. The Paris office, having received a report from New York that so much money had been collected for relief, made out a receipt to cover the amount. The National Office was therefore able to show a receipt for money collected and sent to Europe which was never sent, but instead was turned over to the American Communist party.

The communists quickly learned how to collect tribute. In getting cash the communists do not respect the sacredness of public funds entrusted to them, nor the funds in the treasuries of organizations which fall under their domination. Relief monies, defense monies and union funds, in the millions of dollars, have been siphoned into the party coffers. The Communist party, through years of experience with the Friends of Soviet Russia and kindred organizations, has learned how to hold the confidence of a generous people and how to cover up the loot to prevent scandals and persecution.

The United Front

During the period in which the Communist party operated as an underground organization, they injected themselves into practically every phase of American social and political life. In their activities the communists were guided by an all-inclusive policy based on the tactics of the United Front.

The United Front policy, originated by Lenin after the communist revolutionary upsurge failed to materialize in Western Europe, laid down the basic policy on tactics which the communists in America and in all other countries follow, up to the present time. The policy is both broad and complex, and covers whatever situations the communists might find themselves in. The United Front tactics are used in an apartment house to unite tenants in a fight against an increase in rents, in running the affairs of pro-Soviet satellite governments and in constituting cabinets and ministries in countries where the Communist party is very strong. The policy is so complex and so involved in its detailed application that long theses and programs dealing with it have been drawn up to guide the communists.

By championing unity the communists inject themselves into non-communist organizations and activities. By the skillful application of the United Front policy, the communists have become an important and often a decisive force in movements and actions, political and non-political, from which they would otherwise be excluded. The employment of United Front tactics forced the communists to learn how to deal with persons and movements not in their camp. Thus the communists developed into able negotiators and astute politicians. Once the communists get their toes into the narrow opening of a door to an organization, they usually succeed in squeezing themselves bodily into the organization and either capturing the organization or dominating its affairs.

United Front programs direct that the communists, directly through their own organizations or indirectly through other organizations, propose unity of action in favor of popular issues or in opposition to measures, political developments and government actions distasteful to the communists. The communists thereby create popular movements, involving large masses of people, through which they can project their views publicly on a much broader basis than if they acted independently. Since the communists comprise the only closely knit, disciplined force in a loosely formed movement of heterogeneous, undisciplined forces, they have relatively little difficulty in gaining the upper hand in the United Front. By playing on the vanity of prominent, influential persons, giving them honors, positions and places on committees with pompous-sounding names, and by cleverly exploiting United Front tactics, the communists, in recent years, have won for themselves the leadership of many causes of a progressive and humanitarian character. They have thus surrounded themselves with an army of respectable persons, from every walk of American life, who unknowingly are generous contributors to communist causes, fighters for communist objectives and disseminators of communist ideology.

Romance in the Michigan Woods

Not far from the little railroad station at Bridgeman, Michigan, close to the waters of Lake Michigan, the communist underground during the hot August days of 1922 held its last and final national convention. The Communist party thereafter, by cautious steps, blossomed into an open, legal party. The Bridgeman convention, in spite of its fantastic episodes, marked the end of communist infantilism and the beginning of communist maturity.

The convention took place on the estate of Kar Wulfskeel. A large main house surrounded by a wide open porch, and a number of clapboard summer bungalows nearby, provided accommodations to the nondescript band of communists who had come together with the permission of the Comintern to settle the issues of the underground.

The men and women who arrived at the Wulfskeel farm, at varying intervals, in groups of two, three and four, represented the elite of the communist movement. Included in the convention attendance of approximately one hundred men and women were three emissaries from Moscow.

Professor Walecski, the mathematician and arch enemy of General Pilsudski, headed the Moscow delegation. He arrived still wearing his ill-fitting white linen suit, which was dirtier than usual, cutting a strange figure in American surroundings. Joseph Pogany followed. In appearance he was the opposite of his chief, for he was foppishly dressed and strutted about like a plump pigeon. A journalist by profession, Pogany, during the short-lived Bela Kun regime held the post of Commissar of War and General of the Hungarian Red Army. A ruthless revolutionist and terrorist of brilliant intellect, he carried with him instructions from the Comintern to remain in the United States for the purpose of transforming the Communist party into the kind of an organization Moscow wanted it to be. The third of the trio, Boris Reinstein, formerly an American citizen who had lived in Buffalo, was a congenial-looking gentleman, who spoke in a moderate, hesitant tone, a man close to sixty, exuberant and bubbling over with childlike enthusiasm. He was a power in the International to be reckoned with for he had the ear of Lenin and Trotsky. Reinstein, in addition to being a member of the Comintern delegation, was the special representative of Losovsky, the President of the Red Trade Union International. Reinstein had instructions to do little talking, a hardship for the garrulous man, but to observe closely and gather information on what was happening in America and to report to Losovsky directly on the activities of William Z. Foster—activities which the Comintern and the Red Trade Union International backed up liberally with hundreds of thousands of dollars.

Deep in the Michigan woods a sylvan scene unfolded, not unlike a German beer-barrel outing of the nineties, but without the beer and with much more joviality and excitement. The towering trees were the mute sentinels of a momentous gathering in which the hand of Moscow, over 6000 miles away, manipulated the strings.

The communists were not unlike other human beings gathered together in similar surroundings. When not in session, some romped through the woods while others gathered in groups to tell stories and play poker, pinochle, or other games. There was plenty of good food which was eaten with gusto amidst loud and furious argument and conversation. Romance blossomed too, as the men took women comrades by the arms and lost themselves in the forest. Earl Browder, then a young man in his late twenties, was too engrossed in the concerns of his heart, to notice with what relish the comrades watched his antics. Nor did he hear how they snickered about his love affair with Mother Bloor who was old enough to be his grandmother. They laughed as he wandered off into the woods with her, holding her closely and kissing her faded, wrinkled cheeks.

A factional struggle rocked the convention in the woods: whether to maintain the underground or abolish it. The Comintern decided, since both factions favored legal as well as illegal communist activity, that the American communists should prepare carefully for coming out into the open when conditions in the United States made such a move possible. The American communists were instructed that in taking such a step they must, under all circumstances, maintain an underground communist apparatus through which to engage in illegal, conspiratorial activities.

Moscow further decided on the composition of the leadership of the American Communist party, its specific decisions on this matter directing the Party to include Pogany, alias Lang, alias Pepper, on its leading executive and policy-making committees. By these decisions Moscow left no doubt that she took a serious view of the importance of the American Communist party. Those who try to maintain the fiction that Moscow holds the American movement in contempt are totally ignorant of the facts.

Extraordinary measures were taken to safeguard the convention. Special guards patrolled the village for twenty-four hours a day. The convention grounds were heavily guarded. Watchmen took up posts on the hills to give them a view of the surrounding country. No one was allowed to enter the grounds without proper identification papers. Those attending the convention were prohibited from leaving the grounds. Writing home or mailing love letters was proscribed.

The convention sessions were held in the thick of the woods in the center of a small clearing completely surrounded by small trees. Not a glimpse could be had of the place from the outside. By following a narrow winding trail one came upon it as if by accident. Tables and chairs were provided for the two chairmen and the secretaries who took down the minutes. The Presidium dominated by the Comintern Rep selected the two chairmen, Caleb Harrison for the Ruthenberg minority and myself for the underground majority. The delegates squatted on the ground, Indian fashion, in a semicircle around the chairmen's table. Guards were stationed on the outer rim of the clearing. No one was allowed to leave the sessions without permission. A comrade who had been granted permission to go to the toilet went accompanied by a guard to guarantee his safe return.

At night flaming torches lit up the weird proceedings. In the amber light the gathering took on the sinister appearance of a meeting in a Stygian forest as the flickering lights played with the dark shadows and danced over drawn, serious faces. The rules required that speeches be made in a low subdued voice. The guards reported that the forest accoustics carried a loud, booming voice for miles. But the communists ignored the rule. They spoke with oratorical passion and added emphasis to what they had to say by bellowing lustily.

The delegation from Moscow came to the convention sittings only after the roll call had been taken and all present were vouched for. When the convention adjourned the delegation was the first to leave.

At night, before the lights went out, all documents, books, printed material, papers, membership cards, minutes, records, etc., had to be turned over to the security commission headed by the comrade in charge of communist rackets and money-raising schemes, Alfred Wagenknecht. This precaution was taken to prevent such records and material from falling into the hands of the authorities should the convention be raided at night when the revolutionary hosts were asleep. In the event of a surprise raid, the comrades were instructed to give false names and addresses and to protest vehemently that they were spending their vacations at the place. Special guards were assigned to the Moscow delegation, who were housed in quarters somewhat isolated from the others. Should an alarm require a hasty departure, plans were worked out for that emergency. Their autos were kept in readiness and the guards assigned to them, armed with automatics, were under instructions to shoot their way out with the precious Comintern cargo, should that be necessary.

Professor Walecski, introduced as Comrade Brooks, delivered the opening speech, in an address which took over two hours to deliver. He covered the range of the world affairs of the Comintern and presented the decisions of Moscow on the internal affairs of the American Communist party and how the spoils of office were to be divided. Following his long intellectual tirade, the Comintern's resolution on the American Party question was read. It concluded:

"The underground organization of the Communist party must not sink into disuse, but, on the contrary, must constantly extend its illegal machinery further and further, in proportion to the growth of the illegal party . . .

"The underground machinery of the Communist party is not merely for emergencies, but for constant and permanent use. Down to the lowest unit—the group of ten—every branch and stem of the party structure must continue to keep its secret addresses and meeting places and to use them in constant underground functioning. Every member, no matter what his work in the legal party, must also perform his duties in the underground organization . . .

"Under bourgeois rule, no matter how liberal it may be, a Communist party must never relinquish its facilities for underground press and, under the circumstances now prevailing in the United States, the active functioning of the underground press cannot be abated . . . The legal political party will be able to take upon itself the printing of a large portion of the literature that is not definitely illegal . . .

"The intellectual workers in these legal institutions of the party must be subject to the same discipline, wage scale and regulations as underground party workers. It must always be remembered that the real revolutionary party, the American Section of the Third International, is the Communist party of America [then the underground] and that the legal party is but an instrument which it uses to better carry on its work among the masses. Only through membership in the American Section—the Communist party of America—can American workers become members of the Communist International."

Before the opening session adjourned a dispute arose over the question of whether it was advisable for Foster to come to the convention, as the industrial organizer of the underground to report on trade union matters. Foster, a newcomer in the Party, operated in the trade union movement as a progressive, and emphatically and publicly denied that he was a member of the Communist party. Many delegates were afraid that by coming to the convention Foster might expose the colossal fraud he was perpetrating and thereby injure the campaign in the trade unions which the communists were conducting through him. Foster belonged to a faction that wanted him to report to the convention. Upon the demand of the Comintern Rep the matter was turned over to the Presidium, where, after considerable discussion, and only after assurances were given that every possible precaution would be taken to get Foster secretly to the place, the decision was made directing Foster to report to the convention. But it was too late to cover up Foster's tracks. Detectives trailed him wherever he went. The Presidium did not know that a squad of government agents and Michigan State police had the convention covered. They were waiting until Foster got to the convention before raiding the Wulfskeel farm, for they had been reliably informed that he would attend. The next day Foster arrived from Chicago with the hounds on his heels.

Upon his arrival Foster immediately went into session with the Presidium which honored him by making him a fraternal delegate. All afternoon long he discussed the nature of his report to the convention with Professor Walecski. Foster delivered his report at night.

For three full hours Foster unfolded a weird tale. Like a revolutionary architect he had his blue print on how the old "labor faker" Samuel Gompers, the founder and President of the American Federation of Labor, was to be bodily kicked out of the trade union movement, a beaten and disgraced man. Get into the unions, he told the communists. Bore from within and the unions one by one will fall into your hands. Foster depicted the old line trade union officials as a bunch of nitwits, unconscious ignoramuses, moribund and so lacking in energy and initiative that they could be easily maneuvered and misled into a situation in which the communists could take the unions away from them. He explained how issues were to be projected in the unions for the purpose of arousing the rank-and-file. Step by step he outlined how the communists were to build up their own organization within the trade union structure. He warned the communists to camouflage their fight in the trade unions, to conduct it as a trade union fight, not as a communist fight. He called upon the communists in the unions to hide their identity and establish secret trade union cells in the unions in which the communists got a foothold.

Foster finished. He had made a tremendous impression but no applause broke out when he took his seat. Convention rules forbade it. The amber lights flickered; the tall trees cast their dark shadows. Reinstein, the emissary of the Red Trade Union International, rushed to the speaker's table and warmly shook Foster's hand in appreciation. The convention adjourned for the night. A few couples, arm in arm, lost themselves in the solitude of the woods. Others went to bathe in the nude in the placid waters of Lake Michigan under the stars. Soon only nature's noises, in a harmony of discord, filled the air.

Morning broke the serene calm of the night before. Foster, strolling by himself, noticed a mysterious figure peering through the branches of a thick cluster of bushes. He investigated. Recognition of the man sent cold shivers down his spine. There stood the notorious Spolansky, private detective and government operative who specialized in hunting down reds. A meeting of the Presidium convened immediately and there Foster reported what he had seen. Members of the Presidium charged him with being careless in coming to the convention. Foster, red with anger, retorted with curses and explained that he had taken every possible precaution to cover up his tracks. Walecski, the C.I. Rep, though alarmed and nervous, cautioned against panic.

The Presidium followed his advice. First considered was Foster's presence at the convention. Orders were given to get Foster out of the convention grounds at once. The Communist party and the Comintern could ill-afford to have Foster identified with the communists by having him arrested at a secret underground convention. It would ruin the plans worked out with Foster for capturing the American Federation of Labor and making him its first communist president. Foster left, after being given categorical orders not to proceed directly to Chicago or leave a trail between the Communist party convention at Bridgeman and Chicago, the headquarters of Foster's conspiracy against American labor.

The Presidium discussed the impending raid for hours. Wagenknecht received orders to safeguard all records, documents and material from falling into the hands of the raiders. Only the day before the C.I. Rep had demanded that a census be taken of all present. A mimeographed form to be filled out by all comrades required them to give their real names, their aliases, family histories, professions, years spent in the Socialist and communist movement, connections with other organizations, prison records, strike records, education, languages spoken and whatever other information they considered of value to the Comintern. The C.I. Rep explained that the Comintern wanted the information in order to estimate the character and complexion of the American communist leadership, and for compiling as complete a record as possible of all communist leaders. Walecski did not want such a detailed and complete record of the leaders of American communism to fall into the hands of the authorities. But the eagle eye of the Comintern did not know that on Wagenknecht's committee of three there was one spy in the pay of the government.

The Presidium did a good job in handling the crisis facing the underground convention. Detailed plans were worked out for completing the convention and disbanding without panic before the raid took place. The next morning suspicious faces appeared around the convention grounds. The convention was called into session at once. With clock-like precision every move decided upon by the Presidium was executed without a hitch. The ignorant baby of the 1920 raids had grown, in a period of two years, into a disciplined revolutionary army. The new officers and committees of the Communist party underground were elected and the motion ending the convention was duly adopted. One minute later large limousines, as if from nowhere, came rumbling into the grounds.

Into the first limousine went the Comintern delegation, wrapped in blankets that hid their faces, accompanied by armed guards, fingering triggers, ready to shoot and kill. "Go!" shouted the guard as he slammed the door. The long black limousine shot out of the grounds like a bullet. Automobile followed automobile, each loaded with a crew of underground conspirators. The first to leave were those out on bail, facing trial or awaiting return to prison. Those implicated in shady affairs and marked by criminal records left next, and last went the foreign-born aliens who faced deportation should they be seized. There was no commotion, no disorder; the flights proceeded according to plan.

The American-born and naturalized citizens who had no blemishes on their records were ordered to stay behind. They were instructed to stand up for their constitutional rights as Americans and to protest vigorously against the uncalled-for interference with an American's right to enjoy his vacation as he saw fit.

When the raid took place the indignant, protesting "Americans" were herded into army trucks and carted away. A group of the raiders armed with pick axes and shovels were directed by the spy member of Wagenknecht's committee to the spot where he had buried the records. They dug up the barrel with its precious contents containing the personal histories of the communist leaders, fake passports, codes, minutes, cables to and from the Comintern and the official Comintern decisions on the American Communist party.

The raid on the Bridgeman convention, resulting in the arrest or indictment of every top leader of the Communist party, did not harm the organization. Not one of the leaders or members served time. The communists demonstrated to Moscow and to the United States that they knew how to meet an attack and turn it to the advantage of the movement. The Bridgeman convention marked the end of the infancy of the Communist party and the beginning of its maturity. The American communists, for the first time, had worked out a program for their activities in the United States, which from the organizational standpoint and in its relation to the organized forces in the country, especially the trade unions, was practical and workable. The Communist party, now a factor to be dealt with in the political and social life of the country, faced the future confidently and planned and labored untiringly for its destiny.

CHAPTER THREE

THE AMERICAN COMMUNISTS
DISCOVER THE UNITED STATES

IN THE beginning the American communists dwelt in the skies. They lived in the United States but their hearts and minds were elsewhere. They were caught in the fantasies of the Russian Revolution like children in the wonders of fairyland. But, unlike children who accept the wonders of fairyland as realities for the moment, the communists accepted the fantasy of the revolution as a living reality which became part of their existence and dominated their thinking. The Russian Revolution meant communism, a communism that fitted into a spiritual vacuum and replaced for them the hold that religion had on the spiritual yearnings of ordinary human beings. Communists, to be understood, must be taken as human beings to whom communism, the Bolshevik brand, with its idolizing of Soviet Statism, is a religion to which they adhere fanatically like dogmatic religious zealots. But the communist, unlike a religious person, bases his conduct on the abnegation of religious influences on life. In the communist there is substituted the complete submission of the individual to a materialistic, anti-religious philosophy and to the power of the Communist party over his life.

The political education of the American communists started in Moscow at the Third World Congress of the Comintern, held in the summer of 1921. The Third Congress forced the American communists to face the realities of American life and to base their activities on American conditions. The Comintern sent one of its ablest political thinkers to the United States to transform the American Communist party along the lines laid down by the decisions of the Third World Congress.

Pogany, soon mastering the English language, spent twenty hours out of twenty-four studying the social, political and cultural structure of American life in order to be equipped to bring home to the communists the facts about the country in which they lived. Operating under the alias of John Pepper, Pogany discovered the United States for the communists.

The communists took to the revelation like little children who suddenly come upon a new toy. With the discovery of America, the Communist party developed rapidly. The underground party was quickly liquidated. The illegal work of the organization, however, was not given up, but was considerably broadened and more adeptly conducted. Communism emerged from the cellars to become a serious issue in American life. The communist infiltration and poisoning of American life was on.

What did the human element in Communism consist of at this time? When first organized the communist movement was a foreign-inspired movement. The membership of the Communist party was made up overwhelmingly of foreign-born who were more interested in what was going on in their mother countries than they were with events in the United States. The foreign bloc which constituted the backbone of the early communist movement shared the leadership of the movement with men and women who were American in their origin, but the Americans had to yield to the pressure of the foreign-born elements to hold on to their positions of leadership.

Fully 90 percent of the membership of the Communist party were foreign-born. Only 10 percent were native Americans, and of this small number many were the sons and daughters of immigrants. This classification of the membership of the Communist party during its formative years is in no way derogatory. The foreign inspiration of the movement together with its foreign-born membership did not prevent the development of American communism and its integration into the life of the country.

The membership of the Communist party is fluctuating, ever-changing. Moreover the complexion of the Party membership changed as the movement grew and developed. Besides transforming the individuals who joined the movement the Communist party sought out and attracted elements which the party needed in carrying on its activities, especially in the trade union field. Members were welcomed who had no scruples and no regard for human life. Deals were made with trade union politicians and racketeers in order to gain control of unions, and many of these corrupt, criminal elements were induced to join the Communist party in order that the Party might control them better. Known gangsters were recruited to become members of workers' strong-arm squads, and these in turn were organized into clubs under various names, given an elementary communist education and then drawn into the party organization. Around the Communist party grew an ever-increasing army of shiftless, non-working men and women who maintained themselves with some degree of economic security out of the special services which they were able to render to the Party. These new elements, the heroic Amazons and the men of brawn who wielded the blackjack, the dagger, and the gun, were pampered and glorified. In the eyes of the rank-and-file they constituted the fighting vanguard, the heroes of the movement.

Shortly after the communists had discovered the United States, the communist rank-and-file consisted of idealistic zealots, hardened communist-Bolsheviks, unscrupulous careerists, office holders and the flotsam and jetsam of professional revolutionaries who give direction and color to the Party. The trained army of men and women who could give a beating and take one too made up a special category which supplied the movement with fighting cadres and inspired the membership with confidence and courage. They were the instruments of terror, the comrades through whom the beginnings of American red terrorism took on form.

Civil War in the Unions—The Attack on Gompers

The plot to assassinate the character of Samuel Gompers and to drive him out of the organized labor movement a disgraced and thoroughly beaten man was formulated in Moscow in 1921. The plans were drawn during the sessions of the International Congress of the Red Trade Union International. The American communists who participated in their formulation were Minor, Foster, Ella Reeves Bloor and Earl Browder.

According to previous arrangements, Sidney Hillman, President of the Amalgamated Clothing Workers of America, was present in Moscow to observe the sessions of the Profintern Congress. The vain and ambitious American labor leader fitted into the scheme which the communists had worked out for America. The Russian Bolsheviks exploited his vanity and fired his ambitions. They heaped honors upon him, wined and dined him at special receptions, and Lenin and the other Soviet officials went out of their way to receive him. The wine of flattery worked, for the labor leader from America was convinced that the Bolsheviks considered him a man of unusual ability, a progressive trade unionist who towered above Gompers. Lenin himself entered the negotiations with Hillman concerning the plan to destroy Gompers and take over control of the American Federation of Labor.

Upon William Z. Foster's shoulders fell the responsibility of upholding the American Communist party's end of the grand plan. Before 1921 Foster's name does not appear on the roster of communist leaders. The career of this man who had become the focal point of communist trade union policy is worth reviewing. Since the end of the steel strike in January 1920, which he had led to a disastrous conclusion, he had been more or less a discredited, isolated figure in the American Federation of Labor.

Brooding over his failures, no longer having a worthwhile anchorage in the American Federation of Labor, Foster returned to his first love, anarcho-syndicalism, which he had publicly repudiated during the steel strike. With a handful of followers he organized a syndicalist league to propagate once more the principles and program which Foster personally published in a book on *Syndicalism* written by him years earlier in collaboration with Earl C. Ford. The book gives an insight into the mental quirks of the Foster who here put his fantastic ideas down in black and white, revealing the diabolical currents which, back in 1913, had been running through the mind of America's present-day foremost Communist leader.

Foster's thesis called for violent revolution, the rejection by the working class of political action and the transformation of the unions into fighting revolutionary organizations. He went much further than this by calling for the disorganization of the armed forces in the following words:

"Syndicalists in every country are already actively preparing this disorganization of the armed forces by carrying on a double educational program among the workers . . .

"They are teaching class soldiers not to shoot their brothers and sisters who are in revolt, but, if need be, *to shoot their own officers and to desert the army when the crucial moment arrives.*"

Foster in his pamphlet inveighed against the state and called for its destruction. The syndicalist, said Foster, "is a radical anti-patriot." He summed up his philosophy in the following words: "He [the syndicalist] allows no considerations of 'legality,' 'religion,' 'patriotism,' 'honor,' 'duty,' etc. to stand in the way of his adoption of effective tactics."

Foster stood at the height of his career in the trade union movement in early 1920 when the eyes of the world were focused on the man who led the steel workers in battle against the powerful steel combines. What stature did Foster assume then? The Bolshevik Revolution was a matter of history. The communists dominated the American radical scene. Europe was still in the throes of social upheavals of revolutionary significance. How did these events that should have warmed the heart of the syndicalist Foster affect Foster the A F of L labor leader? Did this champion of the militant minority take advantage of his position as leader of 365,000 steel workers to lead them towards the left? We have the testimony on this matter of William Hard, a keen observer who watched the fortunes of Foster during the steel strike. He reported to the *New Republic* on January 7, 1920:

"I have watched him. He moves slower than his twenty-four unions. He moves actually behind his twenty-four unions, not in front of them. He waits for authority. He follows it inch by inch, day by day."

Before the Senate committee investigating the steel strike, Gompers, testifying about Foster, declared:

"He was a man of ability, a man of good presence, gentle in expression, a commander of good English, and I encouraged him. I was willing to help build a golden bridge for mine enemy to pass over. I was willing to welcome an erring brother into the ranks of constructive labor."

Foster, in his deportment, showed that he was anxious to cross the golden bridge, to deserve the confidence that Gompers had placed in him. At a time when radicals and revolutionary syndicalists, like Foster, had every reason to promulgate and practice their principles because of the revolutionary fermentation going on in the world, he chose to disavow them.

Senator Gillette reminded Foster that he had written articles attacking the labor leaders of the American Federation of Labor as labor fakers and had used the following words:

"The exploits of these labor fakers are too well known to need recapitulation here. Suffice it to say the labor fakers must go."

Foster, cornered, replied that he had no particular labor leader in mind and had made an error. He declared that in his opinion the great majority of the trade union leaders were honest men, in fact more honest than any other group of men in positions of leadership.

That declaration did not prevent Foster, after he had lost the strike, from hurling the invective of labor faker at Samuel Gompers and all the other labor leaders who refused to follow him into the camp of the communists.

When the Senate committee pressed Foster to the wall he squirmed as he repudiated every revolutionary principle he ever stood for. When Senator Borah came to his rescue, he welcomed an opportunity to explain:

"I am one who was raised in the slums . . . *I have no teachings or principles.*"

The man who under oath confessed that he had no teachings, no principles, received from Lenin the most important communist mission in America.

How did Foster, the discredited and forgotten labor leader, who in 1920 headed an organization numbering about a dozen followers, get to Moscow in 1921? That is a story of the operations of Moscow agents in the United States. It has already been revealed that in 1920 Johnson, the Boston Lett, alias Scott, was under specific instructions to bring a delegation of trade unionists to the World Congress of the Profintern to be held in Moscow, in the summer of 1921. He was ordered by hook or crook to secure delegates. Scott had his pockets stuffed with money to facilitate his efforts. But the legitimate trade union leaders turned down Scott's invitations and fabulous promises. Scott had to turn to the extreme left wing radicals in the trade unions who were without official standing and lacked a following. In desperation Scott was forced to turn to Foster who was fast getting nowhere with a vestpocket organization, without funds and followers.

Scott's shekels and Lenin's pamphlet did the trick. Scott showed Foster how with Moscow support his Trade Union Educational League could be developed into a powerful organization and pave the way for Foster to replace Gompers as President of the A F of L. The bankrupt Foster needed little convincing. He badly needed a tie-block to moor to lest he sink into oblivion. Scott subsidized the anemic Trade Union Educational League. Foster received a special invitation to go to Moscow and the funds to get him there. Bought and paid for, in the spring of 1921, a queer delegation, with no roots whatsoever in the American trade union movement, left for Moscow to represent the organized workers of the United States in the name of the Trade Union Educational League. Foster headed the delegation. Earl Browder, his messenger boy and good man Friday, and Ella

Reeves Bloor were his associates, arm in arm. Browder served Foster meekly and loyally until 1929, when the Comintern ordered him to ditch Foster and strike out for himself.

The Bolsheviks with great pomp and ceremony greeted Foster as the outstanding American trade union leader. Foster was so greatly impressed that he admits that in Moscow whatever doubts or misgivings he had about the communist movement were dissipated and that he forthwith became a communist and joined the Party. Foster, unlike Hillman, who was not a delegate but only an observer and who had not joined the Communist party, acted at the Profintern Congress like a disciplined comrade under orders.

Foster, Minor and Hillman put the finishing touches on the grand scheme to take over the American trade union movement. They laid down the program and policy which have guided communist activities in the unions ever since.

The grand trade union scheme worked out with Lenin provided that Hillman should throw his support behind Foster's efforts to build up a broad opposition movement inside of the American Federation of Labor. Since Hillman headed an independent union at odds with the A F of L, he was to use his influence with other independent unions, namely the Railroad Brotherhoods, to win their support for Foster's disruptive efforts in the A F of L. The communists agreed with Hillman that as soon as Foster's opposition movement in the A F of L became sufficiently strong to strike out for power, Hillman's Amalgamated Clothing Workers, the Railroad Brotherhoods and other independent unions were to unite with the Foster opposition in the A F of L to form a trade union bloc for the purpose of making a frontal attack on Samuel Gompers in order to capture the A F of L. In the event the plot against Gompers did not succeed the bloc was to attempt to win the support of the bulk of the A F of L unions for its program. Once a sufficient number lined up in support of the bloc, the bloc was to strike out independently for the leadership of America's organized workers. The communists followed this policy in splitting the A F of L and organizing the C.I.O.

Immediately upon his return to the United States Foster went into a huddle with the leading committees of the communist underground. The greatest secrecy was maintained concerning his activities and movements. On orders of the Comintern, Foster was put in charge of the Industrial Department of the Communist party and made a full voting member of its highest leading committees. He operated in the communist underground under the names of Lansing and Borden.

The Trade Union Educational League, enriched by several hundred thousand dollars in subsidies from Moscow, became the trade union department of the underground, designated by the letter X.

The communists in the trade unions were put in Foster's charge under orders to follow his leadership. All party members who were eligible were ordered to joins unions of the A F of L at once.

Though the communists concentrated on the unions of the A F of L, they did not leave the other unions alone. The communists organized communist factions within such independent unions as the Amalgamated Clothing Workers and the Railroad Brotherhoods and bored from within these organizations as energetically as they did in the A F of L. At the same time they gave the radical revolutionary unions no peace. With one hand they invited the I.W.W. to join the Red International of Trade Unions, and with the other hand they attacked the I.W.W. for being an anarchist, syndicalist organization which sabotaged the efforts of the revolutionary workers to gain control of the unions. They called upon the members of the I.W.W. to desert the organization and join the American Federation of Labor in order to cooperate with the communists in the fight against Gompers. Foster, more bitterly than any one else, attacked the syndicalist beliefs he had held for a lifetime in an effort to discredit the I.W.W. and wreck the organization.

A communist nucleus was formed inside the I.W.W. Outstanding I.W.W. personalities who were in desperate financial circumstances were bribed by giving them paid jobs as organizers for the communist nucleus or paid positions in the Communist party. The ferocity with which Foster attacked the I.W.W. and the independent unions of the left caused a serious rift in Communist party ranks between Foster and the communists who supported the left unions. The independent unions in New York which stood to the left of Hillman had loyally supported the communist cause. The Comintern had approved the organizing of these unions into a federation called the United Labor Council. The leader of the Council and its founder was none other than Joseph Zack, the chief of the trade union department of the underground before Foster entered the Communist party. Joseph Zack later became a member of Foster's personal caucus in the party; was graduated from the Lenin University in Moscow; became an intimate friend of Joseph Stalin and one of his advisers on American affairs, and an important figure in Stalin's inner circle in the Comintern.

Foster demanded that the United Labor Council be abolished, that the independent unions in the council be disbanded and their members forced to join the American Federation of Labor. The comrades in the United Labor Council and in the independent unions fought back. The controversy was submitted to Moscow. Moscow favored Foster on the liquidation of the Council but opposed the liquidation of the left independent unions. Moscow decided that the independent unions of the left should join a special committee set up by the Profintern by which they were to support Foster's efforts in the A F of L. At the same time Foster was given a free hand to destroy the leaders and left independent unions which refused to follow his orders. By such indirection, a practice common to the Comintern, the United Labor Council was soon liquidated and most of the unions which were affiliated with it were destroyed.

Foster, who proved a submissive tool in the hands of the Communist party and the Comintern, played an important role in injecting the communist issue into the trade unions. Though the negative, the destructive side of communism stands out most prominently in the trade unions, one must admit that the communists must be credited with positive and important constructive achievements in the unions. American trade unionism owes much to the communists. The communists have given vitality and force to the issue of industrial unionism, without which the organization of the mass production industries would have been impossible. The communists more than any other force have instilled the American workers with trade union consciousness. By raising in the unions the issue of the organization of the unorganized workers, the communists have been responsible for bringing millions of workers into the trade unions. By raising legitimate political issues in the unions the communists have been responsible for broadening the organized worker's political outlook. Communists have developed new streamlined strike techniques and methods for organizing workers on an industry and nation-wide basis. Communism cannot be combated by ignoring the tremendous efforts in men, propaganda and funds which the communists have invested constructively on behalf of the trade unions.

But all these constructive efforts were, and will continue to be, secondary to the primary interests of the communists as a revolutionary destructive force, and to the interests of the Soviet Union which they slavishly serve. They will sacrifice, as they have done on many occasions, the interests of the trade unions and of the American people to the interests of the Soviet Union.

The trade union line directing the communists to go into the unions and Foster's ascendancy to the trade union leadership of the Communist party brought new forces into the movement, forces which psychologically and in many other ways changed the face of American communism. Foster ushered in the proletarian tradition of the blue flannel workshirt, the leather jacket, the tilted cap, the slouch of the tough guy and the glorification of slang. Minor attacked the concept of morals as a bourgeois institution. Foster rounded out and consolidated Minor's position by attacking intellectuals and intellectualism, by exalting the common, vulgar, ignorant worker. The union slugger was idealized and the men who lived by intellectual pursuits were held in contempt.

The transformation of the Communist party membership was most noticeable in the city of Chicago where Foster maintained the national headquarters of the Trade Union Educational League.

In profligacy and vice, the youthful members of Chicago's leading cadre of professional revolutionists outstripped their elder compatriots. Characteristically blasé and caustically cynical towards life, the youthful champions of communism were already aged in the experience of smut and lascivious dissipation. They poisoned the atmosphere in which they circulated. They imposed their standards upon the teen-aged youths who joined the movement out of the idealistic desire to serve humanity. From Chicago, the lecherous pestilence spread throughout the country, wherever the communists maintained a substantial organization.

The Chicago cesspool among the youth boiled over in 1927 during a plenary session of the Central Executive Committee. All the Party leaders and the leaders of the youth movement were pulled up by their ears when William F. Dunne, by no means a puritan, warned the gathering of the sexual depravity and degeneration which had taken hold of the communist youth movement in Chicago and throughout the country. He bravely took up the cudgels for reform even though, in so doing, he antagonized the influential forces in the youth movement who supported his leadership in the Party. Many of the elder communist statesmen substantiated the Dunne charges. The youth leaders fought back by hurling the same kind of charges against the Party leaders and by declaring that the affairs of the boudoir belonged to the boudoir and had no place in a Communist party which is concerned with political problems. Much bad blood was engendered but no resolutions or decisions were adopted on the matter. The Party could not risk a house cleaning.

Before closing this episode it is necessary to touch on another phase of the same subject. The Communist party is primarily a man's party in spite of the fact that women compose a large percentage of its membership and enjoy equal rights with the men. In the recognized, public leadership of the Party they are negligible. Only two or three women have attained outstanding leadership in the Party organization. Nevertheless women in the Communist party indirectly wield tremendous influence. The friendship of these women is coveted and their animosity feared.

An incident involving the author will throw light on women's status in the movement. In 1919 I was instrumental in organizing the Communist party. A few weeks later I was arrested during the raids conducted by the Lusk Committee, indicted for criminal anarchy, tried, found guilty and sent to Sing Sing Prison to serve a term of five to ten years at hard labor. After being confined to prison for almost three years I was released on bail pending the outcome of an appeal on my behalf to the United States Supreme Court. Returning from Sing Sing to New York after an absence of three years, I was amazed to find how the Communist party had grown and the extent of its ramifications in many organizations. The Party structure had grown into an imposing edifice, the organization and its institutions offering many opportunities to communists to carve out a career for themselves. Communist party members, men and women, were dominated by an ambition not only to work for the Party as professional revolutionists but also to win for themselves places in the Party leadership. But the women comrades in spite of their ability did not reach the coveted places.

One of the ambitious women, the wife of a member of the Central Executive Committee, who gave her services to the Party as an artist, organizer, writer, soap-box orator and propagandist, visited me soon after I returned from prison and before I had had an opportunity to orientate myself to the changes which had taken place in the Party organization. During a conversation dealing with the activities of the movement and the internal situation in the Party she suddenly blurted out:

"Comrade Gitlow you have been away for a long time. Tell me, have you had any contact with women in prison?"

"Yes, on visiting days in the visiting room."

"Oh, I don't mean that. What I mean is, did you have an opportunity for sexual intercourse?"

"That was quite impossible, comrade. Why do you ask me such a question?"

"I will be frank with you, Ben. I like you. I'd like to go to bed with you."

"But that is out of the question. You are the wife of comrade . . . He is an important leader in the Party, and besides, a good friend of mine."

"But you don't understand. Sure, I'm married and also have kids. You and I are revolutionists, we're communists. We believe in each one giving free rein to his or her desires. My friend [husband] understands my position perfectly and has no objections if I sometimes go to bed with another man."

When she discovered, much to her surprise that she was not making any headway she became very serious.

"You are a stranger in the Party, Ben," she continued. "A man makes his way in the Party organization by his own efforts and ability. But not a woman. A woman comrade to get anywhere in the Party must attach herself to a male party leader. Then she will get to know what is really going on in the Party and will be able to command a position that counts. Sure, my man is a party leader. But he never notices me. He is engrossed in his party work and refuses to discuss his affairs with me or take me into his confidence. If I am to gain recognition on my own I must do what the other women around the Central Executive Committee do—sleep with one of its members."

She backed up her contentions with stories about the women who moved about in the Party's top circles and how they got there.

This favored group of Shebas at the center did not make up the majority of the women members of the Communist party. In its rank-and-file women the communist movement has its most fanatical and self-sacrificing followers. They waste their lives in the services of the Party, holding that the cause supersedes all personal considerations. They are endowed with great courage. Communist women play a prominent role in demonstrations where battles with the police are inevitable in spite of the danger of cracked heads and being trampled under horses' hoofs. They make up the large army which distributes millions of copies of communist propaganda. Communist women with bundles of papers, pamphlets and leaflets go from house to house, climb the stairs of tenements and knock on doors in order to leave copies of the printed communist message and to invite and answer questions. You will find the communist women in all kinds of women's organizations, in tenants' leagues, parent-and-teacher associations, in consumers' organizations, in inter-racial movements, in movements against the high cost of living, in all the movements the communists organize for so-called humane purposes, in strikes, on picket lines— everywhere you will find these red Amazons spearheading the communist cause and guarding the interests of the Party.

Most women in the Communist party, due to the demands of the Party on their time, have been forced to give up whatever social and personal life they had outside of the Party before they entered the movement. The personal and social life thus lost is replaced by another supplied by the Communist party. The longer women remain in the Communist party the more dependent they become on the Party's social life. There is no organization in the United States, political or otherwise, in which women are active, that so completely controls their lives as does the Communist party. Once women are caught in the vortex of the communist organization they become voluntary prisoners to a system of physical and ideological control which narrows the sphere of their personal lives entirely to the limits of the Party organization.

Joseph Pogany—Alias John Pepper

Joseph Pogany, alias John Pepper, Short, Lang, and Strong, rediscovered America for the American communists. The Hungarian political Christopher Columbus, special agent of the Comintern, opened up a new world for the American communists. Following the raid on the Bridgeman convention the underground Communist party established a new set of underground national headquarters in New York City. Operating from this secret working center Pepper began a bizarre and amazing career as an American communist which lasted from 1922 to its tragic end in Moscow in 1929, when the final curtain was dropped on his dramatic escapades in Europe, Asia and America. Stalin salted Pepper away by giving him a job in the salt mines to still his voice and doom him to oblivion. To Pepper must go the credit of transforming the romantic sectarian Communist party of the United States into a revolutionary political American party that keeps abreast of the ever-changing social and economic developments of the country.

Pepper's discovery of America did not depend entirely upon book knowledge, though he did read and absorb the contents of thousands of volumes on America. He spent hours in individual talks with the leaders of the movement and with authorities acquainted with the various phases of American life. He visited the district organizations of the Party and acquainted himself with local conditions. He avidly read the newspapers from all parts of the country. He visited the movies, the theaters and night clubs. He got acquainted with the country's popular music, studied its slang and gags. He made an exhaustive study of the population composition of the country to determine how it was divided into races and nationalities.

The more the Hungarian genius studied the country, the more he liked it. Had he not thrown in his lot with the International Communist movement he would have become a super American patriot. This man, illegally in the United States, enjoyed its music, its theaters, its food, its newspapers, its young novelists, its humor, its "funnies," its cigarettes and chewing gum. Though he fought for the proletarianization of the American Communist party, that did not stop him from reveling in the luscious bourgeois life of America. He whetted his appetite like a gourmand and let the tasteful delicacies linger in his mouth the better to enjoy himself.

John Pepper did not confine his associations entirely to communists. He made the American communist leaders realize that to do so was to give up the opportunity of forming the kind of associations which could be of great value to the communists in many respects. He therefore made it a point to confer with outstanding labor leaders, congressional leaders, figures prominent in every walk of American life, authors, bankers, economists, college professors, rich merchants and industrialists.

The snobbish-looking Pepper, who dressed foppishly and loved gold-tipped cigarettes and good cognac, was thoroughly democratic in his conduct toward others. He was what the Americans term a good mixer, one upon whom the life of the party can depend. To a group of communist leaders he once seriously remarked: "Communist leaders should read good romances and novels, first for relaxation and enjoyment and second as a guide to a better understanding of human character. As realistic politicians we must understand the character of the people if we are to deal with them intelligently.

"And furthermore," he continued, "a communist leader must not allow himself to be caught stewing in his own juice. Life will become very monotonous for such a one. A communist must drink good wine in moderation and should not confine his taste to one brand. He must learn to appreciate the different vintages for their intrinsic worth. And so it must be with romance too, comrades. A communist leader must not restrain his passion for novelty—a new, serious love affair every six months is a good tonic for a communist leader. It revives his energy and quickens his impulses. Yes, comrades, it adds zest to life like spice to food."

The working headquarters of the Political Committee were established in a natty four-room apartment in a newly constructed apartment house in the Washington Heights section of New York, just above 180th Street. Here Pepper also established his personal office. He did not live there, for the apartment was kept by Israel Amter, the cabbage-eater, and his wife.

At the Washington Heights headquarters the Political Committee gathered almost daily to conduct the Party's affairs. Around the large table cluttered with papers and cigarette butts gathered Pepper, Lovestone, Foster, Ruthenberg, Dunne, Amter, Jakira, Browder and Katterfeld. Pepper because of his illegal status in the United States, having been smuggled into the country by the GPU, was satisfied, for the time being, to operate behind the scenes.

The Communists Unload a Bag Full of Tricks

Carrying out the United Front directives of the Communist International, the American communists sought allies in liberal, socialist and labor circles by proposing to them joint action in favor of issues and political combinations favored by the Communist party. The men and women who yesterday were denounced by the communists as traitors to the working class today were invited to join hands with the communists in a fight for common objectives. The American communists were advised by the Comintern that the main objective of the United Front was to give the Communist party access to the masses who followed the liberals, the socialists and the trade union leaders, so that the Communist party could separate them from their reactionary conservative leaders. The communists were instructed to carry out the tactics of the United Front in such a way that they could expose and discredit reformist leaders with whom they united. The United Front was in reality a diabolical maneuver on the part of the communists, to gain time, to gain access to non-communist masses so that they could strengthen their own forces, and by raising issues that were impossible to realize, discredit the non-communist leaders in the United Front and thus split the labor movement.

The American communist leaders had no well-thought-out plans on how to initiate the United Front in the United States. John Pepper did. His United Front program called upon the communists to start a nation-wide campaign for the immediate formation of a labor party. He believed that if the Communist party took the lead in bringing about the formation of a labor party and provided it with finances, communist control of the new Party would be assured. Pepper also believed that the labor party should not be confined to the industrial workers only but should also include the farmers. Therefore the communists advocated the formation of a Farmer-Labor party.

Pepper was the first communist to realize that the foreign-born and the American of foreign-born extraction composed an important segment of the population which could be used for the political advantages of the Communist party. He therefore proposed, in addition to the United Front for the formation of a Farmer-Labor party, the initiation by the Communist party of a United Front movement in defense of the rights of the foreign-born, in which United Front movement the Communist party could enlist the organizations to which millions of foreign-born workers belonged. Broadly viewed, Pepper's United Front proposals, proposals which the Communist party accepted, subject to Moscow's approval, involved the three largest population concentrations in the country—the farmers, the industrial workers and the foreign-born. Moscow quickly approved the proposals and supplied the American communists with the cash to carry them out.

In the early part of 1923 the Communist International ordered the underground Communist party to merge with its legal organization the Workers party, to form one united, open and legal Communist party of the United States of America. The Communist party was now fully prepared to undertake responsibilities involved in executing the United Front policy. Four men were entrusted by the Political Committee with the campaign for the formation of a Farmer-

Labor party. Foster, Lovestone, Pepper and Ruthenberg toured the country, interviewing liberals, Farmer-Labor party politicians from Minnesota, trade union officials, heads of farmer organizations, ex-officials of the defunct Non Partisan League, and individuals whose prominence or connections might help the effort to get the Farmer-Labor party started. They spent lavishly and without hesitation the $100,000 which Moscow supplied for this purpose.

The Communist party organization went into high gear behind the campaign for the formation of a Farmer-Labor party. Party organizers toured the country visiting unions and other organizations to enlist their support and to have them pass resolutions backing up the campaign. High-pressure tactics were employed to build up sentiment for a Farmer-Labor party, so that the Communist party could form a committee for calling a national conference to launch the Party. Whenever it became necessary to get important persons to support the United Front for the Farmer-Labor party by offering them jobs and money it was done. In order to line up the Minnesota Farmer-Labor party, the communists used Clarence Hathaway, prominent in the Minnesota Farmer-Labor party and in the Machinists Union. He kept his affiliation with the Communist party a secret and posed as a progressive.

The first national convention to organize the Farmer-Labor party took place in Chicago in July, 1923. Over 500 delegates attended the convention, the overwhelming majority of whom were affiliated with the Communist party. When John Fitzpatrick, President of the Chicago Federation of Labor, realized that he and his labor delegation had been roped into a communist convention by his friend Foster and that, together with the few genuine farmer-laborites, they had been swallowed up by the Communist party, he got hold of Foster and demanded that under no circumstances should the convention proceed with the organization of a Farmer-Labor party.

The committee of four which sat in the balcony rejected Fitzpatrick's ultimatum. Fitzpatrick's labor delegation and the genuine farmer laborites bolted the convention. The communists proceeded with the convention. Amid fiery speeches and a wild display of enthusiasm a luke-warm reform platform which Ruthenberg and Pepper drafted was adopted. The Federated Farmer-Labor party which emerged from the communist womb died soon after it was born.

Following the Chicago fiasco, it became clear that the progressive movement forming around the Railroad Brotherhoods which had the support of the old Senator, LaFollette, was preparing to launch a third party in the 1924 presidential campaign with LaFollette as its standard bearer. The communists were forced to take a stand on the LaFollette issue. Pepper proposed that if the communists could not get the Farmer-Labor party forces to nominate a trade unionist of the left for the Presidency and insisted on endorsing the LaFollette candidacy, the communists in the interest of unity and for the purpose of remaining inside the movement should go along with the endorsement of LaFollette. Ludwig Lore, editor of the German Communist *Volkszeitung,* opposed the endorsement. The matter was turned over to Moscow for a decision.

While Moscow deliberated the moot question of LaFollette's endorsement, the Communist party, through the fake Federated Farmer-Labor party and with the assistance of the leaders of the Farmer-Labor party of Minnesota, conducted a campaign to secure delegates to attend a convention to be held in St. Paul on June 17, 1924, at which a national Farmer-Labor party was to be launched and candidates for President and Vice President of the United States nominated. To obtain an agreement to call the St. Paul Convention the Communist party gave its solemn pledge to the leaders of the Minnesota Farmer-Labor party that they would not oppose the nomination of LaFollette and in the event he was nominated would do everything in their power to elect him.

In the heat of the campaign for the St. Paul Convention orders came from Moscow demanding that Pepper proceed forthwith to Moscow. Pepper packed his valises with documents to back up his position, secured false passports and left for Moscow. But Foster, who had gotten control of the Communist party in 1924, did not trust Pepper. He cabled Moscow that it was advisable that he be in Moscow when American party questions were being considered. Moscow cabled back. Foster also packed his grip and left with false passports for the "Communist Holy Land."

One month before the St. Paul Convention was to open Moscow cabled its decisions. The St. Paul Convention call was approved but the endorsement of LaFollette rejected. The Comintern ordered the American communists under no circumstances to support LaFollette even if it meant splitting the United Front with the Farmer-Labor party people of Minnesota and the progressive trade unionists. Moscow reversed itself in a few short months on the LaFollette matter. It had originally approved the policy of the LaFollette endorsement.

How this decision on a purely internal American political matter was dominated by internal Russian politics shows to what an extent the American Communist party is at the mercy of Moscow.

In the summer of 1924 a triumvirate in the Russian Communist party consisting of Stalin, Zinoviev and Bukharin ganged up on Trotsky and began preparing the grounds for his removal from the Executive Committee of the Comintern and from the leadership of the Russian Communist party. In the United States a group in the Communist party headed by Lore and Juliet Stuart Poyntz supported Trotsky against Zinoviev. This group opposed the communist endorsement of LaFollette. When the LaFollette issue came up in the Comintern once more Trotsky fought against endorsement. Zinoviev, representing the majority of the Comintern Executive, and acting as the mouthpiece of the triumvirate, supported Trotsky's position and reversed himself because he did not want to give Trotsky a political issue. At the same time Zinoviev insisted that the Comintern castigate Lore and his followers in the Communist party even though he supported their policy on a major political issue. Thus the Comintern supported Trotsky on principles but proceeded to act organizationally against his supporters in America. Foster also got a spanking from the Comintern because he had entered into an alliance with the Lore group in order to capture a majority of the National Convention of the Communist party in December, 1923. Since the internal interests of the Russian Communist party were served by these unprincipled moves it did not matter that the American Communist party, forced to break solemn promises, was placed in an indefensible position.

Heaven and hell were turned over to get delegates to the St. Paul Convention. The expense involved did not matter. Moscow gold paid for everything: the railroad expenses, the hotel expenses, the per diem for delegates, the convention expenses, the clerical expenses. Over 600 delegates were present representing all parts of the country. A technical force of over 100 attended to the convention's needs. In addition the Communist party had arranged to hold a Party caucus in St. Paul to take up the latest decisions of the Communist International on American party questions. Every Communist delegate was under orders to attend the caucus. In addition every important Party member and functionary not a delegate had received instructions to proceed to St. Paul in order to be present at the caucus. Fully a thousand Communist party members congregated at St. Paul. Most of them stopped over at the Ryan Hotel, the convention's headquarters. The hotel also housed the secret headquarters of the Communist party from which the convention was manipulated.

Dumping the Farmer-Labor Party Into the Ash Can

At the St. Paul Convention Americans got a lesson in how the long arm of Moscow manipulates its communist puppets in the United States. Those entrusted with the affairs of the United States government failed to appreciate the events, to evaluate their significance. They failed to connect what happened in St. Paul with the methods of Bolshevik politics, which are so carefully labeled the politics of realism. Moscow demonstrated at St. Paul that the Russian communists in all their actions are concerned not with the interests of the working class, or of the Communist party of a particular country, but with Russian national interests, and above all the interests of the Russian Communist party. The world will, through bitter experience, discover that the same considerations will determine Russian communist action in all their spheres of influence whether it be a communist party or a Russian satellite state. The events at the St. Paul Convention made that clear.

When the convention opened, the legitimate farmer-laborites and trade unionists and smattering of liberals present did not know that the communist leaders carried in their pockets orders from Moscow to ditch old man LaFollette. Hathaway, who under false pretenses acted as the leader of the Minnesota Farmer-Labor party forces, and acted as their main negotiator with the communists, was put in a difficult position, for this communist plant had to act as if he was serving the interests of the non-communists at the time that he was using fraudulent and underhanded methods to put the communist proposals across. During a critical stage of the convention the orders of the communist steering committee were so brazen that even the crooked Hathaway was afraid to carry them out. Though in charge of all convention arrangements he disappeared from the convention. When he was finally located, it was in a speakeasy where he had drowned his troubles and eased his conscience with bootleg liquor.

The Communist party packed the convention with hundreds of delegates who represented no one but themselves. They carried with them credentials from a multiplicity of communist organizations which did not elect them, and many of which existed on paper only. The communist steam roller planted its stooges in every nook and corner of the convention hall. These were kept informed on what to do by a host of messengers and secret code messages executed by the waving of the hands. The LaFollette supporters wanted the LaFollette issue settled first. The communists hedged by insisting upon the adoption of program first. The communists had their way. They followed up this advantage by cleverly forcing through the adoption of an extreme radical program which the communists knew beforehand LaFollette could under no circumstances accept, thus making it doubly sure that LaFollette would not accept the endorsement of the St. Paul convention should the convention get out of hand and nominate him.

The program adopted, the communist steam roller proceeded to the nomination of candidate for president in opposition to the wishes of the genuine farmer-laborites. The honors went to Duncan Mc-Donald, a trade unionist of Illinois who cooperated with the communists and accepted their orders. The communists kept the farmer-laborites in line by a clever ruse, giving them the impression that the door was left open to support LaFollette should he accept the new party's program.

But just as McDonald started his campaign as the candidate of the newly launched National Farmer-Labor party, all the expenses of which were being paid out of the treasury of the Communist party, orders came from Moscow directing the Communist party to dump the National Farmer-Labor party overboard by nominating its own candidates—Foster for president and myself for vice president. With the new orders came $50,000 from Moscow, the first installment of a subsidy voted for meeting the expenses of the campaign.

No other political party could engage in such chicanery and double dealing. No American political party could perpetrate such a fraud on the American public and get away with it. But a Communist party that claims it is motivated by the highest ideals did just that and got away with it. What the Communist party did with the Farmer-Labor party movement, in itself an important episode in the history of communist-sponsored United Fronts, is part of a policy based on fraudulent methods and deceptions which is employed over and over again in United Fronts. It is politely called by some "the ever-changing vicissitudes of the Party line."

The Comintern kept Pepper in Moscow for four years. The Comintern returned him to the United States with instructions to unite the Foster group with the majority group in the American party. In 1928 he returned to Moscow to attend the World Congress of the

Comintern as a delegate of the American party. But Pepper, the father of the Labor party policy, did not keep abreast of the internal developments in the Russian Communist party. Stalin had decided to remove Bukharin from the presidency of the Comintern. Pepper worked too closely with Bukharin during the Congress. That was enough to condemn him in Stalin's eyes. A joke made the rounds in Comintern circles in 1929 which described Pepper running about the streets of Moscow with the palm of his hand over his mouth. "What is the trouble, Comrade Pepper? Why do you hold your hand over your mouth?" "Oh!" replied Pepper, "I have made a terrible mistake. Woe is me. I just kissed the ass of Bukharin. I found out too late that I should not have done it." Communists leaders in the United States and in other countries made the same mistake Pepper did—they failed to jump to Stalin's side when Stalin cracked the whip, and like Pepper they all paid dearly for not doing so.

The American Communist party Pepper left behind in 1928 was different from the Party he had come to in 1922. A streamlined Party, ruled by an astute political leadership, directed the communist movement. The rank-and-file members had been transformed from sectarian idealists into soldiers of a disciplined revolutionary party. They had been imbued by Minor with a new morality, that the end justifies the means, and that the Communist party can do no wrong. Inner party politics and factionalism made them realize that the attainment of power within the Party organization is the prerequisite of every good communist. Due to this conception the Party became the arena in which communists fought for place and power in the Party. In the inner Party struggle for power Bolshevik ethics of dog-eat-dog ruled supreme. The Communist party had expanded in all directions, due largely to the hundreds of thousands of dollars in subsidies which Moscow generously provided. The *Daily Worker* was started with Moscow gold, the initial installment being $35,000. The Party had daily newspapers, in Jewish, Russian, Lithuanian, Ukrainian, Finnish, Polish and German, besides numerous weeklies and monthlies in English and other languages. The Communist party's propaganda set-up spent several million dollars a year. In addition the Communist party controlled and dominated numerous unions, organizations, societies and clubs. They poured money into the Party treasury and provided jobs for Communist party members so that they could devote their full time to Party work. The Communist party now rested on a firm economic foundation. Thousands of communists depended for their livelihood, not on the capitalist exploiter, but on the Communist party organization.

The Communists and the Unions

From 1921 to 1928 the money earmarked by Moscow for the fight in the unions went directly to Foster. He was responsible to no one for the spending of hundreds of thousands of dollars. The war which Foster directed in the trade unions had two main objectives, as has already been shown: one, to discredit and drive the leaders out of the unions who refused to support the communist position, and two, to put the communists in control of the unions.

In communist trade union tactics and policies is found the key to their revolutionary strategy. The communists are the most active trade unionists and the busiest trade union organizers because the Communist party recognizes that the unions, with their millions of organized workers, are reservoirs of tremendous potential and dynamic power once the communists can use the unions for their own purposes. The Communist party organization is built on two basic principles laid down by Lenin. Though they seem diametrically opposed to each other, Lenin's organizational principles form the synthesis for the organization of the Party and the conduct of its activities. Lenin held that the Communist party must consist of a militant and trained minority highly centralized and disciplined. He called this minority the vanguard of the proletariat. At the same time he insisted that the Communist party, the Party of the organized, disciplined, militant minority, must be a mass Party, a Party that appeals to millions of people and that can mobilize them for action behind the issues sponsored by the militant minority.

In demanding that the Communist parties of the West be mass parties, Lenin, the revolutionary strategist, knew exactly what he was doing. How could he insist that the communists in the other countries do what Lenin himself did not do? For Lenin's Bolshevik party when he captured power was not a mass party. Lenin made a surprise coup in Petrograd. The bewildered Russians did not understand what it was all about. Before they had time to realize what had happened he used his power at Russia's political center to strangle all opposition and to extend his communist regime over the entire land. Lenin know what worked in Russia would not necessarily work in the capitalist countries of Western Europe and America. He had been an exile in Europe for too many years not to recognize that conditions in the capitalist countries were altogether different. The governments were more stable and better organized. The masses of the people were more educated and were more politically alert because of the democratic privileges they enjoyed. Finally Lenin considered of utmost importance the fact that the workers were politically organized into large Socialist parties and Labor parties and economically into powerful trade unions. He had tried a frontal attack upon the powerful socialist and trade union concentrations of the West and was obliged to admit that the communists had failed to make a dent in them. He knew that the world was on guard against communism. He therefore hammered home into the brains of the communists of other countries that it would be foolish for them in their countries to follow the Russian Bolshevik pattern of 1917. To build mass Communist parties the communists must concentrate on the unions, Lenin declared in 1921. There the communists can not only gain control of industrial organizations which have the power to cripple capitalism but also leadership over millions of workers. Therefore communists everywhere recognize that if a Communist party is to succeed, the question of who does or does not control the unions is not an academic question but a question of the life and future of communism.

Among communist leaders, control of the trade unions encompasses a realization that union control in the hands of the communists enables them to keep a loaded shotgun at the head of the government by using the economic and political power of the organized workers. Once the communists gain decisive control of the country's trade union movement, the communists have virtually established a defacto government of their own. A push of a button on the ninth floor of Communist party headquarters on 13th Street could then silence the wheels of industry and halt transportation on land, over the sea and in the air. The wide network of communications, radio, telephone, telegraph, the press and the postal services, the nerves without which modern industrial life is impossible, would come to rest like dead leaves on a cold, calm autumn day. That is what the communists are after in their fight to become the masters of the trade unions. The moment the American Communist party captures control of the unions in the vital industries of the country, atom bomb or no atom bomb, the stage is set for the overthrow of the American government and world revolution.

Though the American communists have not yet secured the kind of control over the American unions that they are after, the sinister communist government within a government is in operation and has been in operation for over a decade. If the American people were given an opportunity to sit in on meetings of the Political Committee of the Communist party they would enjoy a ring-side seat at the sessions of the Supreme Council of the Soviet United States. They would be amazed at the matters coming up for consideration. The Political Committee sits like a cabinet. It passes judgment and makes decisions on matters affecting the lives of Americans. Not only political matters are considered but other matters also, such as wages, working hours, the speed-up and slow-down of production, new methods of production and industrial secrets and the affairs of management you would expect the Board of Directors of General Motors to handle, with this difference: that the political committee sits as the board of directors not of one industrial corporation but of all of them put together. You would wonder how details which belong in the province of the trade unions find their way into the Political Committee. Your surprise would be followed by astonishment when the Political Committee makes decisions for unions and union officials to carry out. And if you were lucky you would begin to understand how the members of the Political Committee are able to act as they do and why. For you would discover that many trade union officials and members come to the meetings of the Political Committee to place the problems of their unions in the laps of the gods of the Polcom. By listening carefully you would understand that the Communist party has built up an intricate secret organization in all unions, whether the communists control the unions or not, consisting of Communist party members and sympathizers, and that between these secret communist formations in the unions and the Party the closest ties are maintained. Channels of information are established through which a steady stream of information concerning the union and the industry in which it operates flows into the industrial department of the Party. The industrial department sifts the information it gathers and transmits what it considers important or requiring a decision to the Political Committee. Not even the Executive Council of the American Federation of Labor gathers such a voluminous amount of information concerning the unions and their subdivisions as does the Polcom of the Communist party.

The Polcom also formulates the popular issues by which to agitate and arouse the trade union masses. Many of the issues raised by the communists are good issues, progressive issues, but that is not the reason why they are raised. They are raised for the same reasons that a fisherman sows bait—to attract the fish so he can more easily catch them. The communists seek to bait the workers in order to capture their unions and thereby put both the unions and the workers under their influence and domination. The readiness with which the union workers and many trade union officials accept communist trade union issues on their face value accounts for much of the internecine strife and chaos which prevails in many unions.

The communists took their work in the unions seriously. Three years after the communists opened a broadside against Gompers they were already important factors in the United Brotherhood of Carpenters and Joiners of America, the International Association of Machinists, the International Jewelry Workers Union, the United Textile Workers of America, the Amalgamated Clothing Workers, Journeymen's Tailors Union of North America, International Fur Workers Union, Boot and Shoe Workers Union, A F of L, Shoe Workers Protective Union, International Pocket Book Workers Union, International Typographical Union, the Railroad Brotherhoods, the International Ladies Garment Workers Union, the Journeymen Barbers International Union, International Union of Bakery and Confectionery Workers, the Brotherhood of Painters, Decorators and Paperhangers. In addition, the communists had built up opposition movements in the unions of the Building Trades Department of the A F of L and in the unions of its Metal Department. Opposition movements too had been started in the International Longshoremen's Union and in the International Seafarers Union. In many parts of the country communists were a force in A F of L local unions of bookkeepers and stenographers. Most of the smaller independent unions were communist controlled and a communist opposition movement was maintained in the I.W.W. These inroads in the American unions were accomplished, over a period of three years, by a Communist party with a paid-up membership of approximately 20,000. A disciplined communist army can move mountains.

The most notable and dramatic communist war waged in the unions was fought in the United Mine Workers of America where the communists sought to take away from the miners' chief, John L. Lewis, his mastery of the 400,000 soft and hard coal diggers. Moscow insisted that the miners, upon whose work the industrial life of the United States depended, should become the central point of the

Communist party's trade union activity. Moscow backed up its decision on the miners' campaign with an initial contribution of $100,000.

The communists opened the campaign against Lewis by calling him a gangster, an agent of the bosses, a miners' tsar, a thug and a murderer. Every conceivable epithet was hurled against him. The minefields were flooded with millions of bombastic leaflets which in foul, derogatory language blasted away at Lewis's reputation.

In the beginning of 1924 the communists almost captured the United Mine Workers Union. Lewis, in desperation, had to use extraordinary means to prevent the communists' putsch from ousting him from his union. The opposition caucus organized at that convention by the Communist party was attended by almost 1100 bona fide delegates. In the same year the communist candidate for president of the Miners Union, Voyzey, polled 66,000 votes against 166,000 for John L. Lewis. The communists claimed that their vote was considerably higher and charged that John L. Lewis had disenfranchised thousands of union miners and had stolen the election by fraudulently counting the ballots.

When the $100,000 was spent Moscow sent more money—subsidies to continue the fight—subsidies for special miners' papers—subsidies to hold national conventions of progressive miners, to bribe miners' officials and to pay for an army of communist organizers in the mining fields. Before the fight was over, in the year 1928, when the communists organized their own miners' union—the National Miners Union—Moscow had spent over a half million dollars to smash Lewis, and the Communist party increased that sum by an additional $200,000 through special fund-raising campaigns and robbing the treasury of a communist miners' relief organization. But the stocky Lewis with the booming voice and the bushy eyebrows held on to his union. Moscow remembered that when, in later years, it came to terms with Lewis and supported him for the presidency of the newly formed C.I.O.

The Three-Flank Attack

The Communist party employs a three-flank attack upon the trade unions requiring skilled generalship in its execution, based not on the ability of one man, but on the collective intelligence of a staff which includes the best brains of Russia as well as members of the Central Executive Committee of the Communist party and its Polcom. Often

Moscow sent to the United States, besides its own people, skilled trade union experts from Germany, England and France to advise and assist the American communists. The communist general staff is fully aware of the logistics of its war in the trade unions and is amply supplied with funds to take care of its end of the conflict. The attacks on the three flanks of the trade unions are carried on simultaneously, for each one is of importance and serves a specific purpose.

The first one is directed at the rank-and-file members of the unions. Its strategy involves the employment of issues which appear desirable and attractive to the workers, issues that do not sound fantastic and beyond the realm of realization, such as higher wages, shorter hours, unemployment benefits and political demands upon the government. There are times when the communist demands are legitimate. Usually the demands are made sufficiently exorbitant to arouse the opposition of the trade union officials who know that the demands cannot be realized without a prolonged, bitter struggle that would wreck the unions. The mass of the workers, agitated by the communist demands for increased earnings and better conditions, resent the opposition on the part of their officials to the demands.

This agitation around economic and political issues is coupled with a direct appeal to the unemployed workers who, because of their desperate condition, most easily succumb to communist propaganda, particularly that section of the unemployed who are permanently unemployed because of the lack of skill and shiftlessness. The slum elements of the unions become the communists most excellent material for they have lots of time to spare for communist activity. The communists can use them when the other workers are employed. The unionists who work have something to lose; the slum elements have nothing to lose and much to gain. The Communist party can easily satisfy the slum elements by throwing them a few pennies for food. Those among them with ability are recruited into the Party organization and become leaders of the left wing opposition in their unions. Thus is the strategy of the mass approach to the unions worked out in order to win the popular support of the union members for the issues raised by the communists.

The second-flank attack is directed against the union leaders who oppose the communists. In this attack no quarter is given. The trade union official must submit to the demands of the communists or face character assassination and extermination. The most ridiculous charges are made against them, which seldom are warranted. The purpose behind this attack is so to blacken the trade union officials that the trade unionists will loathe and despise them. A persistent hate campaign is carried on at union meetings, at union headquarters, through special mass meetings in the communist and left wing press, by grapevine rumors and by tons of printed and mimeographed material, for the purpose of undermining the workers' trust in their leaders and thus paving the way for a new, a communist leadership.

By this tactic the union officials are forced to take measures against the communists, which the communists use to inflame the workers against their officials by charging the officials with Red baiting and with barring from the unions honest trade unionists and militants who have the courage to fight for the workers' interests. Thus the internal war in the unions which the communists do not control begins as an interminable wrangle and develops into a bloody conflict in which fists, blackjacks, knives and automatics are used.

In the execution of the third-flank attack the communists are masters. This phase may be termed the behind-the-scenes diplomatic war. Here no frontal attacks are made. The attack is carried on in the dark without the knowledge or consent of the trade union membership. The communist rank-and-file is informed and taken into confidence only when it becomes necessary to put them wise as to what is going on so that they can give the non-communist workers a satisfactory explanation of what has happened.

The diplomatic war is conducted by the communist officials with the trade union officials for the purpose of gaining an objective by making deals beneficial to both. In every trade union campaign of significance the communists are busy manipulating behind closed doors. Trade union officials are bought off, sometimes outright with money, more often by supporting them for well-paying posts in the unions. It was done among the miners with a host of miners' officials. Many of these officials hold down important posts today in the C.I.O. as organizers and special representatives. The communists took over the Furriers Union by making deals with officials, with cliques of gangsters, with racketeers and underworld elements. In the International Ladies Garment Workers Union the same tactics were employed.

In carrying out this tactic the communists are not bothered with scruples. They forget one day what they called certain trade union officials the day before. They unite with the worst gangster and racketeer elements even though they have made it a point in their trade union campaign to call for their eradication from the unions. They have made deals on occasions with Lepke, with Benny the Dope, with Al Capone, with Dutch Schultz and other underworld figures of that type to serve their ambitions in the unions. In deals to obtain union advantages for the Communist party, the communists have abandoned principles to secure paid trade union posts for communists. By their actions in the third-flank attack the communists prove that their course in the unions is not guided by principles or by an urge to serve the interests of the workers, but by a lust for power.

But one should not for that reason conclude that once the communists gain control of the unions they will conduct themselves in a manner that will prove detrimental to the workers. The communists are guided by a long-range policy in the unions. They will carry out measures which they formerly attacked as conservative and reactionary in order to hold on to their positions in the unions. They want to hold on to the industrial power which control of the unions give them, the power to cripple American industry whenever that should become necessary.

Strikes—Communist Techniques in the Art of Class Warfare

The Communist party, a party of class warfare, specializes in strikes. The Party foments strikes and injects itself, if possible, into every strike situation, as soon as a strike breaks out. A Party leader, district or local Party official who is lax in going into a strike situation is sharply criticized and often removed from his post. It is the duty of Party officials and organizers in the districts to report on industrial conditions in their territories which are ripe for strike action.

If the employers think that industrial peace depends only upon maintaining satisfactory relations with the unions they are badly mistaken. That situation no longer prevails, for a new factor has entered the industrial field: the Communist party, which has demonstrated repeatedly that it must be accounted for in strike situations. The Communist party employs strike techniques which for dramatic staging and militancy are unequalled. In addition the Communist party has developed its own methods for raising strike-relief funds, for mobilizing public support of strikes, for staging publicity stunts in order to get nation-wide publicity, and for diverting strikes into political channels. The form which mass picketing has taken, its development and spread in labor disputes, is due to the initiative and generalship of communists in picket demonstrations.

The communists are not primarily concerned with the fate of the workers out on strike. It has been drilled into their heads by Lenin and by theses and instructions from Moscow that strikes are never definitely lost and that defeat can be turned into a victory for the Communist party if the Party exploits the strike situation properly. This communist attitude on strikes is part of the wider theory that, under certain conditions, the more violent a worker's demonstration becomes, the more brutally the demonstration is crushed by clubbing and bloodshed, the better for the Party. It has been pointed out to the Communist party repeatedly by the experienced strategists of revolution, that situations in which workers are killed can become great assets for the Party. Should the labor situation become acute, and a state of political instability set in, the Communist party will most surely instigate bloody riots in which innocent people will be killed.

The Communist party does not leave strike situations to chance. An old Bolshevik expression, *Kvostism,* is used in the Party to impress communists with the evils of unplanned, indeliberate action. Translated freely it means that the tail should never be allowed to wag the dog.

Attendance at a meeting of the Political Committee will illuminate the contention that the communists leave nothing to chance. Sitting in the smoked-filled room are the members of the Committee. A girl records the minutes of what transpires. A stenographer takes down verbatim what is said. Copies of the minutes and stenographic transcripts are later dispatched to Moscow. The agenda prepared for the Political Committee meeting by the Secretariat is read. Committee members add additional points to the agenda. When the business of strikes is reached a report is either presented by the head of the Industrial Department or by a Polcom member or by a communist strike leader who is called into the meeting to give a report on his strike.

At the disposal of the members of the Polcom are mimeographed copies of reports by the Industrial Department and the Research Department on the Strike. These are voluminous reports providing the committee members with minute details on all phases of the strike. The Polcom now sits in judgment over the strike like a super industrial cabinet. It has at its disposal information on the nature of the industry involved, the owners and other capitalist interests concerned with its operation. An economic report deals with capital investments, profits, the nature of its products and how they are distributed. A personal history of the chief figures on the side of management is presented and each individual's weak and strong points stressed. The number of workers employed, their racial, religious and national divisions, the wages they receive, the conditions under which they work, their political and other affiliations, their leaders in the unions and in the communal groups to which they belong—all this is covered. The political, social and religious set-ups in the communities involved in the strike are also given. As complete a picture of the strike situation as it is possible to obtain is at the disposal of the Polcom to help it in making decisions.

Besides the written and mimeographed reports the Polcom receives oral reports from Party organizers and representatives assigned to the strike area and from trade union officials and strike leaders. The communists believe that to be thoroughly informed is to be prepared, and the side that is better informed has an advantage over its adversary. The Polcom, the departments and all other committees of the Communist party work on that theory. Fully fortified with information, the Polcom makes decisions which put the Communist party in the middle of the strike situation.

Wherever possible in a strike of major importance which the communists do not lead, they try to get a foothold in the strike by bringing in their strike-relief machinery. By bringing relief to the strikers in the form of food, clothing and shelter the communists win the sympathy of the strikers. The Communists set up relief headquarters in the strike zone, establish food kitchens, bring in speakers and organizers in the name of the relief organization in order to build up the morale of the strikers and get the communist message across. Behind the innocent façade of relief the Communist party sends in an army of communist agents, propagandists and organizers to build up communist influence, and a communist nucleus in the strike. Communist leaders insist that the comrades utilize every strike situation to build up the Communist party organization by recruiting strikers into the Party.

Communist strike-relief work is carried on along United Front lines in order to draw into the orbit of communist influence as many non-communists as possible and thus strengthen the communist base in the strike.

The campaign for the collection of monies for strike relief opens the doors of trade unions and other non-communist organizations to communist speakers and organizers who tour the country in the name of and at the expense of the strike-relief organization. The Party has, in addition, used every major one of its strike-relief campaigns to siphon off hundreds of thousands of dollars collected for strike relief into the treasury of the Party.

The strike-relief strategy was originally worked out by the Communist International which set up an International relief organization, with headquarters in Moscow, known as the International Workers Aid. The responsibility of conducting fund-raising campaigns was turned over to the national branches which the communists organized in their respective countries. The American Communists through the International Workers Aid collected money for the starving workers of Germany, for the Chinese strikers of Shanghai, for the famine strike of Ireland and for a host of international causes. Invariably, with rare exceptions, the monies which the American communists raised for these purposes found its way into the coffers of the Party treasury. The International Workers Aid at Moscow served as a controlling, directing and propaganda organization of communist relief activities all over the world. The first branch of the International Workers Aid in the United States was set up in 1924. All existing communist relief activities and organizations in the United States were put under the supervision of this branch.

The Political Committee exercised jurisdiction over the American Branch of the International Workers Aid and all communist relief activities. During the Passaic Textile strike when hundreds of thousands of dollars rolled into offices of the Passaic Textile Workers Strike-Relief Committee, it was not unusual for the Polcom to make decisions ordering the relief committee to turn over large amounts of the relief money to the Party. The crime of diverting funds raised for the relief of starving strikers was overshadowed by the deception practiced on the workers of holding out a helping hand with bread as bait to ensnare the workers so that they could take over their organizations and control their destinies.

The communists outdid themselves in the strikes which they initiated and led. The outstanding strikes falling into this category, prior to the organization of the C.I.O., were the Passaic Textile Workers strike in 1925-26, the New York Furriers strike of 1926, the Cloakmakers strike in 1926, the Dressmakers strike in 1926, the New Bedford Textile strike, and the Gastonia, North Carolina, Textile strike in

1929. These communist-inspired strikes and many more of them were the forerunners of what followed in the sitdown-strikes in Detroit, in the violence of the fight to unionize Henry Ford's plants, in the bloody war to organize Girdler's steel workers, and in the wave of C.I.O. strikes which plagued the country. At the outbreak of war in Europe in 1939 a wave of communist strikes was started, this time to cripple defense production.

Communist strikes came as a result of prodding by the Comintern. The Comintern insisted that the working class base of the Communist party must be radically changed from a preponderance of Jewish needle-trade workers to non-Jewish workers employed in the basic and mass production industries. Besides concentrating in the unions which operated in these industries the Communist party was directed to initiate a campaign for the organization of the unorganized workers into unions, since the bulk of the workers in these industries were unorganized.

During the meetings of the Polcom at which this matter was discussed questions were raised concerning the methods to be employed in organizing the unorganized. The conclusions reached by the committee laid down the theory that educational campaigns on the necessity of trade union organization, while necessary, are not sufficient; getting organizers into the unorganized fields was considered at best a slow and expensive proposition, and the committee finally concluded the most effective method to be used involved the precipitation of strikes in the unorganized industries. The Communist party worked out a detailed program for the organization of the unorganized which concentrated its efforts among the unorganized metal and coal miners, the workers in the automobile industry with the Ford plants as the main target, and in the marine transport and textile industries.

The Passaic Textile Workers strike was the first communist strike of major importance. It resulted from the fact that the author, then head of the Industrial Department of New York, a member of the National Industrial Department and of the Polcom, had his attention called to a small, one-inch item in the New York newspapers that wage cuts were contemplated in the woolen mills of Passaic. Leaflets were immediately printed attacking the mills for cutting wages, a program of action against the wage cuts drafted, offices opened in Passaic, organizers sent into the territory and a mass meeting called.

The workers who jammed the large hall at the first meeting were immediately called upon, after listening to fiery agitational speeches, to join the union by paying a dollar for the privilege. Communist stooges, planted in all parts of the hall waving one dollar bills, started a stampede toward the platform and the workers were signed up.

The strike was called when the Communist party decided it had enrolled in the rump union a sufficient number of workers in the mills, at the time not more than 10 percent. A committee made up of Communist party members, not one of whom was a textile worker, sat up night and day plotting the strike. The union just carried out the orders which the Party committee gave it. The Party committee, on the eve of the calling of the strike, had before it floor plans of the large textile mills to be struck, plans which indicated where the switches were located which controlled the power, and all other vital information. Like commando officers directing a raid, the Party planned each step, designating who was to shut off the power, how the riotous marches through the mills were to be conducted, who was to lead them, how the timid, hesitant workers were to be bulldozed into going out on strike, and finally, the hour, minute and second when the action should start. The perfect timing worked as if set off by a precision time switch. A tremendous roar resounded through the floors and halls of the mills, "Strike! Strike! Strike!" Workers who knew their cue grabbed poles and clubs, unfurled banners and marched in an ever swelling procession through the huge mill floors, the noise rising in an ever-increasing crescendo, and the great strike which startled the nation and reached the White House and the Halls of Congress was on.

In the Passaic strike the communists showed the country what an all-out total strike was like. They staged militant and picturesque picket demonstrations. Helmets, overseas hats and uniforms of World War I were bought up in large quantities. The strikers and the captains of the picket line who were communists were dressed up in these. They staged huge picket demonstrations behind large American flags led by men who masqueraded as veterans. At night when the strike activities were over for the day the Communist party committee running the strike closeted itself with Weisbord, the young Harvard law student it had brought into the strike situation from Boston. The Party committee demanded that he produce action to dramatize the strike. The Party leaders wanted the kind of action that would make the Passaic strike a national political issue. They wanted news of what was happening in Passaic to reach Moscow in order to enhance the prestige of the American communist leadership.

Weisbord, a vain, egotistical, communist zealot, carried out Party orders. Disorder, on order, broke out. The picture tabloids and other newspapers were duly informed in advance to be on hand to witness the fun. The Communist party strong-arm squad from New York took its place on the picket line. They provoked a fight with the police. Fists and clubs flew. Cameras clicked. Reporters took notes and interviewed Weisbord. That was publicity, national publicity.

The Communist party wanted a favorable press on the strike. Its own publicity people were not getting the proper results. A conference took place at Communist party headquarters in New York at which the advice of an experienced journalist was accepted. An attractive girl reporter, who obliged the male reporters in more ways than one, took over strike publicity. The Party learned and never forgot how glamour and sex can pay off in good publicity.

The communists set up a strikers' relief committee at once. The relief committee did an excellent job of organizing kitchens and feeding the strikers. From the funds collected, enough money remained to colonize Passaic with scores of paid communist organizers and to route others throughout the country, to siphon off thousands of dollars into the Party treasury and to pay for the financing of the Party's factional strifes. One of the directors of the relief organization was under investigation for the theft of a thousand dollars. The Party leaders squelched the matter because they were of the opinion the publicity on the theft might boomerang against the Party.

A Communist party organization sprang up in Passaic where one did not exist before. Every branch of the communist organization, from the Women's Department to the youth section, sent organizers into Passaic to exploit the situation. Even the tiny tots were organized in the Junior Young Communist League and taken out on a school strike.

Other forms of violence backed up the violence on the picket lines. Bombs were exploded at the homes of workers who refused to join the strike. The local Communist party committee at Passaic approved the action but the Central Executive Committee's Textile committee called a halt to the practice, not because it opposed the use of bombs but because traditions in the United States made the use of bombs a dangerous practice politically. The Communist party, however, did approve the explosion of poisonous gas bombs in the

Botany Mills to force out the scabs who were housed there. The Party secured a specialist for the job, a Russian communist from Pittsburg who got a job as a scab in the mill. The explosion of the gas bombs proved very effective, for the scabs came rushing out of the mills coughing violently, holding handkerchiefs to their mouths, and were so terrorized that few returned to their jobs. The proposal to destroy the main valve which supplied water to the Botany Mills was abandoned because the Party learned that the damage would be so great as to cripple the mill permanently. The Party leaders concluded that by such a sabotage job the union closed the doors to an agreement with the mill owners.

Though the Passaic strike was lost it proved that the communists knew how to initiate and lead strikes. The communist strikes that were to follow would throw additional light on communist union activity and strike action.

The communists scored their first successes in the unions in the needletrade unions of New York. These unions with their social democratic traditions and large percentage of radical Jewish workers were order-made for communist penetration. With the exception of the International Fur Workers Union the communists never succeeded in capturing the national organizations of the needle trades even though they dominated the New York unions, the largest in membership and the deciding factors in the industry.

The communists fought bitterly for these unions. The fight for control of the needletrade unions was, in fact, the bloodiest and costliest internal war in labor history. All the weapons in the communist arsenal were used; attack, retreat, counter-attack; stilettos, blackjacks, guns, burning acids, sabotage, assault, murder, demonstrations, mob violence, the breaking up of union meetings, and the raiding of union offices. This was accompanied by the expenditure of fabulous sums of money, the dissipation of millions of dollars of union funds, the employment of lawyers with political connections by the payment of exorbitant fees, the buying up of gangsters and racketeers and their inclusion in the communist front, the bribery of the police and the corruption of the courts.

In the Furriers strike of 1926 the communists showed what they could do when in complete control of an old and experienced union. All the strike leaders with a few exceptions were communists. The public accepted Ben Gold and his union staff as the strike leaders. They were so officially and in name only. The leaders of the Communist party who knew next to nothing about the industry were actually the leaders of the strike. Not a single move was taken without them. What they decided became the policy and law of the strike.

The communist leaders skillfully exploited the factors involved to win the strike and outmaneuver the opponents in the unions opposed to the communists, among whom were the President of the International Fur Workers Union and President William Green of the American Federation of Labor. In order to outmaneuver Green the Communist party raised the issue of the 40-hour week, conducted a national campaign for its adoption by all the unions of the country and forced Green to champion the issue. Through the strike the workers won substantial gains. The settlement was greeted by unprecedented demonstrations of enthusiasm. Communist stock in the trade unions rose appreciably. The communists capitalized on the fact that the communist-led Furriers strike took place at the conclusion of a period of trade union recession, a period in which the unions had lost considerable ground. The Furriers strike broke the passive spell. With the eyes of the trade union movement focused upon them the communists demonstrated that they could militantly and successfully back up their demands for higher wages, shorter hours, improved conditions and better union control of the industry.

The Furriers strike made American labor history in many ways. Ben Gold, the communist furrier, led the strike. This intrepid young man during World War I refused to register for the draft and fled to Mexico to avoid conscription into the armed forces.

The Communist party, before the strike, put one of its members, a clerk without any experience, into the union to assist Gold. After the strike, Gold, suffering from a swelled head, showed signs of independence. The Party showed Gold who was boss by raising the clerk, Irving Potash, to a position of power and authority in the union over Gold, though Gold outwardly continued to hold on to the union's leading position.

Over three million dollars were spent in the Furriers strike, of which only $600,000 went to strikers on relief. The balance went to bribe the police, to pay lawyers handsome fees with which to fix the courts in which strike violence cases came up, to provide for the upkeep of gangsters and special picket squads, for automobiles used by gangsters and sabotage squads, for the upkeep of halls and other expenses. A part of the money was also siphoned off into the Communist party treasury.

The Communist party utilized the Furriers strike to perfect a terrorist organization trained in the art of violence and sabotage. They developed into the shock troops of the Communist party who could be shifted from city to city, from strike to strike, and into situations where the Party needed trained men and women expert in the use of knives, revolvers, blackjacks and poison gas bombs; saboteurs who knew how to ruin merchandise, wreck plants and destroy property. The Furriers strike served to drive home to the Party members the fact that violence held a foremost place in the movement. The long, sharp knife with the pointed blade that snapped out of its handle at the press of a button became a coveted prize of Party members. At headquarters they took them out and displayed them with pride. The strong-arm men who gloated about their bloody exploits were the popular heroes of the red Amazons and were held in high esteem by both rank-and-filers and leaders.

The communists gained control of the Furriers Union by making an alliance with a group of racketeers and gangsters who operated under the name of the Furriers' Civic Club. This group terrorized the union and the industry, exacted tribute from the bosses and depleted the union's treasury for its own gratification. Once the communists had the gunmen and racketeers of the Civic Club on their side, gaining control of the union followed easily, for to oppose the communists meant having one's head batted in or one's throat cut from ear to ear.

The members of the Civic Club who wanted to go along with the communists were recruited into the communist strong-arm squad. The communist gang, however, was not confined to furriers. Communist party members who fitted into such an outfit were conscripted. Its members included communists who came from all parts of the country and from many unions. Included too were all nationalities of the Party. The mainstay of the army of violence and sabotage consisted of a band of intrepid Greeks, members of the Greek section of the Party, fanatical communists who considered what they were doing the highest form of communist activity. And Gold, at heart one of them, assumed the leadership of the gang.

In their lack of feeling and cold cruelty the female members of the gang outdid the men. The sadistic Amazons took special delight in attacking females marked for treatment. They fell upon the victim, kicked, pummeled and scratched her face, dug their nails deep into her womb, ripping and tearing out the hair, and mutilated and lacerated her breasts. When able they ripped off the clothes and left the victim, after her frightful cries had died down, unconscious in a dirty alley or in the gutter. The Communist party gloated over these exploits and looked upon them as the natural consequences of the class war.

At a banquet given in their honor at the end of the strike the Party leaders honored the members of the gang in speeches, praising their work and pointing out the significance of keeping them together as a special organization of the Party. They were hailed as the heroes of the class war and the revolution to come, the shock troops of communism.

The cloakmakers strike, a strike which dragged on for twenty-four weeks, proved that the communists put Communist party interests and orders from Moscow above the welfare of the unions and the interests of the workers. On the eve of the strike involving over 40,000 workers, the author informed the Polcom of the Communist party that the situation was not good for a strike. The Communist party members who were the officials of the New York Joint Board under whose auspices the strike had to be conducted were of the same opinion. Publicly and officially every communist with responsibility in the calling of the strike kept his mouth shut with the exception of Foster, who denounced the communist leaders of the cloakmakers as cowards who were afraid to conduct a militant strike. The other Party leaders listened to Foster rant because cables had been received from Moscow instructing the American communists to foment strikes and give them militant leadership.

Governor Alfred E. Smith appointed a commission to confer with the manufacturers and the union to bring about a settlement of the issues before the strike was called. The Governor's commission secured from the manufacturers terms upon which a satisfactory contract with the union could be signed. The communist officials of the unions, under orders from the Party to call out a strike, rejected the Governor's proposals and the strike was on.

As a result of the strike $3,500,000 of the unions funds were squandered uselessly, the union was thrown into bankruptcy and the workers suffered defeat. Forty thousand American workers were the dupes of communist politics because Moscow willed it.

CHAPTER FOUR

THE COMMUNIST
MERRY-GO-ROUND

ACTIVE fermentation characterizes life in the Communist party. Communists live in an exciting, colorful, exasperating, diversified and desperately intense world. They are caught in the meshing gears of the huge communist machine which dominates the seconds, minutes, hours and days of their existence. On the day they join the Communist party they become voluntary prisoners of a whirling social vortex which separates them from normal relations with the rest of humanity. For a communist, life in the Communist party is complete. The Party not only provides the communist with entertainment but also with health protection, insurance and burial, in the event of death. Painful moments are plenty but never dull ones. The tempo of living is fast and furious. The average Communist party member, always on the go, has no time to hesitate, to think. Only the leaders have the right, within the limitations set by Moscow, to enjoy that luxury. The common herd must absorb the ideas handed down to them like a sponge sucks up water. They whirl around on the communist merry-go-round too blind to see and too ignorant to know where they are going.

Chicken-Coop Morality

In the Communist party and in its youth organization, the Young Communist League, now parading under the name of the American Youth For Democracy, a relentless war goes on against what the communists term petty bourgeois ideologies and influences. Through this campaign the communist organization seeks to tear down respect for the structure of civilization, its ideas, culture, laws, moral standards, customs, religious institutions, patriotism and traditions. The worst insult one can hurl against a communist is to charge that he is a petty bourgeois or permeated with petty-bourgeois ideology and bound in his conduct by petty-bourgeois morality. Among the older comrades who are set in their habits, the campaign does not do as much harm as it does to the youth members who are divided into two age categories—the youth and the junior youth. The junior youth are children ranging from tiny kindergarten tots up to fourteen years of age. Those from fourteen to twenty-five constitute the mature youth. Among the communist youth the anti-petty-bourgeois campaign is devastating.

The little tots, the juniors attending communist Sunday schools, get, under the tutelage of communist youth teachers, most of whom have no education or pedagogic training, a distorted and false picture of life in the United States. They are taught American history which is deliberately colored to break down their patriotism. They are impregnated with atheistic ideas and inculcated with communist ideology. Their minds are crippled in order to develop them into good communist automatons.

In the older youth the breakdown is most noticeable in the field of morals. Their immature minds become so dwarfed and twisted that they believe the best way to prove that they have freed themselves from petty-bourgeois influences is by flying in the face of the moral standards set by society. In this respect the younger boys and girls among them fall under the domination of the older ones and are greatly influenced by them in their personal conduct and attitudes.

First to suffer is the family. Family ties are severed. The communist youth seeks to become an independent agent by freeing himself or herself from family restraints. Some members of the communist youth organization resist the pressure to break with their families. They are the ones with exceptional character and firm family ties. The majority succumb.

The youths are pampered and patronized in order to mold their impressionistic juvenile minds to suit the purposes of communism. The Communist party goes out of its way to make the youth feel that they are the important elements in the movement. This patronization develops youthful arrogance and intellectual conceit characterized by a communist snobbishness which accentuates their moral degeneration. The youthful communist sophists imagine that they are the only communists who are completely free of petty-bourgeois influences and therefore the only true proletarian revolutionists in the movement. They smoke, drink, swear, call the older comrades petty-bourgeois ignoramuses and delight in promiscuous sexual intercourse.

Where did all this lead to? In New York and in other communist centers, the youth built up a communist Sodom and Gomorrah. In New York the wife of one of the outstanding youth leaders, who is today a figure of national and international importance in communist circles, held open house for youth comrades in her apartment in the Bronx. To the house came, whenever they pleased, young communist couples. Here they argued communist politics, sang I.W.W. and communist songs, danced furiously, told dirty stories, sat in the corners and on the floor and necked. When the lights went out the couples collectively undressed and squatted on the floor to sleep. But few slept as the occupants of the chicken coop huddled closely together. Quips and risqué remarks were bantered about in the darkness. And in the few hours remaining to them, couples changed their partners as an example to the timid that they had achieved liberation from the enslavement of petty-bourgeois influences and morality.

This lack of restraint, the freedom based on licentious living, has its counterpart in dependency upon and enslavement to the communist machine in the submission to communist orders from above and in the deadening of the mind with communist ideology. The communist inverted *laissez faire* in personal conduct destroys the spiritual fibre of the communist youth, but to the Communist party that is of no account. The spirit and hopefulness of youth is turned against society. Its energy is used up to furnish the Communist party with a dynamic and courageous youth movement.

Counterfeiting $100 United States Bills

A member of one of Chicago's racketeer gangs stopped before a teller's window in a Chicago bank and presented a new one-hundred-dollar bill for exchange into smaller ones. The teller examined the bill and proceeded to hand out the change. The gangster was so surprised that the teller accepted the bill as genuine, that he halted the teller as he was counting out the change by asking:

"Hey, bud, d'ya think da bill's okay?"

"Sure," replied the teller, examining the hundred-dollar bill again, "but please wait a while, I'll make sure."

A check-up by the bank's expert disclosed that the bill was the most clever piece of counterfeiting that ever came to his attention. As a result of this incident the Federal authorities arrested two men, a German, Hans Dechow, who paraded as Count von Buelow, and Dr. Valentine Gregory Burtan of New York. Dr. Burtan at the time of his arrest was a member of the Lovestone group of communists who had been expelled from the Communist party in 1929. He had been a charter member of the Communist party at its organization.

The German immediately confessed the part he played in the counterfeiting business, pleaded guilty when arraigned and agreed to take the stand against Dr. Burtan. Both were convicted in connection with the counterfeiting and were sent to prison for long terms. The German, however, did not know the source of the counterfeiting. Dr. Burtan knew but did not sing. The authorities therefore were never able to implicate those who were the master criminals behind the manufacture of United States bills that, for their excellence of duplication, have never been equalled in the history of counterfeiting.

Had the Chicago gangster kept his mouth shut a deal would have been consummated between the leaders of the Chicago mobsters and the people Dr. Burtan represented, which would have resulted in the successful floating of several million dollars worth of $100 bills.

The story leading to the Chicago break began late in the year 1932 in a New York speakeasy located in a brownstone house on Sixtieth Street near Lexington Avenue, owned by a former waiter and official of the Amalgamated Food Workers Union and a former Communist party member. The speakeasy proprietor struck up a conversation with a German who was introduced as a Count. The German, a former swashbuckling officer, perfumed, polite, polished and a ladies' man, became a close friend of the speakeasy proprietor.

The proprietor with his past communist and trade union training quickly realized he had an adventurer who would take all kinds of risks to make money, honestly if possible, crookedly if necessary. That the German Count claimed he belonged to the reactionary Stahlhelm and favored the Nazi developments in his home country did not disturb the former communist. The Count confided that he had connections with agents of munition manufacturers and engaged in the dangerous and illicit business of supplying arms and munitions to Mexican rebels and the revolutionary bandits of the South and Central American countries. Dr. Burtan, a friend of the proprietor, visited the speakeasy and was introduced to the Count for a purpose. Perhaps through the doctor a deal could be made with the Soviet government to supply it with shipments of the latest types of American arms, gas bombs and chemicals for use in warfare. The German was informed the doctor had connections and that a deal could be made with an important power by which fabulous sums of money could be made.

Dr. Burtan, a clean-looking medical man, a specialist in heart disease, with excellent hospital connections and a good reputation in the profession, enjoyed a lucrative practice. Mild-mannered, slow in his movements, he did not look the part he played. Behind the calm façade of the medico stirred a restive, adventurous soul permeated with a high degree of idealism and a love for humanity. The Dr. Burtan complex consisted of a driving romantic spirit, coupled with great personal courage, a loyalty to friends that ignored self-interest, plus the quality of being kind to others, especially the poor and unfortunate. A psychologically twisted Robin Hood, steeped in the ideology of communism, that was Dr. Burtan who carried on his exploits in the canyons of hard stone and steel of the modern industrial and commercial Sherwood Forest.

The two men, the opposites in appearance and in the motives for their actions, met. The German, trigger-quick and selfish, with no regard for mankind; brave, adventurous, without principle, interested only in the money he could make by taking dangerous risks. Dr. Burtan, slow and deliberate, a kindly young man with a sensitive feeling for others, fired with a passionate desire for action, for adventure in the service of his principles and ideals.

The OGPU is a weird organization engaged in entangling machinations with all kinds of individuals, even with individuals whose activities run counter to the activities of the communists. In every communist party one member of its powerful secretariat of three is a liaison officer with the OGPU, and for all intents and purposes a member of that organization. In 1929 that member of the secretariat of the American Communist party was expelled on direct orders from Stalin. But he was not expelled from the OGPU apparatus, and has admitted that he remained and worked for the OGPU up to 1936. This man, a leader of a communist splinter group, entered the negotiations between Dr. Burtan and the spurious German Count. At first small deals were made to test out the German. He procured tear gas bombs, stink bombs, and potent chemical bombs for use in strikes and inner union struggles. He also procured powerful tear-gas ejectors fashioned into containers that looked like fountain pens and that clipped into one's pocket just like a fountain pen. If the pen was held before the face of a person a push at the end released a plunger which squirted the noxious chemicals into the victim's eyes and temporarily blinded him.

When the receipt of these things gave assurance that the German could deliver the goods, the matter of securing arms and munitions was taken up with the chiefs of the OGPU in New York, a tall handsome Russian who traveled under the name of Alfred, and a woman of Lettish Russian extraction, who went along as his wife. The deal worked out after many secret negotiations between the OGPU and the Amtorg, the Russian Trading Corporation, provided for the purchase of the arms and munitions wanted, to be paid for by the Soviet government and to be so delivered as to avoid knowledge of the transactions leaking out through the gun-running operations over which the German would take charge. The conference which eventually took place between the Amtorg officials and the munitions manufacturer from Pittsburg broke up because the Russians wanted the types of munitions and chemical bombs earmarked exclusively for the United States government. The German was left high-and-dry without a penny in his pocket.

At that time, the pockets of the OGPU agents were burning hot with new $100 United States bills. They had been cashing lots of them in gambling houses, night clubs, speakeasies and at the Havana race track. The ace agent of the OGPU, Nick Dozenberg, traveled for this purpose, in regal style, between New York, Florida and Havana. But the exchange of the counterfeit bills by such retail methods took up too much time. Besides, sufficiently large sums of money were not realized. The OGPU center in New York decided that a kill on a wholesale scale involving a profit of several million dollars had to be arranged for or the whole matter dropped, for it was too dangerous to change counterfeit bills indefinitely.

The OGPU's interest in American counterfeit money originated in the passport manufacturing plant of the OGPU in Berlin, Germany. The German Communist party sent an expert plate-maker and engraver to work in the passport mill. The counterfeiting of passports proved child's play to him. He got confidential with his Russian superiors and showed them what he really could do. The European money he counterfeited defied detection and easily passed as genuine currency. His chiefs asked him if he could counterfeit American paper money. He answered that he could if the proper paper were obtained. The OGPU had an exact duplicate of the paper produced in a Russian paper mill. The master craftsman went to work and counterfeited American $100 bills. They were easily cashed. But the OGPU still had a problem to solve. How did the United States treasury serialize and number the bills? Nick Dozenberg was assigned to discover how. He appealed to the secretariat of the Communist party to help him get the information, promising them that it would be worth a lot of money to the Party.

The question of using counterfeit United States currency on an extensive and world-wide scale in order to bring about monetary anarchy and a collapse of the capitalist financial system came up for discussion in the Comintern's inner circle and in the Polcom of the Russian Communist party. The idea was rejected because Russia was on the eve of launching the first Five Year Plan, a plan which depended largely on imports of capital goods from abroad for the building up of her industries. Using counterfeit money, the Russians decided, involved risks that might jeopardize the plan. The communists of Russia were not then interested in the collapse of capitalism, they were much more interested in building up Soviet economy with the aid of capitalist technicians and machinery. But since Russia had to build up its reserves of foreign valuta, to pay for the heavy import of goods and services necessitated by the plan, it was decided to give the OGPU abroad a free hand in financing its activities, as much as possible, by the use of American counterfeit money.

The $100 counterfeit bills were dispatched to OGPU centers all over the world from Berlin in Soviet diplomatic pouches which enjoyed immunity from search at borders and points of entry. The bulk of it went to OGPU headquarters in New York.

The former member of the secretariat intrigued the German by giving him a few hundred-dollar counterfeit bills which the German had no difficulty in passing on to others. The communist splinter group chief working with the OGPU knew the counterfeits were good, for the OGPU had paid him in counterfeit bills for his services, which bills he turned over to the treasurer of the group. The money was deposited without a kick-back taking place. The German, when he was confident the bills were good, allowed himself to be drawn into a scheme for the wholesale exchange of the spurious bills into legitimate currency. Nick had so far failed to dispose of the counterfeits in wholesale lots. Bank tellers who were approached and offered $25,000 and more were afraid to go into the proposition. The leader of the splinter group saw a way out. The German informed him he had contacts with Chicago racketeers who were anxious to tie up with a good proposition should it be worthwhile.

On the eve of Burtan's departure for Chicago, the communist splinter group, by an overwheming majority, decided that Stalin's policies in Russia were 100 percent correct. The clubrooms were crowded with jubilant comrades congratulating each other that the group would soon issue a daily newspaper and that Stalin would take their leader back into the Party. The leader did not let them know that the money was to come from his cut of the counterfeiting transaction, if it went through.

Following the exposure in Chicago of the counterfeiting, Dr. Burtan and the German, minor figures in the counterfeiting transactions, paid with their freedom. The master minds behind the scheme went scot-free. Dozenberg, with Burtan out of the way, made off with a glamorous nurse who worked in his medical office, the former wife of a U. S. Army intelligence officer. Dozenberg's communist wife died under suspicious circumstances in China.

The leader of the splinter group dropped the doctor like a hot potato following his arrest. The Communist party in the *Daily Worker* attacked him as a counter-revolutionary oppositionist and a counterfeiter. When Burtan's wife read in the *Daily Worker* that her husband was an ordinary counterfeiter and surmised that the Communist party had decided not to come to his defense, the woman got in touch with Max Bedacht, the Communist party liaison officer with the OGPU, now president of the International Workers Order, a communist fraternal insurance organization. She threatened Bedacht that unless the Party provided her husband with legal defense and gave her money for the support of herself and child that she would tell the world what she knew about the affair. Bedacht called a hurried meeting of the secretariat at which a decision was made to meet the demands of Mrs. Burtan.

Dr. Burtan served a fifteen-year prison term. He had traveled communism's road, from idealism to ideology, from ideology to crime, the road to a devil's paradise in which power built on violence and evil is worshipped and the good in man destroyed.

CHAPTER FIVE

THE STALIN ERA OF UNLIMITED PERSONAL POWER

The communist world superstructure deliberately refuses to recognize the laws of civilized society. The communist parties which constitute the international organization are *ipso facto* criminal organizations which break the law. The question then must be asked: What legal structure holds the world communist organization together? By what written or unwritten code of laws is it governed? But the written constitutions, statutes, laws and rules governing the international communist organization and the communist parties are without substance, for they rest upon no legal or ethical basis. In reality the communists are governed by no legal or ethical jurisprudence whatsoever. In the actual government of the communist organization the anarchy of the jungle prevails. He who heads the pack personifies the law, for his acts and his decisions are binding upon the communist organization and the millions of communists who belong to it.

Defiance of law, repudiation of the spiritual and moral standards which separate man from the beast have produced for the communists an organization in which the communists themselves have no rights, no protection, for there are no rules or laws by which they can guide their conduct. They are the slaves of a brutalizing system, in which might is right, and they end up the helpless victims of that system.

The Soviet Spy System and the Communist Party

The radical movement of pre-communist days put its foot down on police and spies. Membership in radical organizations was denied to policemen, federal agents, industrial spies, military intelligence personnel, agents of district attorneys' offices and stool pigeons. The Communist party inherited this anti-police tradition and Communist party leaders in printed and oral statements made it clear that their attitude to all government police and intelligence agencies was as hostile as that of any other radical organization. But there was, and still is, a marked and important difference, depending on the pole of attraction. The pole of attraction for the communists is the Soviet government. The Soviet police and intelligence agencies are looked upon with favor by the Communist party and are cooperated with to the fullest extent. American communist cooperation with the Soviet police and espionage agencies has transformed the Communist party into a police and spy organization *par excellence,* which operates on the continents of North and South America cheaply and efficiently for its Soviet masters. Included in the Communist party spy network are practically all the members of the Party and a large number of fellow travelers.

As has already been indicated the first communist agents sent to the United States to work with and direct the affairs of the Communist party were men like Scott, members of the Cheka, the first Soviet secret police and espionage organization which changed its name to GPU, then to OGPU, and is today known by the initials NKVD. The report of the Canadian Royal Commission of February 5, 1946, on Soviet espionage in Canada and its links with American and Canadian communists shows how intimate are the ties between the two.

The Soviet police state insists that every communist agent, every consular office, every embassy, every diplomatic mission, every cultural, technical or commercial mission sent to a foreign country include members of the Soviet government's espionage organization and military intelligence organization.

By 1929 the relations between the Communist party and the OGPU covered many fields and countries in the Western Hemisphere. At Montevideo, Uruguay, the OGPU, the Comintern and the Profintern established a center from which to carry on their operations on the North and South Atlantic seaboard and in the countries of South America. By bribing government officials, Soviet spies and communist agents were allowed to operate from that center without molestation. American Communist party representatives traveled continuously between Montevideo and ports in the United States.

Party leaders who went to Moscow conferred with OGPU agents assigned to work in the Americas. On their way back the Americans stopped over at the Russian Embassy situated on Unter Den Linden in Berlin to get last-minute instructions from the Comintern OGPU chief, whose office consisted of a small room on the main floor of the embassy building.

American Communist party members escorting Soviet missions in the United States as interpreters or technical advisers acted as spies for the OGPU. The Communist party has been gathering for years voluminous information on military matters, on industrial secrets, on diplomatic matters and on inner security matters. One member of the Party's Secretariat of three is assigned as a liaison officer between the Party and the OGPU.

In 1927 an expert aerial photographer of the United States Army joined the Communist party. The Party induced him to turn over the knowledge he gained in the Army to the OGPU. He bought up the latest aerial photographic equipment and turned it over to the Russians. Later, the Communist party released him to take up new duties as a permanent agent of the OGPU.

At the request of the OGPU the Communist party screened its members and also leaders. Those suited for the OGPU or Russian military intelligence were separated from the Party organization and turned over to the OGPU.

In 1927 the British government raided the offices of Arcos in London, the Soviet government's commercial trading corporation in England. Scotland Yard came into possession of a dossier which included names with American addresses. The names were unknown in British and American trading circles. When the newspapers carried the list the top leaders of the American Communist party were enroute to Moscow. A number were traveling under assumed names on American passports obtained by a Canadian communist, an OGPU contact in Montreal engaged in the import and export business. Steamship tickets, visas and other details involved in traveling abroad were taken care of by a steamship travel agency operated by the OGPU with offices on East 14 Street.

Upon reading the names, the Communist leaders knew that Scotland Yard had obtained the files of the Arcos OGPU chief. The list was authentic and disclosed the names and addresses of Communist party OGPU agents in the United States and other confidential names and addresses. Included were the names and addresses of the persons to whom code cables were sent by the OGPU, the Comintern and the Profintern. Other names were of persons to whom Russian money was sent for transmission to the Communist party. Scotland Yard also had in its possession the secret codes in which Moscow communicated, by letter and cable, with the American Communist party.

The Comintern acted quickly by branding as forgeries the documents seized in the Arcos raids. The American Communist party followed the same tack and charged Scotland Yard with attempting a frame-up of innocent people. Copies of many of the records given out by Scotland Yard were securely locked in a safe in the office of one of the Communist party's lawyers, whose name and address was also included in the list published in the press. Cables ordered him to destroy all records immediately. New codes were drawn up in Moscow by the OGPU and the Comintern. Copies of the codes were handed over to the secretary of the Party, Jay Lovestone, who was in Moscow at the time. The codes were graded for confidential matters and for matters of the utmost secrecy. The codes covering utmost secrecy were changed every three months, the others about every six months. The top-secret code was entrusted only to the secretary of the Party and he in turn had orders to employ only one girl, as absolutely trustworthy for decoding purposes. An intricate system of numbers and a key board of numbers used in decoding the top-secret code involved so much work that a day's time had to be spent in decoding a small cable.

The ramifications and machinery of the Soviet spy system have been greatly improved. The web spun from the Moscow center spreads all over the Americas. Secret operational centers, tied to the Soviet government's diplomatic and consular offices are in all capitals and important cities. Around them the members of the Communist parties of North and South America, numbering close to 2,000,000, constitute an extensive spy organization which no other government can match and with which no government can compete. The tie-up of the American Communist party with the Soviet spy system, the espionage contacts it maintains on a continental and world scale make the Communist party one of the most sinister and diabolical organizations in the United States. With Draculian cunning for over twenty-eight years, the American communists as spies and agents of a foreign power have gnawed away at the foundations of our liberties. In this sphere the realities and practices of American communism supersede its philosophical and ideological claims to American working class leadership and American revolutionary objectives.

C.I. Reps

In the leading nations of the world and among lesser known peoples; in the Far East, the Middle East, Africa, and in practically all colonial possessions, communist parties of one pattern and one mind function smoothly and effectively. How does Moscow control this gigantic organization with millions of members of different races, nationalities, religions and types of civilization? There is no confusion despite the multitude of languages. Instead unity prevails, based on an ideological coherence that baffles those who seek to understand this incomprehensible phenomenon of communism which transcends the barriers and differences between peoples. Moscow controls this world-wide organization by the following means: one, by the indoctrination of communist ideology; two, by the attraction of Soviet power, which like a magnet draws to it those who have no power and seek it; three, the lavish expenditure of money for communist propaganda and organization, and four, by the direct supervision and control of the world organization by agents and political specialists from Moscow.

By indoctrination, communist ideology so impresses itself upon the minds of those who embrace it that regardless of their origins and differences they think and react alike. Ideology is therefore the starting point of communism, its foundation, for without communist ideology there could be no communist organization.

Second in importance is the attraction of Soviet power. Communism without a state, without a center of political power could not hold together on a world scale. The Soviet government gives the communists all over the world a sense of belonging to and being part of an all-powerful state. The millions who belong to the world communist superstructure are thereby imbued with a sense of dignity and strength that enables them to carry out the difficult and superhuman tasks which the movement imposes upon them.

Next in importance comes the expenditure of money, the filthy lucre of capitalism which the Marxists contend is the source of evil. Yet without the millions of dollars which the Communist power-center spends annually to keep its global superstructure in operation, the communist world organization would fall to pieces. In carrying on communist activities, the question of where the money is to come from seldom worries the movement. Among communist leading circles it is generally stated that Uncle Joe will provide. And Uncle

Joe has been a generous provider who does not fail his hard-working nephews and nieces.

At this point attention will be given to the fourth means employed by Moscow and its application to the American Communist party. It has been shown that Moscow from the beginning, as far back as 1919, took an active part in the affairs of American communism. It not only supplied money but also sent over many emissaries to help organize communist parties in the countries of North and South America. The steps taken by Moscow proved that Moscow considered the Communist party of the United States the key to the extension of communism over the two American continents. In the expansion of communism over the Western Hemisphere the American Communist party acted as the direct agent of Moscow and the recipient and the dispenser of funds allotted by Moscow for that purpose.

The fact, however, that the Communist party of the United States enjoyed a privileged position among the communist parties of the Americas did not mean that the American Communist party was permitted to act as a free and independent agent. The American Communist party was at all times strictly controlled and directed by Moscow through international representatives who were sent by Moscow to the Communist party of the United States. These representatives traveled with credentials issued in the name of the Communist International, the Red Trade Union International, the Moper or International Red Aid, The International Workers Aid, The Young Communist International, the OGPU and in extraordinary situations as the personal representatives of Stalin. The Communist party generally referred to them as C.I. Reps. In addition to the C.I. Reps a steady flow of people, all of them sent by Moscow, came to the United States on specific missions to the Communist party with powers limited to their missions. They were what the Party called "Spets," specialists, in trade union matters, organization, propaganda, farmers, etc. All the Moscow agents at a given time in the United States formed a group which acted as a unit on American party matters. Headed by the C.I. Rep this group of foreigners exercised absolute power over the American party. The Party leadership obeyed its wishes and were in deadly fear of arousing its animosity.

The C.I. Reps were no mere ambassadors of good will, the fraternal delegates from one Communist party to another. They were the plenipotentiary representatives of the Communist world superstructure who carried with them credentials which gave them unlimited powers over the Party, the Party's leading committees and subdivisions, its press and institutions, leadership and membership. The C.I. Reps who exercised the powers of life and death over the communist organization also acted as special agents of the Soviet government and interfered in the affairs of Soviet government agencies in the countries to which they were sent. The C.I. Reps who acted as Stalin's agents were men carefully selected by Stalin for missions of great personal concern to him.

Not all the C.I. Reps sent by Moscow to the American Communist party were Russians. They included Germans, Italians, English, Poles, Swedes, Finns, Czechs, Hungarians and French. Stalin's personal representatives were always Russian. The Moscow representatives to the Communist party entered the United States illegally through Mexico across the Mexican-Texas border; through Cuba via Havana to Florida; via Montreal, Canada, or directly through the port of New York. Most of them returned to Moscow, embarking at the port of New York using genuine American and Canadian passports secured for them in the name of American and Canadian citizens by the underground passport bureau of the Communist party. These passports eventually went into the hands of the OGPU where exact duplicates were forged which, together with the originals, were supplied to its agents and spies for their personal use in traveling over the world.

One of the most important ones sent by Stalin to America was Gussev, a colleague of Lenin in the organization of the Bolshevik party, who came here in 1925. Gussev, a short, chubby man, understood English but did not speak it. He carried on his conversation with the Party leaders in German. He came accompanied by a girl, a member of the German Communist party and the staff of the Comintern OGPU, and by a Finn, named Sirola, a C.I. Rep with a specific assignment to the Finnish Section of the Communist party. Sirola was an outstanding international personality in communist circles, a brilliant scholar, an educator and a man of wisdom and tact. His job was to integrate the Finns in the United States with the Communist party, in order to gain control of the Finnish cooperatives, institutions and property valued at several million dollars. He sought also to array the American Finns against the Finnish government, to use their influence among the Finns in Finland and their financial support to bolster up the puppet Finnish Karelian Soviet as a stepping stone towards the domination of the whole of Finland by the Soviet government.

Gussev adopted the alias, P. Green. The American communists who did not like him called him, "Paris Green." Lulu, the German girl, acted as his secretary and did special reporting on the American party to the OGPU. Green conducted himself with a frigid air, never permitting himself to become angry. In conversing or addressing meetings he spoke quietly, without emphasis. He kept a poker face under all circumstances.

Green worshipped Stalin. Stalin had saved his life during the Civil War in Russia when a military tribunal headed by Trotsky demanded his execution because he refused to carry out decisions made by those higher in command. Stalin intervened, had the case reviewed, reversed Trotsky and saved Gussev's life. In the fight against Trotsky, Stalin had in Gussev an abject slave and supporter.

As early as 1925, when Trotsky was still a power in Russia, Stalin began preparing the grounds for Trotsky's ouster from Soviet politics and life by sending his personal representatives to all communist parties to line them up in the fight against Trotsky. Because of Foster's friendship with Lore, who supported Trotsky, Stalin instructed Gussev to favor the Ruthenberg faction then in a minority in the American party and create a situation that would make it possible to remove Foster from the control of the Party even though he had the support of the majority.

A few weeks later the rape of the majority leadership of the American Communist party by C.I. Rep Green took place at the Party's convention held in Chicago. Before the convention, he called in the leaders of the minority and unfolded Stalin's plans and the secret orders he had given him. Stalin, he informed the comrades, was out to get undisputed control of the Russian Communist party and the Communist International. Stalin, he told them in his careful German, had no use for the "flicken Politik" pursued by Zinoviev in the Comintern. He wanted the Comintern to take a definite stand on the leadership in the various parties of the Comintern and not to waste time with diplomatic quibbling and bargaining to bring about a united leadership. The first step in Stalin's plan for a consolidated communist leadership throughout the world called for the elimination of Trotsky from the affairs of the Communist party of Soviet Russia and from the Communist International.

Green conducted his affairs with the utmost secrecy and care in order to avoid apprehension by the authorities. He used a small, secluded cemetery in Chicago's North Side for conferences with trusted comrades. Seated on a stone vault, amid weatherbeaten tombstones he chewed his gum and talked. It was a macabre setting for the intrigues of inner communist power politics, sugar-coated by the soft-spoken German words of the short, pot-bellied man who was as cold and expressionless as the tomb on which he sat.

In the graveyard one felt a stony chill as Green unfolded the ideas of his master. "Ah, comrades," said Green, the German sentences coming slowly, each word carefully chosen for calculated effect, "Trotsky is an overrated man. His world centers around his own egotistical person. I lived together with Trotsky in exile. I watched him standing for hours before a mirror, rehearsing a speech he was to deliver, scrutinizing his expressions to determine which best reflected his great importance. Bah! there is no place in a Bolshevik movement for such a self-seeking, self-worshipping hero.

"Stalin," he continued, "is different. In him we have the perfect organization man, to whom the interests of the organization come first. Following the death of Lenin he saw clearly that the Party organization had to be defended against the personal ambitions of one man. When Trotsky tried to discredit the role of bolshevism in the Russian revolution and to minimize the part played by the Party of Lenin, Stalin fought back to preserve the name of the Party and the Communist International."

And then dealing with the American Communist party he concluded: "Comrades, watch Stalin. He plans to weld the Bolshevik forces in Russia and throughout the world into a firmly knit, coherent Bolshevik force. He cannot trust Foster because he has played around with Trotsky's supporters, like Lore. Stalin knows how to be loyal to those who fight with him. The fight against Trotsky is only the beginning. Stalin must have more than assurances. He must have guarantees where every leadership of every Communist party in the Comintern stands—with him or against him."

But the leaders of the Ruthenberg faction did not grasp the implications behind the soft-spoken words. For that shortcoming, four years later, in 1929, Stalin kicked them out of the Comintern and had them expelled from the Party. They failed to understand that the fight against Trotsky opened a war by Stalin to remove all communist leaders in the way of his plans to establish his personal domination over the Communist party of Russia and the communist world superstructure.

When the convention opened the Foster faction had a decisive majority. But Foster, the leader of the majority, took no chances. The struggle for power in the American Communist party had become so terrific that Foster feared the Ruthenberg faction would attempt to seize the Party organization by force. Both factions mobilized their strong-arm squads on the eve of the convention and both squads were heavily armed. An internal war threatened which the communists feared would be settled only by bloodshed. Such bloody internal wars were not new in the Comintern. Many factional situations culminated in a resort to arms and assassination. A good section of the Executive Committee of the Finnish Communist party was wiped out by cold-blooded murder and the murderers received the recognition of the Comintern. The national headquarters of the Party which contained the presses which printed the *Daily Worker* looked like an armed camp. Foster's gunmen, armed with automatics and sawed-off shot-guns, jammed the building and carefully scrutinized everyone who entered.

The bloody inter-organizational civil war did not break out because Green, armed with cables which he had directed the Comintern and Stalin to send him, cables signed by the President of the Comintern and by Joseph Stalin, took the starch out of Foster. The cables stated that the Comintern and Stalin had no faith in his leadership and therefore denied him the right to take the majority. The cables exploded like an atom bomb in the Foster camp. Foster was deprived of his majority and the leadership fell into the hands of the minority. Thus the American communists were given a lesson in Stalin's conception of democracy, a lesson which the rest of the world, to its sorrow, will probably learn much too late.

Stalin Takes Over

The communists do not know what they may or may not do. They have no sense of comradeship, no trust in each other. The dark pool is deep and treacherous. Its murky blackness spreads out in all directions and may yet engulf the whole of mankind. The past and present forecast the future. A review of the events of 1928 and 1929 affecting the American Communist party will give the reader an understanding of how this world-wide, extra-legal structure of organized communism works.

In July, 1928, amid great fanfare, the Sixth World Congress of the

Communist International opened in Moscow. To demonstrate the unity which prevailed, the Russian delegates to the Congress, including Stalin, embraced each other while the delegates roared their approval. Dispatches went out to the four corners of the world, that with the elimination of Trotsky from the movement, the Communist world superstructure was more united than ever before. But the picture presented to the public, painted in exaggerated colors, grossly falsified the facts and hid the truth from the world.

The real Congress was not the Sixth World Congress but the Corridor Congress, secretly organized by Stalin, which met behind the massive columns of the Congress hall during the sessions of the Congress. At the sessions of the Corridor Congress Stalin laid his plans and organized his forces to take over absolute personal control of the communist world organization. Before the public Stalin took the little cherubic Bukharin, the president of the Communist International, in his arms and kissed him. Leaving the stage, as the delegates wildly acclaimed this demonstration of affection, Stalin gathered his gang together *in camera* to plot the destruction of Bukharin. The delegates who a few moments before had cheered Bukharin now plotted how to stab him in the back.

At the Sixth World Congress every decision, resolution, manifesto and motion passed unanimously. Unanimously the Congress, supposed to represent the highest communist authority in the world, elected the Executive Committee and officers of the Communist International and in a wild demonstration amid the singing of the *Internationale* in many tongues, the delegates holding their clenched fists aloft, unanimously re-elected Bukharin President. Stalin joined in the demonstrations and added his vote to the unanimous total.

In the United States the members of the Communist party were disturbed by rumors that all was not unity in Moscow, that a serious conflict raged between Stalin and Bukharin. The innocent lambs sent a cable to the Congress asking for an explanation. After receipt of the American cable Stalin appeared before the Congress, arm in arm with Bukharin. In the name of both he presented a resolution on behalf of the Russian delegation and the Polcom of the Russian Communist party categorically denying the rumors and stating that perfect unanimity existed in the Russian delegation and in the Russian Communist party on all matters before the Congress. He branded as falsehoods all rumors that claimed he and Bukharin were in opposition to each other. With the inclusion of the resolution into the records, Stalin smiled, stroked his mustache, took a puff at his pipe and departed to the secret Corridor Congress, where he had a good laugh at what had just transpired. There he conferred with his American stooges, assuring them that when they went back to the United States and took up the fight to oust Bukharin from the Comintern, they could count on his support.

The Stalin caucus of the American Communist party in Moscow consisted of about half of the twenty American delegates to the Sixth World Congress and the American students who were attending the communist universities and colleges in Moscow. These were called together by Losovsky, the President of the Red International of Trade Unions, at the behest of Stalin, and informed that it would pay them to line up with Stalin against Bukharin; he promised that Stalin would reward such loyalty by giving them the leadership of the American party. The top figures in the Stalin caucus were Foster, Dunne and Zack. Of the three, only Foster remains a member and leader of the Party, the other two have been expelled. Of the three, Stalin confided most in Zack, the jovial, bald-headed Czecho-Slovak from America. Zack was the political manipulator behind the scene, not the man to be catapulted into the public leadership of the American party. For that post Stalin wanted Dunne. Stalin liked Dunne. Though an intellectual and a journalist, he looked like a proletarian rough-neck. He was not afraid to use violence, and besides, he was not a Jew. But he had one bad fault. He drank too much. Stalin once shipped Dunne to a sanitarium in outer Mongolia to cure him of his alcolism. In private talks with Dunne during the Congress he solemnly promised him the leadership of the American party. Dunne forthwith cabled the contents of his conversation with the Chief to his cronies in the United States. He got drunk and bragged too much about what Stalin was going to do. The OGPU reported. Stalin crossed him off the list immediately. Stalin then called Foster into a conference and promised the man he had once deposed from the leadership that he would give him the leadership once more if Foster would, upon his return to the United States, make a good fight against Bukharin and the majority leadership of the American Communist party. Foster, his face flushed with joy, thanked the boss profusely, professed his loyalty and promised the Chief to faithfully carry out all his orders.

Stalin kept his plans for the American Communist party to himself and his accomplices. He was not bothered by the fact that the Sixth World Congress had passed a resolution endorsing the majority leadership and that he had voted for the resolution. He kept the Party leaders in ignorance of what he plotted against them. Foster and his associates upon their return home, though in a hopeless minority, started a factional war to dislodge the majority and pushed the campaign against Bukharin. But the majority leadership, by professing their loyalty to the Comintern and to Stalin, were able to thwart their efforts. Foster failed to make good his promises to Stalin.

At the convention of the Communist party held at the beginning of 1929, the majority leadership rolled up a staggering total and elected over 90 percent of the delegates to the convention. The majority, however, reckoned without Stalin's long arm. They felt it soon enough when two C.I. Reps, Phillip Dengel, a German, and Harry Pollit, an Englishman, arrived in the United States from the Comintern. The Young Communist International sent as its Rep a tall, uncouth, not too brilliant, red-haired English lad by the name of Rust. Rust and Pollit are today Stalin's men in the top leadership of the British Communist party.

The two Stalin boys, who were to polish off the American party, arrived on the eve the Communist party convention opened in New York City at the Irving Plaza Hall near Union Square, dubbed by the communists "Red Square." When the convention opened, delegates and Party members crammed every available bit of space so that the audience looked like one congealed mass of humanity. On the small platform crowded the Party leadership protected by a selected band of heavily armed men who at the nod of one of the Party leaders would have torn a person apart limb from limb. The opposition, spurred on by Stalin to make a good fight, came to the convention surrounded by a gang of armed ruffians, prepared to do just that. With the first knock of the gavel on the table, the opposition began, in defiance of the convention majority and the rules of procedure, to demand consideration of a resolution calling for the ouster of Bukharin from the Comintern for his opportunistic, counter-revolutionary views. They filibustered, screamed, stamped their feet, hurled invectives against the chairman and prepared for a battle that would have rocked the communist movement. A fight actually started on the platform when one of Foster's gangsters clouted the Negro, William Haywood, on the jaw, splitting his lip and breaking some teeth. The threat of a bloody battle hastened an agreement between the factions to adjourn the convention in order to give the leaders an opportunity to confer with Stalin's agents.

The conferences with the Reps in which the majority leaders of the Party participated proved to be a weird episode in American communist political history. Dengel and Pollit had never been to the United States before. They knew nothing of American conditions and politics. All they did was to confront the leaders of the American Communist party with an ultimatum from Stalin, from which they refused to budge one iota, for that was Stalin's orders to them. Dengel carried the ultimatum in his pocket, black typed letters on a white sheet of paper, embossed with the seal of the Communist International and signed by the weasel-eyed Finn, Kussinnen, its secretary. When Dengel had it read, he took pains to impress the Americans that the decision embodied the personal will of Stalin. Stalin demanded that regardless of the vote of the Party members on who should lead the Party, the minority must be given the majority leadership of the Party. In unequivocal language Stalin declared that the majority delegates had no right to decide who should be elected to head the American Communist party and that Foster (who had received less than ten percent of the votes) should be elected to that post. Stalin, in his ultimatum, gave the American communists a taste of true communist democracy.

The majority leadership fought back. They refused to accept Stalin's ultimatum. Calling their forces together they informed them that Stalin demanded that Foster be made the secretary of the Party and that Lovestone, the secretary, must be separated from the American Communist party and dispatched to Moscow for special work at the Comintern. The majority leaders, stupefied, assured their followers that Stalin had acted on misinformation, that the opposition had fed him with stories that the Party leadership did not enjoy the support of the membership. They promised their followers that once Stalin learned they had the overwhelming majority and the best proletarian elements, that he would respect the majority and change his mind. Leader after leader prostrated himself before the members in proving his loyalty and servility to the Comintern and Stalin. But none of them could satisfactorily explain why Stalin acted the way he did.

Foster and his faction, smelling the blood of victory, hammered away on the Bukharin issue. The majority leadership in desperation answered that they were loyal to the Comintern and Stalin, and that they did not wear Bukharin buttons. In desperation they asked for a conference with the C.I. Reps. They argued that if the price of retaining their leadership of the American Communist party depended upon their condemning Bukharin they were ready to introduce a resolution of their own against Bukharin, in stronger terms than Foster had done, and would include, in addition, whatever points the Reps suggested.

The talks went on for hours, during the day and far into the night. Dengel and Pollit did not move one inch. They stated over and over again that they had received strict instructions from Stalin that were binding upon them and they refused to use their own judgment. Stalin wanted his pound of flesh. The majority, they insisted, must renounce its majority and accept the minority as the bosses of the Party and as their overlords. The majority leaders in a last desperate effort to appease the Reps introduced the resolution attacking Bukharin and calling for his expulsion from the Comintern. The Reps countered by demanding that the majority leadership abdicate.

The majority appealed against the ultimatum by sending a lengthy cable to Stalin. Upon receipt of the cable Stalin decided to hedge and take a little more time in executing his decision. He sent a cable back to the United States in which he permitted the convention majority to conclude the convention in an orderly fashion by electing the new Central Executive Committee which in turn elected the sub-committees and officers of the Party. He refused to allow Lovestone to be chosen for the post of general secretary and insisted that he be sent to Moscow at once, as originally ordered. The cable concluded that all convention decisions should stand pending a review of the convention by the Comintern. He instructed his personal representatives to remain in the United States in order to direct the affairs of the American party. Pepper, who had been ordered to return to Moscow and was in hiding, this time received Stalin's strict orders to return at once.

Stalin, as these decisions indicate, attached considerable importance to the American Communist party, staking his reputation on bringing the Party completely under his control. At the same time that Stalin sent the cable to the American Communist party convention he used the Communist International against the majority leadership by framing them before they had an opportunity to present their appeal. Stalin had ordered the communist parties of Germany, France, Czecho-Slovakia, England and far-off China, who were ignorant about the affairs of the American party, to pass resolutions condemning the majority leadership. In 1948, the world was treated to almost exactly the same kind of spectacle when the Cominform, (as the Comintern is now called), at Stalin's behest, castigated the leaders of the Yugoslav Communist party. When Tito refused to grovel at Stalin's feet, Communist parties all over the world passed resolutions condemning Tito and his government, although in reality they knew little or nothing about the actual conditions prevailing in Yugoslavia. Like trained circus horses they again responded to the crack of Stalin's whip.

The American delegates who arrived in Moscow seeking justice recognized that a new spirit had taken hold of the Comintern. The little Bukharin had been booted out of the presidency and clear out of the Comintern building. He walked furtively around the streets of Moscow like a frightened ghost. His private Comintern secretary, the Finn in whom he confided, in mortal fear of his own safety, denounced and maligned the man who had been his best friend. Molotov, Stalin's spitting, stuttering drudge, replaced Bukharin in fact, but not in name, as the big shot in the Comintern. Stalin considered the American Communist party question of such great importance that the commission which was formed to hear the appeal included him as a member and Molotov as its chairman. The two outstanding rulers of the Soviet government, a government of over 160 million people, beset with pressing problems and great difficulties, gave up a considerable portion of their valuable time to consider the affairs of the American Communist party, a Party with about 35,000 dues-paying members.

The entire weight of the Communist world superstructure was brought down upon the heads of the leaders of the American party. Stalin appeared in person and stayed on all night until four in the morning in order to put his decision across. He confronted the American communists with the power of his personal dictatorship, the prestige of the Russian Revolution, the pressure of the world-wide communist organization and the might of the Soviet government.

The American Communist party leadership was smashed. Stalin, with one exception, did not yield a point from his original ultimatum. The exception involved the scrapping of Foster. Stalin held Foster responsible for the failure to create the conditions in the American party which would have made it easy for Stalin to carry out his ultimatum at the Party convention proper. He called Foster a cheap speculator who speculated on the outcome of affairs in the Comintern and in the Communist party of the Soviet Union. He accused him of bad faith, of misrepresenting Stalin's position to the members of the

American party. Talking directly at Foster he gave him the uncomplimentary reasons why he no longer favored him for the leadership. Foster like a beaten puppy dog kept quiet.

Stalin had his way. Those who did not submit to his orders were removed from all positions. The American Communist party received orders that if, on their return to the United States, the American communist leaders refused to publicly endorse Stalin's decisions against them, they should be expelled from the Party. Stalin did not trust the new leaders he had put in charge of the Party to carry out his decisions. He selected an envoy and invested him with astounding powers to do the job for him. He was provided with an initial sum of $50,000 dollars, the decision on finances, assuring that whatever sums were needed to rout the opposition in America would be put at his disposal. Stalin selected a Russian who could speak English, B. Mikhailov, a henchman of Losovsky who operated under the name of Williams. Granted dictatorial rights over the American party, he had vested in him the power to take over the property of the Party, to reshuffle the Party leadership and to expel any member or leader. He also had the right to supervise and make decisions on the editorial and managerial policies of all the Party's newspapers and periodicals in whatever language they were published. All Party decisions had to be submitted to him for review and he had the right to veto or change them. He alone enjoyed the exclusive power to make decisions for the Party, on political, trade union, organizational and other matters, the decisions being binding upon the Party organization. A supplementary decision was made by Stalin on the *Daily Worker* which provided that, if the *Daily Worker* fell into the hands of the opposition, Williams was to be supplied with upwards of one million dollars to launch a new daily communist newspaper.

When Williams arrived in the United States he found his task much simpler than Stalin had imagined it would be. The American communists solidly backed the Soviet Union and Stalin. They denounced their former leaders in the words of Stalin as "Hooverites," agents of American imperialism, crooked politicians and counter-revolutionists. Only two hundred followed the expelled leaders out of the Party. Stalin now had the American Communist party securely tucked away in the breast pocket of his Russian blouse. The American communists lost the right to independent thinking and action. When Williams finished his task he was replaced by another. Browder beat the tom toms and made all the noise, but a secret Moscow agent, a Stalin Rep, controlled the works and determined what Browder should say and do. From 1929 to date, Russian commissars have directed the leaders of the American Communist party and determined the destiny of American communism. Stalin's system of personal commissars has replaced the cumbersome machinery of the Communist International in the running of the Communist world superstructure. A president of the Communist world organization is no longer necessary, for Stalin is its undisputed boss.

CHAPTER SIX

MOSCOW DAYS AND NIGHTS

IN MOSCOW, the womb of the communist movement, in the bleak city of sprawling buildings and bizarre cathedrals, the birth pangs of a new era in communism were marked by political strife and bloodletting. The communist merry-go-round suddenly came to an abrupt stop and immediately began a mad whirl in the opposite direction. The communist leaders who were caught off guard were dashed to the ground and destroyed. Such were the fateful days of 1929. Stalin moved rapidly on all fronts. He threw Trotsky out of Russia. He kicked Bukharin out of the Comintern. He purged all the communist parties as he did the American party in order to establish his undisputed leadership over them. He tightened his grip on the Soviet government and made absolute his personal dictatorship. All these measures were instituted with precision and ruthlessness in order to usher in the new era, the sharp swing to the left marked by the launching of the Five Year Plan for the industrialization of Russia and the collectivization of agriculture on a communist basis. With one fell blow the NEP which permitted limited private enterprise was abolished to make way, as Stalin himself declared, for an economic and political policy which would lead to civil war in the villages and in the cities against the bourgeois, petty bourgeois and counter-revolutionary forces seeking to block the plan. The war to put the plan across, he told his comrades, would involve great sacrifices on the part of the communists and great losses in human lives. The communists who packed the crown room of the Tsar's palace listened to Stalin's prophetic words. They were hopeful of the future. They did not see the gathering clouds and the approaching hand of death, for many of them were living ghosts who tomorrow would be dead.

Bukharin—the Fatalist

In 1928 Bukharin was considered, next to Stalin, the most powerful man in the international communist movement. The following

163

year he became an outcast, a man hounded and despised by the communists who had fawned at his feet during his presidency of the Comintern. Bukharin, a short, fair-looking, artistic man with delicate features, spent his leisure in painting and sketching. A mischievous sparkle in his eyes lit up a boyish face that seemed to be always smiling. When angry, his face turned crimson and words shot out of his mouth like red-hot coals. A highly educated man and a scholar, he belonged to the universal Bolsheviks, the men who in exile lived in the countries of Western Europe and in the United States. His human characteristics set him apart from the rest of the Bolshevik clan. The Russian Communist party members called him the darling of the Party, for he was the one outstanding leader they loved and admired.

Bukaharin, in league with Stalin, led the fight against Trotsky in the Comintern. Trotsky came to the Red Hall of the Comintern, portfolio jammed with papers and documents. He sat in the center close to the middle aisle. Next to him sat the Spanish communist, Ninn, who had the courage to support him, a fact Stalin never forgot. During the Spanish Civil War the OGPU got Ninn and gave him the bullet in the back of the neck. Trotsky, beard bristling, eyes afire, understanding every language spoken, and speaking them all equally as well, fidgeted as he listened to the small fry representing their parties speak against him on matters they knew nothing about. He interrupted their tirades with sarcastic interjections under which they wilted, causing them to lose their poise and the ability coherently to continue their arguments.

When Trotsky got up to defend himself no one applauded him but everyone listened, for they knew a great man was speaking who towered intellectually above every other living communist. A slavish adherence to Marxism warped the brilliance of his mind, and his judgment often succumbed to an intense egotism. Trotsky was supreme in debate. He lashed out against Stalin in words of metallic clearness, his phrases delivered with sharp stinging blows. An orator of dynamic qualities, in whom were colorfully blended form, personality, gestures and dramatic presentation, he hammered away at his opponents, now in Russian, now in English, a sharp rap in French and a sledge-hammer blow in German, switching from one language to another with the facility of an acrobat swinging from one trapeze to another. When Bukharin rose to answer him, Trotsky got up from his seat, stuffed his papers into a portfolio, shot a stinging insult at

Bukharin and rushed out of the room as if a windstorm had struck him. That was in the summer of 1927. Trotsky never again entered the Comintern building.

By 1929 Stalin had eliminated most of the powerful figures in Lenin's Bolshevik machine. The team of Zinoviev, Radek and Kamenev, the shining lights of the Comintern, walked in the shadows of Moscow like beaten dogs with their tails between their legs. The revolution prepared to devour its children. With Trotsky out of the way Stalin turned his attention to the men who helped to eliminate him—Bukharin, Rykoff and Tomsky.

Bukharin and his group, branded by Stalin as right wingers, made the mistake of fighting against Stalin's vindictiveness by raising economic and political issues. Stalin, the political boss, countered by unscrupulously using the methods of machine politics against them.

Bukharin voted against sending Trotsky into exile. When Stalin ordered Zinoviev and Kamenev moved out of Moscow and sent into exile to isolated parts of the Soviet Union far from the capital, Bukharin, who opposed the order, secretly visited his old friends, with whom he had suffered persecution and exile during Tsarist days, to bid them good-bye. But Stalin's eyes and ears were everywhere. After that meeting the OGPU hailed Kamenev before Stalin, who grilled him all night long. He read to the cringing man before him what had been said during the meeting with Bukharin. Stalin put Kamenev through a third degree in which he demanded that Kamenev confess to the plot Bukharin had mapped out for a war against Stalin. Kamenev professed ignorance. Kamenev winced as Stalin tore into him with ugly words, charges and threats. Then the man yielded and signed a statement against Bukharin, along the lines demanded by Stalin, in order to avoid the venom and savage brutality of the man who ruled over all the Russians. Stalin thus had in his possession what he wanted.

Stalin did not wait to give Bukharin a hearing and a trial before the Control Commission of the Russian Communist party. Instead he resorted to one of his favorite methods in a fight against an opponent —the use of rumor. Stalin's rumor factory went into operation. The charges which were supposed to be kept secret until the proper organs of the Party had considered them, were whispered about confidentially in government circles, in Russian Communist party headquarters, at the Comintern and in the rooms and lobby of the Lux Hotel. Bukharin was tossed about on the mounting waves of gossip.

While fighting for his political life in an atmosphere poisoned against him with rumors and lies, branded by Stalin as the man who would bring capitalism back to Russia, Bukharin committed a cardinal sin, in the eyes of the uncouth, uncultured Stalin. At a meeting of the Politburo Stalin chided Bukharin and charged him with conduct unbecoming a member of the Politburo. For hours the inquisition dragged on. Bukharin lost his composure, jumped to his feet and in a fit of anger did what Stalin had been doing to him. He berated the boss, and pointing his finger at Stalin shouted: "You are the Ghengis Khan of the Communist party," likening him to the bloodthirsty Tartar despot.

Rykoff, the premier of the Soviet Union, supported Bukharin. A West European, he pleaded the case of the Russian people, demanding that something had to be done to better the lot of the masses. On May Day Stalin punished him by removing him from the reviewing stand on Red Square. Rykoff took up a post reserved for Moscow's local officials. The marchers, when they passed by Rykoff, wildly cheered him for they instinctively reacted to Rykoff's concern for them. When they passed before Stalin they kept a mute silence. Hearing of the demonstrations for Rykoff, Stalin fumed with jealousy and accused the right wingers of using May Day to stage hostile demonstrations against him.

A man who is often mentioned as the probable successor of Stalin should he die had for months been wavering between Stalin and Bukharin. The members of the Russian Communist party felt that should he support Bukharin, Stalin's position would be a difficult one. Stalin toyed with Andreyev's ambitions, promised to shove him upwards by making him a member of the Politburo in Bukharin's place. When Andreyev spoke, Stalin propped himself on his elbows as he leaned over the table on the platform the better to hear what the young man had to say. He looked squarely at him with his steely, penetrating eyes. The crown room was packed with people who sat hypnotized. The muffled voices of the translators making running translations of the speech to communist leaders from other lands added to the dramatic tension. Andreyev did what Stalin expected of him. He deserted Bukharin, tore into his program and delivered a vitriolic personal attack against him to demonstrate his loyalty to the man on the platform who was staring at him. The speech finished, Stalin stretched himself, smiled at the crowd in front of him with an air of victorious satisfaction and clapped his hands, the signal for a thunderous demonstration of approval.

Stalin used the Five Year Plan politically for all it was worth. His propaganda machine, geared in high, whipped the country into a frenzy. Bukharin and his associates, unable to escape the mass psychical contagion which gripped the Russian people, harassed by a ruthless, vindictive regime, beat their chests before the almighty Stalin in confessing the errors of their ways. In obsequious humiliation they bowed before Stalin's omniscience and omnipotent power. But capitulation did not help Bukharin. He had pleaded, in vain, for the adoption of a legal code by which to guide one's actions in the communist paradise, a plea which Stalin rejected as so much bourgeois rot and triviality. Bukharin and his associates were at the mercy of the one man who was the law and the state. Stalin gave them no respite. Rykoff drowned himself in vodka, Tomsky committed suicide and Bukharin with trembling fingers wrote tomes in praise of Stalin. When the time came Stalin had his day. Bukharin and Rykoff were convicted as traitors and a GPU firing squad satisfactorily closed forever a chapter for Stalin.

The Pilgrims to Mecca

Members of the inner circle of the American Communist party referred to Moscow as Mecca, and journeys to Moscow were called "Pilgrimages to Mecca." The American communists, and the communists of other countries also, on their arrival in Moscow were immediately taken to the OGPU office of the Comintern where the short, black-mustached Abram officiated. Before they were allowed to mingle in Moscow's communist society Abram collected their passports, photographed them and gave them new passports, stamped with the seal of the Comintern and countersigned by the Secretary of the Executive Committee of the Communist International. Abram's OGPU office functioned efficiently. In a country where red tape and disorder reigned in most offices, he kept his meticulously clean. A business atmosphere prevailed in a well-ordered room, full of sunshine and free of red tape. The passports collected were deposited in a huge safe with two massive doors. From the safe Abromovitch took the crisp, newly printed ruble notes which paid for Comintern expenses in Russia. The communists from abroad were not informed that by depositing their passports with the OGPU they were putting themselves at the mercy of the Soviet government, for without their original passports they were not free to leave the country.

The passports collected by Abram were afterwards sent to the passport mill of the OGPU where copies were made of them for use by the OGPU and other Soviet government and comintern agencies. Often the communists from abroad, without their knowledge, received for their own use the forged passports in place of the genuine ones. The American communists received free hotel accommodations, and a generous weekly allowance in Russian currency for their personal expenses during their stay in Mecca. This was supplemented with free banquets, refreshments served during meetings, free theaters and other amusements, receptions at clubs, factories and in the homes of prominent Russian communist officials. The trips the American communists took were organized, official trips, never unofficial ones. They saw only what the Russians wanted them to see and wrote what the Russians wanted them to write. A foreign communist in Russia enjoyed the feeling of being part of a powerful government. Most of them lived during their pilgrimage to Mecca in an imaginary world built up for them very cleverly by propaganda and association with the Russian communists. A few of them who saw beyond the tinsel preferred to play blind and to go along with the lie for political and material considerations.

The German Communists ranked second only to the Russians in influence at that time, and of that group Heinz Neumann towered over the other leaders in brilliancy of intellect. Heinz, the son of a Rabbi, had deserted the Labor Zionist movement and thrown in his lot with the Spartacus Bund of Rosa Luxembourg and the junior Karl Liebknecht, winding up finally as the close associate of Max Holtz, the firebrand and terrorist of the German Revolution. When the Holtz uprising failed, Neumann fled to Russia. A lad at the time, he arrived in Russia a physical and mental wreck, and tried to shut out from his mind the memories of the horrors through which he had passed by drinking himself into insensibility. He was attached to the Comintern where Bukharin quickly recognized the intellectual capacities of the lad and took him under his wing like a father, wielding tremendous influence upon the young man. Bukharin had him treated for alcoholism. What the doctors failed to accomplish Bukharin accomplished by patient persuasion. Neumann became a total abstainer.

A student, a prodigious searcher for knowledge, a shrewd political analyist and thinker, a prolific reader, an accomplished debater in German, French and Russian, and sociably a likable fellow, he soon became a power in the Comintern, the right hand of its president,

Bukharin. But the leaders of the German Communist party hated him and were jealous of his achievements because as the confidant of Bukharin, "der Jude Heinz" wielded greater influence in Comintern circles than they did.

Neumann succumbed to the political influences of Moscow and the moral degeneration of communism. He realized that a communist leader of the Comintern, in order to hold on to his position, must determine quickly in which direction the political winds blew from the Kremlin and act accordingly, regardless of convictions and personal ties and loyalties. When the political weathervane pointed away from Bukharin in the direction of Stalin, Neumann was among the first to join the Stalin caucus in the Comintern. He worked to destroy the very man who had rehabilitated him, and saved him from the deteriorating effects of alcoholism. When Stalin gave the signal Neumann did not hesitate to hurl his stinging invectives against the man who had been his best friend and had treated him like a son. He turned on Bukharin fiercely, so that Stalin and the Comintern pack would have no doubts that he had severed the ties forever between him and the man and comrade to whom he owed his life.

Neumann soon learned what many other communists, Russians and non-Russians, learned too late, that Stalin is the objective iceberg of communism, a man devoid of all feeling in the pursuit of his political ambitions. The men and women who today, out of fear, loyally serve him and his personal ambitions, tomorrow may be summarily liquidated. In Soviet Russia everybody owes allegiance to Stalin. Stalin, on the other hand, owes nothing to anyone.

In view of the recent exchange of charges and counter-charges between Russia and the Western powers, regarding who backed Hitler and to what extent, the following episode may be of particular interest.

Just before Hitler took hold of Germany, Stalin admired his handiwork in the organization of the Nazi party and the audacity he used in executing his orders. Stalin entertained the idea that by getting the Communist party of Germany and the Nazi party to collaborate with each other on behalf of a common program he could make a deal with Hitler which would give the Slav-Teuton combination control of the European continent and eventually domination of the world. The leaders of the German Communist party were called to Moscow and under Stalin's orders were forced to draft a program for Germany which included the main points of the Nazi program.

Hitler quickly congratulated the German communists and the Russians for endorsing his position.

Stalin sent the Germans back to Germany with instructions to undermine the Socialist-Democratic coalition in control of the German Republic by instigating armed uprisings and by acts of political sabotage that played directly into the hands of Hitler. Stalin went further. He ordered the German communists to seek a united front with the Nazis for the overthrow of the democratic government. And to see that the German Communist party carried out his directives, Stalin sent as his personal envoy to Germany none other than the former labor Zionist Neumann. No longer the Jew, but the Communist, the Internationalist, Neumann appealed on a program of extreme German chauvinism to Hitler's aryan hoodlums and to Streicher's Jew-baiters to join hands with the communists. Neumann sought also to get individual Nazis, especially group and district leaders and officers of the Storm Troopers, to join the German Communist party by offering them bribes and well-paying positions backed up with Moscow gold.

But Hitler at that time wanted to play a lone hand. He answered the pleas of Neumann and the German Communist party by asking them to give up the Communist party for a truly great German party, letting them know at the same time that only aryan communists would be admitted. Neumann's campaign went into reverse. Instead of the Nazis joining the Communist party many communists, especially from the youth movement, joined the Nazis. After Hitler came into power the movement of communists into Nazi ranks became a flood.

Thus it is extremely interesting to note that Hitler's hoodlums and the communist-trained terrorists were equally responsible for the subsequent reign of terror that was unleashed on the world. And it is additionally interesting when one realizes that it was solely because of Hitler's egotism that Stalin could only admire rather than actively participate in it.

Neumann returned to Russia. Stalin having no further use for him, his downfall followed rapidly. During the purges, in the prime of manhood, the OGPU liquidated him without much ado. He joined his companion Max Holtz in the Red Valhalla. Holtz, as a political exile in Moscow, did not see eye-to-eye with the Bolsheviks. The OGPU murdered him and gave out a report that he drowned in a lake when his rowboat capsized. His body was never found and no memorial meetings were ever held in his honor.

The pilgrims from America to Mecca who had given up their American citizenship to settle in the land of socialism were without exception a miserable lot. They besieged the representative of the American Communist party to the Comintern and the leaders of the Party who happened to be in Moscow with frantic appeals for permission to leave their communist fatherland and return to capitalist United States. They did not give the real reasons for their desire to leave Russia for then they would have to confess that they were dissatisfied with Russian conditions, a confession that would land them in prison as counter-revolutionary agents. All of them who were sick of the Soviet paradise went out of their way to explain how wonderful conditions were in Russia, how happy they were that they had come, and then gave all kinds of family and personal reasons why they should be given permission to return. After the Five Year Plan had been in operation and thousands of Americans went to Russia to build communism quickly, the Party leaders had their hands full handling the cases which came to their attention. One case, typical of hundreds of them, involved an automobile worker from Detroit. He donated his life's savings to the Party in order to get permission to go to the "Holy Land" to help Stalin build a socialist society in five years. In one year's time the bulky Ford worker with the round cheerful face lost his bulk and his smile. Clothed in rags he looked a haunted man who had lost his bearings as he pleaded his case to deaf ears that did not want to hear. To let him return to the United States involved the danger that he might tell the truth about Russian conditions. American citizens of Russian birth, the communists who went to Russia to help in the Five Year Plan, automatically became Soviet citizens the moment they landed on Soviet soil. The others, before they were assigned to jobs, were induced to give up their American citizenship and to become citizens of the Workers Republic of the World. By so doing they became Soviet citizens subject to the jurisdiction of the Soviet government and the Russian Communist party. The Russian Communist party bureaucrats in the factories and in the districts where these former Americans found themselves took special delight in taunting and torturing the Americans who asked permission to return to their native land, and held them up for derision before the Russian workers.

At the plenary sessions of the Executive Committee of the Comintern held in May, 1927, plans were worked out to make the Tenth Anniversary Celebration of the Bolshevik Revolution, to be held dur-

ing the month of November of that year, an elaborate spectacle and a
round of fetes for the spreading of communist and pro-Soviet propaganda in the capitalist countries, on a scale heretofore undreamed of.
The Soviet government set aside an enormous sum of money for that
purpose. Before the leaders of the American Communist party left
for home they held conferences with representatives of the Commissariat for Foreign Affairs. The conferences went over the names of
people in the United States who were to be invited by the various
departments of the Soviet government, by the Russian trade unions
and by the Comintern to come as the special guests of these government and communist agencies to the Tenth Anniversary Celebration.
The plan provided that large delegations from every country in the
world be sent to the Soviet Union. The American communists were
called upon to organize and send one of the largest delegations. The
Russian trade unions were to receive the names of American trade
unionists to whom to send invitations; the cultural departments of the
government, the names of actors, writers, artists, singers, etc.; the
educational department, the names of educators, teachers, professors
and scientists; the health department, the names of doctors, surgeons,
nurses, laboratory technicians, and so on all down the line. The Communist party, the Americans were told, must see to it that each delegation included a sufficient number of communists who could report on
the views and activities of the individual delegates and safeguard
Soviet and communist interests. The members of the delegations who
expressed a willingness to pay their own fare should be permitted to do
so, the Americans were informed; the others would have their fare
paid by the Soviet government and the government would pay all their
expenses during their sojourn in the Soviet Union. The representative
of the Foreign Office declared all the money necessary for the organization of delegations and financing their journey to Moscow would be
supplied to the Communist party through Comintern channels
established for that purpose.

The representative of the Foreign Office explained that the Russians had developed a skill in welcoming visitors and in psychologizing
them by playing on their vanity so that they saw through communist
eyes what the Soviet government wanted them to see. And laughing
he added that the wise neutral people who come to Soviet Russia with
an open mind to see for themselves generally accepted communist
propaganda at its face value and willingly put their names to statements and reports on matters they knew nothing about. Managing the

delegations from the time they left their native country until they reached the Russian border he insisted was the duty and responsibility of the American Communist party.

Speaking in German, he concluded: "People should be chosen for the delegations who will be useful in creating Soviet friendship in the United States. But the composition of the delegation must not be limited to this one objective. There are other important considerations, *nicht wahr?* For example, liberals, unionists, intellectuals and politicians who can be instrumental in extending the influence of the American Communist party when they return home, who can give the Communist party valuable organizational and political contacts should by all means be included. Try to get scientists, highly skilled technical men, engineers, and chemists who can be a source of scientific and technical help and information which we need badly. Finally include in the delegations such individuals who because of their contacts with government departments, with the military and large industrial establishments, can be of valuable assistance to the GPU."

The Tenth Anniversary Celebration came off according to plan. Stalin gave the visiting delegations, made up of thousands of men and women from all walks of life and from all parts of the world, a magnificent pageant. They were wined, dined, entertained and patronized like princes visiting a royal court. Behind the greatest show ever put on display, an army of communists were busy at work, watching the delegates, steering them, molding their opinions, getting them into the predestined grooves from which they were to carry on their work in their respective countries on behalf of the Soviet government and the communist world superstructure.

The communist leaders are always taking trips to Mecca where they report on their activities, submit to a review and criticism of their activities and reaffirm their allegiance to the almighty power which they serve. But the pilgrimages are not confined only to communists. Through the years, thousands of individuals from the United States, who are not communists, have either individually or in groups visited the Soviet Union for specific purposes without ever discovering that the Communist party had been instrumental in organizing the trips. The organization by the Communist party of pilgrimages to "Communist Mecca," with or without the knowledge of the pilgrims, is part of a well-conceived communist plan to build up support in the United States for communist causes and for the Soviet Union. By skillfully exploiting the pilgrimages the American Communist party has drawn into the orbit of communism many distinguished and influential Americans, some of whom have become either regular or secret members of the Party. By the use of these pilgrimages the army of fellow travelers has been considerably augmented and developed into a sinister force which hypocritically denies its communist character and subserviency to the Communist party.

Anna Louise Strong's Letter to Madam Sun Yat-Sen

Anna Louise Strong, born in Nebraska and educated in universities in the United States and Germany is a doctor of philosophy, an expert on city affairs and child welfare, educator and member of a school board, journalist, editor, foreign correspondent, lecturer at colleges and universities, author, poet, organizer of the Moscow *Daily News,* first English newspaper published by the Soviet government, and Soviet apologist and agent since 1922. She became enmeshed in the web of communism to such an extent that she could not free herself when her conscience dictated that she should. Though a woman of unusual ability, endowed with a mind of extraordinary intellectual capacities, yet she faltered and succumbed to the overpowering influences of communism on her mind and soul. She is one of a large army of intellectuals, molders of public opinion, who blindly serve tyranny and a cause which degrades mankind.

In 1927 Anna Louise Strong did not like what she saw in Russia. She was appalled by the Stalin regime. Shocked by the infamous methods used to destroy men high in Soviet life and unable to keep quiet about the treatment of Trotsky, she wrote a letter to Madam Sun Yat-Sen in which she opened up her heart to her friend. She complained bitterly about the turn of events in Russia. She was apprehensive about Russia's future. In words written with passion, expressing a condition of great emotional strain and a conscience deeply hurt, she appealed to Madam Sun to intercede on behalf of justice. One got the impression from the reading of the letter that Miss Strong stood at the crossroads. She had to choose between following her conscience or serving the cause which stood above the individual and his emotional reactions. It was clear from the tone of the letter that the woman did not have the courage to make a decision.

In writing to Madam Sun Yat-Sen, Miss Strong blundered. The widow of China's liberator, living in Moscow, had not the capacity for independent thinking. She lived in a private world of her own in which she was isolated and pampered by the Russians. The communists had a firm hold on the old lady. It was impossible for any one to break down her faith in communism and her loyalty to the Soviet government. Had the letter reached the old lady it would have brought a rebuke instead of an appreciative response to the appeal for justice of a disheartened and troubled woman.

But the Russians took no chances with Madam Sun Yat-Sen. They surrounded her with servants who pried into her affairs. Mail to and from her had to pass through GPU channels first. Strong's letter fell into the hands of the GPU. The investigation which followed involved the Politburo of the Russian Communist party, the Foreign Office, the Communist International and the American Communist party.

A GPU man attached to the Commissariat of Foreign Affairs called upon the leaders of the Communist party to discuss the request of Miss Strong, who was in the United States, for permission to return to the Soviet Union.

"We have intercepted a letter Miss Strong wrote to Madam Sun Yat-Sen indicative of strong Trotskyist leanings on her part. We have given the matter careful consideration. The lady is a very valuable person and capable in her field. We would not like to lose her. What do you think we should do about it?"

The Americans explained that Miss Strong was not officially a Party member but that she had always cooperated with the Party and carried out Party orders when she was in the United States. "She made it a practice," the Americans said, "to visit the national office of the Party upon her return to the United States to acquaint herself with Party policies and to find out the intentions of the Party leaders." They added that just because she paraded in the States as a fair-minded liberal who did not belong to the Party, her writings and lectures assumed an air of objectivity that was exceedingly effective. The Americans insisted that everything should be done to keep the lady in line for she had done trojan work in building up pro-Soviet sentiment and in getting a large number of liberals and innocents to support the Party and its campaigns.

The GPU man of the Foreign Office explained that the members of the Politburo and the Foreign Office felt as the Americans did about her. "She evidently could not make up her mind after she wrote the letter and must have had a change of heart. That is why she asked permission to return. She evidently wants to continue to work with us. But let me assure you the GPU and the Foreign Office are not stupid. Comrade Strong has committed an indiscretion so we will have to find ways to compromise her in order to keep her under our thumb. In the meantime, comrades, we will file this utterly stupid letter from an emotional woman in our archives and say absolutely nothing about it. Furthermore we are not afraid if Comrade Strong visits Madam Sun. We have taken great pains to give her our version of the Trotsky controversy. Regardless of what Comrade Strong may say, Madam Sun will defend our position."

Miss Strong got her permission and returned to Moscow. Never again has she balked at the Party line nor criticized the affairs of the Soviet government. Hers has been a paean of perpetual praise for the actions of the communist world superstructure, reaching high C in praise of Stalin and the Soviet dictatorship. She travels periodically between Moscow and the United States and appears before audiences as a non-communist who leans heavily on the pro-Soviet viewpoint and adheres strictly to the Party line.

Losovsky: the Boss of the Profintern in Action

The international obligations of the Communist party crowd the calendar. These examples are typical of almost all years: The American Communist party leaders went to Moscow in May, 1927, to attend the plenary sessions of the Executive Committee of the Comintern, called in communist circles the ECCI. In November of the same year they attended the Tenth Anniversary Celebration. At the beginning of 1928 a large delegation attended the World Congress of the Profintern and in the summer of the same year a still larger delegation consisting of practically all the top leaders of the Communist party, including its candidate for President of the United States, went to Moscow to attend the Sixth World Congress of the Communist International. At the beginning of 1929 an Extraordinary Commission of the Communist International headed by Molotov and including Stalin and Manuilsky held sessions in Moscow for over six weeks to consider the internal affairs of the Communist party of the United States. In between these dates lesser affairs took place, some in Moscow, others in Berlin and in Paris, dealing with Communist International actions and campaigns, which leaders of the American Communist party had to attend. The European obligations were supplemented by conferences and meetings held in Mexico and Latin America and far-off China. Before the outbreak of World War II the steamers leaving New York harbor for Europe usually carried communists aboard, with faked or forged passports in their pockets, enroute to attend to their inter-national obligations. The communist world superstructure was grinding away in high gear, its concept of one world, a communist world, actually in operation.

The American Communist party sent a large delegation to the Fifth World Congress of the Red Trade Union International. I was made chairman of the delegation. Supposed to be a delegation of trade unionists, not one of us was chosen by a union; all were selected by the Political Committee of the Communist party. The money for our passage and expenses to and from Moscow came from the treasury of the Profintern. Hotel, traveling and living expenses, in Russia proper, came from the same source.

The Congress sessions were held in the large Trade Union Hall of the Columns. Losovsky, the big boss of the Congress, arrived at the hall in the latest deluxe model Rolls Royce limousine, a pearl-blue beauty with exquisite upholstery. A liveried chauffeur opened the door for him as he stepped out of his private rolling palace to direct the affairs of the world's toiling and exploited proletariat.

The chiefs of the Russian Communist party and the Russian officials of the Comintern despised the man, for he came to the Bolshevik party after the October Revolution, as a Menshevik, which is not a good recommendation. Yet he survived all his enemies and lived to see many of them die ignominious deaths. How did he do it? Because he assumed the role of a minor Talleyrand in the communist movement. The man was shrewd and crafty, an organizer of great ability, an inveterate intriguer and as tough and callous as saddle leather. He took personal insults with a smile, was the one man who looked pleased when you spat in his face. Losovsky transformed the Profintern into a personal machine for his own political purposes. His profintern agents kept him posted on what was going on in the communist movement throughout the world. Though head of an organization which was supposed to concern itself with trade union matters, he played communist politics first and attended to his union business afterwards. Lacking the calibre or the background to stand on his own feet, he realized that for his own security he had to attach himself to the leadership of another. He, therefore, early hitched his wagon to Stalin's star and the hitch paid good dividends.

Losovsky is a dirty, unscrupulous fighter, with the cunning of a cat and the treachery of a rat. He instructed the official interpreters of the Congress to garble the speeches of those who opposed him in such a way as to discredit them. He issued press releases based upon the garbled translations. When the injured parties protested he promised to have retractions printed but the retractions never saw the light of day.

He spent money extravagantly to bolster up his personal machine. He turned over to Foster, who acted as his personal agent in the United States, hundreds of thousands of dollars, for which Foster had to account to no one. Foster spent large sums of this money freely to build up his faction in the Party. Losovsky did not object, for he considered such money well spent when it went into the building of the American section of his personal political machine. Nor did Losovsky bother to find out how much of the money thus appropriated by him for trade union purposes was misappropriated for personal purposes. The more a communist leader stole the more certain was he of his loyalty. It was Losovsky's method of bribery and corruption. Money scandals involving the disappearance of large sums of money have been common occurrences in the international communist movement.

All the countries of North and South America were represented by large delegations. When other Russian Communist leaders had their eyes focused mainly on Europe and Asia, Losovsky had his focused on the Americas. In the fertile fields unplowed by the others he went to work and built up for himself a strong following. Months before the Congress opened, Mink, who paraded as Losovsky's son-in-law, a taxi driver from Philadelphia, toured the South American countries for delegates. He rounded them up by hook and crook and dispatched them to Moscow. Most of them did not know what the Congress was all about, but they knew how to deliver a speech prepared for them and, most important, how to vote right.

The Congress marked an historical turning point in Communist trade union policy. The Congress, in anticipation of the launching of the Five Year Plan then being drafted by experts for the Politburo, made a sharp left turn, departing from the policy laid down by Lenin in 1920, directing the communists to bore from within the conservative unions. Losovsky called for a break with that policy. He directed the communists to leave the unions and organize revolutionary unions, red communist unions.

In between Congress sessions the delegates were treated to a continuous round of elaborate parties, entertainments and banquets. The

Russian unions did the entertaining. The communists were not bothered by the fact that the Russian people were tightening their belts, that women formed lines in front of cooperatives at four o'clock on cold Russian mornings, shivering for hours, waiting for the stores to open in order to get a pint of milk. Meat was unobtainable and beyond the reach of the Russian worker. Privation and want showed their ugly faces.

The communists sat in warmly heated dining halls, listened to sweet music, devoured costly food and guzzled liquor by the bucketfuls. The banquet given by the Profintern in the Hotel Metropole climaxed the weeks of revelry. Around a spouting water fountain shimmering in the bright lights of hundreds of colored bulbs tables were set to accommodate over 2000 guests. Each table contained large platters of princely food, arranged in towering designs, garnished with tropical fruits and fresh vegetables out of season. In between the platters were stacked bottles of the rarest and most expensive vintages of Russia, wines, champagnes, brandies, vodkas, cognacs, whiskies and liqueurs. A large orchestra hidden behind the palms supplied music. Here the shabbiness of Moscow, the drab life of its struggling people, disappeared in a show of affluence worthy of the pompous royal court of Louis XIV of France.

Losovsky appreciated the value of sex in politics. He picked his feminine staff for their glamour. They arrived at the banquet dressed in exquisite low-cut evening gowns of silks and satins, sporting ermine and mink capes, displaying sparkling jewels, their naked arms laden with exotic gold bracelets encrusted with expensive gems. Here was no proletarian festival. The nervous waiters, sweating profusely, danced around tables making sure of serving every whim and desire of the guests. As soon as one bottle was emptied another replaced it. Toast followed toast. Entertainers appeared before the drunken guests —singers from the opera, sword dancers from the Caucasus, jugglers from the Crimea, peasant troupes from the Ukraine. But the reveling communists drowned out the performers with laughter and shouting. The guests danced furiously around the fountain. Comrades were thrown into the air in the Russian custom, amid shouts and hurrahs, and caught in extended arms. Fights broke out amongst the tables as the hours wore on. From a tame frenzy the party developed into a bacchanalian festival. Drunken men and women threw each other into the cold water of the fountain. They screamed and yelled as they rolled over each others' wet carcasses on the slippery dance floor.

Bedlam reigned as the hall resounded with the strains of the orchestra and the discordant singing of drunken voices.

With the dawn, the affair broke up. The weary advance guards of the proletariat dragged their heavy, shaky feet out of the hall. Crimson were the heavens over the Kremlin walls. In the restaurants workers sat holding hot tumblers of unsweetened tea in the palms of their cold hands. Here and there one bit into a bulka or a piece of black bread, just doughy bread with no butter or jam smeared on it. They stared at the bleak walls and munched away. The god of materialism reigned and inequality stalked the land.

Dark Clouds—Moscow 1929

Russia is a country that is supercharged with politics. And Moscow, the bastard amalgam of western European civilization and a mixture of Byzantian and oriental cultures, is the political hot-bed of the world. In no other capital does so much information on world affairs flow into the departments and organizations which deal with world problems. Information comes to Moscow from the world's capitals and from the remotest corners of the globe. Moscow gets the reports on matters of major importance all the way down the scale to matters of no apparent importance whatsoever. This information is sifted by special departments in the Foreign Office, by the bureau of the Communist party of Russia dealing with International affairs, and by departments of the Comintern and Profintern which still function in spite of the announcement that the two organizations have been abolished. In addition Moscow receives from the communist parties of all countries special reports and interpretive material on the political, social and economic affairs of their respective countries. An army is at work gathering information for the Soviet government which no other country can afford to duplicate. In the United States this army consists of the 100,000 members of the Communist party, a host of fellow travelers, agents of Soviet military intelligence and of the NKVD, the members of all Soviet governmental diplomatic and commercial agencies—everyone connected with the Communist party and with the Soviet government acts as a spy and gathers information for Moscow. The voluminous information received by Moscow is, after it is thoroughly sifted, centralized for digestion by a staff of political and economic experts and presented to the Russian rulers in such a form that they can get a comprehensive picture on world affairs by which to guide their foreign policy.

Though there may develop differences of opinion on foreign affairs, the government publicly presents only one viewpoint, for it cannot very well be otherwise in a totalitarian state. There is just one individualist in Russia and he is Stalin. On foreign affairs as well as on domestic affairs he must make the decisions, lay down the policies. Everybody else must carry them out. That is why, when the political winds blowing out of the windows of Stalin's office change, the city of Moscow reacts to the change immediately. When changing political winds presage foreboding times ahead, the population feel it in their bones and a communist arriving from abroad senses it immediately.

The Moscow of 1929 was not the Moscow of 1927. The Comintern building looked as if a hurricane had swept through it. Bukharin was gone, a has-been. Piatnitsky, the head of the organization department, who built up the Comintern, afraid that Stalin would put his head on the chopping block, suddenly developed a serious illness and had himself sent off to the Crimea to a sanitarium and thus stayed the hand of Stalin. New faces appeared in all the departments. The old ones disappeared. Nobody inquired why or what happened to them. The leadership of every communist party had been reshuffled or was in the process of being reshuffled. The list of condemned communists against whom stinging resolutions of rebuke had been passed by the Comintern and endorsed by all Communist parties included the outstanding leaders of Communist parties and famous figures in the Comintern.

Woe to the condemned. No one greeted them. No one dared to speak to them, not even their closest personal friends of the day before.

Many communists from the smaller nations and from all European countries, with the exception of England, who were suspected of opposition to Stalin or who failed to measure up to the requirements set by Stalin or had been too friendly with Bukharin were, against their will, detained in Moscow. The involuntary exiles were permitted to stay on in their rooms in the hotels and received the regular stipend given communists during their stay in the city. They were given absolutely nothing to do. Their trek each day to the Comintern building, where they waited in the commandant's room for a pass to see the Comintern officials in order to have their cases considered, proved useless as the days dragged on into weeks and the weeks into months. The comrades they knew well refused to be seen with them or to talk to them. Their letters were confiscated by the GPU and they received no letters in return. Though they had the freedom of the city and were not confined behind iron bars under lock and guard, they were worse than prisoners, for not one of them knew his fate. Doubts turned to fear which assumed monstrous forms and which, with the boredom of isolation, undermined their mental equilibrium. Two Czechs, in the Hotel Bristol, sought freedom from the physical and mental torture of their solitary confinement by committing suicide together. Others too strong to surrender did likewise. Many recanted, swore allegiance to Stalin and threw themselves at the mercy of the Comintern. They accepted perilous missions to Korea, Japan and other graveyards for communist emissaries in preference to exile in Moscow as an ostracized communist. Many were liquidated by Stalin's personal GPU guards following which a report was given out that they met death by accident. In the purges which followed later, large numbers of foreign communists in Moscow were rounded up and liquidated without the formality of a hearing or trial. In the Comintern apparatus only a few remained—the few who were able to fix up their fences and remain in Stalin's service.

The case of the German communist Brown should interest Americans. Brown, real name Ewart, exercised considerable influence in the German Communist party. With the ousting of Brandler and Thalheimer, and later of Ruth Fischer and her husband Maslov from the leadership of the German party every one in the Comintern knew that Brown was in line for the leadership. Because of his proletarian background, the active role he played in the early communist uprisings in Germany, the honesty and sincerity of the man, Brown had the overwhelming support of the rank-and-file members of the German party. But Comintern politics ruled otherwise and Thaelmann, the bully, was chosen instead.

Bukharin liked Brown, for Bukharin was the one man in the Comintern to whom the human bonds of friendship sometimes counted. Bukharin appreciated the fact that Brown, the uneducated worker, by dogged determination, had under great difficulties educated himself and become a cultured person. In 1927 Brown headed the Anglo-American Commission of the Comintern and was subsequently appointed by Bukharin as the C.I. Rep to the American Communist party. His mission in the United States finished, Brown returned to Moscow and obtained permission to resume his activities in the German party. A money scandal involving Thaelmann and his brother-in-law in the stealing of hundreds of thousands of marks from the Party, a scandal which Brown was instrumental in exposing, gave him a majority of the Party's Central Executive Committee and the leadership of the Party.

But Brown committed the cardinal sin of acting independently on who should constitute the leadership of the German party, without first taking up the matter with Stalin. In a rage Stalin took the matter up in the Politburo of the Russian party and ordered the entire Central Executive Committee of the German Communist party and its district leaders and important functionaries to pack up and leave for Moscow immediately. Stalin vindicated Thaelmann and rebuked the Germans in the severest terms. Brown and those supporting him who had been most active against Thaelmann were removed from their posts and ordered to remain in Moscow.

Brown joined the involuntary exiles in Moscow. Confined to the Lux he was afraid to go anywhere. His girl friend, a buxom, good-looking German stenographer working in the Comintern apparatus, loved him madly. She defied communist precedent, ignored the ban of ostracism placed on her comrade, and slept with him and comforted him. The brave girl did much more: she fought on his behalf with all the important people in the Comintern.

Brown heard that the leaders of the American Communist party had arrived in Moscow to argue their case before the Comintern. He knew the Americans well and sent his girl to arrange for a meeting.

About 1 A.M. there was a knock on the door of the room in the Lux where the Americans were meeting. A frightened girl entered, dressed in blue silk pajamas. She spoke in a whisper. Wouldn't the American comrades who were under fire also meet with Comrade Brown? "He wants me to let you know that he is very anxious to meet his American friends because he feels strongly that what he has to tell will be of benefit to them. Should you be willing the meeting can be arranged, with the greatest degree of secrecy."

Some of the Americans present objected most strenuously to a meeting with Brown. They were Moscow residents at the time. The leaders, however, who knew that they were up against it, agreed to meet with the doomed man.

The meeting took place a few hours later in the same room. The Brown who entered was not his jovial and happy self. Before the Americans, in the dimly lighted room stood a broken and frightened man who hesitated a few moments before he took a seat. The boyish, mischievous eyes were bloodshot. The lips trembled as he spoke halt-ingly, with great emotion and effort. He steadied himself, straining every nerve in his body to prevent a breakdown in a torrent of tears. He measured his words as he spoke in German:

"Comrades, to continue the fight is useless. The Comintern is too powerful. In spite of everything it does, the decisions and actions with which we disagree, it is still the Comintern, the one organization in which the toiling masses of the world have faith. It is their only hope. Comrades, I have been dealt with most unjustly, but as a revolutionist, a communist, I must not allow my personal feelings to stand in the way of the greater and more important issues confronting mankind. I would be unworthy of being called a communist if I did.

"Comrades, being a communist, I cannot go against the Comin-tern, for the Comintern is my life. I was born a worker, whatever I am I owe to the workers' movement. As a child of the movement there is no life for me outside of the movement. Since Stalin saw fit to remove me from my Party I have struggled with myself many nights and days. The inner struggle, for a comrade in my position, is a pain-ful experience, the nights one spends alone with frightful thoughts and the darkness. I have weighed everything; I have reviewed the past and tried to fathom the future and have come to one definite conclusion—to submit. That is the course I have chosen. For me to do otherwise means to accept an existence without an anchorage—death. Comrades, I speak most earnestly. I will crawl on my knees before the Comintern. I will do everything they ask me to do just so long as I remain in the fold. The years will blot out the past, of that I am certain, and the future will vindicate me."

He paused for a few moments. The bloodshot eyes looked glassy in the glow of the small incandescent bulb. The lips parched under the strain of his emotional effort. He rested his hands on the table to stop the fingers from shaking. They kept on quivering. The man who wanted to live not for himself but for the cause finally summoned up enough strength to conclude:

"Comrades, and I say it with the deepest sincerity, do not fight against the Comintern. I plead with you to do what I have decided to do, submit. Don't allow yourselves to be destroyed and lost forever to the movement. I implore you, summon the courage to throw yourself under the discipline of the Comintern. The future, comrades, is with the Comintern and not with you."

Brown went to the Comintern. He ate crow. He condemned himself and his past actions in Germany and elsewhere. He lashed out against the Americans who refused to submit. The poor man counted on a movement and not on the man who was the movement. Stalin never forgave Brown for trying to oust his flunky from the leadership of the German party. The Comintern decided to keep Brown out of Germany and out of the affairs of the German party. He was sent on the most dangerous missions to India, the Far East and to Brazil. In Brazil he fell into the hands of the Brazilian government, which had been tipped off that he was plotting a revolution for the overthrow of the government. The Comintern gave Brown orders to do just that. He was arrested with Pires, the Secretary of the Brazilian Communist party, and sentenced to a long prison term, the Comintern did little to defend him. Deserted by the movement he served, he rotted away and died in a Brazilian dungeon. The score for Stalin was settled.

Moscow's Communist Underworld

Moscow, like every other capital in Europe, has its underworld. The pickpockets on the Tverskaya are so numerous and have such slippery fingers that few foreigners escape having their pockets picked. There are robberies, hold-ups and murders galore. Beggars, bands of Gypsies, orientals from the Far East, Mohammedans from the south, a colorful army of cut-throats and bandits converge on the city from all directions and give the "Militza," the Moscow police, no end of trouble. When darkness comes, the Tverskaya, Moscow's Broadway, and many other busy thoroughfares fill up with overpainted prostitutes ranging from teen-agers upwards, who crowd the sidewalks and boldly accost every male they approach. They satisfy their customers in the dark alleys off the side streets. Those who can afford it go to the public bath houses where accommodations are provided without any questions being asked. But this underworld is overshadowed by the political underworld which grew large and ominous as Stalin began tightening his grip on Russia.

The Communist political underworld germinated in the soil of bolshevism, sprouted out of the soil which nurtured it and blossomed forth in all its glory when Stalin got complete control of the Russian Communist party. He transformed the Party into his own personal instrument; transformed the Central Control Commission and the district Control Commissions, empowered to try and judge Communist party members, into his personal agencies for persecuting Communist party members. Stalin now had an instrument in his hands, an instrument he soon proved he could use effectively, through which he could force communists to agree with his policies or face the consequences of being hailed before the Control Commission as criminals plotting the destruction of the Party and the State. Stalin's control commission system has been inaugurated in every communist party and functions in the United States precisely as it does in Russia, with this difference—it has not the authority of an American Soviet government to back up its decisions, and Eugene Dennis, the General Secretary of the Party, is not yet the Stalin of America.

To fully understand the communist political underworld and to grasp its entire significance it is necessary to have some knowledge of how Stalin, the political boss operates, for his methods are today the accepted methods throughout the communist world superstructure. Stalin carefully selects as his subordinates, for leading positions in the Russian Communist party and in all other parties, those whose records can be used against them, should that ever become necessary. When the leaders of the Russian Communist party and the Comintern clamored for the removal of Losovsky from the Profintern, Stalin stepped in and retained him, for he could always use Losovsky's record as a Menshevik to kill him politically. He kept the crook Thaelmann in the leadership of the German party for the same reason. When Piatnitsky demanded that Browder be punished for causing the Comintern to lose millions of dollars in China, Stalin personally stepped into the case, saved Browder and made him the leader of the American Communist party.

Stalin, the astute political boss, does not depend on the use of one tactic to keep an iron grip on the Russian party and the world communist movement. He uses many tactics. He instituted the "dog-watch-dog" system in the Russian Communist party and later throughout the international communist movement, by giving every important Communist party official an aide whether he wanted one or not. The aides, appointed by Stalin, spied on the officials, and the officials, also Stalin men, spied on their aides. The aides did much more than just spy on their chiefs. They insisted that their chiefs energetically carry out the Party line by making suggestions and introducing motions for the record. With insidious cunning records were built up, by the aides against their chiefs, of incompetence in office and failure to carry out the Party line. Thus Stalin has filed away in his archives a case against every Party official of importance. All he has to do when he wants to remove an official is to produce the record and call upon the aide to prefer charges against his chief before Stalin's hand-picked Control Commission.

As the political underworld took on shape its methods and forms were applied to the communist parties of all other countries. From the day Gussev, the personal representative of Stalin, arrived in the United States in 1925 the American communist leaders lost the little independence they enjoyed.

From 1924 to 1929 Stalin busied himself with building up a private army of his own within the OGPU. His association with the police set-up and methods of the Soviets goes back to the early 1920's when he headed the Commissariat of Inspection. His acts then, which aroused the ire of Lenin, acts which the sick Lenin did not have the power to suppress, foreshadowed the future developments. From among spies and stool pigeons of the Commissariat of Inspection, from the ranks of the Party and from the OGPU, Stalin carefully selected the individuals who were to organize and officer his private OGPU army. The men who made up this army, known in Party circles as Stalin's OGPU guard, had to accept loyalty to Stalin above all other loyalties. The guards came into existence without any official government decision ordering their organization and without the approval of the Russian Communist party. At first they operated without official standing. The early raids upon the Trotskyists from 1927-1929 were carried out by Stalin's private guards without the matter being brought to the attention of the Politburo. Soon Stalin's private OGPU guard assumed functions that transformed it into a state within a state, which dominated the affairs of the Russian Communist party, the Soviet government and the OGPU of which it was a child. Its sinister authority extends beyond Russian borders into every country in which the communist world superstructure has an organization. The Communist party of the United States obeys its dictates. Through this agency of the political underworld Stalin holds the reins of the world communist movement firmly in his hands.

The dissolution of the Communist International in 1943, Stalin's gesture to President Roosevelt, which F. D. R. took at its face value, did not mean that the Russians agreed to put an end to Communist propaganda and activities in other countries. It simply meant that the affairs of the Communist International in the United States were to be transferred to the supervision of the political underworld, a change which has tied up the Communist party more directly with the OGPU than heretofore.

The political underworld has been responsible for the elimination of Stalin's foes everywhere. The assassination of Trotsky, the mysterious disappearance of hundreds of communist oppositionists in Europe, Asia and America attest to the efficiency of the global criminal operations of this camarilla of spies, assassins, bandits and political blackguards.

An American Builds Up Soviet Industry in Siberia

A successful American businessman, an outstanding technician in his line, Russian-born and a former democratic socialist, fell under the spell of the propaganda associated with the Five Year Plan. He actually believed that the Soviet government, through the Five Year Plan, put the principles of socialism concretely into practice. Overcome by a desire to help in a constructive way in the building of socialism, he sold his lucrative business and converted all his property and assets into cash. Thereafter he negotiated a deal with the Amtorg Trading Corporation that he be allowed to go to Russia to help them reorganize and establish, on a sound technical and business basis, the manufacture of the products he knew so much about. Having severed his ties with capitalism he embarked overjoyed at the prospects of his practical socialist mission.

On a cold winter day in 1930, he arrived in Moscow. The head of the department in charge of his activities met him at the station. After depositing his luggage at the hotel, his chief invited him home for dinner. On leaving the hotel the American businessman was escorted to a brand new limousine. The back seat being occupied by the chief's wife and two other persons he rode with the chauffeur who had held the door open for him as he entered the auto.

He greeted the chauffeur with a friendly smile. "Tovarich, I am an American. I am very glad to make your acquaintance."

But the chauffeur was not communicative. He just nodded his head and attended to his driving.

"Tell me, tovarich," continued the American, "how are things in Russia now that the Five Year Plan has been launched? You know, in America, things are not so good. Factories are at a standstill. Millions of workers are without jobs. Because we can produce too much people are starving. I'd like to have an opportunity to talk to you about it since you are a worker. Perhaps you will get an opportunity to come to see me at my hotel tonight after the dinner is over?"

"Sorry, tovarich," replied the chauffeur, "I will not be able to come," the tone of his voice giving evidence that he was annoyed by the conversation. The American businessman did not understand.

The elaborate and luxurious quarters of his chief seemed incongruous in a land struggling to build socialism and establish equality for all. He gaped with astonishment at the woman who took an expensive mink coat off her shoulders. For a moment he imagined that he was not in a workers' country but at a bourgeois affair on Park Avenue. The lady of the house smiled at him and took him by the arm. "My dear Amerikanski tovarich, since you are going to stay with us for a long time, allow me to acquaint you with the ways of our country. It is not proper to take servants into your confidence or to talk to them on the basis of social equality. They may get exaggerated notions about their importance. Servants, after all, must know their place."

The American winced. He could not credit this evidence that snobbery based on class distinctions prevailed in the land of socialism. The American traveled from city to city and from province to province putting factories in shape, introducing better techniques, teaching workers how to do their jobs properly and saving tons of valuable raw material from spoiling because of improper handling and storage. He saved the Soviet Union millions of dollars and had the factories turn out a product from which Russia realized millions of dollars more from the export trade. He had a job to do and did it well, giving the land of socialism his invaluable experience and knowledge. But what the American idealist who loved the plain people of Russia saw in his travels broke down his spirit, and doubts replaced the positive convictions he had once held.

An assignment, his last, found the American in charge of a factory in an isolated Siberian town situated in a timber producing area. The factory hugged a wide, rushing river. From the windows of his office the American could see the river banks, the edge of the forest and the railroad station.

Hunger gripped the countryside. The workers who managed to come to work barely dragged themselves along. The river abounded in fish, the common food of the workers. But the fish in the stream belonged under socialism to the government fish trust. The fish trust had to meet the increased quotas set for it in the Five Year Plan. Workers caught fishing were arrested and severely punished as enemies of the state, for stealing state property. The fish trust, determined to meet its quota, to satisfy the record, cast its nets into the stream and hauled out mountains of fish. But the starving populace of the surrounding communities got none of it. Fish piled high waited for railroad cars in which to be transported inland. The freight cars did not come. The sun beat down upon the fish, heavily guarded by soldiers to prevent the people from stealing some of it. The fish rotted. The stink rose to the heavens. When the fish had rotted so that it was no longer suitable for human consumption it was carted away and dumped on garbage heaps.

The Siberian winter set in and snow piled deeper and deeper on the frozen countryside. Long freight trains arrived, not with food or goods but with a human cargo—a cargo of peasants. The American watched the scene from his office window. OGPU chiefs, in fur hoods covering heads and ears, and dressed in long fur coats which brushed the white snow that crunched beneath each step of their heavy fur-lined boots, were shouting and waving their hands in a bedlam of loud orders and confusion. A regiment of OGPU soldiers, warmly dressed, surrounded the freight cars and the railroad station with fixed rifles. The American grabbed his hat and coat and hastened to the station. He watched the unloading of the carloads of human flesh. He saw peasants from the south of the Ukraine, accustomed to mild balmy weather jump out of the cars. Miserable wretches they were, dressed in tatters with paper and rags tied around their feet. There were among them old men with white patriarchal beards as well as the middle-aged and young. They were the hard working peasants of the soil who had resisted collectivization and had been rounded up by the OGPU and shipped to Siberia to help gather in the lumber to meet the enormous requirements of the Five Year Plan. The trees had to be cut down in the cold wastes of Siberia. In order to meet the quotas set, the peasants were rooted out of the soil, herded into filthy box cars like cattle and shipped to the frozen wilderness of Northern Siberia to work as slaves in the lumber camps managed by the OGPU.

Tears welled in the American's eyes as he watched the despondent, lost men come out of the cars, their shivering frames hunching against the icy fingers of the cold north wind. There was no weeping, no complaining. The figures of the doomed stood in silence, silhouetted against a bleak gray sky while the curses of the OGPU rent the air.

One long winter day followed another. The American had accustomed himself to the lonely scene. He stood at his window and looked beyond his vision in search of an answer for his troubled soul. Every day there were stiff-frozen corpses in rags. The Siberian winter was now reaping the harvest. The OGPU delivered the rigid human icicles that once were men on a flat springless cart drawn by two horses. At the place of burial the horses stopped. The driver tilted the wagon over with a long wooden bar, and the dead peasants found peace and security at last.

The American businessman who loved the common people could not stand what his eyes saw. It was not morbidity that made him look at the scene. Inside him was a force beyond his control, one that gave him no peace. He hugged the window like one obsessed, to see the peasants arrive and the corpses buried. Perhaps he thought that an accumulation of imprints upon his mind would give him the answer he was seeking. The American broke down. His hair turned white prematurely. Deep lines formed on a face that before was smooth and unwrinkled. Socialism, he had always believed, must be measured by human values, in the good it brings to the common man. He suddenly came to the realization that in Soviet Russia socialism operated in defiance of human values and rested on a foundation of unprecedented human misery. The void that remained, when the ideal upon which his spiritual life depended was shattered, frightened the man. Penniless and disillusioned, he returned to America.

The Tyrant

Stalin presented the 1929 Party conference with a grandiose plan for the industrialization of Russia and the development of agriculture along socialist lines. The conference had before it a blueprint of socialism, a scheme of planned economy never before entertained by any major power. Hopes ran high. The communists pledged themselves to tackle the job to transform Russia into a mighty unconquerable industrial country. The fact that the communists were convinced that war would soon come to the world hastened the adoption of the plan, for the communists believed the war would be directed against them. They figured that to survive a war they must have guns, tanks, airplanes, explosives, and the machines and raw materials with which to turn them out. Criticism of Stalin's plan was therefore easily swept aside.

Before two years had gone by, the breakdown of industry, the curtailment of the manufacture of light industry and consumers' goods, the frightful war against the peasantry to force them to accept collectivization of agriculture and the extraordinary measures taken by the OGPU police state to force the population into line, created such resentment, so much discontent, that the regime of Stalin hung in the balance. Red Army units made up of the sons of peasants were sent into the villages to shoot peasants. Many of them rebelled. Assassinations of communist officials were frequent occurrences. In any other country not ruled by a totalitarian dictatorship, the man responsible for policies which brought such calamities upon his country would have been removed. Under cover there was plenty of grumbling in Russian Communist party circles, among the military and in the government offices. Had Stalin at the height of the crisis taken full responsibility for what had befallen the country, he might have been removed and another dictator put in his place.

But Stalin did not admit he had made a mistake. On the contrary he emphatically declared that his policy was correct and the only policy for Russia. He lashed out against the small fry in the Russian Communist party, the petty officials, the dumbheads as he labeled them, who did not understand the policy and made a mess in carrying it out. By such an attack on the mass base of the Russian Communist party, Stalin put the entire membership under fire. It must be kept in mind that in Soviet Russia, the Communist party is the motive factor of Russian political life, the dynamic driving force in its economic structure and in the government. The effects of his attacks against the Communist party membership created a most desperate situation for Stalin. The usual cleansing of the Party was now not enough, for to permit those driven out of the Party by the "chiska" to remain at large constituted a threat to his power should they be organized against him. Stalin was left no other alternative than the purging of the Communist party organization from top to bottom. In firm control of the OGPU, he decided to use it ruthlessly, without mercy and decisively. The Society of Old Bolsheviks, Lenin's patriarchal guardians of communist orthodoxy, was swooped down upon like a den of criminals and its members were either shot or sent to concentration camps in Siberia to waste away the few days remaining of their lives. Great heroes of the Russian Revolution were thrown into dungeons, forced to confess that they were traitors and then shot. Every section of the Russian Communist party from the highest committee, the Politburo, down to the smallest nucleus was carefully combed by OGPU agents, and communists suspected of opposition to Stalin's policies were by the hundreds of thousands hustled off to OGPU dungeons where they were grilled and tortured and finally either liquidated or sent off to concentration camps. Stalin emerged the ruler supreme, omnipotent, hailed by those in the Party who survived as "the cosmic ruler of the universe."

The names of the prominent Bolsheviks who died in an insane stupor because of the special measures the OGPU used against so-called communist traitors are legion. History has these names on record. But history has not recorded how or why these men signed their lives away.

The Method

The question is often asked, "How does the OGPU do it?" What sinister methods do OGPU inquisitors use to make outstanding communists confess to the commission of fantastic crimes against the Soviet government? Why did old Bolshevik revolutionists, like Bukharin, Radek, Zinoviev, Kamenev, Sokolnikov, Tukhachevsky, Rykov, Krestinsky and many more like them, who defied persecution during Tsarist days in courageously fighting for their opinions, capitulate to Stalin by self debasement? They went to death, each one of them signing his name to a confession which, if true, damned them as diabolic, unprincipled plotters—traitors who deserved their punishment.

But the confessions were too much of one cloth, the same thread and the identical patterns going into all of them. That is what makes their veracity unbelievable. Then why did these communist revolutionaries play such degrading, such cowardly roles before Stalin's political police?

Finding an answer to the above questions have stumped political thinkers and psychologists as well. It has been said that Yagoda, the skilled pharmacist who headed the OGPU, and by whose handiwork many of the confessions were obtained, had established a special chemical laboratory in which toxicologists produced deadly, quick-acting poisons and drugs to debilitate the functions of the brain and nervous system. The liquidation of Yagoda, on his own confession, as the instigator of the poisoning of Gorky and others establishes this fact. The demise of Yagoda does not mean that the laboratory he had established has been abolished in the OGPU. It still functions, carrying on research into the delicate mechanisms of the brain and nervous system and how certain drugs can affect its functions one way or another. Drugs may have been used to transform the brains of the victims into putty in the hands of the OGPU.

Some have held that the victim is confined in a specially constructed cell that is painted in striking colors and surrealist designs in such a way that the confined person loses all sense of form and distance. The cell appears to have no walls, ceiling or floors. The prisoner feels that he is caught in a horrible kaleidoscopic whirl of brightly colored geometric projections, which are perpetually changing their forms, colors and positions. Such cells were actually used by the OGPU in Loyalist Spain during the Spanish Civil War.

The appearance of the men in court during the mass trials belied the use of drugs to undermine their sanity. Not one of them looked like a man who had been driven into a state of psychopathy because of months of isolation in a monstrous, colorful, whirling surrealist cell. Evidently the OGPU used other methods upon them, methods just as diabolical, which forced them to capitulate and confess. To understand the power of the OGPU over communists, the communist mind must be first understood.

The men who confessed were, most of them, loyal communists who had devoted a lifetime to the movement. They had lived in poverty, had experienced great hardships and had spent years in prison and in exile. They knew what it meant to be suppressed and hounded by the police. The mere act of suppression or police brutality could not break their spirits. They had the courage to fight for their convictions. Yet they failed to stand up and defy the suppressive measures used by the Communist party and its political police against them.

Persons who have never been members of the Marxian movement cannot comprehend the power wielded by Marxian ideology over the individual. Under communism the grip of Marxian ideology becomes even stronger because it is bolstered up by the power and grandeur of a Marxian political state. Under communist rule, therefore, the ideological control of the human mind is so strong, and the associations surrounding that control so powerful, that few individuals can break with it decisively. Many who break with communism, who leave the Communist party and refuse to abide by its discipline, are unable to free themselves from the ideological concepts of communism, with the result that they continue to think and react like communists. They remain Marxians even though they break with communism and because of that fact the communist movement continues to have a hold on them psychologically and ideologically.

This fact explains why many socialist Marxists, who are anti-communist, who for years have been the object of communist attacks and persecution, in such critical political situations as we have in Europe, accept the communists as a progressive working class force and unite with them against the so-called anti-working-class reactionary opposition. European socialists have often preferred to go into coalitions with the communists than with legitimate democratic forces, even though modern history has given them ample proof that once the communists get power they will ruthlessly eliminate the socialists who do not bow before their rule.

If Marxian ideology has such a strong hold on ex-communists and socialists how much stronger must be its hold on the communist faithful, especially on the Russian communists who have made a Marxian revolution in Russia and have put their communist theories into concrete form. To drive communist ideology out of the minds of such men is practically impossible. Take the example of Leon Trotsky: Persecuted by the communist state he helped to establish; driven by its ruler from one country to another; his supporters forced to commit suicide, purged, hounded and murdered; the communist press of all countries filled with lies about his activities; charges concocted against him as a traitor who conspired with Fascists and Nazis for the overthrow of the Soviet government—and yet, though the communist Frankenstein which he had built up was crushing him, though he recognized the police character of Stalin's communist regime, he nevertheless remained a prisoner of communist ideology to such an extent that he failed to see that the inevitable consequence of a communist, totalitarian dictatorship was the flourishing police state of Stalin. Trotsky blamed Stalin and continued to support the system that made Stalin the personal expression of its virtues and vices.

The OGPU, understanding the communist mind, started with the premise that the Russian communists Stalin ordered them to purge were ideologically communists and slaves to the Communist party. In dealing with the communist mind the chiefs of the OGPU stood on firm ground, for they were all communists and members of the Party.

The holy trinity worshipped by the communists consisted of Marx, Lenin and the Communist party. After 1929 the name of Stalin was compounded with that of Lenin, transforming the holy trinity into Marx, Lenin-Stalin and the Party. The Russian communists look upon their Party as the supreme organization not only of the Russian proletariat but also of the world's proletariat. Stalin, speaking of the Russian Communist party, declared: "Without the Party as the essential guiding force, there cannot be a lasting and firmly consolidated dictatorship of the proletariat. Because the Russian communists understand this important and fundamental role of the Communist party upon which the existence of the communist government is predicated, their belief in the Party and their worship of the Party organization exceeds rational understanding."

To communists, the Communist party organization is much more than a political Party. Their conception of the Party is that of an organization of unlimited boundaries and omnipotent power which deals with every phase of life. The Party therefore stands above the individual. In the eyes of Communist party members, Party decisions are vested with supernatural omniscience. Here we have the strange paradox of modern times: that communists, Marxian materialists, with a pronounced atheistic outlook on life and history, adopt a profoundly religious attitude towards a temporal man-made organization. To the communist the Party is Godly and fanatically worshipped as such. The communists inside Russia and outside have built a halo around the Russian Communist party, holding that the Party of Lenin represents the final word in wisdom and cannot err. Russian Communist party decisions, no matter how they are arrived at, are considered infallible by the communists of all countries. And every one of the Russian communists purged by the OGPU had such an attitude towards the Party.

The question necessarily arises, how does the OGPU operate to get confessions from communist leaders who are not ignorant rank-and-filers, but intellectuals with brains and minds of their own?

Stalin is an astute political tyrant. He is no wavering idiot. He realized that in order to hold on to his power in the face of the débâcle of his policies, he had to demonstrate to the country that his enemies in the Communist party who opposed his policies were in league with reactionaries and Fascists from abroad to wreck his program of socialist reconstruction in order to overthrow his regime. Since the foreign plotters were beyond his reach and could not be seized by the OGPU it became absolutely necessary to produce the Russian plotters. The Russian plotters had to be sufficiently important personalities connected with the Communist party and the Soviet government to dramatize the extent and seriousness of the plot. Only by producing such figures could an hysteria be whipped up in the country by which Stalin and his supporters could consolidate their positions and retain their power.

So, loyal old communists, renowned for their Bolshevik orthodoxy, were seized by the OGPU during the dark hours of the night, surrounded by a squad of OGPU soldiers with rifles mounted with glistening bayonets, and marched off to prison chambers reserved for political offenders. The OGPU now gets to work on the mind of the imprisoned communist in its clutches. The arrested communist is isolated, kept in a cell by himself for weeks. No one sees him and he sees no one. Contact with the outside world or with counsel is denied him. He is given no papers and no books. The man is an animal encased in a box. He has the pleasure during his conscious hours of staring at the walls and thinking.

The eventful day arrives when he is taken from his cell for an interview with the OGPU chief assigned to the prison. The conversation is cordial, like that between one comrade and another. The victim complains against his isolation. He wants to know what he is being charged with. The chief on the other hand is very sorry for what has happened. He assures his victim that it will not happen again. The OGPU man ponders the question: Why has the man before him, his old friend in the Party, been detained? "Oh! that matter will become apparent after due discussion," he replies. A discussion follows on the situation in the Communist party. The chief reports that in spite of all difficulties the Party policy is working out remarkably well. He tells the prisoner that it is too bad that he failed to see the wisdom of Stalin's program. He finds fault with the prisoner who as an old Bolshevik should have known that the Communist party comes first and that once the Party makes a decision it must be obeyed and carried out. The discussion proceeds in a friendly manner and covers a wide range of subjects, from inner Party politics to personal matters. Nothing definite is reached during the first conversation. In dismissing the prisoner the OGPU chief shoots a passing hint that perhaps the comrade will think matters over. He assures the prisoner that in the meantime he will see to it that papers, magazines and books are supplied to him. The game of cat-and-mouse is on. The prisoner returns to his cell puzzled for he has learned next to nothing on why he is being detained. He has his suspicions. But he has not yet been handed the official charges. He has not seen or heard the indictment.

Life in solitary now becomes a little more pleasant. He receives Party papers which carry glowing accounts of the tremendous progress being made by the Party under the leadership of Stalin. He gets official Party reports which substantiate what he has read in the press. The reports from the Comintern prove that not only the domestic but also the international policies of Stalin are working out admirably well.

From time to time the lesser chiefs of the OGPU visit him. They supply him with cigarettes, drink a glass of tea with him, pass on some confidential bits of information and discuss inner Party affairs. All of them want to know why he broke with the Party. They give enthusiastic accounts of the strides the Party is making, of the successes achieved in overcoming difficulties and defeating the oppositionists in the Party and among the non-proletarian elements in the country. The conversations, bolstered up by printed and typewritten material supplied to the prisoner, have an important objective—to build up the importance of the Communist party and to play down the position of the individual as picayune in comparison.

The mind of the communist prisoner is being carefully molded by the OGPU in such a way that he realizes that the Communist party is engaged in a terrific struggle to build up socialism. Stalin is pictured as the great hero and leader, who had the vision and the courage and the organizational genius to mobilize the country for socialist construction in agriculture and industry. Under Stalin the Soviet Union would soon outstrip the leading capitalist countries, including the United States. Stalin forges ahead in spite of the opposition of saboteurs, inside and outside of the Soviet Union. It slowly dawns upon the prisoner that his detention might have something to do with the sabotage of the Five Year Plan.

What the prisoner did not know but would soon find out was that the OGPU had manufactured a case against him and other prominent comrades, involving them in a conspiracy against Stalin and the government.

After weeks of conversations and discussions the prisoner is informed that he, together with others, has been arrested for conspiring against the Soviet government in the formation of an anti-Soviet bloc. The smooth words of the OGPU now give way to threats. A demand is made that the prisoner confess to the part he played in the conspiracy. The prisoner listens dumbfounded.

The prisoner professes his innocence. The accuser reiterates. He demands that the prisoner sign a confession and threatens to keep him in solitary confinement until he does. During all these lengthy proceedings the accused has not had the advice of counsel and has had no contact whatsoever with relatives and friends on the outside. The OGPU lets him know that in Russia it is not only the accused who pays for his crimes but also his family and dear ones as well. The principle of collective guilt is a monstrous weapon of terror in the hands of the OGPU. The prisoner shudders but refuses to give in. As he protests his innocence and demands justice he is sent brusquely to his cell.

More pressure is exerted against the prisoner. Secrets about his personal life are disclosed to him. The OGPU presses him to confess or else they will make public everything they know about his personal character. The threat of character assassination by disclosing ugly secrets about his habits has been used in the Russian Communist party and in the Comintern repeatedly to hold communists and fellow travelers in line. Prominent artists and writers have been forced against their will to spearhead communist united front movements by the threat that if they refused their perverse sexual habits would be disclosed. The communist prisoner knows this and shudders.

The prisoner is dragged out of his cell at all hours of the day and night. He is awakened when he falls asleep and is interrogated in his cell. The OGPU does not employ physical torture against him by stringing him up by his thumbs, or by welting him across the back or by making him kneel on his bare knees on a damp cement floor covered with caustic, cutting, salt crystals. Against prominent communist political prisoners such methods are not used. The pressure is mental torture that seeks to exhaust and destroy the mind and the spirit. The incessant banging away through conversations, the interruption of ideas by accusations, questions, interpretations, bits of news, etc., the endless hagglings and discussions kept up for weeks, are bound to break down the mental fiber of the strongest-willed mind.

The communist prisoner rails and weeps. He pleads his innocence. He proclaims his loyalty to the Communist party and to Stalin. When they appeal to his communist integrity he calls attention to his long record as a Bolshevik and a disciplined Party member. The OGPU derides his record. They harp on the one theme, "Confess to your crimes. The quicker, the better." The prisoner remains adamant.

A day arrives when the OGPU presents the protesting communist prisoner with a choice bit of information. The prisoner is seated comfortably in the chief's office, opposite the chief, who is surrounded by his aides sitting in easy chairs. The prisoner is handed a cigarette and a glass of hot tea. A wan nervous man faces his inquisitors. The OGPU chief begins:

"My dear comrade, I am sorry you did not take my advice in the first place. Had you confessed it would have saved us and you a lot of trouble and pain."

This declaration is followed up with an account of the conspiracy with which the prisoner is charged. Every detail is stressed. The chief concludes by informing the prisoner that his best friend and collaborator has denounced him for the leading part he played in the criminal plot against the Soviet government.

The prisoner recognizes an old police trick used during Tsarist days. When the Tsar's political police wanted to break down a stubborn revolutionist and make him plead guilty they confronted him with a story that his friend had betrayed him to the police. The prisoner, an old communist war horse, does not fall for such tricks and he tells the chief off accordingly.

"But my dear comrade, you are badly mistaken. Allow me to assure you it is not a trick at all. We of the OGPU are communists. We do not use Tsarist police methods," replied the chief. "I have here, as you see, the written confession of your friend. You can verify the signature, if you like, and read it."

Trembling hands grab up the typewritten pages. He reads but cannot believe his eyes. "The whole thing is preposterous. How could a comrade put his name to such an infamous document fabricated out of lies? It cannot be true."

"But it is true," calmly remarks the chief. "I realize that the disclosure of the plot is a shock to you. But why not be objective, comrade, and discuss it. The Party, I warn you, takes it very seriously."

Discussion of the document begins. Hours and hours of discussion without end during which the prisoner is shown more signed confessions, more documents to discuss and argue about. The prisoner is stubborn. He refuses to yield after days of arguments.

In a final effort to break down the prisoner's resistance he is taken to a room and left by himself. After wondering what the new move is all about a fellow conspirator is brought in, his friend who signed the confession. The door is bolted and the two are left to themselves. One eyes the other with distrust and skepticism. They are not certain of each other. Besides both know that in OGPU rooms the walls have ears. The first prisoner does not dare open his mouth. The "criminal" who has signed his name to a long confession, having nothing to lose, begins. He asks personal questions and complains of the treatment he has received. The prisoner who has not confessed listens. Through his mind rushes the thought that he must talk to some one who is not a member of the inquisition. He is also worried about the confession that he is certain his friend has signed under duress, and must find out the reason why. Finally he summons up enough courage to ask:

"Did you sign a confession?"

"Yes."

"How could you put your name to such lies?"

"But I am not the only one who has confessed. Haven't you? All the others have. If you read mine you must have read theirs also."

"What you have done is heinous. What made you involve your friends in such a preposterous frame-up?"

"Be rational, comrade. As old Bolsheviks we have always maintained that the needs of the movement come first; that the Party stands above the individual."

"But the Party cannot do that to us. It has not the right to ask us to agree to our own destruction."

"You should have thought of that before you began opposing the Party. Don't you realize comrade, we have made a terrible mistake. Stalin was right and we were wrong."

"But I have admitted my mistake. I capitulated and came out in support of Stalin's policies. What more does Stalin want?"

"So did we all confess our errors, but we did so with our tongues in our cheeks. We entertained reservations at a time when the Party, our Party, was engaged in a desperate struggle with the enemies of socialism. At such a time, a time of civil war, there is no room for reservations. The Party has the right to demand and get the undivided loyalty of every Party member. We must act like soldiers in the front lines. The commander gives the orders. We must obey regardless of the consequences to ourselves. That is the A B C of communism."

"But my dear comrade, you are not talking to a child who has just joined the Consomols. You are talking to a man who knows the Communist party because he helped to organize it and therefore knows the political limitations of the Party."

"Don't talk like Zinoviev. You know what happened to that fool when he allowed his vanity to overrule his communist judgement."

The prisoner who has not yet confessed keeps quiet. The one who has confessed eyes him sharply. The first one is thinking about Zinoviev, Lenin's closest friend and collaborator. He had been arrested too, had confessed, was then brought to trial, found guilty, and executed a little over a year ago. Frightful, he thinks, that I should be in the same predicament. He asks himself, "What is going on in Russia that such outrageous methods must be employed by the Party against its own members?"

The prisoner holds his throbbing temple between the palms of his hands. He feels the blood spurting through his arteries. If he could only end the madness of it all, the worthless futility of his existence.

"I see that you are distressed," remarks the second prisoner. "So was I. Why prolong the agony? Don't you realize that life for us has run its course? Why continue to oppose the Party? Who are we and what are we without the Party? Fading shadows without life and substance. Bourgeois individualistic sentiments will get us nowhere. Pity for ourselves will lead us into an emotional swamp supported by the quicksands of fantastic illusions. Don't you understand in this tragic hour of our careers that we cannot put our individualism above the collective will of the movement? Come comrade, be rational."

The prisoner who has not yet confessed paces up and down. Thoughts like hammer blows seem to beat against the walls of his head. Into the moments of silence crowds an eternity. The blood rushes in a hot stream through his body. Drops of sweat gather on his forehead, yet a cold chill runs down his spine. He feels he is going to collapse, that reason and sanity will leave his battered brain. "No," he reasons, "I cannot go on this way. I cannot live down a life which has ended in a colossal mistake." His knees shake. He feels he will fall in a dead faint to the floor. He steadies himself at the table. He looks through wild bloodshot eyes at the other prisoner, the comrade who just stares at him. They do not speak. Two doomed communists face each other. One has already resigned himself to his fate. The other has not yet been able to make up his mind. He finds his tongue and screams for the jailer.

The prisoner is taken back to his cell. He drags his heavy feet through the long corridors. The OGPU, in the adjacent room, have heard everything. They are fortified with additional knowledge. That knowledge they will use in a psychological war of nerves to batter down the will of the man and to force him to capitulate. The weary prisoner who drags his tortured corpse along will have no peace of mind until he does. No trial will take place until his signature is on the dotted line of a confession which will be dictated by the OGPU and upon which the prisoner will elaborate after he is resigned to his fate.

The psychological war against prominent communists is usually conducted over a period covering many years. The Communist party conducts that war energetically day after day without a letup and without mercy. The war against Bukharin started in the fall of 1928 when Bukharin in his article in *Pravda,* "The Notes of an Economist," dared by innuendo to criticize some of Stalin's economic policies. A year later, in a letter to the Central Committee of the Russian Communist party, Bukharin recanted and capitulated to Stalin. But the war against him as the leader and mouthpiece of the right wing continued. Nine years later, in 1938, he was brought to trial a confessed "traitor" to his country, who "collaborated" with the Nazis and was executed. The psychological war against Bukharin ended when the bullets of an OGPU firing squad spattered his blood against the red brick walls of the OGPU prison courtyard. A year later Stalin signed the pact with Hitler and began a period of collaboration with the Nazis which ended only with Hitler's invasion of Russian territory.

CHAPTER SEVEN

ORGANIZED CONFUSION

AS HAS already been pointed out, Stalin took over the American Communist party, lock, stock, and barrel, in the middle of May, 1929, by a series of decrees promulgated by him and read before the ECCI by Molotov. At Stalin's direction the Soviet Foreign Office called in the press services supplying news to the United States and gave them the story to cable to the "capitalist" press before the decisions were officially cabled to the *Daily Worker* and the membership of the American Communist party. Stalin's personal rep, endowed with dictatorial powers over the American party, his pockets stuffed with Moscow gold, left immediately for the United States, traveling on forged passports. He operated in the United States under the aliases of Carl Wall and Williams.

Three factors now determined the life of the American Communist party. Stalin's viceroy, Wall, ruled the Party with an iron hand. The economic crash of 1929 created new and greater opportunities for the communists. The Five Year Plan for building socialism in Russia dictated the political line which the American communists had to pursue on the domestic scene.

The line of the Five Year Plan, in the Comintern, the decisive line of political policy for all communist parties, was known as the line of the third period. What was the third period? The Comintern held that the third period as distinct from the second period marked the end of capitalist stabilization in the world, the period in which capitalism would march to its grave to be buried by the victorious revolutionary hosts of communism. It marked the beginning of the period when the communists would proceed from defensive to offensive action. For the communists the third period marked the beginning of a revolutionary era, in which the communists were to take advantage of the world crisis of capitalism to foment civil strife in their respective countries, with the objective of developing the disorders into a revolutionary situation leading to the destruction by force of capitalist rule and the assumption of power by the communists. Stalin emphatically insisted that the United States was not exempt from the developments of the third period. He lashed out against the American communists who maintained that the United States was not faced with an immediate revolutionary situation, by branding them as exceptionalists who did not understand the third period. They were cowards and apologists for American imperialism, he declared, who refused to see that the United States was on the eve of decisive revolutionary developments.

Following the meeting of the ECCI, at which Stalin took over the affairs of the American Communist party, a joint meeting of the Comintern Executive and the Profintern Executive formulated plans for the launching of a revolution in Germany for the overthrow of the Weimar Republic. Emissaries were selected from all the important communist parties and ordered to proceed to Germany to assist the German communists in organizing the revolutionary uprising, so that they could learn from first-hand experience the dynamics of revolution for future use by their own parties.

But what the non-Russian Comintern emissaries to Germany were not told was that Stalin's plans for Germany called for the stirring up of wide-spread revolutionary disturbances throughout the Reich short of actual revolution. Other motives dictated Stalin's policy. Practically half of the leadership of the non-Russian communist parties had been purged out of the Comintern. The Comintern was badly split and demoralized. Creating a revolutionary situation in Germany and dramatizing it would put new life and enthusiasm into the Comintern and thereby justify Stalin's assumption of power over the Communist world organization. It would at the same time make good propaganda at home for consumption by the Russian masses who were being called upon to make tremendous sacrifices for the Five Year Plan in order to complete the socialist stage of the communist revolution in Russia. It did not matter to Stalin and the rulers of the Comintern that the German masses were being deliberately misled into revolutionary battles in which thousands would lose their lives. The artificially created communist revolutionary uprisings in Germany in the early thirties before Hitler came into power, inspired by the internal politics of the Comintern, were directed against the democratic government of Germany and helped to weaken the German democratic base, so that the victory of Hitler became inevitable.

Under the lash of C.I. Rep Mikhailov, alias Williams, Stalin's boss of the American Communist party, the Party was overturned and re-organized in order that the American communists could play their part in the historically important developments of the third period. Dr. Jacob Mindel, a morbid dentist, chairman of the Control Committee of the Communist party of the United States, ferreted out the heretics in the organization. The dentist's actions as presiding judge of the highest judicial tribunal of the Communist party were supervised by the Lett, Charles Dirba, the technical head of the Organization Department and the OGPU man in the Party. Dr. Mindel, the high executioner, with the watch dog, Dirba, sitting close by, interrogated the Party leaders and all communists who played important roles in unions, fraternal organizations, veterans organizations, colleges, churches, schools, women's organizations etc., to determine their loyalty to the Communist party line and Stalin. The inquisition carried on to purge the Communist party was conducted under the innocent and misleading name of the "Enlightenment Campaign." Those whose answers failed to satisfy the C.I. Rep or the Control Committee were thrown out of the Party and denounced in the Party press as renegades and traitors to the working class. The Communist party leaders were required to back up their oral statements of loyalty with written confessions of faith, and these in turn were also published in the Party press. When the Party purge was completed Dr. Mindel received orders to leave for Moscow where he was to give a report in person to the Comintern and the OGPU of the work of his Control Commission. In Moscow the work of the Control Committee of the American Communist party was integrated with the OGPU, and Mindel, a full-fledged member of the OGPU, returned to the United States. The purge successfully carried out, the American Communists were now ready to face the test of the third period. In the beginning of 1930 the Communist party made the following declaration:

"The struggles of 1930 and the coming period which will undoubtedly be of much greater proportions than those of 1929 will be predominantly political struggles with the class lines sharply drawn—with ever larger sections of the working class facing, not relatively small sections of the bourgeoisie, *but locked in struggle with the capitalist class as a whole and its most powerful instrument of domination—the state power.*"

These were no empty words. The communists meant what they said. They were translated into directives for action in which violence and bloodshed followed. By 1929 the Communist party operated a large number of revolutionary industrial unions which were affiliated with the Trade Union Unity League, headed by Foster. The TUUL, as the league was called, acted as the American section of the Red International of Trade Unions and constituted the Trade Union Department of the Communist party. The important communist unions were: the National Miners Unions, the Needle Trade Workers Industrial Union, the National Textile Workers Union, the Marine Workers Industrial Union, the Amalgamated Food Workers of America, the Food Workers Industrial Union, the Auto and Aircraft Workers Industrial Union. The communist unions in the TUUL were joined by communist inspired and organized opposition movements operating in the A F of L and independent unions. In addition, the communists organized special committees which conducted campaigns for the organization of the unorganized workers into unions to be dominated by the communists, in the steel, chemical, oil and other basic industries. This extensive trade union organization, through which the communists were making a serious bid for economic power, was thrown into the activities of the third period campaign.

The economic depression of 1929 did not deter the American communists. When the legitimate trade unions, because of the increase of unemployment, were bankrupt and too weak to fight, the communists stepped into the trade union picture and proved they could arouse unionized and unorganized workers to strike militantly and ferociously for unionization and better conditions. Defying the impotent labor leaders, the communists instigated strikes in automobile, coal mining, textile, shoe, clothing, marine transport industries and in agriculture. They took full advantage of the economic depression years and demonstrated that they knew how to capitalize on unemployment, economic chaos, social stagnation and discontent. When, in 1930, the unemployed in the United States reached the 10,000,000 mark, the communists were feverishly working to organize the unemployed and thereby establish their hegemony over them. They were out to convert the struggles of the unemployed for work and relief into predominantly political struggles against the United States government. They were going to demonstrate to Moscow that the period of decisive revolutionary struggles was not confined to the European countries alone but included as well the most powerful citadel of capitalism— the United States.

Fight or Starve!

On January 11, 1930 a manifesto was issued to the unemployed calling upon them to organize against unemployment, the speed-up, and wage cuts. The central slogan of the manifesto printed in bold headlines read, "WORKERS DON'T STARVE! FIGHT!"

Simultaneously the organization of the communist youth, the Young Communist League, called for "active participation in the liberation struggles of the oppressed peoples against imperialism," backed up by "revolutionary work in the bourgeois army through the organization of nuclei [Communist party cells in the army], revolutionary circles and groups."

In January 1930 a large delegation of American communist leaders headed by Foster were in Moscow getting last-minute instructions on how the American communists were to foment disorders in the countries of the Western Hemisphere.

On January 14 the communists began the organization of unemployed councils throughout the nation under the auspices of the Trade Union Unity League. Communist party headquarters in all parts of the country were thrown open to the unemployed. Those who were homeless were permitted to sleep in the headquarters and were served hot coffee and sandwiches by friendly communist girls.

On January 15 the Communist International issued a call to all communist parties throughout the world to organize impressive revolutionary demonstrations of the unemployed. The date was finally set for March the 6th in order to give the communists of the various countries sufficient time to complete the preparations involved in getting the unemployed to demonstrate.

The communists gathered the unemployed together by whatever methods brought results. They harangued them with speeches. They fed them. They assigned them to odd jobs in the unemployed campaign or around Party headquarters, giving them twenty-five cents and a half dollar a day. They fought to get relief for them at welfare agencies. A thousand and one subtleties were used—successfully.

Spearheading the unemployed movement were communist men, women and children who made up a motley crew of poorly dressed, haggard looking, yet fierce and determined fighters. They swooped down out of nowhere on state capitols, city halls, court rooms and welfare agencies demanding relief. They carried placards with flaming slogans, shouted diatribes against the capitalists and the government and were spurred on by cheer leaders.

These demonstrations were not spontaneous or accidental. Every one of them was carefully planned. The communists knew exactly what they were after. Official Comintern instructions stated: "These demonstrations should not make for the traditional meeting place but for such places as government buildings, parliaments, town halls, barracks . . ."

What kind of demonstrations the communists should organize was also the subject of official directives from Moscow which stated: "The appearance of the demonstrations is very important. They must have a revolutionary and proletarian aspect, they must be effective. This requirement is met by demonstrations straight from factories of workers in their working clothes, of cripples and invalids of the imperialist and civil war, demonstrations of women workers, orphans, etc. . . ." Moscow demanded that the demonstrations be militant fighting demonstrations. "It may be observed," went on the instructions, "that a worker who does not yet dare fight against the police is ready to fight against the strike breaker . . ."

The instructions which called for a fight against the police detailed how the communists, through fraternization and by infiltration, could undermine the morale of the armed forces. The communists were given orders to organize their own military formations under the camouflaged name of "Workers Defense Corps." "These defense corps," emphasized Moscow, "should not be secret fighting organizations within the Communist party but united front organs of Communist, non-Party and Social-Democratic workers. If possible they will be legal, if not they must be established despite their prohibition."

The Workers Defense Corps in the United States were organized secretly. They were not given an appropriate name and put into uniforms as the communists did similar organizations in the European countries. Conditions in the United States were not yet ripe enough for such a bold move. Instead they were organized into groups of eight, consisting of communists and non-communists. Every group of eight had a leader who was called a captain. The leaders were all communists who received special training and took their orders from the Communist party. The leaders controlled and trained their groups of eight. The steel rod which held the defense corps together was the members of the secret strong-arm organization which was organized by the Communist party following the end of the Furriers Strike.

The members of the defense corps were taught how to fight the police. They were trained how to strike the leg of a horse with the sharp corner of a stick or iron bar in order to throw the mounted policeman. Instructions were given on how to resist policemen by mugging and slugging them. They were shown how to disarm the police by seizing their clubs and blackjacks. Members of the defense corps, like their comrades in the Red Front in Germany, were egged on to get souvenirs of their fights with the police, such as police badges, brass buttons torn from uniforms, caps, clubs etc. These were cherished by the defense corps fighters and proudly displayed before envious communists at Party headquarters. Girls were instructed to stick long pins into their berets which at a moment's notice they could pull out and use effectively against horses, police and detectives as they surged back and forth with the crowds fighting the police. The premeditated idea was to infuriate the police, to call forth retaliation by the police, forcing them to resort to extreme police brutality in order to create a scene of mob frenzy compounded of acts of bloody violence against swirling, screaming, frightened, scattering forms of men, women and children.

Women communists were taught how to yell hysterically, in rasping, fiendish calls, in order to create a panic and give the impression that a massacre was taking place. Some fell in an assumed faint before policemen; others jumped at the police and tore at their faces with their nails. Strategically scattered among the demonstrators were the men and women communists who supervised the demonstration. They understood the psychology of the mob, knew how to keep the demonstrators in line and how to whip up their enthusiasm and courage. They acted among the demonstrators like cheer leaders at a football game. They yelled the slogans, got the mobs to repeat them and egged them on to fight and resist the police. Close to the head of the procession marched the Communist party strong-arm men, the communist advance guards who feared nothing. If a line of police attempted to halt the demonstrators, the communist cheer leaders loudly called upon the demonstrators to push onward amid boos and curses against the police. The members of the defense corps watched their captains for the sign to go into action and the captains waited for the signal from the officers of the advance guard. At a given signal from the Communist party leader in charge, the demonstration would go into action. Suddenly a few wiry communists would spring out of the mob. With lightning speed one would welt a policeman on the back of the neck. Another would snatch a club out of a policeman's hand and begin swinging it over the owner's head, while another would heave a rock among the police. Pandemonium would break out. The demonstrators would press through the police lines. Now the militant revolutionary battle of the hungry unemployed against their "heartless government and its brutal police" was on. Fighting would break out on all sides. Screaming, hysterical women would fall into dead faints. A new force suddenly would come upon the scene—the communist red cross. Wounded demonstrators would be grabbed up by members of this group and taken to first aid stations at which red nurses and communist doctors officiated.

To the Communist party demonstrations such as these are serious business for through them the communists are participating in the initial stages of the American communist revolution. The communist rank-and-file are getting a needed baptism under fire and learning at the same time what will stand them in good stead later on. During the depression years, Americans who watched the communist unemployed demonstrations, witnessed in a miniature form how a communist revolution can start and develop into a full scale operation to bring down in ruins the powerful structure of the United States government.

Credit for coining the central slogan for the unemployed campaign, "Starve or Fight!", must be given to a widow, a communist who inherited millions from her husband. Left childless, she induced the head of the New York Communist party organization, who was a member of the Central Executive Committee and the husband of one of her secretaries, to sleep with her. Part of the connubial deal involved generous contributions and large loans to the New York organization which was badly in need of money. When the baby was born, the mother refused to disclose the name of its father, claiming she had chosen a mate who physically and mentally assured a healthy progeny, that her baby was a eugenic baby. The scandal of the eugenic baby rocked the top circles of the Communist party because the wife of the New York leader, herself childless, brought charges against her employer that she had used her money to buy and corrupt an outstanding Party leader. The Politburo told the complaining wife, a Party member, to keep her mouth shut and informed the rich widow that the Party would not interfere in her personal affairs and that she would be protected from all scandal-mongers. It was the mother of the eugenic baby, this woman surrounded by affluence, who, in the luxurious comfort of her drawing room, wrote the pamphlet on the unemployed in which she coined the phrase "Starve or Fight!" The pamphlet published by the Communist party appeared under that name.

The communists pounded into the heads of the unemployed that the capitalist world was against them, that the police, the courts, the armed forces, Congress and the President of the United States were the enemies of the unemployed and hostile to the demands of the jobless for adequate relief. Communist speakers and organizers harangued the unemployed with the idea that if they wanted to eat and to work at decent wages they had to fight. The communists marched up and down the streets in demonstrations of the unemployed shouting in unison without stopping, "Starve or fight! Starve or fight! Starve or fight!" ad infinitum.

On the eve of March 6 the Communist party manifesto to the unemployed called upon them to demonstrate; it called upon the workers in the factories to lay down their tools and join the demonstrations of the jobless. It called upon the workers to resist and fight the police and to defend the Soviet Union, the worker's paradise, where unemployment does not exist.

March 6 made history. Over 100,000 people congregated around Union Square in New York City. Communist plans called for a fight with the police. The comrades had received instructions on how to provoke the police. The fight with the police started as planned. It was the signal for the three top communist leaders of the Party, Foster, Minor and Amter to grab a taxi and proceed to City Hall to present the demands of the unemployed to the Mayor. The demonstrators on Union Square who were being chased and clubbed by the police were ordered to proceed at once to City Hall to back up the delegation to the Mayor. The communist delegation, though they failed to see the Mayor, insisted on going through with their demonstrations. Every attempt on the part of the communists to hold a meeting on the steps of the City Hall or near by was broken up by the police. The defense corps broke up into groups which fought the police all over City Hall Park. Foster, Minor and Amter were arrested. But the communists were satisfied. They had made national history. They proved to the unemployed that the police and the government opposed them. The communists had their baptism in blood and demonstrated to the Comintern and the Russian people that the workers in the wealthiest and most powerful capitalist country in the world were ready to fight against starvation and their capitalist oppressors.

New York was not the only city in which communist-directed demonstrations of the unemployed took place on March 6. Demonstrations occurred in hundreds of cities from New York to California and from Duluth down to the Gulf of Mexico. The communists had succeeded in rallying millions of workers to follow them on the unemployment issue. From March 6 on they were the undisputed leaders of America's jobless millions. Success in this field gave the communists a distinct place in national, state and local politics. It opened for them the front door into the most significant trade union development, that of the organization of the C.I.O.

The communists were good generals. They did not rest on their March 6th laurels. They immediately issued a call for a National Unemployed Conference to be held in Chicago on July 4, for the purpose of forming a consolidated national movement of the unemployment. The July 4 Conference was ushered in by violent demonstrations and bloody battles which took place on the eve of the conference in all parts of the country.

On June 29 a fight broke out between Garveyites and members of the Communist party and the Young Communist League who were staging an open air rally in Harlem for the purpose of enrolling unemployed Negroes as delegates to the July 4 Conference. When the police stepped in to prevent a riot the communists attacked the police. At the end of the bloody battle, a Negro communist, delegate to the Chicago conference, lay in the gutter dead from a bullet wound.

Another open-air demonstration next day in New York's Latin-American quarter resulted in a furious battle. The communists wrested the clubs from the policemen and started swinging them over the policemen's heads. The police drew their revolvers and started shooting. A Latin-American worker, Gonzalo Gonzales, was shot.

The favorite song in the Comintern was that of the German Communist party, *Blut Muss Giessen*. "Blood Must Flow" had become a living reality for the American communists. The Chicago July 4 Conference opened with a riot in which the unemployed, led by Communists singing the *Internationale,* marched through the streets and fought fierce running battles with the police. Over 2000 delegates packed the convention hall, approved the communist program on the unemployed situation, launched a national organization of the jobless and elected the communist slate of officers presented to them by the communist steering committee.

One month later in Moscow the Fifth World Congress of the

Comintern challenged the capitalist world in the following words, delivered in the keynote address by Losovsky: "The Red International of Trade Unions will know how to lead the masses under the red flag of the Comintern in the fight for the dictatorship of the proletariat and for the victory of communism in the whole world."

The fifty delegates to the Congress from the Communist party of the United States stood on their feet and wildly cheered the call for world revolution. The fifty American communists represented the strategic industrial areas of the United States and every important industry. The composition of the American delegation put meaning into Lenin's admonition to the communists to turn every factory into a revolutionary fortress. Three delegates came from the National Textile Union, four from the National Miners Union, three from the Marine Workers Industrial Union, one of them George Mink an OGPU agent and gunman, two from the Auto Workers Industrial Union, three from the Metal Workers Industrial League, plus delegates from the lumber workers, the shoe workers, the building trades, the laundry workers, construction workers, chemical workers, furniture workers, the agricultural workers and six delegates at large selected by the Political Committee to head the delegation. The cost of sending one delegate to Moscow and returning him to the United States in transportation charges alone cost a minimum of $750.00. His wages had to be paid to dependents in the United States during his absence, and money had to be paid for his upkeep in Europe enroute to Moscow and back and for his living expenses in Moscow. The cost of sending a delegation of fifty to Moscow totals at least $75,000, every penny of which was paid by Moscow and not one cent by the Communist party of the United States.

On the return of the delegation to the United States the class war battle-front burst into action. The leaders of the Communist party and the communist trade union officials arrived in the United States from the Comintern Congress kicking at the traces. They had the latest orders and instructions in their pockets. They knew how much money Moscow had decided to give the Party for its major campaigns. Everybody was raring to go. And go the Party did, on a wild rampage up and down the country.

In September the fight against evictions began. Whenever one of the unemployed had his belongings moved out on the sidewalk, the communists, as if from nowhere, appeared on the scene and proceeded to put the belongings of the dispossessed back into the vacant apartment. If the janitor protested he was brutally beaten up. If the landlord tried to interfere he got a blow on the head from a blackjack. If the sheriffs tried to uphold the court's eviction order they were given a stiff fight. Finally the arrival of the police on the scene caused a riot of major proportions because the communists were by now seasoned fighters against the police and could give a good accounting of themselves.

The communist-led unemployment demonstrations did not subside. They were held almost every day in the week all over the country on a local and neighborhood basis. They were held before welfare agencies, on public squares, before government buildings, at factory gates and before the offices of large corporations. When a number of the demonstrators were arrested the communists came in droves to the court room. They sat in shirt sleeves, leather jackets and dirty clothes. The communist lawyers were under instructions not to proceed along legal lines but to make propaganda. The communists who packed the court room sneered at the judge and scoffed at the prosecutor. The communists on the witness stand defied the court, spoke in contemptuous, sarcastic tones and harangued against the police and capitalist justice. It took courage to carry out such tactics, a courage mixed with idealism and rascality. It expressed itself in a snobbish proletarianism. Here was revolutionary fanaticism in action, a fanaticism which under favorable historical conditions sways the mobs and exerts tremendous dynamic power, the power to move mountains and send mighty governments to their graves.

The communists are a mobile force. In spite of the tremendous effort put into the campaign for the unemployed they did not neglect their other activities. On the contrary the other activities were stimulated by what was being done among the unemployed. A demonstration on behalf of the foreign-born was staged in Washington. Led by Mother Ella Reeves Bloor, then over seventy years old, many times married and actually the mother of many outstanding communist leaders, the demonstration tried to storm the United States Congress. The police interfered. A bloody riot broke out within the sight of the Capitol dome. Tear gas and pistols had to be brought into play to finally subdue them. The communists were jubilant. In the skirmish they had gained their objective of showing that the government was arrayed against the millions of foreign-born who had made the United

States their home. They viewed what happened as an experience in the class war, part of the struggle against the capitalist state, the forerunner of greater and fiercer struggles to come.

The following words of Bukharin, spoken in 1930, are worth pondering over: "The defense of the dictatorship of the proletariat and of the entire grandiose socialist construction, the fruits of heroic efforts of the working masses and the Party, is for us [the communists of all countries] the highest law of proletarian devotion to which everything must be subordinated." Bukharin expressed what every loyal communist solemnly believes in. He expressed the communist law of fanatical devotion by which every communist becomes an abject slave to the Party machine. This law of blind devotion to everything the Communist party does keeps in human bondage not only the communists of the vast Eurasian empire known as the Soviet Union but also the communists of the United States and of the entire Communist world superstructure.

Trying to Wreck the Banks

By the end of 1930 the banks began to feel the disastrous effects of the depression. Many closed their doors, among them the Bank of the United States on Fifth Avenue at Fourteenth Street, close to the National Headquarters of the Communist party. A run on the bank followed in which the dejected, angry depositors clamored for their money. Excited communists rushed into Party headquarters and reported the situation to the leaders. The leaders went into a huddle and immediately decided on a course of action. The communists loitering around the headquarters were gathered together and given instructions to rush to the bank and lose themselves among the depositors. Parading as fellow depositors, who had lost their life's savings, they were told to arouse the anger of the crowd and at the same time spread rumors that other banks were soon to follow the example of the Bank of the United States. The communist leadership hoped thereby to create a panic among the people and cause a serious run on all banks in the city that served as the financial center of America. They believed that by so doing they could bring on a financial catastrophe that would rock the economic foundations of the country and undermine the stability of the government.

But the communist leaders did not act like fools. They backed up their destructive policy with a constructive program calculated to incense the small depositors against the banks and the large depositors. They urged the formation of an organization of small depositors. They got communists who were depositors in the Bank of the United States to start such an organization. The plan was to start with the small depositors, who greatly outnumbered the large depositors. The communists demanded seizure of the deposits of the larger depositors to pay off the small depositors dollar for dollar. They called upon the government to arrest the bankers and hold them as criminally responsible for the bank failures. They demanded the immediate nationalization of the banks, and that the government should turn the banks over to the workers' organizations which were to control them democratically.

In this matter, it is interesting to note that in 1927, Foster, the Chairman of the Communist party, appeared before the Executive Committee of the Communist International with a proposition that the communists favor the institution and organization of labor banks. Foster maintained that the workers, through their trade unions and cooperative organizations and by the ownership of labor banks, could obtain for their own purposes a large slice of capitalism and in the end use the financial structure of capitalism to finance a proletarian revolution. The Comintern Executive laughed him out of court. The policy followed in 1930 was the direct opposite, for it rested on a set of proposals which, if adopted, would bring about the financial collapse of the United States with all its disastrous and profoundly disturbing political consequences. If it meant the loss of billions in savings to the American people and greater unemployment and privations for the American workers and their families, on an unprecedented scale, it was just what the communists wanted and what they were planning for.

Blood and More Blood—The Washington Hunger March

By the end of 1930, in less than a year's time, the communists had built up their unemployed councils into a national movement which corralled millions who were ready for action and were not afraid of the leadership of the Communist party. In the years 1931 and 1932 the communists showed the country what they could do with the unemployed.

But the communist leaders were not given a free hand. The Communist International was greatly concerned with American developments. American communists leaders were called to Moscow every few months to confer with the Russian communist leaders on what to do in America. At these conferences the Russians decided to back the unemployment efforts of the American communists heavily, with money and with expert advice and direction. The original plans for a hunger march of the unemployed on Washington were worked out at these Moscow conferences.

The Comintern set aside $100,000 to finance the hunger march on Washington. With the money came a host of Comintern organizers and a C.I. Rep and a Profintern Rep to direct the campaign. The idea was to hold hunger marches on a local scale which were to culminate in a national movement for a hunger march on the nation's capital. Hunger marches sprouted up suddenly in all parts of the country like mushrooms in a field after a shower.

In St. Louis the hunger marchers took possession of the City Hall. When the police tried to eject them, the desperate men and women spurred on by their communist leaders fought back. Only by smashing heads and using tear gas did the police finally succeed in getting them out.

In New York the hunger marchers massed around the City Hall in an attempt to take possession of the place. When refused admission they yelled, "To hell with the law!" and threw themselves at the police.

In Los Angeles 10,000 hunger marchers fought the police a running battle for hours.

In Akron, in a howling blizzard, the communists led 4000 hunger marchers to the City Hall.

On January 25 seven state governors met at Albany, New York, to discuss the unemployment situation in their states. Communist-led hunger marchers converged from all parts of New York State to demonstrate and riot before the governors.

May witnessed the beginning of unauthorized strikes in the coal fields of Pittsburg, Kentucky, West Virginia and Ohio. The communists provoked the strikes and led them in defiance of the miners' union. The strikes were turned into desperate, bloody struggles. The strikers, egged on by the communists to engage in violent direct action, fought pitched battles with sheriffs and coal company deputies. Scores of miners were killed.

Every day witnessed new hunger demonstrations. The communist-inspired unauthorized strikes started in the coal mining industry now spread to steel and textiles. Everywhere the communists were fanning the flames of discontent and everywhere there were violent battles, clubbings, arrests, shootings and death. The class war was on. There was no neutral ground. The communists gave no quarter and sought no quarter.

By the beginning of August the communists felt that they had spilled enough blood and that the hunger situation in the land had been sufficiently dramatized to issue the call for a national hunger march on Washington. The Hunger March Manifesto declared: "All these demands and these means of struggle are only the first steps towards organizing the power of the toiling masses completely to overthrow the system of capitalist slavery and starvation and to reorganize the whole of American society on the basis of the welfare of the people . . . the basis of socialism. The dictatorship of the working class must take the place of the dictatorship of the powerful finance capitalists."

The maximum organizational strength of the Communist party was mobilized for the march on Washington. Included also were all the organizations which the communists controlled. Elaborate detailed instructions were worked out by the Central Executive Committee in collaboration with the C.I. Rep. The International Labor Defense mobilized its resources to defend those who ran counter to the law. The Workers International Relief received orders to supply sleeping quarters and food along the line of march.

The communists opened a National Unemployed Conference in Washington on December 6, a day before the hunger march was scheduled to arrive at the capital. Every organization with which the Communist party was connected sent delegates—cooperatives, the Communist party, the Young Communist League, the Young Pioneers, the Trade Union Unity League, the International Workers Order, Communist Unions, A F of L unions and independent unions, workers sports clubs, workers clubs, the League for the Defense of the Foreign Born, the Friends of the Soviet Union, the United Council of Working Class Women, the Workers Ex-Servicemen's League, cultural organizations, church groups, Negro organizations, college groups, school groups, the Unemployed Councils, etc., etc. Over 4000 men, women and children delegates packed the conference.

Maps were printed of the routes the hunger marchers were to follow and at what points they were to converge. Each section of the country received concrete instructions on how to transport its quota of hunger marchers to the capital. The New York communists had to provide a minimum of ten automobiles and eighty-seven trucks. The marchers from points west of St. Louis converged at St. Louis and from St. Louis proceeded to Washington. The Middle West and Pacific Northwest converged at Chicago. The main streams of marchers left from converging points at Boston, Buffalo, Chicago, Philadelphia and St. Louis. Transporting 10,000 hunger marchers in hired trucks, feeding them, hiring halls en route, legal fees and other expenses cost the Communist party before the march was finished over $200,000.

The marchers did not proceed to Washington like sheep. En route they made propaganda, staged demonstrations, resisted the authorities and enrolled new recruits. The communists displayed generalship. They learned much about the country and, more important, what was needed to arouse the people in different sections of the country. Some day they may use what they learned on the National Hunger March in a way that will startle and wake up the country.

A week before the hunger marchers were to descend upon Washington a delegation of the Hunger Marchers entered Washington for two purposes, one to present to President Hoover the demands of the hunger marchers and two, as a scouting party to get the lay of the land. The delegation didn't get to see Hoover. They attempted to picket the White House and were arrested. The communists enlarged upon Hoover's refusal to see them, charging that he slammed the door in the face of starving men and women who wanted to present their case to him. On reaching Washington the 10,000 hunger marchers chanted "Hunger Hoover" over and over again. The most popular slogan drafted by the communists indicated that they expected a real outburst of violence at the nation's capital, for it read, "The Hoover Program—A Crust Of Bread On A Bayonet."

But contrary to the expectations of the communist leaders all went off peacefully. The leaders appeared before the conference and orated against the government. The hunger marchers arrived on schedule and marched through the streets of Washington. They cursed Hoover and booed William Green as the fascist president of the fascist American Federation of Labor.

The C.I. Rep secreted in a Washington Hotel room turned purple with rage. The plan to bring about in Washington a massacre of the hunger marchers as a result of provoked violent clashes with the authorities did not materialize. Perhaps the cold winter blasts had something to do with it. Climatic conditions made it impossible to keep the hunger marchers indefinitely in the capital. They were given orders to return home, following the routes by which they came. The enraged C.I. Rep called the communist leaders together. He lashed out against them, charged them with being cowards and with deceiving the Comintern. The leaders, terror-stricken, admitted their mistakes and shortcomings. They promised that the next time it would be different, a fact they proved without the shadow of a doubt eight months later. The Communist party leaders, having no further business in Washington, checked out of the fashionable hotels and left by pullman train for home.

Getting Hoover's Goat

The Bolsheviks never got over the fact that they had to depend on the enormous amount of relief supplies shipped to Russia by the United States, the distribution of which was supervised by Hoover, to extricate the communist fatherland from a famine. To be saved by American capitalism at a time when Russia's communist rulers were plotting the destruction of the capitalist world was too bitter a pill to swallow. Even though they accepted his services, they charged that Hoover was guided by ulterior motives. The Bolsheviks in the Comintern charged that Hoover distributed the supplies for political purposes, seeking to tie in with his relief activities a movement for the overthrow of the Soviet government. They held Hoover personally responsible for the overthrow of Bela Kun's communist regime of Hungary, charging that as Chairman of the European Relief Council he financed and fed the Hungarian counter-revolution. The Russian Communists boasted that the Cheka, whose agents honeycombed the Hoover relief set-up in Russia, would prevent him from achieving his counter-revolutionary goal. Ever since that time the communist leaders of Russia, whose regime was saved by the splendid relief job Hoover did, have conducted a vicious campaign against Hoover which has not relaxed in its fury for the past twenty-seven years.

The economic crisis following the crash in Wall Street in 1929 gave the Comintern the opportunity it was looking for. Hoover was the President of the United States. They could exploit the situation by blaming Hoover for the world's economic ills. They unloosed against him a campaign of personal abuse, with the objective of destroying him as a public figure for all time. Comintern orders directed the American Communist party to carry out this plot of character assassination. Stalin himself started the campaign against Hoover in 1929 when in his address to the American communists he branded former leaders of the American Communist party agents of Hoover.

The Communist *Daily Worker* featured caricatures of Hoover with exaggerated jowls. They nicknamed him "Prosperity Herb." Under one of Hoover's pictures the following appeared: "Workers, don't you remember way back a year ago—how Hoover brought us 'all' prosperity? Five million workers without jobs now; lots of wage cuts, etc., rather punches us below the belt, eh? But Hoover should worry, look at those fat jowls! Don't miss any meals, does he?"

On another occasion they stated: "The loudest-mouthed of Hoover's liars was Henry Ford." A picture of Hoover fishing had him dubbed the "Fat Fisherman." They charged that Hoover spent personally for his own family $4000 a year for milk while workers' babies died of starvation. A Communist party manifesto in bold type was headed: "HOOVER DECLARES WAR ON THE WORKING CLASS." In the communist press, before meetings of unemployed, on street corners, in union halls, wherever communists congregated Hoover served as the target of a venomous mud-slinging campaign. He was pictured as a lyncher of Negroes, as a policeman with a club mashing in the brains of workers. Hoover was the arch imperialist, the fascist, the agent of Wall Street, plotting wars of aggression. The communists were determined to make Hoover the scapegoat of the world's economic crisis, the leader of world reaction, a man to be hated by the people. In a large measure they succeeded.

1932 saw the outbreak of important strikes under communist leadership—the strike of the Kentucky coal miners, strikes of needle trade workers, textile workers and numerous other strikes scattered over the country. In the Kentucky strike a communist youth organizer, Harry Simms, twenty years old, of New York City, not a coal miner, was murdered. His body draped in a red flag rested in state at the New York Workers Center. Young and old communists passed by the bier and vowed to take revenge against the Hoover terror.

The same year witnessed the mighty "Hands Off China Campaign" directed against Japan and the United States. The communists charged that Hoover was conspiring with Japan for the purpose of provoking a war against the Soviet Union. Earl Browder sent out instructions, in the name of the Executive Committee of the Communist International, to all Communist party nuclei and organizations that they hold demonstrations in the name of the Hands Off China

Committee in front of all Japanese consular offices and the Japanese Embassy in Washington. In his letter to the Party members Browder quoted directly from the decoded cables sent by the Comintern to the American party. Weinstone, a member of the Political Committee who aspired for Browder's job, realized that Browder had made a serious mistake in exposing the hand of the Comintern in an action which was supposed to be conducted by the liberals. Weinstone believed he could have Browder removed from the general secretaryship of the Party. But the ambitious Weinstone reckoned without Stalin. Browder was Stalin's man. The matter reached Moscow for a decision. Browder received a mild rebuke for not being careful. The one who brought the charges was denounced as a factionalist and removed from active participation in the affairs of the American party by detaining him in Moscow for a long time. In Chicago, the demonstrations in front of the Japanese consulate turned into a riot. The Communist party goon squad came armed with short stubby wooden clubs with sharp spikes sticking out of their ends, which ripped through the police uniforms and tore the flesh.

The Hands Off China Campaign wound up in Washington before the Japanese Embassy. The communists demonstrated and paraded in defiance of the government's express orders. The placards denounced both Japan and Hoover. Massed before the embassy a riot broke out. Men, women and children were unceremoniously clubbed by the police who in turn also got a severe beating. Communist fighters were now seasoned soldiers. They tore into the police and sent scores of them to the hospital. The communist leaders had made good their promise to the C.I. Rep that they would make things hum in Washington the next time they got a chance.

The Campaign Against Henry Ford

In Detroit the communists concentrated on organizing the automobile industry. Political Committee minutes are full of lengthy decisions on the unionization of the industry and Henry Ford. Communist party records show that since 1927 the Communist party had received hundreds of cables from the Comintern and the Profintern dealing with both. Moscow wanted action, not oratory and resolutions. They insisted that the communist campaign for the organization of the industry be conducted in such a way that Henry Ford would be exposed as the most brutal exploiter of labor. These orders and directives from Moscow to the American Communists to undermine the reputation of Ford came at a time when Ford had agreed to take into his plants many Russian technicians, mechanics and engineers for the purpose of teaching them the American techniques in mass automobile production. Ford, too, supplied the Soviet government with tractors and automobiles and was instrumental in setting up one of the Soviet Union's first modern automobile plants.

But the Comintern did not like Ford. His theories on mass production and his advocacy of high wages geared to production gained too much popularity among the workers of Europe. The Comintern countered Ford's popularity by charging that Ford's speed-up methods undermined the health of the workers and represented an excessive rate of exploitation. They held that the Ford system was a system of industrial feudalism based upon the exploitation and enslavement of the workers. They called the Ford system rationalization and contrasted it with the system of socialism which prevailed in Russia. They had communist Marxian economists write special books on the subject, based on the theme of "Ford or Marx."

The Communist party of the United States had to prove the truth of the Marxian hypothesis of the Comintern by involving Ford in a violent class war conflict. They were under strict orders from the Comintern to embroil Ford in a struggle with his workers which would expose him as a trade union buster and slave driver. The communists were determined to teach "Old Henry, the speed-up king," as they called him, the "loudest-mouthed liar of Hoover's liars," a thing or two before they got through with him, regardless of what it might cost.

In March the communists of Detroit started a hunger march, supposedly of Ford workers, against Ford's Detroit plant. The Young Communist League and the Communist party mobilized their goon squads, defense corps and the gangsters from the unions they controlled. The plan for the attack upon the plant included cleverly worked-out tactics calculated to focus the eyes of the country on Detroit and Ford. Though the hunger march was staged under the auspices of the Detroit Unemployed Council, the Political Committee, through the Detroit District organization, led the affair. The line of march stretched for over a mile. The communist-led unemployed gathered at Oakwood and Ford, coming in trolleys that were jammed with rough and boisterous crowds of men who yelled curses and vulgar insults at Henry Ford. They refused to pay their fares when they alighted from the cars and told the conductors to collect the fares from the "old sonovabitch Henry Ford."

A battle royal started when the police attempted to arrest those who refused to pay their fares. The police had their hands full as the communists fell upon them in earnest. Heavy bricks started to fly in all directions. One leveled at Harry Bennett, the personnel manager of the Ford Company, hit him in the head and knocked him unconscious. The men the police succeeded in arresting were rescued from the police and the arresting officer laid low with a terrific blow from a cut-off pipe end. An attempt to disperse the crowd by turning the water hose on them infuriated the milling mob and inspired it to fiercer resistance. The police shot volleys from their revolvers over the heads of the rioters. Instead of breaking up and fleeing, the men, exhorted by their communist leaders, gave the police no quarter. The police then fired in earnest, using their riot guns and machine guns. The surging mass of humanity stopped in its tracks, turned around and fled. Four men lay dead, three were in a dying condition and thirty-five were wounded. Among the dead lay Joe York, a dreamy-eyed lad of nineteen, the Detroit District Organizer of the Young Communist League. An additional argument was added to the issue of Ford or Marx—blood.

The communist broadside to the country declared: "The Ford-Murphy police slaughtered the hunger marchers. Ford is responsible for the massacre." Browder called Mayor Frank Murphy, "the champion demagogue and chief agent of the auto bosses." The Communist party manifesto issued following the event held that, "Henry Ford, the richest man in the world, is responsible for the death of the four workers and the wounding of many others who came to demand bread and milk for their children."

Had the police not interfered with the demonstrators, the communists would have gone through with the second part of their plan which called for the seizure and occupation of the Ford Plant. Once inside, the communists were prepared to defend their seizure of the plant from vantage places behind windows and by using the machines as barricades, the instructions being not to give up without a terrific struggle and only after turning the huge plant into a shambles.

But the raging class warfare inspired and led by the Communist party did not end with the Detroit massacre. It flared up in many parts of the country. Communism in 1932 was a national phenomenon, its policies national, its activities nationwide. Riots marked May Day celebrations. In the sleepy city of brotherly love the communists sent ten of Philadelphia's finest policemen to the hospital. Following right after May Day a massacre occurred in Chicago's Melrose Park as a prelude to the opening of the National Nominating Convention of the Communist party. An unemployed demonstration led by the communist candidate for congressman-at-large did not wait for the police to attack; instead it took the offensive and pounced upon the police. The police lined a crowd of the demonstrators against a wall and riddled them with bullets. Nine, including the communist candidate, were shot down.

The Communists Take Over the Bonus March

In May 1932, the campaign against Hoover took on added significance. A spontaneous movement sprang up among the veterans of World War I for a march on Washington to force Congress to pass a bill granting a bonus to veterans. The communists were not in the picture. The C.I. Rep called the Communist party leaders together and demanded to know why the communists had missed up on this development. He called their attention to the fact that a year before, at the National Conference of the Unemployed, a resolution drafted by the Communist party demanding the immediate passage of a bonus bill had been passed unanimously. The Party leaders were on the spot. He read them the contents of a cable from Moscow which demanded that the communists organize a bonus march of their own on Washington and take steps to get control of the movement which had already been started. The C.I. Rep also informed them that the Comintern was sending a special representative from Moscow who would supervise the organization of the movement and direct it and that he was bringing with him the funds necessary to finance it.

The communists veterans' organization in May, 1932, came out publicly for the bonus, coupled with a vicious attack upon the American Legion and the Veterans of Foreign Wars. On May 19 the communist Workers Ex-Servicemen's League formed a Provisional Bonus March Committee and set June 8 as the date for a march on Washington. Emanuel Levine, an ex-Marine and the organizer of the California district of the Communist party, headed the Joint Provisional Bonus March Committee in charge of all arrangements. The Communist party members of the provisional committee met daily with the special rep of the Comintern and the national leaders of the Communist party to formulate plans and work out strategy and policies.

In less than two weeks' time the communists were on their way to Washington from New York, Chicago, Seattle, Los Angeles and Detroit.

The Communist Bonus Marchers arrived in Washington hell-bent for trouble. When General P. T. Glassford, Washington's Police Chief, charged the communists were plotting to start a riot, the communists called him a liar. On June 8 over 11,000 veterans marched down Pennsylvania Avenue.

The government had set up camps to house and feed the veterans. These camps, dubbed by the communists the Anacostia Mud Flats, housed the original bonus marchers who were not under communist leadership. Attempts to exclude the communists from these camps failed.

The legitimate leaders of the bonus march sought to get consideration of their demands by lawful and peaceful means. The communists had other ideas. A struggle between the two forces followed. The communists charged that W. W. Waters, the originator of the Bonus March and the leader of the veterans, maintained his leadership with the aid of the police. In order to gain control themselves, the communists demanded the holding of new elections for the choosing of commanders and the formation of communist-dominated rank-and-file committees to determine policy and make decisions.

The largest and toughest gang of communists came from Illinois. They staged a rank-and-file revolt in the large Illinois contingent, kicked out the commander and put a communist in his place. The police, fully aware of the trickery and rough-house tactics used by the communists, arrested the new commander. The communists retaliated by charging that the high command of the Bonus March was composed of stool pigeons and police agents who were betraying the veterans.

The communist high command met secretly in one of the fashionable hotels. The high board of strategy included the members of the Political Committee of the Communist party, the C.I. Rep Emanuel Levine and the communist heads of the veterans' delegations of the Workers Ex-Servicemen's League. The communist high command demanded that the leaders of the veterans who refused to comply with the orders of the communists be driven out of Washington. They laid down a policy calling for violent demonstrations in harmony with militant class warfare and demanded that the veterans be kept in Washington until hell freezes over in order to exasperate the government and force the hand of Hoover.

On June 18 the famous manifesto made its appearance, a manifesto every word of which was carefully gone over by the communist secret board of strategy and approved by the representative of the Communist International. It called upon the 20,000 veterans to pursue the policies laid down by the communists. Captioned in bold type, "Only Mass Action Will Win Bonus Fight!" a quarter of a million copies of the manifesto were distributed in Washington.

Immediately afterwards the words of the manifesto were backed up by action. In defiance of police orders to the contrary the communists led 3000 veterans to the Capitol and stormed the Capitol steps. So quickly was the feat executed that it caught the Washington police by surprise. That audacious demonstration, in defiance of government authority, marked a signal victory for the communists by demonstrating to the veterans that the communists meant business.

Results in bringing about changes in the command of the veterans quickly followed. The *Daily Worker* reported the next day that, "the militant fighting policy of the Worker's Ex-Servicemen's League triumphed here today when the veterans of Camp Bartlett ousted the fascist leader Everett and voted for Pace." Pace was at the time a leader of the Detroit organization of the Communist party.

After the assault on the Capitol the communist secret board of strategy met and mapped out further moves, moves which called for the seizure of government buildings to provide living accommodations for the vets. They decided that the vets be bivouacked on the Capitol grounds by bringing in beds and field kitchens with an eye towards storming and seizing the Capitol.

Eleven days after the communist bonus marchers entered Washington they began the actual seizure of a dozen United States government buildings.

"On to the Capitol," screamed the communists. "Over the bridge, comrades. The Senate is going to defeat the bonus bill. Everybody to Washington." The famous stampede to the Capitol started. Thousands of vets, a human mass of sweating, angry, howling men jammed the Capitol steps. Thousands of others crowded into the Capitol plaza. But nothing happened. The police did not interfere. The veterans cooled off as the hours went by and eventually returned to their camps.

The communists were patient. They could afford to wait for the explosion to take place.

On June 21 fully 5,000 veterans, led by the communists, stormed empty government buildings, seized them, lodged the veterans inside and put the communist, Pace, in charge of the commandeered buildings.

The communist high command decided that the time was now ripe to expose the hand of the Communist party in the bonus fight. A mass meeting took place under the joint auspices of the Communist party and the Workers Ex-Servicemen's League. The meeting cheered the communist demands for the veterans and outdid itself in heaping abuse upon President Hoover and the non-communist leaders of the veterans. Developments came fast and furious. Waters charged that the communist gang led by Pace which seized the Illinois contingent were drunkards guilty of misusing veterans' funds. The communists, now in the driver's seat, kicked Waters out of command, put Thomas Kelly in command for a few hours and then took complete charge of the Bonus March movement.

The newly installed communist command of the veterans broadcast calls throughout the nation urging more bonus marchers to march on Washington. The communists had succeeded in keeping the veterans in Washington almost a month. The mood of the veterans got uglier from day to day. The communists' leaders were then firmly in the saddle. On July 5 Earl Browder declared that the veterans were the shock troops of the unemployed. Said he, "The Bonus revolutionary force in Washington is the most significant beginning of the mass struggle against the deepening consequence of the crisis." On July 7 the communists seized Camp Anacostia and immediately called for a march on the Capitol. On July 8 Vice-president Curtis and Garner, Speaker of the House, denied the vets the right to march on the Capitol. On July 14, Pace at the head of 10,000 veterans marched on the Capitol. A communist committee invaded Curtis' office.

On July 18 the vets stormed the Washington court house.

On July 22 the veterans refused to get out of the Capitol.

On July 25 the fight with the Capitol police took place. Veterans were clubbed and arrested.

On July 28 the government went into action. General Douglas MacArthur, Chief of Staff of the United States Army, stepped in to prevent serious bloodshed after a fight between communist-led veterans and police resulted in the death of one veteran and the shooting of an innocent bystander. Tanks and troops opened a drive to push the BEF out of Washington. It was just what the communists wanted. It was what they had conspired to bring about. Now they could brand Hoover as a murderer of hungry unemployed veterans. They could charge that the United States Army was Wall Street's tool with which to crush the unemployed and that the government and the Congress of the United States were bloody fascist butchers of unarmed American workers.

The communists attempted to regroup their forces in order to resist General MacArthur. At a conference of veterans on July 29, in Old Masonic Hall, while James Ford, Communist candidate for vice-president, exhorted the delegates to resist the U.S. Army, the place was raided and Ford and forty-two others were arrested. The raid closed the communist siege of Washington. The Communist party issued a manifesto which ended, "Down With Hoover's Wall Street War on Vets." The first phase of their campaign against Hoover was over. A new man would soon enter the White House to usher in a new phase of American political history. But the communist phobia against Hoover will last as long as Hoover lives.

The Red Front

The Communist party of Germany, for years, maintained a military organization known as the Red Front. Hitler patterned his Storm Troopers organization after the Red Front. The Red Front drilled, practiced rifle shooting, studied the tactics of street fighting, was staffed with officers like a regular army and had secret stores of arms and ammunition. In 1933 the Communist party of the United States decided to build up a Red Front organization in the United States to supplement the Defense Corps which were already established. The responsibility for building the Red Front fell upon the Young Communist League. To overcome the suspicions of the authorities, the organization called itself a sports organization.

The organization was divided into two parts: The Red Front and The Young Storm Leaders. The communists adopted the name of Young Storm after Hitler's Storm Troops, for the groups which included children up to and including fourteen years of age. Those above fourteen were enrolled in the Red Front.

The *Red Front,* the paper of the organization, claimed that: "The

Red Front is an organization that builds up the body of youth in a disciplinary way." Indeed, those who joined the Red Front soon found out that they joined a military organization, run on a military basis by officers who were trusted communists, and whose orders were military orders that had to be obeyed as such.

The organization program stated: "The Red Front defense organization calls to you to engage in the class struggle and fight against fascist machinations in the United States." Once a youth joined the organization, it did not take him long to find out that by "fight" his communist officers meant "fight" in the full sense of the word, with clubs, knives, revolvers, hand grenades, rifles and machine guns, whenever that should become necessary. By fascist machinations was meant any action of the capitalist government of the United States and its subdivisions, the Army, Navy or the police, which the communists decided to oppose with counter-measures involving the use of force and violence.

"The Red Front" continued the declaration, "takes in all honest proletarians regardless of race or color. In order to prepare our bodies for greater resistance we have the following activities: Swimming, track running, jumping, baseball, boxing, wrestling, jiu-jitsu, cudgel throwing and hiking."

The Red Front practiced military marching, and jiu jitsu to use on police during demonstrations and on picket lines. Cudgel throwing involved throwing a cudgel at the horse of a mounted policeman so as to strike the horse on his foreleg and break it. The Red Front practiced how to throw hand grenades, how to throw missiles during a demonstration. The gymnastics were secondary to the lessons in the use of firearms and military tactics.

Declared the *Red Front:* "Groups in every factory is the first step for the fight against fascism." Thus they gave added significance to the Party slogan: "Turn every factory into a fortress."

Said the *Red Front:* "The question of anchoring the Red Front in different factories and shops, railroads, etc., is of the greatest importance. The dashing to pieces of the whole apparatus of government is, in the period of revolutionary uprising, thus easier to accomplish!"

A first aid section, made up almost entirely of female communists and communists medicos, served the Red Front groups whenever that became necessary.

The young storm troopers were trained to act as messengers, and to spy on enemy concentrations. The German Red Front had discovered that by using children they could get messages out from besieged groups, for the children had no difficulty in crossing the lines of fire and getting across enemy lines. Through children they could keep contact with general headquarters and with fighting groups widely separated from each other. These tactics were being taught to the red storm troop children in the U.S.

The emblem of the storm troop was a clenched fist on a red background with "Red Front" in bold letters on top and "U.S.A." below. The cloth circular insignias were either sewed on the shirt sleeve or on the breast of the brown shirt.

The main slogan of the organization which the Red Front thundered lustily as they raised their clenched fists was: "With the Red Front for a Socialist Soviet Republic." And they felt they were bound to get it by dashing the government of the U.S.A. with their military might.

The editor of the official magazine of the Red Front, a Party member, whose name remained a secret, like the names of all other officials and staff officers of the organization, overstepped his bounds. The Communist party ordered the November, 1933, issue of *Red Front* withdrawn from publication, and all issues not yet sold destroyed. The Party sharply condemned the editor for implying that there were 16,000,000 Germans of American birth in the United States who were strongly subject to Nazi influence. It also charged that the editors of the paper were anti-Negro because they printed as a headline a quote from the Nazis: "Jews Half Niggers——Nazis."

The Communist party declared: "To publish such a quotation from the agents of the cut-throat Hitler regime is an insult to the Negro masses and is a vicious form of white Chauvinism, regardless of the intent of the authors. . . . The next issue should contain the most searching analysis of the error and on the basis of self-criticism an attempt should be made to overcome the damage done by such objectively fascist and Chauvinist propaganda. In correcting such errors, the Communists inside the Red Front must realize that they have a heavy responsibility to the organization and to the whole working class."

The editors were severely reprimanded by the Party leaders for printing a Nazi statement and were accused of objectively serving the Nazis. But the Communist party leaders had no criticism of the Red Front organization which followed the pattern of the Nazi storm troopers in calling its children's division, "The Young Storm Leaders."

Demonstration By Murder

As far back as 1925, the communists were directed by the Comintern to take to the streets. Every political demonstration of protest, whether on a public square or around the office of a Consulate, in front of the office of a large corporation, or a picket demonstration before City Hall, Congress, the White House or other government buildings, was hailed by the communists as a move to capture the streets. In 1932 the order, "To the streets," became a mania as demonstration followed demonstration. "The streets are ours," shouted the communists. "We defy any one to drive us off the streets."

But the streets, the communists discovered, were not yet theirs. Others had the right to dispute their authority in New York in neighborhoods where the communists considered themselves supreme, namely, Harlem, the Bronx and the lower East Side. The socialists and the Trotskyites had the audacity to come to these restricted territories with their soap boxes and step-ladder platforms for the purpose of holding open-air meetings. That the police permitted such meetings to be held did not phaze the communists. They held that the streets in these neighborhoods belonged to them and they determined to keep all other organizations from using them, free speech or no free speech.

No sooner did a platform make its appearance in one of the specified neighborhoods than the communists appeared with a platform, either in the name of the Communist party or the Unemployed Council. They rigged up their platform close to the other and started a commotion by shouting their lungs out. The communists surrounded the platform of the so-called intruders as the communist gangsters pulled out their pocket-knives, cudgels and iron pipes. The communists started heckling and pushing against the platform in order to topple it over with the speaker. Women communists, close to the platform, screamed and spat upon the speaker.

The hecklers shouted abusive and insulting remarks. In a few minutes a fight started. The platform toppled over, speaker and all. The men with the knives and iron pipes went into action. The literature of the intruders was torn up and scattered. The enemy dispersed, the communists cheered, sang the *Internationale* with raised fists and conducted a meeting on their own behalf.

Those who had their meetings broken up by the communists

protested to the American Civil Liberties Union in the name of free speech and civil liberties, but the American Civil Liberties Union was such an ardent champion of civil liberties for communists that it did absolutely nothing to have civil liberties guaranteed to those who were opposed by the communists.

The socialists who had good trade union connections took matters into their own hands. From the unions, a strong-arm squad was recruited which accompanied the socialists to their street meetings. When the unsuspecting communists came, they got the beating of their lives and retreated. The communists thereupon charged the socialists with being fascist butchers.

The Trotskyites also learned what to do. They formed an alliance with the Industrial Workers of the World, who hated the communists like poison. From the Wobbly Hall they obtained seamen, lumberjacks, stevedores and migratory desperadoes, all itching to put their hands on the communists who, they charged, wrecked their organization. The beating they got from the Trotskyites, on the lower East Side, angered the Communist party leaders, for it had international implications. The leaders of the Communist party had promised that under no circumstances would they permit the Trotskyites to get a foothold in the United States. They swore that they would treat the Trotskyites like rats and traitors. They did just that, turning many a Trotsky public meeting into a bloody battleground. When Stalin feared that Trotsky would get an opportunity to visit the United States, the American Communist leaders had to promise, before the executive of the Comintern, that his first public appearance would be his last.

A Party decision ordered the leaders of the downtown section of the party to create a situation by breaking up the next Trotsky street meeting on the lower East Side in a way that would enable the Party to inflame the inhabitants of the district with lynch spirit against the Trotskyites. On the night of August 20, the Trotskyites erected their platform on the corner of Seventh Street and Avenue B. The Party, already prepared, went into action immediately. A platform of the Unemployed Council rose right next to the Trotskyite platform. Communists representing all the local communist organizations on the East Side came along, singing lustily as they marched behind their respective banners. The surging, singing, howling crowd surrounded both platforms. The poor Trotskyites were greatly outnumbered. A fight took place. The Trotskyite platform was rushed and demolished. The communists had gained possession of their streets. But what the mob below did not know was that on the roof of the tall tenement a number of communists were hidden in the dark shadows of the building's cornice. Below, another communist, standing aside from the crowd, waited to give a fateful signal. The signal was given when the communists controlled the corner with their own people. Heavy cobblestones of granite came hurtling down in the darkness. One communist, Nick Kruzuk, a simple ordinary worker, was taken to the hospital where he died of a fractured skull. Another, Michael Semon, a hard working Slav, died in the hospital the next morning. The crowd dispersed. The street corner that the communists had occupied a moment before was abandoned and people rushed terror-stricken into hallways. The communists added another memorable date to their revolutionary calendar.

On the afternoon of August 24, the demonstration called forth by this tragedy took place; the communists, 20,000 strong, marched through the streets of the lower East Side to Union Square. With raised fists, they repeated after their cheer leader: "Death to the Trotskyites. Death to all Renegades." Not marching were the two simple workers whose murder called forth the demonstration. They lay mute in their coffins. The days of class struggle were over for them. They had no way of knowing that the organization to which they belonged, which was shouting for vengeance, had murdered them. Such premeditated murders of communists by communists had taken place before and were considered justified by the political objectives of communist necessity. They will be repeated—the time, the place and the circumstances will be different—the incentives the same.

Communist Social Life

In the early part of the 1930's, before the Communist party tied its fortunes to the New Deal, the dues-paying membership of the Communist party fluctuated between 50,000 and 60,000. The periphery, that is, the circle of followers and supporters around the dues-paying membership numbered at least 150,000. Through communist control of unions, fraternal organizations, clubs, unemployed councils, veterans organizations and communist united front political organizations, built around concrete issues like the League against War and Fascism, the communists wielded an influence among upwards of a million people.

What does the social life of the members of an organization

which wields such tremendous influence in the political and social life of the country consist of? Do they live like other people? Are their habits the same? Communists eat, sleep, breathe, drink, smell and walk like all other human beings. It is as a social animal that they differ.

The communist lives in a social organization all his own, which he holds above the social organization to which all other persons belong. His social organization is the movement, concretely the Party. Outside of the Party, outside of the communist movement, the communist has practically no social or personal life of his own. Whatever he does centers in the Communist party organization. Even the hours he spends working for a livelihood are the concern of the Communist party; in fact, one of its main concerns, because the Communist party seeks through the organization of its membership in the industrial, commercial and other establishments to build a core within the framework of the country's industrial, commercial, cultural and political structure. Like termites the communists and their supporters and followers eat away at the foundations on which the country rests, transforming the supporting beams to a pulverized dust that will make it easy for the communists, when the opportune time arrives, to topple the structure over.

To begin with, the communist movement succeeds in doing what no other organization has so far been able to do. Upon the members it takes into its ranks, the Communist party performs a feat in psychological transformation by freeing them from frustrations and a sense of inferiority. What mental therapeutics has accomplished only in a small way, the Communist party, as far as its membership is concerned, has accomplished on a large scale. From the leaders down to the humblest, most backward, ignorant Party member, we have the living examples of the Communist party's psychological handiwork. The communist man is convinced of the messianic power of his way of thinking, of the superiority of his intellect and of the ultimate justice of his conduct. He is imbued with the idea that he is called upon to serve history, that the future belongs to him.

In the communist movement, nobodies become somebodies with a purpose. The doldrums of life are transformed into violent currents which stimulate the emotions, and change life for the Party member from a dull purposeless state of inactivity, into a state of agitated purposeful activity and interest.

Practically every moment of a Party member's living day is spent in purposeful activity for the Communist party. The average Party member carries on Party work in the neighborhood in which he lives, among the tenants in his house; at the shop or office he has special communist duties to perform. If he is a union member, he attends union meetings, and Party faction meetings of the union to which he belongs. Most likely he is an officer and has additional responsibilities and meetings and conferences to take care of. After work he has Party meetings, conferences, demonstrations, picket lines to worry about. He also belongs to a communist fraternal organization, to a labor party, to a number of communist front organizations. To all he must give his time. Then, there is the Party school, cultural activities, lectures, dances, singing groups, dramatic groups in which he is active. Interspersed with all this activity are social affairs, parties, cocktail parties, card parties, run by the Party organization directly and by hundreds of organizations which cluster like huge bunches of grapes around the Party organization which acts as a powerful stem holding them all together. Lucky is the Party member who finds time to wipe his nose and catch more than three to four hours sleep a day.

The Party member is too busy to think; he is too excited, too agitated. He keeps flitting about as the Party directs, at a feverish pace. He has no time to contemplate, to think or to worry about himself. The Party winds him up and keeps him going. Party life is hectic, but not dull. The Party member thrives on this activity.

There is also the dangerous part of Party activity, such as fighting in demonstrations, leading oppositions in unions where one's life is in danger, defying the Government authorities, doing communist work in the factories where, to be caught, means losing one's job or committing various acts of violence.

The Communist party, which claims to work for the elimination of all class divisions and distinctions, maintains a caste system which divides the Party membership into castes as widely separated in their social contacts and life in the Party as the residents of Park Avenue luxury apartments are from the tenement dwellers in the slums of the lower East Side.

The national leadership of the Communist party, centered mainly in New York, represents the upper crust. The top national leaders lecture to and talk down to the Party rank-and-file, but do not associate with them. This upper crust is divided into two parts. The inner core of the Party is a small select group made up of the top Party leaders, their wives or girl friends, a few of the rich Party members, C.I. Reps, top emissaries of other communist parties who happen to be in the United States, the chief Party lawyers, and a communist doctor or two. In this select, greatly restricted group, the real affairs of the Party and its relations to the world communist superstructure and the Soviet government are matters of conversation intermingled with the dirt and real politics of the Party organization. The communist upper crust is seldom seen at the many affairs which the rank-and-file attend. They may attend special affairs for seamen to demonstrate to the Party membership that they consider work among seamen of great importance. They will condescend to attend a banquet given for the special benefit of the strong-arm men and gangsters of the Party, for a communist leadership without the mailed fist and the hand that can wield the dagger or the gun is like a general who must depend upon an army to fight with its bare hands. Large social affairs, like concerts and dances, which the Party organization as a whole attends, affairs which attract from 5,000 to 20,000 workers, they also attend in order to show themselves off like movie actors at the opening night of an important picture or play. Otherwise, the upper crust meets socially in the sumptuous apartments of rich communists.

Around the upper crust is a much larger group, the powdered-sugar-coating on the crust. This group is made up of communists and non-communists who hew to the Party line so religiously that it is impossible to determine at what point they cease to be communists. Among them are the writers, the artists, the communists of means who own and operate lucrative businesses, favored communist trade union officials, influential liberals, government officials, Russian Embassy and consular employees, the national heads of front movements, ministers, musicians, Park Avenue people—to boil it down to a single characterization, communist café society, the Red Bohemia that gushes over and around the communist leadership of the United States. Here the communist leadership mixes with the upper strata of capitalism and wallows in the luxurious abundance of wealth. From its exploitation the Communist party obtains important contacts with leading phases of American life. Through it, the Party leadership gains influence in circles which would otherwise be closed to them. Through Red Bohemia, the communist leadership is able to tap financial resources of great benefit to the Party. Red Bohemia, which centers in New York, is nevertheless a national institution which covers all important centers of the country. It has outposts in the universities and university towns, in the large industrial centers, in the exclusive resort spots of Florida and California, and in the movie colony of Hollywood. Links connect Hollywood's Red Bohemia of script writers, actors, producers, and directors with the Party leadership, and through them with Party interests. From the movie colony, the communists have gained prestige in the entertainment and cultural world, and something very substantial besides—hundreds of thousands of dollars yearly for a period of over twelve years. Through Red Bohemia, the communists have tapped, besides Hollywood and Broadway, the lush pickings of Park and Fifth Avenue society, and have entered and influenced the book publishing, newspaper and radio fields.

By introducing a famous star from Hollywood, an author of note, or any one of hundreds of famous celebrities from Red Bohemia to the rich lady whose husband is in the upper income brackets; by arranging that the celebrity be a guest at a big party, planned for one of the many causes in which the communists are interested, top communist leaders gain easy access to penthouse society. As they sip cocktails from delicately stemmed cocktail glasses, their eyes are no longer focused on the lower depths. In settings meticulously and expensively arranged by interior decorators, among men who count their money in six digits and over, among women who flit around in expensive clothes and jewels, the communists have opportunities for gathering in sheckels for the communist cause on a scale they never before dreamed of. Mingling in such society gives them a political, social and commercial standing of which they can make excellent use. At parties like these, the communists learn many things. Before long, selected agents of the OGPU are also present, in order to gather what information they can and to make friends with the men and women whose influence might prove useful for Soviet espionage.

The Party soon developed a technique for handling the people in the upper brackets in a more efficient and more organized fashion. Chosen Party members, whose membership in the Party was kept a dark secret, were fitted out exactly as the movies do a poor girl who suddenly inherits riches. Elaborate apartments were furnished for them in the exclusive sections of New York. In each apartment a bar was erected and stocked with the finest wines and liqueurs. Party members who were waiters were secured to act as bartenders and waiters, others as cooks and servants. In these apartments cocktail parties for good causes were held to which the golden butterflies were invited. One night of each week was set aside for open house. Here penthouse society mingled and rubbed shoulders with Red Bohemia, and had a marvelous time as it was being fleeced.

A member of a dance group knew just how to ogle a fat industrialist in such a way that his cheeks turned pink and his heart bubbled over for the poor exploited proletariat. A young artist, sipping cocktails with an overstuffed and overpowdered lady, expounded on the role art played in combatting fascism as he impressed her with the fact that she ought to really do something about it.

The money rolled into the Communist party coffers. United front movements could be organized and financed for every kind of a cause. There were plenty of people to be secured to decorate letterheads with their names, as members of national committees or boards of directors. The Communist party in society was an organization with the kind of influence that counted in dollars and cents.

Hob-nobbing with rich and fashionable society had no effect whatsoever on the outlook of the communist leaders. To their credit, it must be stated that they did not succumb to the corrupting influences of bourgeois society. On the contrary, they so influenced the society circles with which they came in contact, so changed the outlook of the gentlemen and ladies with whom they sipped cocktails, that they transformed them into the financial pillars of the Party and subservient agents of the communist cause. Like good jockeys, the communist leaders steered the society horses in the direction of the communist goal. Park Avenue was important enough, but more important was the winning of the trade unions, getting an ideological grip on the youth in the schools, colleges and factories, organizing the farmers and agricultural workers, getting the hegemony over the millions of foreign-born and Negroes—that was the major and unforgotten objective of the communist leaders who hoped thereby to make the Communist party a mass party, the leader of millions of ordinary citizens, the average Americans. To this stupendous job and to Soviet espionage, the communist leaders devoted most of their energy and time. They concentrated on the masses—the great reservoir of power upon which the fate of history hangs. The communist leaders, believing in a conscious dynamism based on the power derived from the control of the masses, hope, once they get that control in the key and decisive economic and political sectors of the United States, to turn the wheels of American history sharply and violently in their direction.

CHAPTER EIGHT

SCHOOLS FOR REVOLUTION

PRIOR to the outbreak of World War II, the leaders of all communist parties were called together by the Executive Committee of the Communist International for a secret session to consider the new situation confronting the communist movement. The executive of the Comintern, certain that war would break out soon, imposed heavy responsibilities on the communist parties of all countries. But no intimation was given that Stalin would come to terms with Hitler. The secret session considered how the Comintern could safeguard its interests and continue its activities during a period of war when, in addition to the curtailment of civil liberties, boundaries were closed and the ordinary means of communication no longer available.

When Hitler crushed the German Communist movement, it became necessary to move the Comintern GPU headquarters from Berlin. New contacts, new codes, new methods of communications and new OGPU squads had to be organized. The headquarters were established in Denmark. An American communist, George Mink, played an important role in setting up the new Comintern GPU headquarters at Copenhagen.

The Executive of the Comintern declared that with the outbreak of a European war certain, a war bound to develop into a world war, the problem would be infinitely more difficult. The foreign communists, however, were assured that they had nothing to fear and that the interests of the Comintern would be well guarded. Particular attention was called to the fact that in the last ten years, over 100,000 students had been graduated from the communist universities, schools and academies in the Soviet Union, and had been integrated in the framework of the OGPU.

Many of the outstanding communist political figures in the Balkan countries, in Italy, Greece, Czecho-Slovakia, France, Bulgaria,

Austria, China, India, Indo-China, and in the South American countries, have been trained in Russia's communist academies.

Heading the list is the Lenin University, established in 1926 for the purpose of training communists of leadership quality. Making up the student body of the Lenin University, were communists from every country in the world. Klement Gottwald, the communist president of Czecho-Slovakia, is one of the better known graduates of the Lenin University.

In 1926, when the school first opened its doors, the Communist party of the United States sent a small contingent of ten students. The following year, twenty students were sent, and after that from forty to fifty students a year.

The Lenin University lived on funds supplied by the Soviet government. The students' transportation to Moscow was paid for by the University. Americans received $50 a month for the support of their wives and $25 additional for each child. In addition, the students received 50 rubles a month for spending money. The Lenin University provided its students with the best living quarters in Moscow. The building on Verevskaya 15, face to face with the British Embassy, in a section set aside for embassies, was one of Moscow's most modernized buildings, supplied with steam heat, hot and cold showers, modern plumbing facilities and other refinements missing in most of Moscow's buildings.

The students' living quarters were excellent. They were supplied with ample clean linen, and the food served was plentiful and good. The students also got free laundry service and were provided with free entertainment and travel. The theater, opera and concert halls were for the students to enjoy as they saw fit.

On arriving in Moscow, the students received a perfunctory entrance examination, for they had come on the specific recommendation of their Parties. Since most of them were already trained Party leaders, they had no difficulty in answering a few questions on economics and on the Communist party, how it is organized and how it functions.

All passports and papers were taken away from the students and turned over to the University's manager, who in turn placed them safely in the hands of the GPU. The students received a special identification card which served as a passport inside of the Soviet Union. This identification card was similar to the one issued to members of the Central Committee of the Russian Communist party and was like the card Stalin himself carried in his pocket. After three months, the student became a regular member of the Communist party of the Soviet Union. The Party to which he belonged before he came to Moscow lost all control over him. He gave up his allegiance to his own Party and transferred his allegiance to the Communist party of Russia.

The director of the University, Madam Kirsanova, the wife of Yaroslavski, who replaced Bukharin as editor of the *Pravda,* was a plump, ruddy-complexioned woman who made up for what she lacked in feminine charms by her political acumen and authority.

The curriculum consisted of courses covering Marxian economics, the history of the Russian Communist party, an extensive study of labor history covering the labor movements in all countries, agrarian problems, including the colonial question and the history of Russia, with special emphasis on the history of the Russian Revolution.

The material covering these subjects was translated into the various languages with which the students were familiar, mimeographed and bound into volumes. In addition, the school housed a large library. The books which the students had to read as part of their studies were to be had in the library in many languages and in dozens of volumes.

In addition, the Lenin students had access to the library of the Karl Marx and Lenin Institute, the outstanding library of its kind in the world—a library which was built up as a result of the indefatigable efforts of the greatest Marxian scholar in Russia. This was Rassanev, who was rewarded in the latter thirties by being liquidated by an OGPU firing squad as a fascist traitor of the Soviet Union.

The theoretical program was supplemented by a program of practical work, a program calculated to graduate a well-rounded communist political leader and agent of the Soviet Union.

In the first year, during the summer months, the students are assigned to a factory near Moscow. The student is given a job at a machine like an ordinary worker. He becomes a member of the union which has jurisdiction over the factory, and functions like a communist proletarian in the works. He attends shop committee meetings, union meetings and communist nuclei meetings in the factory in order to get a first-hand idea of how such meetings are run under a communist dictatorship. But student activities are not limited to the worker, his union, shop committee and Party cell. The communist student is given an opportunity to study how industries are managed under a communist dictatorship. He meets with the factory's manager and attends the meetings of the committee which directs management affairs. He studies the techniques of management, the handling of personnel, production problems and hundreds of other matters involved in the complex techniques of modern production.

The Lenin student, as soon as he is assigned to a factory, finds that the OGPU plays an important role in the running of Russian industry. Connected with every factory is a special division of the OGPU. He learns that the plant itself is heavily guarded by OGPU soldiers with fixed rifles and bayonets, that the passes issued workers, allowing them to enter the factory gates, are changed each week and are given out by the OGPU.

The student is initiated to secrets which are kept from the other workers and from the public generally. The student discovers that every large industrial plant has auxiliary buildings separated from the plant, which are under the strictest surveillance of the OGPU. In these heavily guarded buildings, technicians are engaged in making dies and tools for converting the plant to war production at a moment's notice. All these shops, on a small scale, turn out munitions and guns and other military equipment.

Thus the Lenin student learns that a communist country does not believe in peace and maintains itself on a war footing at all times.

Having acquainted himself with the affairs of industry the first year, the second year the student is sent to the seat of a provincial government to learn how a branch of the Soviet government functions. By this means the Lenin student grasps the fundamentals of communist government in action; of dictatorship à la Russe.

A number of Lenin students are allowed to indicate their preference. Should they pick Baku, they are constituted into a group and sent there. The director appoints one of their number the *starester,* or leader of the group. The starester is always one of Kirsanova's favorites, or a student who has demonstrated that he is the most politically awake and trustworthy student among the group, the one who can best be trusted to look out for Soviet interests.

On their arrival in Baku the students are met by government officials. They board limousines, are put up in the best hotel and feasted like important dignitaries. Many a provincial Soviet government has been ousted and its members replaced by others due to reports made by Lenin students on their return to Moscow.

Baku, the grim oil city of Moscow, is an ugly affair without sewage or modern facilities. In the summer it is hot and the stench from the garbage and sewage which piles up is terrific. One of the students, speaking of the city, declared: "Baku is a big city of 200,000 population. The whole town stinks."

The students are attached to the Presidium of the Baku Soviet, and are then divided up so that the many departments of the government can be attended by the students assigned to them. When the time permits, the students are called together by the starester to give a report on the departments they attended, so that the student body as a whole can get a composite idea of how the Baku Soviet functions.

The students, not permitted by the government officials to bury themselves in laborious study of the workings of the government, are entertained at numerous elaborate social festivities arranged in their honor. They soon forget the stinking city, for they are guests at the newly built colony for the Soviet officials and their families on the cool shores of the Caspian Sea. Here, they find billets containing attractive, comfortable rooms. The cottages in which the officials live are cozy and bright with sunshine. The club houses, the tennis courts, the large swimming pool, the outdoor restaurants are in sharp contrast to the gray, overcast, hot, ill-smelling city beyond.

Between the officials and the city's population, a marked separation is noted. The hostility between the officialdom and the sweltering mass of humanity that grumbles as it works is reflected in the remarks of the officialdom about the backwardness of the masses. To them they are the ignorant peasants of yesterday, who know nothing about communism, who must be watched and cannot be trusted.

The student becomes aware that once he is away from the city, the hostility takes on a more ugly form. When the student indicates a desire to visit villages fifty miles outside of the city, the government officials tell him that to do so is dangerous. The Mohammedan tribesmen, he is told, are bandits, murderers, and to venture outside the city gates is dangerous without a military escort.

The Lenin students, nevertheless, learn much about the practical, the un-theoretical, un-idealistic side of communist government. They are taught concretely how to maintain and execute the power of government under a dictatorship should they be called upon to do so in their own country.

In the third year, the students' most important year, the students remain in the city of Moscow, the center of communist world power. The students are attached to one of the commissariats of the Soviet government, as for example, the Commissariat of Foreign Affairs, the Commissariat of Labor, the Commissariat of Agriculture, etc. The most promising students, those who have demonstrated that they have what it takes to boss a country, are attached to the personal staffs of the principal leaders of the Comintern, including Stalin.

Gottwald, the President of Czecho-Slovakia, was attached to Losovsky. Joseph Zack, an American communist, served with both Stalin and Losovsky.

In the last six months of the third year, the students are attached to important missions of the Comintern to other countries. Thus the Lenin students get a rounded knowledge of the operation of a Soviet dictatorship. They learn the methods the great communist leaders use in conducting their affairs, and they are trained to handle concrete problems in other countries for the communist world superstructure.

There is no other school in any part of the world that gives such a thorough, well-rounded training in the methods of fomenting revolution, gaining power, setting up a dictatorship, operating a government under a dictatorship, and handling the forces of oppression. In addition, the Lenin University gives the student a theoretical basis and a very adequate background in international power politics. The graduates are the well-trained ambassadors of world communism, the skilled agents of world revolution.

During the three years, the Lenin student is also drilled and trained in military science, OGPU espionage work and sabotage. The agenda includes a course on the organization of combat groups, how to induct people into their formations, and the training techniques which must be used.

A military cabinet, made up of Red Army instructors and specialists, is attached to the school. A special room is set aside by the military cabinet, which contains small arms, machine guns of all the important makes of all countries, tommy guns, grenades, land mines, booby traps, etc. The students are taught everything they must know about those instruments of death. They are taught how they are manufactured. They are given instruction in taking guns apart, cleaning them, repairing them and reassembling them.

The school has an enclosed rifle range where the students practice on the various weapons, not so much to be able to hit the target, for that is considered secondary, but rather to get used to the noise, so that they can grow accustomed to being under fire.

The riding academy near the school is under the supervision of the military cabinet, so that the future communist leaders of world revolution may learn how to sit on a horse, ride him, organize cavalry units and train cavalry formations. An old Tzarist Cossack, an expert horseman who crashed his *nazlika* against the back of many a revolutionary demonstrator, yells his orders to the Red horsemen of tomorrow.

Another department of the military cabinet trains the student in the use of sabers, swords, bayonets, daggers and all kinds of weapons in which the sharp edge of cold steel is used.

The OGPU teaches special subjects to communists from other lands who hope to organize a communist political police patterned after the OGPU in their own countries.

The Lenin students are taken out by OGPU instructors to an abandoned track of railroad on the outskirts of Moscow to learn how to operate railroads during a revolutionary uprising and how to sabotage and destroy them should that become necessary. The students man the locomotives and learn how to drive them. In addition, they are shown how to derail locomotives and cars as part of a course in sabotage methods.

The students learn how to convert a train of cars into a military train and the techniques involved in its operation for offense and defense. The OGPU instructors also take the Lenin students to the locomotive works to teach them how a locomotive is constructed, to acquaint them with the parts that go into its making and to give them training in essential repairs.

The Lenin graduates selected by the OGPU for work in their organization get, in addition, specialized training in OGPU schools.

The military department instruction is, on the whole, comprehensive and quite complete, for communists hold that a knowledge of military essentials is necessary for the successful conduct of a revolution and for defense after the revolution.

The military department, after the Lenin students complete their preliminary studies on firearms, takes them to Red Army armories and camps where they learn about artillery and other matters from Red Army officers and instructors.

Military professors from the Red Army Military Academy visit the school to lecture to the students on military theory and operations.

Students are taught military topography. They are shown detailed military maps of important European and American cities, and are asked to pick out the key points for attack in the event of a revolutionary uprising. They are taught what counter-measures should be taken in a revolutionary uprising, against the police, the militia and the army. They also get a good education in the art of psychological warfare. They are drilled in what a minority group can do in the armed forces to undermine morale and make the soldiers resist their officers. What the Russians 'and other revolutionists have learned through bitter experience, amplified by expert military knowledge and enriched by the new tactics that have been developed by the Red Army, are matters on which the Lenin students receive detailed instruction.

The students hear experts on guerrilla warfare; Russians, Chinese, experts from the Balkan countries and from Spain expound on guerrilla tactics. These also teach the students how, under guerrilla conditions, they are to procure arms, manufacture munitions, commit sabotage, use dynamite and make bombs and explosives of all sorts.

Others teach the Lenin students how to form Red Guard units and later how to replace Red Guard units by the formation of Red Army regiments and divisions.

On the question of repression and the use of Red Terror, the students are told that terror and repression are worthless if not complete and ruthless. No compassion, they are told, must be shown in tightening the grip of the communists once the upper hand has been gained.

Out of the Lenin University every year come trained revolutionary leaders, communists who know what they are after, how to get it and what to do after they do get it. They are men to whom the revolutionary goal they are after is everything, and everything else is subordinated to that goal. These trained revolutionary men and women have a will to rule and a heart as cold and as cruel as the weapons of violence and destruction which they employ.

The OGPU has the first call on the Lenin students on graduation. After the OGPU has made its selections, a few are taken by the Comintern and the Profintern and added to their staffs. The rest are sent home to their respective countries to take up the responsibilities of communist leadership. Every Lenin University graduate is an OGPU contact, and through them the OGPU has valuable contacts abroad, contacts who know the essentials of OGPU methods.

Those drafted by the OGPU, and they include some of the ablest communists from outside Russia, are integrated into the OGPU apparatus and their ties with their respective communist parties and countries are severed. They must take the solemn and strict OGPU oath and become citizens of the Soviet Union. After special training in OGPU schools, they get their assignments and from Moscow fan out in all directions covering all parts of the globe.

The Lenin school is just one school. It is the school of the communist elite, of the selected few who are favored by the communist world superstructure. There are others equally important, and because of their mass character, perhaps more important, for in those where large numbers of revolutionary professionals are trained the general pattern of the Lenin school is followed, even though the courses as a whole are not as extensive and advanced. Often students in these universities who exhibit unusual capabilities are transferred to the Lenin University, where the accommodations, food and social life are much better. Besides, Lenin students enjoy the unusual privileges accorded only to top leaders of the communist movement.

The leading theoretical and scientific school of the world communist superstructure is the Academy of Red Professors. This is strictly a school for intellectuals. About one hundred students attend its courses, which require seven years of hard intensive study and research to complete. Students for the Academy of Red Professors are not taken directly from the communist parties. They must take a preliminary course, somewhat in the nature of a Marxian B.A., which takes two years. One cannot become a Red Professor in less than nine years of laborious work.

The Mid-European University caters to communists coming from the Balkan countries, from the smaller nationalities of the Soviet Union, from countries contiguous to the Soviet Union, and to a specified number of students sent by the communist parties of Europe, the United States and Canada. The American communists sent a large number of Negro communists to this university. About 2000 students attend this university. Stalin took a personal interest in the Mid-European University, for here were included by far the largest number of students from the Slavic countries. In the Comintern it was known as Stalin's pet. Away back in 1926 and 1927, when the University was first founded, Stalin began laying his plan for a Pan-Slavic block of communist nations to dominate the whole of Europe.

Two important universities were devoted entirely to the training and development of Communist leaders for China. The Far-Eastern University and the Sun Yat-Sen University together take care of approximately 5000 Chinese students. The Chinese students are given a much better military course than is given to the Lenin students. The Chinese students, upon entering the universities, are enrolled in a special Red Army brigade.

To all intents and purposes, the two communist Chinese universities in Moscow constitute a miniature Chinese West Point. The Chinese are drilled and trained like cadets of the officers' training schools of the Red Army, with one exception—much greater emphasis is placed on guerrilla fighting.

Madam Sun Yat-Sen is the patron saint of both universities. In Moscow it is her custom to meet, together with Stalin, the Chinese communist delegations and groups which come to Moscow regularly for conferences on Chinese affairs.

In Leningrad, the OGPU runs a mysterious school. The school is not publicized. Few know about the school and the few who do seldom speak about it. For here the fine art of sabotage is taught to those who have passed an exacting screening to determine whether they are fitted for the kind of work in which they are to be trained. The communist students learn how to dynamite a bridge, derail a train, set fire to warehouses, seize and make use of existing telegraphic and radio communications. In this school the communists learn how to fight the police during demonstrations, and develop the militancy and courage of the demonstrators. The methods of gangsterism are improved upon, and lessons given on how they are to be applied. Here a devil's brew is concocted and served out to the students, a brew of crime and violence mixed together in a sadistic hall of horrors in order to produce the strong-arm men of the blackjack, dynamite and automatic. The German Communist party had thousands of these desperadoes who spearheaded street brawls, riots, and armed uprisings in Germany in the early thirties.

In the Spanish Civil War, the communists put their Russian-trained saboteurs into a special battalion to eliminate the forces who opposed the communist domination of the Republican cause. Many American communists who went over to Spain with the Abraham Lincoln Brigade served with this battalion of terror and murder.

These Russian-trained communist commandos form the iron core of the resistance movements of Europe. They are kept in readiness in every European country. Given the signal, they will set Europe to the torch. Desperation and hunger may yet give them the opportunity to put the whole continent under the sway of the hammer and sickle.

In the Frunze Military Academy, in the section dealing with foreign military problems, thirty percent of the students are made up of communists from other countries. Here, the general staff of the communist fifth column is trained. In this academy, Tito got his military training. In this academy, a group of Spanish communists have been trained who hope, through the overthrow of the Franco regime, to get the upper hand in Spain. Here were trained Hungarians, Bulgarians, Czechs, Germans, Frenchmen, Italians, Poles and Greeks who, today in their respective countries, head armies of trained soldiers and security police. The time is fast approaching when communist totalitarianism will seek world domination by force of arms. When that time comes, it will count its armed legions in Europe and Asia at over forty million men.

Another OGPU school is in Vladivostock.

A large university is maintained in Tiflis for communists of the Near and Middle East.

Before the outbreak of the War, the Comintern had under consideration the establishment of another university in Baku, to be devoted to the training of communists for the Near East, Northern India and India.

The Soviet schools for the training of professional communist revolutionary leaders form an important part of an educational system which stretches clear around the globe, for in practically every country the Communist party runs schools patterned after the schools in Russia.

During the Spanish Civil War, the communist world superstructure sent thousands of communists from all countries into Spain to get practical experience on how to carry on a civil war. Virtually every known Communist party leader of the United States as well as of other countries embarked for Spain to take a part in the running of the Spanish Civil War. In this way the communist world superstructure was able to bolster the theoretical knowledge of communist leaders by practical, concrete examples in a bloody civil war which involved large scale military operations and the interplay of politics on a world scale. The international communist movement, thanks to its training schools and universities, does not rely upon the revolutionary idealist who is guided by ideals and abstract theories. It relies upon a staff of highly trained officers. Given half a chance, they will conquer and communize the world.

The outbreak of World War II temporarily halted the operation of the world communist educational system. Though the names of many of the educational institutions have been changed, and they have been shifted from one locality to another since the end of the war, the system as it existed before the war is unaltered. Many of the old schools, the more important ones, have been reopened and their work is carried on secretly on a much more extensive scale. The Schools in the Soviet Union are augmented by the establishment of new educational institutions in the satellite countries, Red China, and in all other countries where communist parties operate.

The communist educational system has shifted its emphasis to the military prerequisites and problems of communist education, in preparation for the war which the communist world superstructure views as inevitable. The numerous military academies in Moscow and throughout the Soviet Union are crowded with communists from all countries, the largest contingents coming from the satellite nations.

As a result of the Cominform rift with Marshal Tito, the outside world learned, for the first time, that behind the iron curtain several hundred communists from Yugoslavia were attending military academies for the training of officers, and that a much larger number of members of the Yugoslav young communist organization were attending various communist schools. Here we have an indication that the world communist educational system is operating full blast, and that in its schools are enrolled a much greater number of students than before the war. Before the war Yugoslavia supplied at most a score of students. Additional proof that the world communist educational system operates on a grand scale also comes from Germany. Selected German students, many of them former Nazis, officers in Hitler's armies and officials of his party, have been educated and trained by the thousands in the communist schools in Russia and sent back to Germany to serve the communist world superstructure in the hub of the world where the conflict between communism and European civilization takes on an acute form. What is true of Yugoslavia and Germany is true of all the satellite nations and it holds equally good for the communist parties of all other countries. Knowing the system for what it is, if the reader wishes he can, in his reading, substitute Cominform for Comintern and NKVD for OGPU in the entire certainty that what he is reading is true today.

Before the war, a preserve on the outskirts of Moscow, consisting of fifteen square miles, was set aside for the building of a new Lenin University with campus, military training grounds, and housing units, able to accommodate 10,000 Lenin students at a time. Here the Lenin University planned to turn out, on the average, three to four thousand graduates a year.

Such educational projects are not activated by desire for ostentatious display nor do they stem from the Russian urge to perpetuate the glory of Lenin's name. Rather they are proof that the communist slogan of world revolution is not merely a slogan but is a realistic goal. The training of hundreds of thousands of professional revolutionary leaders is one of the important practical steps to achieve it.

CHAPTER NINE

RESPECTABILITY AND SUCCESS

THREE events, one in the U.S. political field, the other in the economic field and the third in the international field of diplomacy, established the American communist movement as a factor in the political, social and economic affairs of the country.

American communism owes its rise to prominence to the election of Roosevelt as President in 1932, to the organization of the Committee on Industrial Organization in 1935, to the recognition of the Soviet Union by the United States in 1933.

Though Roosevelt's New Deal program and organization ranks first in immediate importance to the growth of communism in the United States, the organization of the C.I.O. from the communist standpoint is much more basic and of lasting importance to the movement, even though the organization of the C.I.O. without Roosevelt's blessing and endorsement would never have taken place. The recognition of the Soviet Union facilitated Soviet and Comintern penetration of the United States and opened wide the doors for the infiltration of the government by communists and their satellites drawn from a growing army of fellow travelers.

Communist endorsement of the Roosevelt administration and the New Deal did not come suddenly. When Roosevelt was Governor of New York State, the communists kept up an incessant barrage against Roosevelt as a reactionary tool of Wall Street. In 1932 the communists nominated Browder for president to run against Roosevelt. Browder charged, in his campaign speeches, that Roosevelt's election would mean a continuation of Hoover's reactionary hunger policies. The communists branded the first Roosevelt Cabinet as "the new Wall Street hunger and war cabinet." Of Henry Wallace, who was appointed Secretary of Agriculture, whose pro-Soviet line today receives the most active support of the communists and the endorsement of Soviet Russia, they had this to say: "This Wallace is an alleged friend of the farmer. He hails from Des Moines, Iowa, and inherited the publishing racket of his father, Henry C. Wallace, who was Secretary of Agriculture under Coolidge. When old man Wallace got the Republican job from Coolidge, he resigned as editor of *Wallace's Farmer* in favor of his son who now takes the old man's job in the Roosevelt cabinet. This Wallace family is connected with bankers and grain speculators in the Middle West and the publication, *Wallace's Farmer,* shared in millions gypped from the farmers by the Harvester trust."

"Wallace," declared the communists, "wants to make Roosevelt a dictator to boost prices for the benefit of the trusts, thus hitting the poor farmers on the land and the workers in the city."

Roosevelt and the New Deal were characterized as follows: "Yes, the 'New Deal' may prove to be fascism. This smiling India rubber liberal in the White House is destined to destroy all remaining American liberals."

Earl Browder, General Secretary of the Communist party, on July 8, 1933, delivered this blast: "For the working class the Industrial Recovery Act is truly an Industrial Slavery Act. It is one of the steps towards the militarization of labor. It is a forerunner of American fascism."

The communists, in 1934, branded the Wagner Bill as "Roosevelt's company-union club against the workers."

Browder, at a press conference during the Eighth National Convention of the Communist party, characterized Roosevelt as follows: "Roosevelt is the most effective agent Wall Street has had in several years." When a reporter asked him, "Is there no difference between Roosevelt and Hoover?" He answered: "Yes, there is a difference. The masses feel it in their stomachs. The masses have less food, less clothing, more inadequate shelter now than they had under Hoover."

The communist May Day Manifesto screamed: "Against the New Deal Fascism and War."

Of Mrs. Eleanor Roosevelt the communists had this to say: "The only girls Mrs. Roosevelt really knows, are those in her own set; the millionaire families with their parasitic debutante daughters, who participate in orgies that not even Hollywood could duplicate." Nevertheless, when the Party line changed and the communists wedded the New Deal, they did not hesitate in enlisting the services of Eleanor Roosevelt in many of their outstanding united front causes.

What took place to change the line of the communists towards the New Deal? The answer is not to be found in the United States.

Basic policies for the communist world superstructure originate in Moscow, not in the United States. No leader of the American Communist party would dare, on his own, propose such a revolutionary change in communist policy as that involved in the support of Roosevelt and the New Deal. The anti-Roosevelt policy, which was continued without interruption up to the fall of 1935, had its inception in Moscow and was supervised in the United States by a delegation of three C.I. Reps who were sent to the United States for that purpose.

Neither Browder, Foster, Dennis nor any other American communist leader has the authority or the guts to initiate a basic line of policy for the American Communist party.

To understand how the change in line came about, one must keep in mind that at the beginning of 1933 Hitler came into power. The communist world superstructure had made many overtures to the Nazis. The Nazis used these overtures to their advantage, but never once agreed to unite organizationally with the communists nor to give up their promise to root bolshevism out of Germany.

At first, Stalin and most of his advisers were of the opinion that Hitler's day of power would be of short duration. Stalin himself ventured to predict that the rise of Hitler to power would lay the basis for a communist revolution in Germany, because once the democratic institutions had been wiped out by the Nazis there would be no other alternative left the Germans.

Stalin had weighed the advisability of making a Bolshevik revolution in Germany in 1929 and 1930. In fact, communist emissaries by the thousands, representing all communist parties, including the Communist party of the United States, were sent into Germany. From the United States went H. M. Wicks, Ford, George Mink, Charles Krumbein, and scores of American students of the Lenin University. Secret information went out to all communist parties of the world, notifying them of the expected communist revolution in Germany. The highly confidential reports outlined the tasks of the communist parties in all countries in support of the revolution. A secret Comintern bureau had been set up in Germany, headed by Dimitrov and Bela Kun. In the Comintern, the Bureau was known as the Western European Bureau of the Comintern. The German Communist party which, in normal times, was subsidized to the extent of from three to five million American dollars a year, an enormous sum for Germany, through the Western bureau of the Comintern was more heavily subsidized by counterfeit and legitimate currency than heretofore. The money poured into Germany by the Soviet government represented an enormous sacrifice on the part of the Russian people and a terrific strain upon the country.

The world communist superstructure poised nervously for the shot that was to be heard round the world, a shot that would throw the world capitals into a state of fear and panic. But Stalin got frightened. The Five Year Plan put a heavy burden upon the country. Russia was not prepared for the consequences of a German communist revolution. Stalin was afraid to risk the possibility of a war with the capitalist powers at a time when Russia was in the process of building up her industrial war potentials. Word went out, "No German Revolution." Most of the communist agents of revolution from other countries either returned to Russia or went home. The Western bureau remained in operation, as a branch office of the Comintern.

The communist world superstructure suffered a severe blow when the Communist party of Germany succumbed to the blows of Hitler. Many of its leaders succeeded in fleeing to Moscow. Large numbers of its members, especially from the youth organizations, went over to the Nazi party. More than half of the top leaders and most of the secondary leaders who numbered in the tens of thousands and constituted the backbone of the Party were confined to concentration camps, and eventually died from brutal Nazi treatment or were executed.

But, when the collapse of Hitler did not take place, when it became clear to the communist world superstructure and to Stalin that Hitler knew how to consolidate his forces, they realized that the adoption of a policy to meet the new situation created by Hitler became absolutely necessary.

To lump all capitalists with Hitler did not work. For Hitler was attacking the liberals, the socialists and the conservative trade unionists as ferociously as he was attacking the communists.

Comintern orders went out early in March, 1933, to all communist parties directing them to form anti-fascist congresses and instructing the communist parties to take steps to form united fronts with socialists and others for that purpose. But, how far these united fronts should go had not yet been worked out. The World Congress of the Comintern, held in Moscow in July, 1935, tackled that question.

Present from the United States were Foster, Browder, Gil Green, representing the Communist Youth Organization; Sam Darcy, a graduate of the Lenin University, and the district organizer of the California District; and Martha Stone, a young girl originally from Minneapolis who had been active in strikes and unemployment demonstrations since 1929.

Foster played second fiddle at the Seventh World Congress, for the Comintern gave the center of the stage to Browder, Gil Green and Sam Darcy. Foster did not like it but he kept his mouth shut.

The Seventh Congress startled the world with two proposals—the call for the formation of a people's front, and an invitation to the Catholics of Germany to form a united front with the German Communist party against Hitler.

The people's front tactic marked a distinct departure in Communist policy on an international scale. It had been followed to some extent in China before 1927, when the Comintern worked together with the Kuomintang in China. Now, the Comintern had broadened and developed the policy on an international scale. The Communist International directed all communist parties in their respective countries to start negotiations with all progressive and liberal forces in the capitalist countries to form a coalition against the right, the reactionary and fascist forces. Powerful people's front movements developed in France and in Spain during the civil war. The application in the United States, due to the differences between American and European political conditions, took on a different form.

The Seventh World Congress ended in the latter part of August, 1935. The plenary session of the American Communist party was set for November 22, 1935, at which time the new policy was to be presented to the American communists; a policy worked out in detail with the C.I. Reps who were sent to the United States for that purpose.

By September it was already known in communist circles that negotiations were proceeding behind the scenes, between certain elements in the New Deal and representatives of the Communist party, which had for their objective a basis on which the communists could throw their support to the New Deal. The New Dealers, in preparation for the 1936 presidential campaign, were anxious to build up a mass base for Roosevelt independent of the regular Democratic party. Through the Russian Embassy in Washington, and together with key figures around Harry Hopkins and Sidney Hillman, talks were held as to how this could best be done.

It was recognized that only the Communist party could supply this group with the inspirational fire that was necessary to set a mass movement afoot. Such support, they figured, assured Roosevelt's chances for re-election. A coalition with the left, they held, would bolster up their position with the administration by strengthening the independence of Roosevelt in his dealings with the conservative democrats, who might balk against supporting the radical measures which they advocated and which they were certain Roosevelt would support.

However, before the communists fell in line, they wanted to know what they were to get out of it. Communists are hard realists, and shrewd political tradesmen.

By September, 1936, the question of communist support of Roosevelt so upset Communist party rank-and-filers, that the *Daily Worker* answered the question, "Is it true that the Communist party will support Roosevelt as a lesser evil to the more reactionary groups like Hearst and the Liberty League?" in the following manner: "No! The Communist party from the very outset of the New Deal has consistently exposed Roosevelt's anti-working-class aims. The development of the New Deal is towards fascism and war and not towards 'socialism' as is claimed by Hearst and his crew of red-baiters."

This answer served three purposes; first, to prevent publicity in the press of the country on the negotiations; second, to stimulate unofficial discussion among Party members, in order to prepare them for a change of line, and third, if the negotiations should fail, to continue the anti-Roosevelt anti-New Deal line as if no negotiations had taken place at all.

The communists were in a good bargaining position. They had plenty to offer. They could put 25,000 trained organizers and political agitators into the field. They had the undisputed control of the movement of the unemployed. The vote of the unemployed, swung one way or another, meant victory or defeat for an aspiring presidential candidate. They had demonstrated before the doors of the White House that the communists controlled the mass youth movement, that the communist-controlled and directed American Youth Congress was a political force to be desired. The communists had organized the League against War and Fascism a few months previously. Included in the new organization were the liberal and progressive forces and an impressive section of the organized labor movement. April witnessed the organization of the League of American Writers. Writers of note—novelists, journalists, dramatists, and poets—from all parts of the country were present. They applauded Browder, who greeted the Congress in the name of the Communist party in these pointed words: "It is with these thoughts that the Communist party greets this Congress of American writers. We are all soldiers in a common cause."

At a July conference in Chicago, called to consider the formation of a third Party to support Roosevelt, Marcantonio was present and so was Congressman Ernest Lundeen of Minnesota, a paid under-cover agent of the Communist party. The communists had much to offer in the trade union field. They had demonstrated that they could organize workers under the most adverse circumstances. Their activity in the trade union field was nationwide, and they controlled a considerable segment of organized labor in unions of their own, in independent unions and in the AF of L.

In addition, they had good contacts with the foreign-born workers. The communists were the first to recognize the important role the foreign-born workers played in the political life of America. They had organized the League to Protect the Foreign Born, an organization through which the communists defended the rights and interests of the foreign-born. They had, in addition, organized a fraternal organization on an international basis called the International Workers Order, completely under Communist party control and under its political and ideological leadership, which in a few years rose to an organization of 150,000 members. They were foreign-born and constituted the militant communist wing among the millions of foreign-born in America.

Moreover, the communists had numerous papers and magazines, women's organizations, veterans' organizations, cooperative leagues, and women's shoppers' groups. All these political assets the Communist party put on the bargaining table during the negotiations. They had plenty to bargain with, many aces in the hole, and found no difficulty in raising the ante.

What took place in the fall of 1935 makes astounding reading. The Communist party was guilty of perpetrating a campaign of political deceit and fraud upon the American people, unmatched in the annals of American history.

The communists, under Comintern direction, were hammering out a people's front, American style. They knew what they were doing. They were not sacrificing communists' interests, but bolstering them up. The Seventh Comintern Congress slogan: "The United Front Is the First Step to Revolution," was being put into effect in a practical way, in the only way in which it could be done in America. In October, the deal with the New Dealers was consummated. From then on developments proceeded with machine-gun rapidity.

In October, at the Atlantic City Convention of the AF of L, John L. Lewis broke with William Green on the issue of organizing the mass production industries on a vertical, industrial union basis.

Lewis, who had for years consistently fought the communists and sought their exclusion from the trade union movement, overnight became the hero of the communists, the outstanding militant and progressive trade union leader in the country. He resigned as vice-president of the American Federation of Labor and formed the Committee of Industrial Organization, which was later to be transformed into a rival of the AF of L under the name of the Congress of Industrial Organizations.

John Brophy, who for years had worked with the communists and had spearheaded the communist drive in the United Mine Workers to oust Lewis from the miners union, was appointed, by Lewis, as director of the new committee. The communists interpreted the move as an invitation to come into the C.I.O. and into it they came in droves, with their organizational techniques, with their driving force and energy, and ideological baggage.

Lewis went all out for Roosevelt and the New Deal. Roosevelt reciprocated by appointing Lewis as one of labor's big three members of the Recovery Administration. The President advised with Lewis on the labor platform for the presidential campaign. It followed inevitably that communist support of Lewis was tied in with communist support of Roosevelt.

Gerson's historical article favoring the New Deal as the lesser of two evils appeared on October 5, 1935. From that day on the usual caricatures of Roosevelt that adorned communist papers disappeared, together with sharp criticism of his administration. The communists, however, did not openly and straightforwardly identify themselves with the New Deal. They maintained an artificial line of difference between themselves and Roosevelt.

On January 1, 1936, Morris Childs, an editor of the *Daily Worker,* one who had the confidence of the Party's inner circle, wrote: "The Republican and Democratic parties have shown, in their actions, that they are the political company unions of the employing class. These Parties can be as little depended upon to defend the workers as a company union in the factory."

On the same day, the Communist party declared: "Support of Roosevelt plays into the hands of reaction. Lewis' cry for his re-election aids anti-Labor forces.

Behind the façade of opposition, however, the Communist party moved heaven and earth in unions, fraternal organizations, clubs, and in all other organizations with which they had contact, to get them to endorse the position of Lewis.

On January 28, the communists had secured such a hold on the Knickerbocker Democrats, an organization of progressive Democrats in New York, that they succeeded in having the organization come out with a sharp condemnation of Ex-Governor Alfred E. Smith and the Liberty League, which included mild criticism of the New Deal along communist lines.

On February 1, 1936, Browder, as general secretary of the Communist party, attacked both President Green of the A F of L, and Lewis of the C.I.O., for supporting President Roosevelt, and called for the organization of a National Farmer-Labor party, but he emphatically stressed that, under no circumstances, would the communists break with the workers who chose to support Roosevelt, thereby indicating that support of Roosevelt had communist blessing. Browder followed this position by a speech in Chicago on February 16, dealing with the opposition of the communists to the reactionary Republicans and the Liberty League, in which he characterized Roosevelt as follows: "Roosevelt roars like a lion in his speeches against them, against the reactionary monopolies, but in his deeds he is like a running rabbit." It was the communists' contention that by supporting Roosevelt as they were doing, by getting the left wing and progressive forces in the labor movement and outside of it to prod him on, they could give the running rabbit, Roosevelt, a backbone which they believed he needed badly.

The Communist party carried out its dualistic political policy by nominating Browder for president and Ford, a Negro, for vice-president, to run on the Communist party ticket. After he was nominated, Browder declared: "The only way to force Roosevelt to fight and put up any resistance is to have a strong force to the left of him." And that was precisely what the communists did in the 1936 campaign. Their staff of competent organizers, expending hundreds of thousands of dollars, got a strong force to the left of him securely entrenched in the New Deal political machine. Thus communists, and those who followed the Party line, were in a position first, to exert pressure upon the New Deal administration and second, to become recipients of political plums in the government.

On the night before election day, the Communist party held a gigantic campaign rally in Madison Square Garden. Browder, flinging all restraint aside, shouted: "President Roosevelt's election will be a rebuke to the worst reactionaries, but is no guarantee against the further progress of fascism in America."

The New Deal forces with whom the communists were working could not afford the open straightforward support of the Communist party. The communists too had nothing to gain by such a tactic. Where votes that counted could be swung, they were in a position to swing them for Roosevelt, and they were determined to get paid for most of it. By such a political strategy they put themselves in a position in which they could bargain effectively, make political deals and place their people in important posts in the New Deal political machine and in important strategic government positions. Only the Communist party leaders would know who their people in the New Deal really were.

This tactic received generous support from the OGPU. Now the OGPU had a chance to get right inside of the most powerful capitalist fortress in the world. Money was forthcoming by the bushelful; the Party established liaison between Washington, New York, the OGPU and the Russian Embassy. For maintaining the Washington communist front in proper style, establishing and maintaining contacts, the OGPU spent close to $1,000,000 a year. Washington society and Washington politicians and government officials soon enjoyed a pleasant acquaintance with Communist Bohemia, sophisticated intellectualism, and an array of communist girls stylishly dressed, who paraded their glamour seductively and made use of their charms for a purpose.

The communists of Union Square discovered Washington and liked it. Communist headquarters, on Thirteenth Street, had links to the Russian Embassy, links to the Administration, links to Government departments and bureaus, links to the State Department; it rubbed shoulders with Washington society and it suddenly found itself exceedingly respectable.

The worries the communists had when Litvinov made his famous agreement with Roosevelt, in order to secure recognition of the

U.S.S.R. by the United States two years before, were forgotten in the wave of prosperity which hit the Communist party.

In his letter to Roosevelt, Litvinov categorically promised the President, "Not to permit the formation or residence on its territory of any organization or group and to prevent the activity on its territory of any organization or group or officials of any organization or group—which has as an aim the overthrow of or the bringing about by force of a change in the political or social order of the whole or any part of the United States, its territories or possessions."

The day after this agreement on the part of the Soviet government to refrain from subversive activities in the United States, and from supporting a political Party like the Communist party which was definitely implied in the agreement, the communists issued the following blast:

"In this country the Communist party section of the Communist International, basing itself on the principles of Lenin and Stalin, will more determinedly than ever strive to win the American workers to the revolutionary way out of the crisis, for the emulation of the Soviet Union and its revolutionary victories . . . and for the final overthrow of the capitalist war mongers."

But the American communists were worried. They were afraid that Litvinov had promised Roosevelt too much, in order to get recognition. Litvinov's letter, if the Soviet government lived up to it, meant the end of Soviet support for American communist activities and the dissolution of the Party.

The communist blast served notice upon the United States that the Party was not bound by Litvinov's agreement. Headquarters, on Thirteenth Street, immediately got in touch with OGPU representatives and presented their worries to them. A private meeting was arranged between members of the Secretariat of the American Communist party, Litvinov, and the chiefs of the OGPU apparatus for the United States, which maintained secret headquarters in New York. At this meeting, Litvinov assured the frightened communists that they had nothing to worry about. The agreement, he explained, was between Governments and not between the United States government and the Communist International. Not having specifically referred to the letter, Litvinov went on to explain that the Comintern is not restrained by the Soviet government and is free to carry on whatever activities it deems necessary. "After all, comrades," he concluded, "you should by this time know how to handle the fiction of the tie-up between the Comintern and the Soviet government. Don't worry about the letter. It is a scrap of paper which will soon be forgotten in the realities of Soviet-American relations."

Following this memorable secret conference, Litvinov held a press conference. Asked about the Communist party of the United States, Litvinov gingerly replied:

"The Communist party of Russia doesn't concern America and the Communist party of the United States of America doesn't concern Russia."

Litvinov knew the reverse to be true, for he knew that at every national convention of the Communist party of Russia, the only Party permitted in the Soviet Union, the Party that is actually the Government of the Soviet Union, reports are diligently made on the American Communist party.

At the convention of the Russian Communist party, in 1939, B. Z. Manuilsky, the representative to the United Nations of the Ukrainian Soviet Republic, who was then the real boss of the Comintern behind Dimitrov, its chairman and figurehead, reported on the Communist party of the United States as follows:

"Considerable progress has been made by the Communist party of the United States of America. By doing everything possible to assist in shaping the class movement of the proletariat and in its breaking away from the bourgeois Parties, its membership has grown from 20,000 to 90,000.

"Its membership has grown because it has, by its work, assisted in strengthening the industrial unions, which have as many as 4,000,000 members [meaning C.I.O.] and, because it has conducted tireless and patient work among 3,500,000 workers under the reactionary leadership of the American Federation of Labor, for restoration of trade union unity on the basis of the class struggle. One of the Party's fundamental defects is that its contacts with the masses of farmers and the farmers' movement are still weak."

Evidently the Communist party of the United States did concern the Russian government, for the American party, next to the French Communist party, had risen to second place among the communist parties outside of the Soviet Union and it was treated accordingly by the Russian communists and subsidized accordingly.

But Litvinov, chuckling to himself good-naturedly, continued to give the reporters the line, when they asked him how his agreement with President Roosevelt to refrain from propaganda would affect the Communist International:

"The Third International is not mentioned in this document," Litvinov smiled broadly. He was apparently ready for the question and continued, "You must not read more into the document than was intended."

Litvinov proved that the Russians had sized up the President of the United States, and knew how much they could get away with. Later, the Russians were to appease Roosevelt on this matter by publicly announcing the dissolution of the Comintern, but only after the changes in the international situation made it necessary to conduct the affairs of the Comintern on an entirely different basis.

Who Uses Whom?

The communists, from the fall of 1935 up to the end of World War II, played ball with everyone who would play ball with them. The honeymoon with respectability was interrupted only for the brief period of the Soviet-Nazi Pact from August, 1939, to June, 1941. The New Dealers, the Bohemians, the intellectuals, the liberals, and the trade unionists, especially John L. Lewis, learned much from their relations with the communists. Many of them who imagined that communists, in association with others, would lose much of their revolutionary uncompromising characteristics were sadly disillusioned. Those who thought they could exploit the communists for their own purposes found out, much to their sorrow, that the communists were on the end that was doing the exploiting. The communists, like prostitutes who pick up companions on the street, were not being misled. If they were to be seduced, it would be done with the communists' knowledge and desire for such seduction, because it would be profitable and result in good dividends for the communist cause.

Individual communists may have been corrupted by the association with respectability but the Party as a whole remained true to the movement and its goal. Those who were corrupted by the association in large numbers were the non-communists, who were foolish enough to imagine that they could use the communists for their own purposes.

Through association with the communist movement, rational

people were turned into irrational people. Honest democrats, who believed in the democratic tradition of the country, fell for the totalitarian principles of the Soviets. Liberals who preached "one world" wanted that world to be dominated by the Soviet and its communist phrases and slogans. The communist practice of character-assassination became the stock in trade of American intellectuals. Truth for them was a matter of red coloration, not of honesty. If the litmus paper, by which they judged ideas according to their chemical analysis, turned red, indicating communist approval, it was okay with them. If not red, then it became fascist, reactionary and something to be denounced and fought.

For a long time communism penetrated and poisoned American intellectual and cultural life. Through the Newspaper Guild, which they controlled, the communists had access into practically every important newspaper and publication in the United States. Through their organizations of writers, actors, dancers, artists and cultural clubs, they were able to bludgeon the writer, the liberal, the artist, the actor, the teacher and minister, to do their bidding because to fight them, or remain neutral, involved the danger of being publicly disgraced as a red-baiter, a fascist, a reactionary, or a mercenary.

It will be shown later on, in the chapter dealing with the C.I.O. and the unions, that the communists did not, during their honeymoon with respectability, abandon their basic field of operations, the trade unions. The events in China, the Spanish Civil War, the revolts in the Latin American countries, in all of which the Communist party of the United States took an active part, prove that the Communist party never abandoned the communist goal of world domination by the communist world superstructure.

The Communists Go to Spain

The communists fought for big stakes in the Spanish Civil War. Stalin believed that the Spanish communists, who had always been an insignificant factor in Spanish political life, might, with the aid of the Soviet government, gain control of the destinies of Loyalist Spain. If Franco had been defeated then a communist Spain would give the communist world superstructure control of the Iberian Peninsula, a foothold in Western Europe, access to the Mediterranean and the Atlantic Ocean, a gateway to Africa, and a frontier with France at a time when the French communists hoped the Popular Front Government, in which they were participating, would succumb to communist domination; a communist Spain would put a communist power at Portugal's backdoor, a country the Soviet government did not like; give the communists access to the rich mineral deposits of Spain so essential in the production of war matériel, and influence with the Spanish speaking countries of the Western Hemisphere. Stalin considered the gamble was worth-while if the communists could get away with it without involving the world in war at a time when the Soviet Union was not prepared for it. The communists played two horses at the same time. They played the Spanish horse for what they could get out of it while they worked feverishly behind the scenes, mainly in Berlin, trying to fix up their fences with the Nazis. Communists are geniuses in conducting diametrically opposed policies at one and the same time. They have done so repeatedly in international affairs just as the American communists have done so repeatedly in the execution of domestic policies on the American scene.

The Communist International acted with the speed of lightning in the Spanish Civil War. Before many months had gone by, an International Brigade had been organized by the Comintern, with André Marty, the French communist, its figurehead. Behind Marty, Russian political and military chiefs of the OGPU operated as the decisive force, representing the interests of the Soviet government and the communist world superstructure. Orders went out to communist parties all over the world to send Party officials and capable Party members to act as staff members, commissars and officers of the International Brigade. Additional orders went out that recruits be signed for active service with the International Brigade, among whom should be an appreciable number of reliable Communist party members. The trek of communist agents to Loyalist Spain began.

Before the year was up, in the latter part of 1936, Minor was on his way to Spain, presumably as the correspondent of the *Daily Worker*, but actually as one of the many representatives in Spain of the Comintern and also to take care of American communist party affairs in Spain.

Committees of all kinds were immediately formed in the United States, such as the joint North American Committee to Aid Spanish Democracy, and the Friends of the Abraham Lincoln Brigade, for the purpose of raising funds. By the first of the year 1937, medical units started leaving the United States for Loyalist Spain. Special Committees were formed to raise money for that purpose. One Committee, the American Society for Technical Aid to Spanish Democracy, deserves special mention for it was formed to facilitate OGPU operations in the United States. The Committee publicly announced that its purpose was to raise funds to send American skilled workers to Spain. The chairman of the Committee was William E. Browder, brother of Earl Browder. (A sister, Mary Browder, was an OGPU agent and one of its code experts, which indicates the tie-up of the Browder family with the OGPU.) The Executive Secretary, in charge of the office, was Rebecca Grecht, a Communist party official and member of the top inner circle of the Party. Its nominal secretary was John Howard Lawson, dramatist and script writer for the movies, and a Communist party member. Waldo Frank, author, served as Chairman, and Paul Crosbie, Communist party official, as Vice-Chairman. The Board of Directors, numbering some who were not communists, included: Michael Blankfort, Van Wyck Brooks, Malcolm Cowley, Kyle Crichton, Joseph Freeman, Ben Gold, Harry Hart, Lester Cohen, Lewis Mumford, George Sklar, a Lenin University alumnus and OGPU operative, and Alexander Trachtenberg, also a Communist party member.

The first American recruits for Spain were gathered together secretly. They were immediately formed into military units, officered by Communist party members, and trained in the art of warfare. In training soldiers for Spain, the Communist party of the United States trained and prepared itself for revolutionary civil war. The first public announcements that Americans were fighting in Spain appeared in May, 1937.

The first contingents of Americans to arrive in Spain were organized into the American Battalion of the International Brigade, the nucleus around which the Abraham Lincoln Brigade was formed. The Washington Brigade was formed later and the two merged into the Washington-Lincoln Brigade.

American Communist party officials in Spain acted as staff members, intelligence officers and political commissars. George Watts, a Communist party organizer, as political commissar of the Abraham Lincoln Brigade, exerted tremendous power. John Gates, one of the top leaders of the Young Communist League of the United States and political Commissar of the Fifteenth Brigade, ruled it with an iron hand—to arouse his ire meant flirting with death. Robert Minor, surrounded by a staff of American communist journalists, communist aides and spies, received his orders from the higher command of the OGPU. In turn, he made sure that the orders were carried out by the Americans. No deviation from the Communist party line and the line of the OGPU was tolerated. Communist spies mingled with the members of the American brigades and immediately reported back to the political commissars or to Robert Minor any bit of conversation that seemed suspicious or any act which, in their opinion, violated the Party line.

Non-communists, who did not fall in step with the communist position, soon found out, in OGPU prisons and before firing squads, that it did not pay.

The most feared man among the Americans, and among Spaniards and others as well, turned out to be a man who reached Spain via the United States where he was active as a C.I. Rep to the Italian section of the American movement. In Spain, this communist adventurer had an opportunity to prove what metal he was made of. Sormenti, on his arrival in Spain, immediately became an important cog in the OGPU apparatus. The OGPU attached him to the Fifth Regiment, the regiment around which the communists built the Spanish Peoples Army. Sormenti assumed the Spanish name of Carlos Contreras. Before long the Commissar of the Fifth Regiment rose to the rank of Major. Around him were gathered all the hard-boiled gunmen and cut-throats of the American Communist party who were in Spain—the gunman George Mink, who was a pioneer Communist party organizer on the water front, the South Slavic gunmen of the Party from the Chicago District, selected Greek strong-arm men from New York, communist miners from the anthracite and Pittsburg area, Bulgarians from Detroit, and Lithuanians from Chicago.

When orders came from OGPU staff headquarters in Spain to liquidate the Trotskyites in the Loyalist cause, this group from America went to work with cold precision to carry out the orders. Sormenti, alias Major Carlos Contreras, George Mink and a gunman from Chicago, outdid themselves. They shot and killed right and left. The group gloated over their exploits. George Mink was responsible for the assassination of a Spanish anarchist philosopher who was greatly admired and loved by the anarchists throughout the world. The man happened to be a dear personal friend of Carlo Tresca, the Italian-American anarchist who had been collaborating with the communists on the Spanish issue. When he was acquainted with the facts and it was conclusively proven to him that Carlos Contreras and George

Mink were personally involved in the assassination and that George
Mink had fired the bullet that killed the man, a feud broke out between Tresca and Sormenti, which ended with the assassination of
Tresca. The feud was, in the opinion of the author, a contributing
factor but not the direct cause of the assassination, as the author will
attempt to show later on, when dealing with the Tresca murder.

Over 25,000 communist officials, representing practically every
Communist party in the world, were moved into Spain. Headed by
the OGPU, they constituted the communist backbone in Loyalist
Spain. These 25,000 communist agents are better agents today, because
they have trained under fire. They have learned how to translate theories and programs into action. They have learned first-hand how
OGPU methods are concretely applied. They have learned the art of
warfare and the essentials of military leadership. They participated
in maneuvering in a government in which the communists were
among the weakest elements in such a way that the Spanish communists became a leading political factor, and the non-Spanish International communist aggregation in Spain the real leaders and bosses
of the Loyalist government. Had Russia been industrially and mili-
tarily strong enough to match its strength with the democratic capitalist West, the communists would then have struck out for mastery
of the world. But the Russians were not prepared. Stalin knew that
and held back.

But, for the communist world superstructure, participation in
the Civil War in Spain had advantages which the defeat of the
Loyalist forces did not wipe out. What the communists learned in
Spain, they applied to their own countries. In the satellite countries
which the communists now dominate, the communist rulers are men
and women who had been trained in Spain. In the countries where
a communist contest for power is imminent, communists with experience in the Spanish Civil War stand ready to give the signal to start
civil war. In the Latin-American countries, where communist movements are making big strides, and where Sormenti, alias Major Carlos
Contreras, is operating today, the skillful direction of the movements is in the hands of communists who spent years in directing
civil warfare in Spain. The communist army trained in Spain is not
disbanded. The communists have not been softened by respectability.
All depends on what turn history takes. The communists are prepared
to go into action on a grand scale, should that action coincide with the
interests of the Soviet Union.

The C.I.O. a Landmark in Communist Infiltration and Organization

The organization of the C.I.O. owes much to the communists. By driving a wedge into the American Federation of Labor, the communists hoped to gain a dominant position in the trade unions of the C.I.O. and the leadership and control of millions of workers in the nations' basic and mass production industries.

The origin of its organization goes back to Lenin's time. It has already been shown that when Lenin sensed an immediate proletarian revolution was not imminent in Western Europe, he abandoned the call for immediate insurrection and directed the attention of the world's communists towards political action and the capture of the conservative and reactionary trade unions. A direct assault upon the reactionary trade union fortress, which was the communist policy in the United States in 1919-1920, gave way to Lenin's more subtle policy of boring, like termites, within the reactionary American Federation of Labor.

Here again, many novices dealing with communist policies reach simple conclusions by taking a given communist policy, at a given moment, on its face value. Communist policy is never simple. It is always complex and paradoxical. Besides, a momentary policy is always tied up with a long-range basic policy. It accounts for the many twists in Party line, which confuse and confound so many people.

At the time Lenin directed the attention of the American communists to the necessity of working inside the American Federation of Labor and stood against the splitting up and destruction of the organization, he conferred in Moscow with Sidney Hillman on a plan to speed up and bring about the destruction of the American Federation of Labor.

American Communist party officials, together with Foster, participated in the discussions which resulted in a plan whereby forces outside of the AF of L, in the independent unions, together with progressive forces built up by the communists inside of the AF of L, were to unite to either wrest control of the AF of L from the reactionary leaders or, failing that, to destroy the AF of L and build a new organization on its ruins.

Two reasons accounted for the failure of Lenin's plans. Hillman got frightened when he returned to the United States. He played around with the communists, flattered them and gave them money, but failed to carry out his commitments to Lenin. Foster, entrusted with carrying out the plan in the AF of L, was a novice who had just entered the communist movement. He stupidly interpreted the policy as one of loyalty to the American Federation of Labor under all circumstances. His execution of that policy threw the communists into opposition with the radical trade union forces, upon whose collaboration the successful prosecution of the plan depended.

But Lenin's plan was never abandoned. Friendly relations with Sidney Hillman were never jeopardized. Moscow corrected Foster's mistake.

The communists were forced to make peace with the independent trade unionists and the radical, revolutionary trade unionists who refused to go along with Foster. Moscow called for the formation of a trade union bloc. Moscow went so far in demanding the formation of a trade union bloc in the United States, that in a secret, confidential letter to the American party the President of the Comintern suggested that it might be advisable to consider the liquidation of the Red Trade Union International to further the policy.

With the organization of the C.I.O., the question of the liquidation of the Red International of Trade Unions again came to the fore. During the war it went out of business, but only after Moscow laid out plans for the formation of a new international trade union organization. Such an organization was formed with the blessing of Moscow, known as the World Federation of Trade Unions. The AF of L, however, stubbornly refused to participate in its affairs. The C.I.O. joined it.

The new organization is a much more effective medium for Moscow and its world communist superstructure, for it permits the communists to function in the international trade union field behind the façade of the World Federation of Trade Unions, an organization which includes unions from fifty-six countries with a total dues-paying membership of 65,500,000. The Russian trade unions momentarily make up the largest single factor. But the Russian trade unions are trade unions in name only; they are Soviet government labor agencies which have no freedom or independence and are completely under the thumb of the Russian Communist party. The communists, through the World Federation of Unions, operate very effectively in the trade unions on a world scale and from headquarters that are situated in Paris and not in Moscow. In addition to the Russian unions in the World Federation of Trade Unions, the communists dominate the

French unions, a considerable section of the British trade unions and the C.I.O., the unions from Bulgaria, Poland, Italy, Czechoslovakia, the Latin-American and Asiatic countries and elsewhere.

American representatives from the C.I.O., under the leadership of Sidney Hillman, went to the organization conferences of the World Federation of Trade Unions with the blessings of the United States State Department and helped set up an organization which gives the agents of the communist world superstructure strategic positions of tremendous power, for they possess the means of crippling the industrial life of the democratic world through strikes for political purposes, thereby driving the forces of organized labor into the camp of communism. Hillman failed Lenin in 1922. Later, he carried out his bargain with Lenin, splitting American labor and organizing the C.I.O. In agreement with Stalin, he extended the bargain to include the world. In surrendering the world's trade unions to the communists, Hillman was helped to a considerable extent by the British trade unionist, Sir Walter Citrine, who became the first president of the World Federation. Without the inclusion of the C.I.O. as the representative of American labor, and the British Trade Union Congress as the representative of British labor, the organization of the World Federation of Trade Unions would have been impossible. They gave the new organization the non-communist, non-Russian trade union base, which the communists needed so badly.

Since its organization in the latter part of 1945, the World Federation of Trade Unions, on all the major international questions confronting the labor movement, has hewed closely to the Party line. It has defended the interests of the Soviet Union and the communists in Germany, in China, in the Near East, in Japan, in Trieste and in Greece. Its Secretary and head, Louis Sallant, hangs on to the communist line like a fish which has swallowed the bait hook, line and sinker. The Executive Board of the World Federation is firmly in the hands of avowed communists and those who have been baptized by the communist holy water.

The communist world superstructure is busy consolidating this organized force of sixty-six and a half million trade unionists for the coming struggle with the democratic world. Hundreds of thousands of communist functionaries, in all countries of the world, are busy in the World Federation, using its structure for their quisling operations. In France, the communist world superstructure has poured millions of dollars, millions that were not spent on the rank-and-file, for propaganda. The millions were spent to buy up and to corrupt the trade union officials and intellectuals in the French labor movement, who serve as a bridge to the masses. These impoverished souls have sold their integrity and principles for a mess of communist pottage, in return for which they feed the masses who trust them communist lies straight out of the communist propaganda factory.

France is an example of what goes on everywhere else on a similar, though lesser, scale, because France holds a very important spot in the world designs of the communists.

In the United States, due directly to the initiative of the World Federation, a Soviet-American Trade Union Committee was set up in October, 1946, with four members of the Russian unions, and five members of the C.I.O., namely, Philip Murray, R. J. Thomas, Frank Rosenblum, Lee Pressman and Michael Ross. The Russian communists thereby gained access to the C.I.O. with its six and a half millions of American workers.

The gears of the communist world superstructure mesh perfectly as the massive communist organization machine operates in scooping up one vantage point of power after another.

The ease with which the C.I.O. was organized was due to two factors. One, it had the official sanction and support of the New Deal Administration; two, the dominant leaders of the American Federation of Labor were out of step with the new developments in industry and labor, developments which called for the application of new techniques in the organization of labor and for new forms of trade union organization and struggle.

John L. Lewis, whose union of coal miners operates in an industry which is closely tied up with the industrial development of the United States, early recognized that the times called for a decisive change in trade union methods and policy. He displayed a keen sense of political values and realized that the New Deal, if it were to survive, needed a popular base and that it could secure that base only through an alliance with unions organized in the mass production industries. His one mistake was a mistake of necessity. To organize the unorganized industries on an industrial basis, he needed the zeal and the self-sacrificing spirit of an army of organizers imbued with a working class psychology and devoted to its cause. These he needed badly and in a hurry. They were to be had only in the camp of the communists. Lewis, the traditional opponent of the communists in the trade unions, prepared to work with the material he disliked in the hope that, after the organization was well established, he could either force the communists to do his bidding or else eliminate them from the C.I.O. organizations they helped to build. He was mistaken. When Lewis went along with the communists in the C.I.O., it was all right with them. When the communists supported the Hitler-Stalin pact, at the outbreak of World War II, and opposed the pro-British policies of the Roosevelt Administration, they went all-out in support of Lewis' isolationism and opposition to Roosevelt. But, after Hitler invaded Russia, the communists changed their line. The imperialist war became a peoples' war and Roosevelt the champion of the people. But, when Lewis refused to make the turn, the communists took full advantage of their new position of strength with the Roosevelt Administration, lined up solidly behind Hillman and gave Lewis the boot out of the C.I.O.

Hillman, on the other hand, was that one man in the American trade union movement who kept his quarrels with the communists on a family basis. Like husband and wife, they had their tiffs and spats, but they always kissed and made up. The communists treated Hillman and his union as sacred territory. The communists went so far, but no further, and Hillman retaliated by always keeping the door open to them. In disputes involving communists in other unions, Hillman was often called upon by the communists to intercede for them. Hillman maintained his contacts with communists close to the inner circle of the Communist party of the United States; he carefully guarded his friendship with Soviet officials and top Russian communists.

The communists really went to work on the C.I.O. following Lewis' fall. The communist propaganda machine now had a big job mapped out for it, a job which called for the use of its advertising technicians in every field of propaganda. Into the hopper went trained communist propagandists, orators, scribes, personal contact men and women. Into the field went thousands of communist industrial and political organizers, who knew the intricacies of union organization, from the calling out of a strike to the leadership of a picket line, from the employment of rough-house tactics to the intricate maneuvering and strategy by which communist control over unions and their membership is secured. Over this structure, unique in the history and life of American labor, sat a few men, the general staff of the Communist party of the United States, representatives of the

Comintern with ties to the OGPU and the clever chargé d'affaires of the Russian Embassy, Constantine Oumansky.

In organizing the C.I.O., the communists did a good job. No job was too small or too large for them. They took the risks together with the glory. In the thickest and most desperate battles for the organization of the workers, before auto plants, steel mills and rubber factories, the communists were found in the thick of the fight, in the forefront of the battle.

The lessons the communists had learned in Passaic, in Gastonia, in the coal regions, on the water front, in the San Francisco general strike, they applied to the organization of the C.I.O. They outdid themselves in extreme action for they knew that behind every communist picket captain, stood the New Deal Administration, which acted like a very powerful ally.

The country got a taste of militant trade unionism, in the drama and violence which followed. Picket lines were transformed into tense spectacles in which the human actors were pitted against gigantic industries; violence, when it flared up as it did in the strike against Little Steel, resulted in the bloody Sunday of May 30, 1937, when the pickets were fired upon by the Chicago police. Four pickets lay dead in the grass stubble before the plants they wanted to picket; over 100 were wounded. The stubborn Thomas M. Girdler soon met his master on the field of industrial warfare, John Steuben, Communist party organizer of the Youngstown, Ohio, section of the Communist party.

Steuben, Russian by birth whose real name was Rizak, joined the Young Communist League when he was about sixteen years old. He spoke English poorly with a decided accent, had practically no schooling or educational background and knew absolutely nothing of the country of his adoption and its people. That was in 1927. No one, at the time, took the smiling, bashful little lad seriously. In the Party, he learned quickly that a communist must be a political weathervane, must turn quickly with every turn in the Party line. He quickly learned all the tricks of political maneuvering and deception and soon counted for something in the Party machine. Ten years later, the general staff of the Communist party decided to pit the pygmy Steuben against the giant Girdler.

In the ten years' interim, Steuben, the professional revolutionist, had learned much. He had been trained as a Party organizer to handle all kinds of situations and to deal with men. With Browder, Foster,

Stachel, Hathaway and the C I and Profintern representatives standing in back of him, and backed up by the Party machine, Steuben knew he could not go wrong, for it was in the cards that every avenue open to the Communist party and the C.I.O. from Moscow to Washington would be used to help him bring the "tsar" and "tyrant" of Little Steel to his knees.

Everywhere the communists were active. In Detroit, the communists tried out a new technique in industrial warfare. The communists seized the factories by staging sit-down strikes. The country was treated to a preview of things to come, of how the communists intended to seize the factories by occupying them from the inside and converting each factory into a fortress of the communist revolution. The communists were not innocents in trying out this tactic. A spineless, pusillanimous administration let them get away with it. They have learned much from the tactic. The plans for seizing American factories when the time is opportune have been stored away in the minds of the communist leaders and in reports filed away for safe keeping in the Comintern archives. The one thing the communists learned in seizing the factories is, that it can come as the result of an ordinary trade union dispute. Once in control of the factories, should the communists decide to hold on to their occupancy by force of arms, the country faces the alternative of either destroying its seized factories or capitulating to the communists.

The Detroit district of the Communist party holds a unique position in the Communist party organization. Since 1929, the ablest Party organizers have been put in charge of its affairs. Stachel, a key man in the communist inner circle, served as organizer of the Detroit district. In the Detroit district are also to be found some of the oldest and most capable communist trade union officials and Party organizers, men and women who have been purposely sent there from other districts. These operate together with key foreign-language specialists and trained technicians, who act as industrial spies..

New Years, 1937, the communists celebrated by occupying the motor plants. Twenty-six thousand workers went out on strike in the plants of General Motors and occupied the plants. Before the week was up, 100,000 men were out on strike. In two more days, the number jumped to 135,000 and plant after plant was occupied—the largest plants, all of them monuments to American engineering genius and enterprise.

Maurice Sugar, a labor lawyer, top man for the Communist party in Detroit and one of its secret members, was so enthused by the success of the Party policy in the sit-down strikes, that he wrote the words and composed the music for the inspirational song of the sit-down strikers:

> "Bring me my robe and slippers, James,
> Pull up my easy chair
> Bring me my pipe and cushions, James,
> I'm not going anywhere,
> Let me have Peace and Quiet, James,
> Free from noise and din
> And send my regrets to Mr. Sloan
> Just tell him I'm staying in."

The Communists Cover the Water Front

The importance of ocean-going transport to the communist world superstructure received special attention at the hands of the Comintern and the Profintern as early as 1925. Plans were worked out in Moscow for the organization of port bureaus and seamen's clubs in all the leading port cities of the world. Money was set aside to pay for the expenses involved and special Comintern and Profintern representatives were dispatched to the communist Parties of the countries in which the ports were located, to take up with the respective Parties how the directives from Moscow were to be carried out. Upon the city of Hamburg, Germany, fell the honor of becoming the headquarters of the seamen's network of the communist world superstructure. Here an elaborate international headquarters soon came into being which served as a world exchange for seamen, regardless of the flags under which they served. Attached to the Hamburg Port Bureau and to the Headquarters Staff was a special squad of Russian and International OGPU agents, who kept a close eye on the activities of the Hamburg seamen's center and, who also used its facilities to ship out OGPU agents all over the world and to keep up a steady surveillance on the world's commercial shipping as well as naval activities.

In May, 1932, the communist world superstructure held, in Hamburg, its first International Congress of marine workers, longshoremen, rivermen and fishermen, to consider how to replace the old methods of organization with new modern techniques which would bring results quickly.

The American Communist party had already responded in January with a declaration that "the perspective of future developments and possibilities of struggle, the close control maintained by the government, the tremendous array of forces and the importance of this industry in defending the Soviet Union, place enormous tasks squarely before the Marine Workers Industrial Union (the name of the first communist union in the maritime industry, later to become the National Maritime Union, affiliated with the C.I.O.), and demands that the Communist party turn its face sharply towards the water front. . . ."

This significant statement pointed out that the communist waterfront campaign was anti-U.S. government and linked to the interests of the Soviet Union.

Port bureaus were immediately established in the more important ports. The port bureaus were seamen's exchanges from which the communists carried on their activities to gain control over the native seamen and to establish connections with seamen who landed in the ports from other countries. Communist seamen who had official communist business to transact on landing in port immediately made contact with the port bureau. Many OGPU agents did likewise, for the man put in charge of the port bureau was always a communist, either a member of the OGPU or had, secretly working with him, an OGPU agent.

In the United States, George Mink became the official representative of the Profintern for carrying out its program on the water fronts of North and South America.

Mink, always armed with a loaded automatic, covered thousands of miles of water front in his global travels. The man had no education whatsoever. He could not write. Whatever reports he had to make were made orally and then written up by others in proper form. His conduct proved obnoxious to the rank-and-file sailors, and to most of the people with whom he came in contact, including communists. Yet this uncouth, ill-mannered, ignorant Moscow representative, endowed with so much money and power, had a shrewd innate intelligence, bolstered up by the ability to size up the weaknesses in others. He fought with the cunning of a wild cat, had no scruples in beating down either friend or foe, and if cold-blooded murder was in order, did not hesitate to commit it.

To Mink goes the credit of making the first real, worth-while connections on the Atlantic and Pacific Coasts of North and South

America. With him begins the Communist organization of the water front of the United States. Almost simultaneously with the establishment of the port bureaus, the seamen's clubs came into existence and, later, the seamen's water front sections of the Communist party.

The most colorful communist organization on the water front, the Seamen's Clubs, were opened up in New York, New Orleans, San Francisco and Seattle. The club served during the day as a lounging place. The seamen checked their belongings and baggage free of charge, a service which they greatly appreciated and which cost the Communist party very little for the returns it brought, for a seaman out on the high seas was sure to return for his luggage once he hit port again. In the club rooms, communists sat around to start up conversations with sailors who had time on their hands, conversations in which they "wised them up" on the unionization of the industry and filled them with guarded communist propaganda. The literature spread on the table consisted of general printed matter mixed with a lot of communist newspapers, books and leaflets. The social affairs, arranged by the club, attracted the sailors most.

Section organizers were instructed before the club opened to assign attractive communist girls for special work at the seamen's club. The girls were given to understand that getting hold of the water front got top priority in the Party. Above all, the girls were instructed to see to it that the lonely sailors, who craved companionship with the opposite sex, should be made to feel at home and given a good time. The girls danced and obliged the lonely seamen. Soon the word got around on the water front that if you wanted a good time with a swell "broad" without paying for it, you could have it by going up to the seamen's club on Saturday night.

The Party overcame the deficiency in seamen by sending large numbers of selected Communist party members to sea. Most of them made just one trip in order to acquaint themselves with the seamen's lingo and to learn just enough about a ship and the sea to pass off as a bona fide sailor. These synthetic sailors, trained communists, who knew what the Party was after on the water front, became the backbone of the Party among the seamen and the drive to get them all organized into a powerful national seamen's union.

The Communist party owes its position of great influence on the water front, in a large measure, to the Pacific Coast developments centering around the leadership of Harry Bridges, an Australian. The Communist party bolstered up its organization on the Pacific Coast by sending in one of its ablest organizers, a man with plenty of Moscow experience, a graduate of the Lenin School—Sam Darcy, and by establishing a special daily newspaper, the *Western Worker,* in San Francisco with a competent staff of journalists. Success beyond the wildest expectations of the Party came on May 8, 1934, when the longshoremen announced that they were going out on strike for wages of $1.00 per hour and a thirty-four-hour week in place of the 85c an hour and a forty-eight-hour week. The action, under pressure of Harry Bridges and the communists, was taken over the heads of the leaders of the AF of L. Harry Bridges' rank-and-file action committee of the International Longshoreman's Association immediately called upon the longshoremen to set up rank-and-file action committees on all the docks. The rank-and-file committee plan of strategy originated with the communists and was used by them to inject themselves into union situations and in calling outlaw strikes. The strikes on the docks soon spread to all the ships in the harbor. On May 11, the communists succeeded in getting the seamen of 750 ships to vote in favor of a strike under the auspices of the Communist Union, the Marine Workers Industrial Union.

Harry Bridges, as chairman of the strike committee, immediately assumed public leadership. Through his leadership, all the communist agencies were brought into the strike, such as the International Labor Defense for defending the strikers legally, and the International Workers Aid, a Moscow agency for organizing relief and feeding the strikers. The *Workers World,* the communist daily, edited by George Morris, a former top leader of the Young Communist League, whose real name is Morris Yussem, gave the strike the full backing of the paper. With the communist agencies, which Bridges invited into the strike situation, came an army of communist organizers, propagandists, speakers and, what was of tremendous importance, trained strong-arm squads.

The Communist party general staff put great hopes on the 'Frisco strike. They had prepared plans to develop the strike into a general tie-up of the Atlantic and Pacific coasts. They desired to demonstrate to Moscow that they had already enough of a hold on the water front situation to stop and cripple an industry essential to the industrial life of the country and to its welfare.

Communist plans called for turning the San Francisco strike into a militant violent expression of the class war. The Communist party had the manpower in 'Frisco to do just that. Violence was not long in breaking out. A battle took place on May 15 in San Pedro in which two longshoremen were killed.

The next day the teamsters, dock clerks and marine engineers joined the strike.

The communists again led the strikers in battle against the police. They used rocks, planks, iron pipes; the class war in 'Frisco was on. The strike spread. Masters and mates joined the strike; so did the ship pilots.

On May 18, the dockers stormed a ship loading war materials for Japan. They broke through police lines, they boarded the *Oregon Maru* and took possession of her, a signal demonstration to Moscow that in its fight with Japan, water-front workers were on the side of the Soviet government.

The Communist party took no chances on a slip-up in 'Frisco. They sent their top leaders to the scene to direct affairs and to advise Bridges—Roy Hudson, William F. Dunne, Jack Stachel and, later, the leader of the Party, Earl Browder.

On July 5, in a battle with the police, in front of International Longshoremen's Association's Hall, the police used their guns, firing from behind telephone poles. Fifteen participants were wounded and two killed. The communist leadership decided to use the affair to call out a general strike in the name of their union, "The Marine Workers Industrial Union."

By July 13, the general strike initiated by the Communist party, spread so rapidly that it included all the marine workers' unions, the teamsters, slaughter-house workers, boilermakers, iron workers, whole-sale-house employees, taxi drivers and butchers. The Communist party cried: "The Race is now between the elements centered in the strike committee and the reactionary elements in the Labor Council [AF of L]."

On July 15, the general strike became official on a motion of Harry Bridges. His motion provided that the general strike include the entire San Francisco Bay region, including the cities of Oakland, Berkeley, Richmond, Alameda, Palo Alto, Redwood City, San Mateo, Sausalito, San Rafael, and other towns along San Francisco and San Pedro Bays. Over 125,000 workers responded to the call. San Francisco was turned into a dead city overnight.

Harry Bridges became the hero of the communists and his picture, for the first time, was published in the *Daily Worker*. President William Green, of the AF of L, denounced the strike. The police retaliated by enforcing strict police regulations. Gangs wrecked union halls and burned the editorial offices of the communist paper, the *Western Worker*. The communists were satisfied. The 'Frisco general strike was a landmark in the class struggle. It demonstrated better than a million reports to Moscow that, given the opportunity, provided the objective situation was right, the communists could paralyze the industrial life of America and lead the workers from purely strike activity into the political strike and then on to revolution. Browder, reporting on the 'Frisco general strike, declared: "Under the pressure of the most intense terror and persecution, raids on Party offices and auxiliaries of every kind, smashing of office equipment, arrests, raids on homes of individual comrades, etc., we can say the Party functioned throughout this period without a single break. Most Party units met every day or two throughout the entire period. . . .

"As to the political character, the political adequacy of the Party leadership, we must state, there would have been no general strike in San Francisco but for the work of the Party; there would have been no general marine strike."

Following the conclusion of the strike, Darcy and Browder went to Moscow to report on the strike personally. The Moscow leaders were extremely interested. If such a communist-directed general strike could take place in the conservative United States, where the workers have little or no radical traditions, it was important for the communist world superstructure to learn the lessons in tactics and policies involved, directly from the American comrades. Darcy made the detailed report. He claimed credit for every stage in the development of the strike situation in San Francisco, from the organization of Bridges' rank-and-file committee to the calling out of the general strike and its conduct. American communist stocks rose high in Moscow as a result of Darcy's report.

The lesson to the American people is, as I have said before, that the Communist party of the United States is not a nuisance which Stalin tolerates, as some apologists for Russian communism hold, but one of the key Parties in the communist world superstructure; a Party made up of members who have long ago grown out of their swaddling clothes into adept revolutionary conspirators, trained and prepared for the problems confronting them. And, what Moscow knows should add to the American people's estimation of the American Communist party, for the gentlemen of Moscow have full confidence in the ability of the American Communist organization, not only to meet the problems of the country but also, should the occasion present itself, to undertake a struggle for power with the mightiest and strongest capitalist nation in the world.

Guide Posts to the Future

Stalin wrote, on the immediate tasks of the communist parties, the following:

"If, therefore, the communist parties wish to become mass parties, *capable of setting revolution afoot,* they must create intimate ties between themselves and the trade unions, and must find support in these industrial organizations."

Stalin is emphatic and categorical. Without support in the unions, communist parties cannot make a revolution. Getting control of the unions is, therefore, the number one task of the Communist party. By getting control of the unions, the communists mean getting control of the unions in the decisive, the basic industries of the land, the industries upon which the economic life of the country depends.

Through the organization of the C.I.O., the communists achieved this objective. A campaign may succeed within the C.I.O. to eliminate known communists from positions and membership in C.I.O. unions. The government, through its special agencies and by enactment of legislation, may take upon itself the power to cleanse the unions of communism as a step towards security and the preservation of the state. But both courses will fail to dislodge the communists from the foothold they have gained in the C.I.O. unions. The bulk of the communist membership and their followers will remain in the unions, as will a considerable number of trade union officials who carry out Party orders. The Party has anticipated both the move by the C.I.O. officially, and by the government, by having its forces in the C.I.O. unions just melt into the membership where they now operate as trade unionists and not as communists. When the occasion arises the closed buds will suddenly burst open and the communists will appear once more in full bloom.

The communist forces in the C.I.O. unions cannot be treated as a foreign importation. In their ranks are to be found hundreds of thousands of workers of native American stock. You cannot take out of the basic industries of the United States close to two million workers and deport them from the country. It is this communist force in the C.I.O. unions that the country will have to learn how to deal with if it wants to survive as a democracy.

But communist trade union strength is not confined entirely to the C.I.O. They have considerable strength in the American Federation of Labor also, and in the independent unions. The communist arm that holds the hammer is very strong indeed. The arm that holds the sickle which depends upon the organization of the American farmers is far from being as powerful, but the communists are working day and night to build up their strength in the rural communities and on the farms.

To maintain its trade union machine in such a way as not to expose the connections between the Party and its trade union people was no easy matter. Domestic communist trade union policies had to coincide with Moscow's interests. The Party was bodily tied up with a world-wide communist trade union machine. What the American communists did had to jibe with the objectives of the world-wide machine. This position of the American Communist party makes the development of trade union policies and the control of the trade union machine by the Party an exceedingly difficult task, especially when directives from Moscow run counter to the patriotic sentiments of American workers.

Blunders by communists often caused trade union officials, who followed the Party line, to change their position. A classic example is the Maritime Union. The Maritime Union, organized by the money and efforts of the Communist party and Moscow, was recognized as a communist union. Its president, Joseph Curran, fronted the union and for years bolstered up the Communist party machine in the organization. He fought those who fought the communists. On trade union policies and on political issues, he was one with the Communist party, as a record covering over ten years of union activities will prove. But, when the communist general staff tried to maneuver Harry Bridges into a position where he would become the king pin on the water front of the Atlantic as well as the Pacific coast, Curran resented the move, fought back, and broke with the communists.

But the strong communist position in the C.I.O. did not depend only upon its support from the rank-and-file and on the men it had in the national administration, but also on the contacts it had in the various departments of the C.I.O. In all the departments, the Communist party had key people and through these key people, an army of communist clerks carried on the routine work of the organization. To discover them, now that the Communist party has gone underground in the C.I.O., and to root them out, will take a major operation by a skilled surgeon. Philip Murray is not that surgeon; nor has any one come forward in the organization to do the job.

The communists are wonderful chameleons. When it suits their purpose, they can change their colors immediately. Many communist officials in the C.I.O. unions have already taken off their communist robes and donned the robes of the anti-communists. Others will support the most rabid anti-communist resolutions in order to remain in the seat of power. It is a tactic of retreat not new to the communist movement. It was carried out in the war against Gompers, when Gompers sought to expel all communists from the AF of L. It is being done today on a much wider scale and more skillfully.

Only the communist union officials, who are publicly identified with the Communist party, will not disavow their communism. Such officials are few in number. One can count them on the fingers of one hand, because the Communist party made it a policy, before the organization of the C.I.O., to hide the Communist party affiliation of its trade union officials. In an extreme emergency, union officials publicly identified with the Communist party may, after being directed to do so by the Communist party, come out and denounce communism. It has already happened in one important union of the C.I.O., and will probably happen in more, should that be necessary. Only an old standby of the Communist party, like Ben Gold, will remain openly identified with the Communist party, come what may, for it is quite impossible for him to change, unless he breaks completely with the Party organization and is willing to take the personal risk involved. The first time a communist union official of Gold's type gives an indication that his communist loyalty is cracking, his life is not worth the cost of the ink involved in scratching his name on a piece of paper.

Wheels Within Wheels

Browder, at the height of his glory, coined a phrase, "Communism is 20th Century Americanism," a phrase which cost him, among other things, the leadership of the Communist party. The phrase, immediately picked up by the advertising geniuses of the Party, became the outstanding slogan of the period of respectability.

During this period, the Party did not change its ties to Moscow and communist objectives were not sacrificed. Methods were changed in certain directions; communists used the language of conciliation which made possible collaboration with New Deal forces and with liberals and progressives in both the Democratic and Republican parties. The communists had little difficulty in attracting people from all walks of American life who were willing to go along with the communist-New Deal-C.I.O. forces in America, and with the Soviet Union in the international field. This amalgamation of opposing elements in the social structure developed into a dynamic left force, that greatly aided the Communist party.

Those who fluttered like mesmerized moths in the radiance of the red star, were classified into categories by the communist political and organization department, and organized into so many different organizations serving so many causes—international, national, state and local—that it is quite impossible to keep track of them. Some of the organizations were fly-by-nights, called into existence for a momentary purpose only to disappear soon thereafter in the communist ether. Others were of a more lasting nature, enjoying an existence of a year or two, before going out of business. A few organizations were of a more permanent character. The outstanding one is so definitely communist, that there is no need for camouflage—the International Labor Defense, of which Congressman Vito Marcantonio is the chairman.

The influence exerted by the Communist party, through its transmission belt organizations, explains what has been puzzling to many students of the Communist party: why communist political influence is felt in strata of our population numbering millions and why the Communist party, in election campaigns, is unable to register this influence in votes.

This phenomenon, long ago recognized by the communists, explains its organization schemes and strategy. The communists realized that advocating a simon-pure communist program would lead to isolation and sterility. They found out soon enough that American people were not impressed with the principles of communism and opposed the revolutionary means advocated to obtain them. The bitter pill of communism had to be sugar-coated to get the American people to swallow it and had to be fed to them in minimum doses.

Hence, the transmission belt organizations are formed for this purpose on the initiative of the Communist party, around specific, concrete issues and not on the Communist party program. Thus the Communist party that polled only 80,000 votes in the national election of 1936, nevertheless did register and organize approximately 4,000,000 unemployed for unemployment insurance. The Communist party did succeed, through the American Labor Party in New York State which it dominates, to get over 400,000 votes for the Communist-endorsed candidates of the A L P and, in New York City, to elect two communists to the City Council. In elections in California, and in other sections of the country, the communists have demonstrated that, under certain favorable local conditions, they are good vote-getters also. It must be kept in mind that a large percentage of the communists who jam Madison Square Garden meetings and similar meetings throughout the country are unnaturalized foreign-born. Were they citizens, they certainly would vote communist. But this group is steadily decreasing in percentage to the communist total, due to the increase in the number of native-born and naturalized communists.

The Communist May Day Parade, in New York City, with red banners held aloft, with thousands of cardboard slogans carried by the marchers, sways in colorful pageantry through the streets. Over 100,000 men, women and children, singing revolutionary songs and shouting defiant slogans against the Government and capitalism, are in the line of march. This is no paper-box opéra bouffe organization. On display is the manpower, the heart and soul, the fanatic fire that can overheat the social boiler to the point of explosion. One hundred thousand tramp on hard cobblestones and asphalt pavements; tomorrow there may be millions stamping out the institutions of American freedom and the traditions of American life.

In the marching 100,000, we see the ramifications of the communist movement, the Party organizations, the unions under communist domination, the transmission belt organizations, the one-thousand-and-one deceptions under which the world communist superstructure operates in the United States.

Of the 100,000 in the march, in the late 1930's, only 10 percent were members of the Communist party. The others were followers. Among the followers, were many AF of L unions, which later conducted campaigns against the communists. Some have left the communist ranks permanently, but the gap left by the unions which have permanently deserted the communist ranks has been more than filled by new unions which have entered the communist fold. It is important to register the fact that trade unions and socialist organizations, which profess a definite anti-communist bias, nevertheless agreed to join in a communist directed parade, a parade, in its spirit and complexion, stressing the ambitions of the communist world superstructure. These presumably anti-communist, but ideologically Marxian-dominated organizations found no contradiction between their support of communist May Day and their public disavowal of the cause. Here, America experienced a minor manifestation of what Europe has experienced in a big way, that is that in almost every great social and political crisis the anti-communist left has deserted the united cause of democracy and the fight against totalitarian communism to join hands with the communists. The tragic situation is repeating itself today in Germany, France, Italy, Poland, Czechoslovakia, Greece and Finland, and is bringing about the split and disintegration of the British labor movement. The liberals in Europe have, in large numbers, been so overawed by the Red totalitarian colossus, that they have lost the faculty of recognizing the essentials of liberalism which rests upon the foundation of individual liberty and the limitations of the power of the state. They have become the fighting-mad apostles of a police state which seeks, through skillful fifth column penetration and by political and military aggression, to dominate the world.

The American communists have made a start. From 1936 to 1945, a period of almost ten years, interrupted only for the months in which Stalin collaborated with Hitler, the communists of the United States succeeded in creating the people's democratic front, a front which extended from the Communist party to the White House. Evidently the elements of European political disintegration, expressed in the popular front movement of France in the weakening of national patriotism and security, are also to be found in the United States, for the Communist party made use of these elements in setting up a people's democratic front through which it bolstered up the administration and enhanced its own power. A political Party which can maneuver so skillfully, in a land among whose people communism is not popular and who have little or no Marxian traditions, is a political Party that must be reckoned with in the future.

Plain People

All kinds of people go into the making of a Communist party. The movement attracts them from all walks of life. They come from the lowest economic levels up to the highest. Young men, who were hobos before they joined the Party, who never had a nickel to their name, rub shoulders in the Party with the scions of wealth, who have inherited millions from their parents, which they are bent on spending for the Communist cause in America.

This story concerns itself with just an ordinary family man, one of the plain people who, before he joined the Party, worked as a cook in a restaurant. A good family man, he loved his wife and two daughters, one fourteen, and the other sixteen years of age. He worked hard to provide for them and was a scrupulously honest, God-fearing man. A native of Greece, he found contentment in the United States and was happy. But, what John P. did not know was that in 1928 the Communist party had organized a communist shop nucleus in the restaurant. A communist mimeographed shop paper soon made its appearance in the restaurant, which magnified the workers' grievances and called for the institution of reforms, including better and cleaner washrooms, free laundry service for waiters and cooks uniforms, better food, and an item or two of communist propaganda. The communist nucleus got a shop committee elected, which was instrumental in getting the union's business agent to back up the communist demands for reforms. John P. became duly impressed when the boss granted the communist demands one after another. The demands were just demands and practical. Conditions for the workers were greatly improved. The head of the communist shop nucleus, a waiter, and the cook became friends. The waiter worked hard on the cook to make him a Party member. He supplied him with the communist Greek paper, with books and propaganda, invited him to meetings and made it a point to look out for the cook's interests in the restaurant. Before the cook had time to realize it, he became a member of the communist shop nucleus and was assigned for general Party work to the Greek section of the Party.

In 1929, the Party purged itself of dissident elements who refused to conform to Stalin's dictates to the American Communist party. The purge hit the leadership of the Greek federation hard. From the small Greek forces in the Party, new leaders had to be found. The Greek cook suddenly and unexpectedly found himself promoted to a position of importance. He now became a big shot in the Greek Federation and in the communist faction of the foodworkers union. The simple man, who had no time to actually study what communism was all about, soon became caught in the whirl and activity of the movement. Being honest and idealistic, he transferred his religion to the communist cause, giving himself up entirely to the movement.

Being a good communist, he also drew his wife and two daughters into the movement. Communism with him became not only an ideal, but a way of life. The family, like so many other families in the communist movement, was not long in gaining recognition, especially the two handsome daughters, the one just entering womanhood and the child of fourteen.

The father was too busy with Party work to notice what was happening to his family. The mother was now engrossed in Communist Women's work, and did not pay attention to her daughters; they were in good hands, the comrades were taking care of them, both had joined the Young Communist League, and reported to their parents that they were having a wonderful time and doing good work for the cause.

One early morning the mother returned home from a day and night of communist activity. The oldest daughter was not at home. Evidently, she was engaged in Party work and would be home shortly. But the next morning there was no sign of the girl. She asked the younger girl what was up?

"Oh, don't worry, mama. Mary received an invitation of the youth organizer to go to a convention in Philadelphia over the weekend. She'll be home Monday all right."

"But why didn't she let me know?"

The teen-ager giggled, "But, mama, you were so busy, she had no way of reaching you."

On Monday, the mother asked her daughter where she had been.

"To Philadelphia at a youth convention. I had a wonderful time."

With whom did you stay?"

"With Fred, the organizer. You know him. We shared a room together."

"But you should not have done it. You are a young girl. Some day you will have to marry."

The girl laughed: "Mama, you a communist, how could you be so bourgeoise? Besides, I am old enough to know what I am doing."

Then it happened again and was repeated over and over again. A miner's conference in the Anthracite, an important gathering in Pittsburg, a trip to Albany, sometimes with one male comrade, then with another. The mother became exasperated, the father a little too, but he was so busy working for the revolution, in the union, among the Greeks and in the restaurant in which he cooked, that when told, the fact disturbed him for a moment and then was forgotten in the maze of problems and responsibilities that worried his tired brain. One day the older daughter confronted her parents with an announcement that she was leaving home, that she had found a friend in the Party and was going to live with him.

"What, married!" exclaimed the mother.

"Well, not legally according to bourgeois custom. You may call it that, but we prefer to consider it otherwise."

The parents were dumbfounded. The suddenness of the information struck their simple souls sharply and left them speechless.

The father was not feeling too well. He had carried his communist work in the restaurant to such extremes, that he now found himself without a job. To get another one, during a depression when 10,000,000 were jobless and pounding the pavements, was no easy task; to go on relief, when one had worked all one's life and never idled away a day, injured one's pride, soured a man to the very pit of his stomach.

The wife complained to the father, who became moody and angry and said that the girl was old enough to know what she was doing, that in the Communist party such marriages were not unusual and that many communist couples got along very nicely.

A year went by; the family of three had plenty of communist work to do to absorb their time. After a day of meetings, demonstrations, arguments, excitement, mother and father returned home, exhausted and mentally tired. If the mother thought about her daughter's action, she kept it to herself. The family was on relief and Comrade John P., in addition to his other duties, became a leader in the communist unemployed councils. The months passed; the fourteen-year-old daughter was now fifteen, a handsome buxom maiden with luxurious wavy brown hair, a pleasant smile and an olive smooth complexion. A girl like that could not help being a favorite among the YCLers. Life for her in the Party was one round of joyous excitement.

One day, mother and father took time off from Party duties and returned home early in the evening. Opening the door, they were aghast to see their fifteen-year-old daughter naked, in bed with the section organizer. The man and girl, startled, pulled the sheet over their nudity.

The mother screamed: "What does this mean?"

The girl motioned to her parents to leave. They went into the kitchen.

Comrade organizer got up, dressed and sneaked out of the room.

The daughter put on a robe and followed her parents into the kitchen.

"No need for a scene, mama. The comrade is leaving."

"But why did you have to do this to disgrace yourself and the family?"

"Don't be fools. He is my comrade and friend. We intend to live together. You have been in the Party long enough not to be blind. When you love someone in the Party, you just go and live with him. The other girls do it and I don't see what is wrong with it."

"But you are too young to marry."

"Don't get sentimental. You're not a bourgeoise. We are communists, we don't believe in the bourgeois institution of marriage."

"You are talking nonsense, child. You know nothing of life. Don't try to meet life with communist theories."

"Mother, there is no use talking. I've a mind of my own. I will live my life the way I see fit."

The father found his tongue. "Daughter, I have struggled many years to bring you up as a nice, respectable girl. I had hoped one day to enjoy the happiness of seeing you well married."

The girl burst out in hysterical laughter. "You, father, you talk like a scissor bill. I could expect such language from a shopkeeper, not from a leader of the Communist party."

"Stop your nonsensical prattle," screamed the father, angrily. "As long as I am boss of the house, you will conduct yourself as a decent girl should. Do . . ."

The mother interposed, and grabbed the man in her arms to restrain him.

The girl looked defiance at her parents. "You talk like a fool, papa. What can you do? We're on relief. There are millions of families like ours. No, I believe in the movement. I am going to live with Comrade Paul. As friends, we will get along together very nicely."

The family of two went on in a barren, uninspired existence. The mother continued her communist activities. The father brooded over the fate of his once happy family. He expressed doubts over certain policies at communist meetings. His doubts were answered with sharp, abusive attacks. They charged that he showed strong deviationist tendencies, that he acted like a concealed Trotskyite. Others pleaded with him to mend his ways and to get back on a firm Leninist-Stalinist basis. Alone, he brooded to himself. It was all too confusing. He did not understand what it was all about. Why did he become a communist? He could not answer. Why did he give up his religion, his belief in God, to join the Party? Puzzled, he was sure of one thing, that he alone was responsible for the fate that had befallen his family. Had he been like other men, he would still be working and the family would have been as before, happily together. Theories might be all right for Stalin and for Browder, but he was only a cook. One could not expect him to theorize about the world situation and everything else. After all, he was just a simple man who wanted to live and let others live.

One day, the wife returned home alone. She smelled gas and rushed into the kitchen. A horrible sight met her eyes. Her husband was hanging from the light fixture by the neck, his face a death mask of muscular contortion and pain.

And, on July 4, 1938, the General Secretary of the Communist party orated:

"We express this fusion of American tradition with Socialism when we sing the *Star Spangled Banner* and the *Internationale* together, when we decorate our platform today with the flag of our democratic revolution of the eighteenth century and the red flag of the socialist revolution of the twentieth century. This is the meaning of our slogan: 'Communism is twentieth-century Socialism.'"

CHAPTER TEN

THE SAME DANCE—
ANOTHER TUNE

THE communists took Marxism out of the realm of Utopian idealism and political abstraction to build a powerful world revolutionary movement so fluid and flexible, so devoid of illusions, moral scruples and ideals, that often the erroneous conclusion was reached that the communist movement had departed from its basic principles and abandoned communism altogether. Such an analysis of the communist movement was based on momentary factors and not on an over-all historic and long-range view of the movement. The communists have set themselves the goal of dominating the world for communism. The starting point is the Soviet Union, through which they control a stupendous slice of the earth's pie, fabulously rich in natural resources and inhabited by a population of over 160,000,000 people. To communists, the maintenance of Soviet power is the first consideration, for without it the extension of communism on a world-wide basis is impossible. The tactics of Stalin and the Soviet leaders, regardless of how far removed they may be from the basic principles of communism at a given time, are therefore accepted without question by communists everywhere as the policies safeguarding the interests of the Soviet Union. Defending the Soviet Union from its enemies at home and abroad, in a world of conflicting ideologies and in both open and disguised opposition to capitalist nations of great industrial and military power, requires both wisdom and shrewdness in the formulation and execution of policies. The communists quickly realized that in the intricate game of international politics, the following of a narrow sectarian course, hewing strictly to the line of abstract idealism and circumscribed by theoretical principles, leads to disaster. They, therefore, follow the road of expediency whenever necessary, explaining and justifying their actions by the use of communist theories and principles which condemn opportunistic expediency.

Stalin is the master communist politician and strategist. That is why he is the boss of the Communist party and the dictator of Russia. Stalin is not a Cossack who is a master of horsemanship, yet he proved to the world that he could ride two horses, going in opposite directions at one and the same time.

Stalin did not let his left hand interfere with what his right hand was doing. On the one hand he called upon the democratic world to adopt the policy of collective security in order to isolate and restrain the fascists; and on the other hand, he worked even more determinedly to make a deal and reach an agreement with the Nazis. The communist world superstructure, under direct orders from Stalin, in Europe, Asia and America, advocated the union of all anti-Fascist, anti-Nazi forces in a people's front. In the United States, the Communist party formed the People's Democratic Front of the C.I.O., the New Deal and the communists for the same purpose. Litvinov, Soviet Foreign Minister, championed this course, a course which won him international renown as the father of collective security.

At the same time, Stalin and the small group in Russia that enjoyed his confidence had other ideas, for Stalin was not putting all his money on collective security—the democracies did not appeal to him. It was no secret in top Russian communist circles that Stalin was greatly impressed by the ruthless precision with which Hitler consolidated his power when he purged Nazi ranks of dissident elements. Negotiations with Hitler were strictly Stalin's business. Only his most trusted lieutenants were assigned to this highly confidential task. The world communist superstructure was kept completely in the dark, as were the communist parties in all other countries. Stalin feared that if news of his desire to form a working partnership with Hitler ever came prematurely to light, his plans in that direction might be wrecked for good and the communist movement dealt a blow from which it could not easily recover.

To put across the Nazi deal, Stalin had some housecleaning to do in his own Party first. He had to remove every element in the Party who, in his opinion, and in the opinion of his close advisors, might oppose his pro-Nazi policies. He had to create the situation and the reasons justifying a purge of men and women of great political stature and prominent in the revolutionary history of Russia; he had to prepare to purge figures who had held commanding posts in the Russian Communist party, in the Comintern, in the GPU, in the trade unions and in the Young Communist International. He had to prepare the country for the liquidation of the ablest generals of the Red Army staff, including a number of great popular heroes of the Russian people.

Stalin is never impetuous. He moves deliberately and always with a well-prepared plan. On December 1, 1934, an assassin's bullet killed Kirov, boss of the Leningrad section of the Russian Communist party, an intimate of Stalin, a power second to Stalin in the inner circle, the one man everybody who knew Russian Party politics predicted would inherit Stalin's mantle after he died. Kirov's popularity had grown in the Party and in the land because he displayed certain liberalizing tendencies so unusual in the cruel and severe regime of the Soviets. Kirov sought to conciliate the dissident Bolshevik elements and opposed the institution of the death penalty against Old Bolsheviks. He was assassinated under the most mysterious circumstances, and many authorities on internal Russian Party affairs hint that Stalin himself, through the OGPU, arranged the affair.

Kirov's death was just what Stalin needed to create the hysteria in the country necessary for the purges which he planned. What followed is one of the darkest pages in modern history, for the victims of Stalin's purges were accused of the very crimes of which Stalin, himself, was guilty—collaborating and conspiring with Hitler.

Walter G. Krivitsky, a high official of Soviet Military Intelligence and of the OGPU, charged that in December, 1936, he came upon evidence that proved conclusively that Stalin executed Russia's military genius, Marshal Tukhachevsky, and his associate, as German spies, at the very moment when Stalin himself, after months of secret negotiations, was on the verge of closing a deal with Hitler.

For the first time, Stalin's line of policy towards a rapprochment with Hitler was not embodied, as had been the occasion heretofore, in long drawn-up Comintern theses and resolutions. The communist parties were not sent code cables or long coded letters of explanation and instructions concerning Stalin's Moscow-Berlin line. Not even the OGPU agents in foreign lands or the Russian Embassies were given an inkling as to what was going on. Stalin took no chances on gumming up the delicate machinery of his Hitler negotiations; yet it is unfair to state that he did not take measures to enlighten the communist world superstructure of an impending important change in policy. It was not done directly, but indirectly, in a manner which made it incumbent on the communist leaders in foreign countries to use their heads independently for once.

In 1934, the communist world superstructure had built up an extensive international organization around the slogan of "Fight against War and Fascism." In the United States, Moscow spent over $150,000 to organize the League against War and Fascism, and sent special emissaries from abroad for that purpose. Suddenly, with no explanation and upon special orders from the Comintern and the insistence of the representative of the Communist International, the name of the organization was changed to the American League for Peace and Democracy. Stalin already had a secret deal with Hitler. He had promised Hitler to give up the fight against fascism and war.

Many ex-communist students of the communist movement read between the lines of news dispatches from Russia, and interpreted events such as the dropping of the slogan of the "Fight against War and Fascism" as a proof that Stalin had given up the fight against Nazism and had come to a working agreement with Hitler. When they made their conclusions public, they were most bitterly denounced by the communists. The American Communist party leaders completely misjudged the implications of the new orders from Moscow.

Browder was too engrossed in his inflated importance, too overcome with his own pompous phrases, to grasp the significance of the change involved from a fight against fascism to just an ordinary stand for peace and democracy. The other American Party leaders were too busy listening to Browder for a clue as to its implications; but none was forthcoming from the American oracle. The American communists were totally ignorant of Berlin-Moscow developments.

In spite of the fact that at the 18th Congress of the Russian Communist party, held in March, 1936, a congress which will go down in history for indicating how far a Communist party can swing to the extreme fascist right, Stalin clearly indicated to the world and to the communist leaders of other countries the road he had decided to take in the struggle between Western Democracy and Nazi barbarism and totalitarianism. The pattern of Hitler's despotic inhumanity, with its gospel of hate and bloody repression, did not concern the *Pravda* or the Congress. In his speech before the Congress, Stalin ridiculed the idea that the Rome-Berlin Axis was directed against the East (against Soviet Russia). He knew what he was talking about, because he had his secret agreement with Hitler safely tucked away in his pocket. He ridiculed those in the Western democracies, who wish-fully hoped for a march by Hitler on the Soviet Ukraine. He screwed up his eyes and knowingly grinned as he emphasized: "The Germans have disappointed them cruelly. Instead of a march further on to the East against the Soviet Union they have turned West, if you please, and demand colonies."

The line, crystal clear, of Soviet-Nazi collaboration failed to make an impression on the American communist leaders. For their stupidity, Stalin is not to blame. He went as far as he could in making his position clear; if the world and the American communist leaders failed to draw the proper conclusions and were misled, it was their own fault.

Some of the American communist leaders, in defending their ignorance of the Berlin-Moscow line, brought to their defense, before the chagrined Rep of the Comintern, the 1939 May Day Manifesto of the Comintern. Did not the Manifesto call for opposition to Nazi-Fascist aggression, did not one of its main slogans call for "Down with Fascism and Wars of Plunder"?

But the Comintern Rep laughed into their worried faces. He called the perturbed Browder a fool, and directed attention to the fact that the *Daily Worker* of May 3, 1939, carried a Moscow dispatch that Stalin had removed Litvinov as People's Commissar of Foreign Affairs and had put Molotov in his place. Such a removal, he pointed out to the American, was tantamount to an announcement to the world that the line which Litvinov followed had been scrapped and a line out of harmony with collective security and collaboration with the democracies had been adopted.

A little chronology will expose the dilemma of the American communist leaders. They acted as if no change in Soviet International relations had taken place.

In April, 1939, the American Communist party conducted a vigor-ous campaign against isolationism and called for the most active participation of the United States in the internal affairs of Europe and Asia.

On May 27, 1939, Browder came out flat-footedly for a continua-tion of the New Deal and for full support of the New Deal in the presidential elections of 1940.

On June 14, Browder reported popular sentiment throughout the United States in support of a third term for President Roosevelt and intimated that the movement for a third term had the support of the communists.

On July 9, the communists declared that the Finnish elections marked a strong rebuff to Nazi penetration.

On August 20, in a statement on policy, the communists declared: "Here in the United States our course must be clear. It calls for backing the President's foreign policy to the hilt [a policy then opposite to that of the Soviet Union] and trying to make the United States, in collaboration with the Soviet Union, a determining factor for world peace."

On August 21, Moscow reported that it had signed a trade pact with Nazi Germany. The American communists declared the signing of the pact frustrated the plot of the Munichmen and the Rome-Berlin Axis for a war against the Soviet Union by splitting them, but saw no basic change in the international line of Stalin, for on the same day the following jingle was prominently displayed in the *Daily Worker* as part of the communist campaign to have Roosevelt run for a third term:

> "Mr. Roosevelt won't you please run again
> For we want you to do it
> You've got to go through it
> *Again."*

Then the bombshell exploded. The Soviet Union concluded a political pact with Nazi Germany, announced by Tass in the following terse words: "After conclusion of the Soviet-German trade agreement, there arose the problem of improving the political relations between Germany and the USSR. An exchange of views on this subject which took place between the governments of Germany and the USSR established that both Parties desire to relieve the tension of their political relations, to eliminate the war menace and to conclude a non-aggression pact."

The first one to read the news over the ticker was Paul Novik, editor of the Jewish daily, *Freiheit,* the Jewish communist newspaper. He crumpled up the ticker sheet in anger and said it was a dastardly bourgeois trick. Beads of perspiration gathered around his forehead. He was speechless for some time. "After all," he reasoned, "the United Press would not go berserk on such an important piece of news." He went to his desk and looked at the bulldog edition of the New York *Times;* he read Ferdinand Kuhn Jr.'s correspondence from London with an August 21 date line. It stated:

"The deadliest high explosive could not have caused more damage in London than the news late tonight that the Nazi and Soviet governments had agreed on a Non-Aggression Pact behind the backs of the British and French military missions in Moscow."

He rushed to the editorial offices of the *Daily Worker* in the same building. There was panic. Sam Don, whose real name is Donchin, the actual editor and boss of the *Daily Worker,* was present.

Novik presed Don for a line of policy. In consternation he asked: "How should the news be treated?" Others, standing around, said: "We will be mobbed by the workers." Many communists who had read the early editions of the metropolitan papers besieged the offices of the *Daily Worker* with telephone calls.

Donchin, pale as a ghost, did not know what to say. Browder had gone out of town for a vacation. The other leaders of the Party, Foster, Minor, Stachel, including the Representatives from Moscow, were unavailable.

When Alexander Bittleman, the theoretician of the Party, its Russian expert and the man who reads all the Russian papers in order to know how Moscow thinks on every subject, was confronted by the frantic editors, he did not know what to say either. He gave an order that a meeting of all the Party editors of all the Party papers and magazines should be held on the ninth floor that very afternoon, at which time he would outline the Party policy to them.

The room was jammed with the members of the editorial staffs of the Party's press. But Bittleman had nothing new to say. He reiterated the Party's stand in favor of collective security, in favor of a campaign against Hitler and in support of the New Deal. For the first time in his life, this theoretician, who was always so positive in explaining Soviet policy, hemmed and hawed, stuttered and coughed and finally had to admit that the leaders of the Party had received no official word from Moscow. He was informed by the agitated editors that an answer must be forthcoming soon, because Party members, besieging the editorial offices, were frantically demanding that they must know what to say. They told Bittleman that the Party members could not go on facing the enraged workers without having answers for their questions.

An interesting scene occurred in the offices of the *Freiheit,* the Jewish communist daily. One of the best known Party leaders among the Jewish workers in the garment sections of New York is Sam Lipzin. The Party used him to get false passports from the U.S. State Department on which Comintern representatives like Gerhart Eisler and GPU agents traveled. For years he had led the Communist faction in Sidney Hillman's Amalgamated Clothing Workers of America. His life was completely bound up with the workers in the Garment Center of New York. There he could be found gesticulating and arguing almost every day in the year. If any man was in a position to know the effect the pact had upon the Jewish workers, Lipzin was that man. On the morning of the 23rd, he came rushing into the *Freiheit* office, hair disheveled, breathing heavily and much agitated. Turning to Novik, who in those memorable days tried to avoid everyone who came to the office, he exclaimed:

"The workers are making a revolution against us. They are driving us out of the market. What has Stalin done to us? Why did he sign the Pact? Everything we have built up for the last twenty years has been destroyed. I tell you, we are going to be stoned."

Novik turned around on his heel, red with anger: "How dare you speak that way! Get out of here right away!" He threw the frantic Lipzin out of the *Freiheit* as a bum is thrown out of a saloon.

Among the top leaders of the Party, the members of the Political Committee and the district organizers, there were no desertions. They held on to their posts; kept sending cable after cable and waited for Moscow's official word. They were worried and puzzled when no word came.

But among the rank-and-file, the Pact proved devastating. The Party membership at the time was about 100,000. The *Daily Worker* unit, which had a membership of thirty-five, made up of intellectuals, reported that six of its members resigned.

The same proportion were resigning from the other units. The Party suffered, on a national scale, a fifteen percent loss in membership. Over 15,000 members left the Party.

It must be kept in mind that the Communist party is organized on a totalitarian basis. Members are not permitted to voice criticism against the leadership and its policies. To utter an exclamation against Stalin brought about one's expulsion from the Party. The members came together to take orders and carry them out, not to voice an opinion. Yet, at the meetings at which the Pact was discussed, members were violent in their criticism and heaped abuse upon the Party leaders; member after member pointedly asked the Party leaders whether, if the workers did not want to follow Stalin into the camp of Hitler, Stalin wanted them to sacrifice the workers for the Nazis.

Radzwanski, one of the editors of the *Novy Mir,* the Party's Russian language paper, head of the Polish section of the Party, formerly secretary to Dzerjinsky, the founder of the OGPU, a fanatical Bolshevik, threw up his hands in the Party office and exclaimed: "This, that they have done to us, cannot be worse."

Markoff, the director of the Party's school, the Worker's School, kept quiet, but to a few of his most intimate friends he conveyed his great disillusionment over the signing of the Pact. Under the constant pressure of Party pleadings, he gave in, supported the Pact, and then succumbed to a heart attack.

Harry Gannes, the foreign-affairs expert of the *Daily Worker,* inwardly opposed the Pact, but in the columns of the *Daily Worker* became its most outspoken advocate.

A number of members on the staff of the *Freiheit,* including some of the trade union activists, not only resigned from the Party, but attempted to carry on a campaign among the Party members and sympathizers for a repudiation of the Pact and Stalin's leadership.

The poor American communist leaders, who were left to their own resources, without official instructions from the Comintern or from the OGPU or the Russian Embassy, floundered in the dark for two days and did not know what to do. The ninth floor of Thirteenth Street was in bedlam. The editorial offices of the communist *Daily Worker* and all other communist papers were swamped with inquiries. For forty-eight long hours, the communist leaders argued and debated about the line. Something had to be done and done quickly, or else panic would break out in the Party and the Party would suffer serious, irreparable damage.

On August 23, the *Daily Worker* printed, in bold type on the first page, this announcement: "As we went to press Monday night, a bulletin came in from Berlin saying that a Non-Aggression Pact had already been concluded between the Soviet Union and Germany."

Still the Communist party leaders did not know what to say.

On the 23rd of August, a stop-gap article to reassure the Party members, written by the communist scribe, Harry Gannes, declared (the Pact had already been signed), that the talks going on between the USSR and Germany were a blow to the second Munich and ended:

"Today, the Socialist USSR, reviled, maligned and slandered, yet growing stronger and stronger every hour, is more and more heading mankind away from the abyss along the safer road of human progress and victory over the dark forces of reaction, treachery and war."

Pinned down in an interview with reporters of the press, the next day Browder called the Soviet-Nazi Non-Aggression Pact a weapon for peace. At the same time, he went out of his way to impress upon the reporters that he was not sure the Pact would be signed because he had not yet been officially notified. The coded cable he expected from the Comintern, notifying him of the fact with instructions on what kind of line to follow, had not yet arrived.

The Communist party leaders realized they had to act, that they could no longer delay taking a definite stand on the question. In quarters where the Communist party had been very influential, ground was being lost rapidly and many communist supporters were deserting the movement and denouncing the Party.

At last when the Communist party received the line from Moscow, it came out in full support of the Pact as a blow against Munich treachery and aggression.

A membership meeting was called in New York. Members came to the meeting in an ugly mood. Hathaway laid down the Party line, stressing that the Pact smashed the Berlin-Rome-Tokyo Axis, and that it was no alliance with Nazi Germany.

All the Jewish leaders of the Party were called together for a secret special meeting. Foster, the Chairman of the Communist party, presented the new line. Instead of defending himself, he launched into a sharp attack upon the Jews, declaring that they were narrow and chauvinistic in their viewpoint on the Pact. The Jews in the Party, he charged, because of Hitler's anti-semitism had allowed that to determine their attitude and had lost sight of the bigger and by far more important political considerations involved. He demanded that the Jews take a stand as communists on the question and not as Jews. The tension in the meeting held the Jewish leaders glued to their seats. Many showed the strain of great mental and spiritual agitation— hands clutched the chairs in front of them tightly. The top leaders of the Party had come to club the Jewish leaders into submission, not to argue the question with them.

The Communist Jewish leaders were torn between two loyalties, loyalty to their people, who were the innocent victims of Nazi anti-semitic bestiality, and loyalty to the cause of communism, upon which they had placed their hopes for the liberation of all mankind, including the Jews.

Foster gave them no time to think. He pounded away at them with blows that stung. They knew that to oppose Foster meant to be made a target for vicious attacks and to be driven out in disgrace from the movement they had given their lives to serve.

When Foster finished, a resolution endorsing the Soviet-Nazi Pact in unequivocal terms was presented for adoption. Foster insisted upon an immediate vote. The Communist party does not allow its members the privilege of taking time in making up their minds. The Communist party leaders who were Jews had listened to Foster. Now they must vote for the resolution; abstaining from voting for the resolution or voting against it was tantamount to expulsion from the Party.

The few who asked questions or expressed their doubts, during the discussion, became the targets for attacks by the Party leaders, who were unrestrained in their abusive viciousness against them. They were given to understand that the Jews, more than any other element in the Party, were expected to give the new line their whole-hearted and enthusiastic support. Foster summed up with the full weight of Stalin, the Soviet Union, the Comintern and the Party in back of his words, and bludgeoned the Jews into complete submission to the resolution.

On August 31, nine days after the pact with Hitler, Molotov, in his famous speech defending the Pact, declared:

> "It is really difficult to understand that the U.S.S.R. is pursuing and will continue to pursue its own independent policy based on the interests of the people of the U.S.S.R. and *only their interests*."

The American Communist party supported the policy enunciated by Molotov, a policy based on Russian nationalistic interests alone.

Molotov, in the same speech, sneeringly spoke of the British, who were to stand alone as the bulwark of democracy against the Nazi barbarism, in the following insulting words: "We would like to see what fighting stuff they are made of," words which were greeted with loud laughter by his listeners. Molotov knew what he was talking about, for *the next day* World War II broke out, when the Nazi legions invaded Poland.

Browder knew the tune he had to sing. He shouted for the United States to keep at peace and stay out of the war. John L. Lewis came out as a staunch isolationist. He rallied the C.I.O. behind the slogan, "Keep out of War. Give Jobs to the Unemployed!" The communists rushed to the support of Lewis. Lewis' isolationism played right into their hands, for it enabled them to use the weight of the Communist party organization in a drive to get the C.I.O. unions to back John L. Lewis. They were, therefore, able to hold on to their unions, to swing them into line and even to extend their influence among the strong isolationist and pro-Nazi forces of the country.

The communists, however, did not break with Roosevelt immediately. The United Electrical and Machine Workers Union, with a membership in 1939 of 210,000 workers in the plants, destined to produce defense materials for the United States and war matériels for the democracies fighting the Nazis, called for a third term for Roosevelt. This union was solidly controlled by the communists. Later, when President Carey sought to have the union follow the line of Roosevelt, after the communists broke with Roosevelt, he was ousted from the presidency and another elected in his place who supported the Party line.

On the day war broke out, the Communist party held a National Emergency Conference in Chicago, in which they called upon President Roosevelt to prevent the involvement of the United States in the War by maintaining a stand of strict neutrality and by following the action of the Soviet Union.

On September 17, the Soviet Union entered the war by invading Poland. Two days later the National Committee of the Communist party of the United States issued a manifesto to the American people, calling upon them to "Keep America Out of Imperialist War." In this manifesto the Polish government, fighting the Nazis, was severely attacked and the invasion of the Red Army hailed as an act of self-defense on the part of the Soviets.

The slogans of the manifesto carried not one word about fighting against Nazism.

When Molotov, in a speech to the Red Army, declared to the nations of the world, "that the U.S.S.R. stays neutral in war, while calling upon troops to cross the frontiers and liberate their blood brothers in Polish territories," the American communists hailed Molotov's declaration of blood-brotherhood and hailed the Red Army as a crusading army of liberation.

But the Communist party did not yet break with Roosevelt. The communists still called upon the American people to unite around the New Deal and its progressive policies, while at the same time the Communist party opposed all of Roosevelt's moves for national defense and in support of the democracies fighting the Nazis. In October, the Roosevelt administration, irked by the Communist party's position and the sniping of its General Secretary, Earl Browder, moved against the Party by arresting Browder on a charge of passport fraud. The honeymoon with the New Deal temporarily came to an end. The Communist party came out vigorously against F. D. R.

Browder was arrested on October 24, 1939. On the 29th of October, Mike Gold expressed the new position of the communists towards Roosevelt in the following pungent words: "Well, is this the end of the Roosevelt ride?" Answering his own question, Gold concluded: "So, thanks for the ride, Mr. President! It was really swell, while it lasted, but though you have gotten off the wagon, I don't see how the ill-clothed, ill-housed and ill-fed can give up so easily."

And two days later the American communists emphatically endorsed Molotov's speech to the Supreme Soviet of October 31, in which he said:

"One may accept or reject the ideology of Hitlerism as well as any other ideological system, that is a matter of taste. . . . It is, therefore, not only senseless, but criminal to wage such a war for the destruction of Hitlerism, camouflaged as a fight for democracy."

The Communists Turn Isolationists

Overnight, the communists turned a somersault. They abandoned their position as internationalists who called for the adoption of a policy of collective security against the fascist aggressor. They now called upon the country to stay out of the war. They attacked Roosevelt's defense program. They fought against selective service. They did all in their power to keep the American armed forces small in number and inadequately armed. They fought bitterly every measure adopted by the country to bolster the position of the democracies, and did everything in their power to wreck lend-lease.

The communists quickly found new forces among those who had been pro-Nazi and pro-German before the outbreak of the war. They joined hands with the isolationist forces, whom they had, before Russia's signing of the Pact, branded as reactionary Nazi-Fascist bands.

The communist scribe, Mike Quin, coined the slogan, in November, 1939, "The Yanks are not Coming." Bridges' District Council, No. 2, of the Maritime Federation, issued the pamphlet "The Yanks are not Coming" and in three weeks' time distributed over 30,000 copies on the Pacific waterfront.

Before the year was up, the communists had overcome the disadvantages of the new pro-Nazi line and were on the march once more. New peace organizations were shaped on the wreckage of those formed in alliance with New Deal forces. The American Peace mobilization replaced the League for Peace and Democracy. Among the youth, in the unions, especially in the C.I.O. where the communists' position coincided with Lewis' isolationism, the communists made progress.

Throughout the unions, the communists circulated "The Peace Proclamation of Labor." In the industrial heart of America, western Pennsylvania, over 100 prominent trade union officials of AF of L and C.I.O. unions signed the proclamation which ended in these defiant words:

"We serve notice on Wall Street's financiers and industrialists that American Labor will never underwrite their loans and credits to foreign interests with the blood of our people. The Yanks positively are not coming."

The communists, in adopting a course of isolationism, had not isolated themselves from the trade unions. In Detroit, the C.I.O. locals of the auto workers were busy distributing thousands of pamphlets "The Yanks are not Coming." The plants in which they were operating were already in defense production or being converted into defense production. The communists controlled the Plymouth plant and the Bohn Aluminum plants. The union paper for the Dodge plant, the *Dodge Main News,* printed a poem, "The Yanks are not Coming." John L. Lewis called upon Congress that the pledge to keep America out of war must be kept. Philip Murray took the same line the communists took in attacking Roosevelt's budget call for national defense expenditures. The Workers' Alliance, the organization of 3,000,000 unemployed workers, served notice that it would have to reconsider its endorsement of Roosevelt for a third term. The National Maritime Union lashed out against President Roosevelt and supported the position of John L. Lewis and the communists.

In the communist press, the anti-Nazi line was buried under an avalanche of attacks upon Imperialist France, England and the U.S.A.

The May 1, 1940, Manifesto of the Communist International laying down the International Line of the communist world superstructure lashed out against Great Britain and France, against the socialists and trade unionists, who did not support the Nazi-Soviet line, called for revolutions in the colonies of France and England. Not one word appeared calling for a fight against fascism and nazism, and it ended in these words:

"Down with Imperialist War! Down with Capitalist Reaction! Peace to the Peoples! Long live the U.S.S.R., the bulwark of peace, freedom and socialism."

The National Convention of the Communist party of the United States, held on May 30, 1940, declared that the communist-New Deal coalition was dead, "Only the Communist party will come before the masses fighting for peace." Its platform, in no equivocal terms, called for "a fight against the Defense Program and M-Day plans."

Detroit—the Communist Laboratory

In Detroit, the industrial heart of motorized America, in 1939, 1940 and 1941, during the first three years of the defense program, the communists showed what they could do in the city's gigantic plants; plants in which the miracles of mass production turned out airplanes, their motors and parts, blitz buggies, tanks and motorized military equipment. They demonstrated what they could do in a city where American engineering genius went into the construction, machining and tooling of new defense plants, which sprouted up like mushrooms after a heavy shower. Day and night American workmen, efficient and productive, swarmed like busy ants in and out of the huge factories. And in this important city, so vital to our national security, was to be found the greatest communist penetration of American industrial life.

It has already been shown that the red siege of Detroit was started at the initiative of the Communist International as early as 1924. By 1938, the Communist party had become a recognized power in Detroit, due to the organizational and political genius of William Weinstone, who streamlined the Communist party organization and applied new techniques in the organization of Detroit's mass production industries. Browder, the General Secretary of the Communist party organization, was afraid that Weinstone was getting too much prestige, and when Homer Martin, President of the C.I.O. Auto

Workers Union, adopted an anti-communist position, he blamed Weinstone for permitting such a situation to develop and removed him from Detroit. Patrick Tooey, who replaced him, the Party's trouble-shooter in the coal fields, an American of Irish extraction, was well known in Moscow, for he had been a delegate to the Comintern and Profintern on many occasions. Tooey lacked the intellectual background of Weinstone and his political sagacity. He nevertheless had excellent qualities, for he rose from the coal pits to the top ranks of the Party. He understood the psychology of workers, spoke in an effective manner, and was an intrepid fighter.

But the Detroit organization was never left entirely to one man. The communists maintained a crew of able organizers in the city at all times. The three outstanding figures in the Detroit communist inner circle, besides Tooey, included William K. Gebert, a Pole and leader of the Polish section of the Party who served in Detroit as the special agent of the Political Committee of the Party; Maurice Sugar, one of Detroit's outstanding labor attorneys, and Joe Kowalski, a Pole, who for many years edited the Polish communist paper, *Glos Ludowy,* Voice of the People. The United States government had deported Kowalski on his own request to the Soviet Union. When his services were badly needed in Detroit, the Comintern decided that he should return to the United States.

Kowalski took the bold step and returned illegally to the country that had deported him as a dangerous, subversive alien. When the United States sought to deport him once more, the authorities were unable to do so. The Soviet government refused to accept him on the grounds that he was a Polish, not a Russian citizen, and the Polish government, not wanting a dangerous communist, refused to recognize him as a Pole. Kowalski, the man without a country, established himself in Detroit. An innocent-looking book shop on Woodward Avenue served as a smoke screen for his operations, and secret headquarters were maintained in a large room in the rear of the store.

Here, Kowalski gathered together all the information that came to him from the Detroit industrial empire. Technical-industrial information and trade secrets of great value were turned over to the OGPU and by them transmitted to Russia. In the back room were held the secret meetings of Party officials and communist trade union officials and organizers, who planned the industrial warfare against the giants of American industry such as General Motors, Ford and Chrysler.

Maurice Sugar, an outstanding labor attorney, is the public figure of Detroit's communist brain trust. Maurice Sugar has also been in Russia. For years, he was the chief council of the International Labor Defense, the communists' legal defense organization. He operates a legal mill in his spacious offices at the Barlum Towers, where promising communist lawyers learn how to utilize labor laws and the courts in the application of communist strategy. Sugar's office handles much of the legal business of Detroit's labor unions, thereby giving the communists access to important and confidential union matters and legal supervision of their negotiations with the employers.

Sugar is an old Party member, whose communist affiliation was a carefully guarded secret for many years. He had an automobile worker arrested on criminal libel charges, because he had distributed a leaflet which charged that Sugar was a communist. The worker won a verdict of "not guilty" because it was proven in court, beyond the shadow of a doubt, that Sugar was a communist. Sugar is always consulted on Detroit matters by the top communist party officials. Parading as an impartial, pro-labor attorney, Sugar sought to be elected a Recorder's Judge, with the backing he received from the C.I.O. and AF of L unions.

Everything the communists did in Detroit was done according to plan in much the same way as a military high command carries on its operations. The plans were first formulated in Moscow, the working out of the details left to the American communists. Never, in important matters, were the Detroit communists left on their own. Special emissaries were sent by the Comintern and by the Party's national office to guide them.

The communists were a dominant factor in the C.I.O., and it might be interesting to note the general set-up at that time.

One of the most energetic communists in the Automobile Workers Union was John Anderson, a Scotchman from Glasgow, a dynamo of activity who spends from twenty to twenty-two hours each day for his trade union and communist activities. In 1930, he was the communist candidate for Governor of Michigan. He was the leader of Local 155, which has jurisdiction over the tool and die shops, a key industry because a shut-down of the tool and die shops, which employ the most skilled mechanics of the automobile industry, would cause a most serious bottleneck not only in the automobile industry but in the defense program as well.

Nat Ganly was another who wielded great power in the Union

and in the Communist party and the Young Communist League. He was a mere youngster away back in the early 1920's when he acted as Israel Amter's office boy. In those days of underground communism, Ganly operated under his true name—Nathan Kaplan. He was, for a short time, secretary of the Young Communist League and also representative of the League to the Communist Youth International at Moscow.

Nat Ganly is no longer the thin, raw-boned lad of twenty years ago. He has an expanded waist line and likes to smoke large fat cigars. When he was business agent of Local 165, he dominated the Council of Small Parts Shops. This council had jurisdiction over the numerous factories, which produced strips, metal mouldings and small parts. By striking these plants, the communists could shut down the whole automobile industry.

Ganly early discovered how important it was for communist trade union leaders to control jobs. He held that a trade union official, who is in a position to supply a worker with a job, is bound to obtain and keep his support. Ganly made arrangements with employment managers to supply them with the workers they needed whenever they required them. In obtaining these privileges for himself, he gave concessions to the employers. The Ganly system has been followed wherever possible by Communist trade union officials. By controlling the livelihood of workers, they are able to rule despotically over the workers. To give a specific example, one of many: Joe Green obtained a job in the Ainsworth Manufacturing Company, without the assistance of business agent Ganly. He started work at 7 A.M. and was politely discharged at 7:30 that morning, because Ganly called up the firm and demanded that he be fired. Green supported the opposition in the union.

The Bohn Aluminum plant in Detroit, of utmost importance to defense production, manufactured the bearings and vital aluminum parts for automobiles, motorized army equipment, tanks, marine engines, airplanes, etc., and employed between 11,000 and 12,000 workers. A communist Soviet dominated this plant. Here, sabotage against the Defense Program was widespread.

Fred Williams, alias Jack Wilkes, alias Jack Wilson, was the boss of the local union and the business agent. Williams never worked in the industry. Before he became business agent, he was employed in the Kercheval Assembly Plant of the Chrysler Corporation.

Williams was a member of the Executive Committee of the Communist party of Michigan. He was carefully trained by the Communist party for his trade union duties. In the Communist Workers School of New York, he received special instruction on how to organize Party units in the large industries, in the art of sabotage and in the duties of communists in the war industries during a war emergency.

The key plants of the Federal Mogul Corporation were also in communist hands. The Secretary of the local, that has jurisdiction over its 4000 employees, was a communist by the name of Casimer Stawasozynski.

Local 205, U.A.W.-C.I.O., which has jurisdiction over the plant of the National Automotive Fibres Company, also was communist controlled. As a result of a strike at this plant, all the Chrysler shops making automobiles had to shut down because the upholstery that goes into Chrysler cars was produced by National Automotive Fibres. The strike was conducted in the communist twentieth-century stream-lined manner. Sound trucks bellowed out instructions to the pickets. A staff of picket officers from generals down kept the pickets going twenty-four hours. The management had to shut its doors and finally capitulate by signing on the dotted line.

The power in the Dodge local was its Secretary, John Zaremba. The local he dominated, one of the largest in the union with a membership of 30,000 workers, enjoyed great prestige among automobile workers, for it was the pioneer in organizing the industry. Uncle Sam can thank his stars that Hitler caused the communists to change their line, for the communists were in a position to do tremendous damage by sabotaging the tank parts, cartridge shells and other products essential to defense which the Dodge plants manufactured.

The large Packard local was 100 percent communist controlled—not a bad union melon, for the Packard plants employed about 40,000 workers. Packard manufactured the new Rolls Royce air-cooled airplane engine for both the United States government and Great Britain. In addition, it manufactured motors for large torpedoes and gas motors for naval craft. Out of the Packard plants have gone plans of military equipment to Stalin's OGPU, which both the United States and Great Britain desired to keep secret.

The power in the Packard local was Ed Lindahl, President. The opposition candidates of delegates to the convention of the Automobile Workers Union were decisively defeated by the communist slate.

The communists also controlled most of the key departments in the Briggs plant, where upwards of 30,000 workers were employed.

The main obstacle in the path of the communists in the Briggs local was its former President, Emil Mazey, now general secretary of the U.A.W. In a maneuver to gain control of the local, the communists threw their support to a transition candidate for President, a non-communist, and succeeded in eliminating Mazey, thus removing the chief obstacle to their control.

In this local, in which the communist and anti-communist forces were about equal, an election scandal took place in 1938.

In the election conducted by mail, the communists obtained in advance a copy of the ballot and forged duplicates of it in their own print shop. The union sent out to each member entitled to vote a ballot, together with a self-addressed postage-paid return envelope, in which the voted ballot was to be enclosed and mailed back to the committee in charge of the elections. This envelope, issued under a permit of the United States Post Office, was also forged. Since in every election a large number of members do not vote, the communists mailed back to the election committee, in the forged envelopes, a sufficient number of the forged ballots to carry their slate in the union elections by 100 votes. The matter was called to the attention of the United States Attorney General and the Post Office Department. The postal inspectors assigned to investigate the case reported a true case of flagrant violation of the postal laws. But the guilty parties were never brought to justice.

Wyndham Mortimer, in those important years the ace in the hole of the Communist party, was sent to the Pacific coast by the United Auto Workers Union-C.I.O. to organize the aircraft industry. The numerous strikes which took place there can be traced directly to his activities.

Acting as the official communist industrial Commissar on the Pacific coast, he won such high opinion in the Party that they slated him to take the place of Harry Bridges, in the event the government deported him. Mortimer gained his reputation as the international director of the large Flint General Motors local, in which dues were $1.00 a month, the local keeping 67 cents out of every dollar. The local, when he supervised its affairs, had over $300,000 in the treasury. The money disappeared. How? The members of the local did not know. Many who should have known claimed that thousands of dollars of the union's funds were siphoned into the Communist party treasury.

Sam Baron, who was a delegate of the Office Workers Union

to the AF of L convention in Atlantic City in 1935, has this to say about Mortimer: "As a delegate to the 1935 Convention of the AF of L convention in Atlantic City, and as an organizer of the Socialist Group in this Convention, it was necessary for me to discuss various political questions with Mr. Stachel and Mr. Weinstock [Weinstock is the Communist party whip in the AF of L Painters Union], who represented the Communist party. During one of the sessions between us, Mr. Stachel asked me whether I had any objection to their bringing another person with them to attend one of the meetings. Upon their arrival they introduced me to the third person as a good communist, Mr. Wyndham Mortimer."

If questioned, Mortimer will deny membership in the Party. Practically every communist trade union official is under orders to deny membership in the Communist party. The communists are determined to hold on to the unions by every kind of subterfuge. They know that control of the trade unions through communist officials gives them influence over thousands of workers, concrete political power, and access to millions of dollars in rich union treasuries. The Communist party, therefore, considers it better to hide one's communist identity than to lose these opportunities. And of much greater importance is the fact that as trade union officials, the communists can lead the workers into left political channels and thus harness them to the communist movement.

The Murray Body was one of the first plants to settle a strike by giving the union increased wages, a closed shop and the check-off. The local union was communist dominated, the president of its twenty thousand members, Lloyd G. Jones, a Communist party member.

The West Side local, which, in addition to the Kelsey-Hays plant, included the workers in a large number of small plants, was one of the largest locals of the union, with a membership close to 50,000. Walter Reuther, then a Norman Thomas Socialist, hailed from that local. Reuther proposed a plan to the government for the decentralization of the defense program by utilizing the numerous small plants dotting the country.

Reuther, in 1940, called himself a revolutionary socialist. He cooperated and collaborated, as did the C.I.O. as a whole, with the communists on trade union matters and on political matters also.

Walter Reuther, President of the United Automobile Workers Union, and his brother were, however, among the first C.I.O. officials to fight against the communists in the Automobile Workers Union and in the C.I.O. as a whole.

All this does not begin to give the picture of the grip which the Communist party, during the critical years of the Defense program, had on the industrial life of Detroit. The Communist party's control was strongest at the base of Detroit's industrial empire, in the factories where the men and women worked, for the majority of shop stewards were under its control. The stewards take care of the complaints between management and the workers and are responsible for seeing to it that the union contract is lived up to, and that union interests and control are safeguarded in the shops. Generally the union provided one steward for every fifty workers. In the Ford plant, the union contract called for the appointment of one steward for every five hundred workers.

Control over the shop stewards, many of whom were communists, gave the Communist party industrial power based upon the men in the factories. The communist shop stewards acted like labor Tsars. They used high-handed methods against those who opposed them and against workers who refused to pay union dues or carry out union orders. What the communists did in Detroit's factories is an example of what kind of treatment the public will get once the communists gain control over the government. During the lunch hour, it was not unusual to see workers escorted out of the plants by a committee of stewards, roughly handled and warned never to return to the plant again. By the use of self-assumed authority, defying human decency, and legality, the workers were bulldozed and kept in constant fear of being deprived of their livelihood.

In 1941 the communists were determined to turn Detroit into the outstanding communist city in America. The communist chiefs met in Detroit, following their victory over Ford, and mapped out a war against the American Federation of Labor in order to bring the industries and services which the AF of L controlled under their hegemony. Marked for attack were the AF of L unions of transportation, of county and municipal Civil Service employees, teamsters, construction workers, and workers in the food industry.

The communists held strategic economic bases, not only in the automobile industry, but also in other industries. They had successful drives under way to organize the retail and department stores and white collar workers. The communists had already succeeded in organizing the clerical workers of R. L. Polk Co. into a union which

they dominated completely. This company, the largest directory printing firm in the country, gathers and compiles vital statistics, especially
of an industrial nature. The communists, through the union, have
sent spies into the firm as workers to gather valuable information for
the Communist party and the OGPU. The firm was organized by the
calling of a strike engineered by the Wonders Club, a club of the
Young Communist League of Detroit. Acting upon instructions, Mary
Page, alias Mary Reed, secured a job at Polk's. A strike soon broke
out. The firm tried to counteract the communist-called strike by
granting a wage increase. The communists retaliated by claiming
that their militant action caused the firm to make the offer. They
rejected the firm's offer and forced the company to sign a contract
which granted increased wages, the closed shop and the check-off. In
the N.L.R.B. elections in Polk's, before the strike was called, the
communist-dominated United Office and Professional Workers Union,
C.I.O., won by a mere ninety votes. That slim majority gave them
job control and 100 percent control of the union, from the president,
Miss Muriel Jenkins, down.

The victory put the communists in a position to staff all the
C.I.O. unions in Detroit with communist office workers. They also
took advantage of the settlement with the Polk Co. to colonize the
firm with communists.

In addition, the communists followed up their victory over the
Polk firm with an energetic drive to organize Detroit's Federal, State
and Municipal Government office workers.

There was much more to the campaign to make Detroit a C.I.O.
town than appeared on the surface. Behind the effort loomed a political scheme to capture the local government and the government
of the State of Michigan as well. If successful, the communists believed these political gains in Detroit and Michigan would assume
great national proportions and enable them to establish a C.I.O.
government in Washington. The communists backed up their political hopes by the realities of the Detroit situation.

There were, at the time, close to half a million C.I.O. members
in Detroit. Most of them were citizens and voters. Politicians have a
deep respect for votes. Detroit's politicians were no exception. Without
votes a politician cannot operate. And in Detroit the C.I.O. dominated
by the communists had the votes. These votes, communist political
strategists knew, could not be swung for the Communist party, but
they could be swung for Democrats, Republicans and independents.

By controlling the political power of the C.I.O., operating through Labor's Non-Partisan League, therefore, the communists held a menacing whip over the politicians.

But the communists were not content to operate through their own Party, and Labor's Non-Partisan League of the C.I.O. They began applying the tactics they used in penetrating the unions to the Democratic and Republican parties, particularly to the organizations of the Young Democrats and Young Republicans.

Thus, in Detroit, the communist fifth column took form, depending on the proposition that whereas individual treason is recognized, collective treason is not, when it is cloaked as trade unionism and non-partisan politics. As for the politicians, the communists counted on their doing nothing because they were so greedy for the votes which communists, through their control of the C.I.O., could give them.

The people of Detroit were not aware that their city was in the grip of a communist conspiracy, a conspiracy which the local government and the management of industry were unable to deal with at the time. This new phenomenon in American life was graphically demonstrated by the victorious blitzkrieg against the Ford Motor Company. Through the unionization of Ford, the communists gained an iron grip over labor in a company that had defense contracts for jeeps, tanks, airplanes and other defense equipment. They gained that control at a time when they were doing everything in their power to undermine the defense program. The story behind this signal victory gives an idea of the political and social implications of communist penetration of American industrial life.

The campaign against Ford was a communist one. The fight against Ford, as has already been shown, began years ago in the Comintern. The first step was to colonize the Ford plants with communists and close communist sympathizers. Then followed a consistent, energetic campaign to win the support of the Ford workers and to recruit as many of them as possible into the Communist party, or in the secret rank-and-file groups in the Ford plant, which the Communist party had organized.

Every important Party leader who visited Detroit gave time to the Ford situation. Every organizer of the Detroit district—Rudy Baker, John Schmees, Albert Weisbord, Harry Raymond, Owens, Weinstone, and Pat Tooey—concentrated on the Ford campaign.

In the campaign to discredit Ford, and to slander him as the worst opponent of Labor in the United States, the Party succeeded admirably, because of the errors Ford himself committed and the inability of a large industrial organization, operating on an individualistic basis, to cope with the complexities of labor relations.

Before the drive started, it was generally accepted in Detroit that it would be a test of what the Communist party could do in the field of labor organization. Had the Party failed, it probably would have marked the beginning of its decline in Detroit.

That Ford was not antagonistic to labor organizations, was known to every labor leader in Detroit. When Homer Martin, the first president of the C.I.O. Auto Workers Union, was engaged with the communists in a fight for the control of the union, he had assurances from the Ford Company that they were prepared to deal with the union. The communists prevented this, because they wanted to destroy Martin's leadership first. Martin was no match for the communists. The communists forced him out of the union and took matters into their own hands.

Michael F. Wideman Jr., who had always cooperated with the communists, was put in charge of the drive on Ford. He placed the communists in strategic positions and gave them a free hand.

The main organizer on the Ford battle front, sixty-five-year-old William McKie, an Irishman, had plenty of spunk, lots of courage and a capacity for indefatigable work. The Communist party honored him at a dinner for his twenty-five years of activity in the labor movement, for zealous, fanatical devotion to the Communist party.

The Communist party set up plant committeemen in the important departments of Ford who got their orders direct from Bill McKie. The Communist party gave McKie an assistant organizer, Paul Brooks, who never worked at Ford, a Finnish-American communist, whose real name was Paave Kruks.

On the eve of the Ford strike, in the early part of April, the communist Commissars from New York flew into town from that city—the main emissaries being Roy Hudson and William Foster, the Chairman of the Party.

The Communist party had a nucleus in the Ford River Rouge plant of close to 700 communists and close sympathizers, most of the sympathizers coming from the International Workers Order, a communist fraternal organization. Foster ordered this nucleus broken into smaller units. He insisted that all the unreliable elements, suspected of being spies for Ford, be organized into a separate unit.

Hudson and Foster worked out the strategy on how the strike was to be pulled by the Communist party Plant Committeemen. The communists were well prepared for the strike, for the Party had in its possession a complete set of the blueprint plans of the plant. They knew all the vulnerable points, and where the power switches were. They had also a detailed blueprint of the underground cable lines which tunneled the plant. A proposal that trained saboteurs enter the underground passageway in order to sever the cables was seriously considered for hours and finally rejected as being too dangerous because it would inflame public opinion against the strikers.

The details worked out for the strike were checked and re-checked by the Political Committee and Secretariat of the Communist party. The Communist party applies to industrial warfare a system of mobile tactics to be used by forces which the Communist party has built up and which can be mobilized at a moment's notice. The mobile guards of gunmen, knifers, goons, sluggers, saboteurs, acid throwers, etc., first came into existence after the victorious furriers' strike of 1926. Since then they have been augmented into a virtual army of over a thousand men. They strike with lightning speed, like a Panzer division, spreading terror through the ranks of the workers as they disperse and confuse the police and industrial service men. They do not fear the police, for they have been trained to fight and resist them.

In addition, the communists had built up a flying squad in Detroit proper. A large number of "flying aces" work in the Briggs plant. The day before the strike took place at Ford, the union officers of the Briggs plant obtained permission from the firm, which was engaged on defense orders, to release these men from their jobs. Communists with cars, mainly from the states of Indiana, Illinois and Wisconsin, but from points as far east as New York, were ordered to descend upon Detroit. A system of scouts and messengers was established, as well as first aid stations.

A Communist party decision directed that the strike should be called at the zero hour just as the midnight shift leaves and the day shift enters. This created the impression that all the midnight workers had joined the strike. At the same time, all plans were made to prevent the workers of the day shift from entering the plant. On the night the strike was to be called, hundreds of communist mobile guards, wearing Ford Company badges, which the communists procured, entered the plant as regular workers of the midnight shift. Many of them carried baseball bats and other weapons under their jackets. That week the supply of baseball bats was depleted in Detroit. One wholesale house sold out its whole supply. Organizer McKie, prominently wearing a Ford badge, was among them, giving the orders and seeing to it, like a general at the front, that nothing miscarried.

An ugly mood prevailed inside the huge River Rouge plant. The Negroes in the plant who were sympathetic to Ford, because the Company gave them an equal opportunity with the white workers, resented the union's attack on Ford. They armed and barricaded themselves in the plant. They were going to protect the Company which gave them well-paid, skilled jobs. They were going to show their appreciation of the welfare work which Ford had supported in the Negro community. They were afraid once the union came in, they would lose their standing, and the privileges they enjoyed.

So they waited, as the dark hours of the morning passed, to give blow for blow. Had not the Company interfered and induced the Negroes to desist from fighting, that situation would have ended in a bloody battle inside the plant that would have spread out in the city and broken into a frightful race war.

When the zero hour came, the communists surged through the plant, brandishing baseball bats. The power was shut off. Thousands of automobiles, tooting their horns, jammed all the approaches to the factory gates. Workers of the day shift found all entrances blocked. Workers who insisted on going in were surrounded by goon squads, who belabored them with clubs, loaded pipes and baseball bats. It was a miniature of Hitler's attack on France, when he purposely had all the roads jammed with fleeing refugees so that the French army had no freedom of action. In this case, instead of refugees, the roads were jammed with stalled communist cars. The first phase of the blitzkrieg successful, the second phase soon followed.

The law enforcement authorities looked on. In fact, they went out of their way to serve C.I.O. interests. C.I.O. political pressure was evidently stronger than law and order. The Ford Company had to shut its River Rouge plant. An arrangement had to be made to let some men in, in order to keep the machinery in working order so that production could start once the strike was over. Governor Wagoner decided that only workers with C.I.O. passes should be permitted into the plant. Under that order the State police excluded Ford Company officials from entering the factory, for they too had to get permission from the C.I.O. This ruling did not stop the communists from issuing passes to non-workers, to their trained saboteurs, who did enter the plant. They left in their wake a mess of wreckage. The finest machines and tools were destroyed. The sabotage, photographic records of which are available, proves how efficient the communist saboteurs were. What they did cost the company hundreds of thousands of dollars and forced the plant, after the strike was over, to shut down until replacements were made.

The Ford strike victory was much more than a victory for the organizing techniques and strike tactics of the Communist party. When the Ford strike is viewed as part of the general situation in Detroit, when it becomes part of a picture of what the communists succeeded in accomplishing in one city at a time when they were seeking to undermine the strength and security of the country in the interests of the Nazi-Soviet coalition, then the picture as a whole is seen in its proper perspective. What happened in Detroit shows how deep the roots of communism go, how its poisonous vines creep over a great American city and obtain a stranglehold on its political, social and industrial life. Detroit proved that in dealing with the Communist party, the country deals not with a legally constituted political Party, but with an intricate, complicated conspiracy, based on a web of domestic and international entanglements, difficult to trace, from which it derives its directives and power. Once the communists can duplicate nationally that which they succeeded in doing in Detroit, American liberty will hang in the balance, for the communists will be in a position to strike successfully at the foundations of the American way of life.

How Bob Minor Was Made Acting Secretary of the Party

The communists were not fooled by the New Deal's soft line towards the communists. All other administrations had absolutely refused, knowingly, to issue passports to communists. Well-known communists, if they wanted to leave the country, had to travel on false passports under assumed names. These passports were secured in a number of ways. One method was to have a communist who was not known and who, in appearance, looked like the communist leader who wanted to go abroad, apply for a passport in his own name. As soon as the passport was issued to him by the State Department, the passport was turned over to the Party office, where the photograph of the person was removed and the picture of the leader who was to use it put in its place. The New Deal administration changed all this and, through the American Civil Liberties Union, the State Department let it be known that all known communists who applied for American passports would obtain them.

American Communist party leaders did procure and use such passports. But, when they left on important secret missions, they preferred to use fake passports, because only through fake passports could they cover up their tracks and prevent the authorities from knowing of their secret trips to Moscow and other capitals. Bittleman and Jack Johnstone traveled on fake passports on secret missions to Mexico, Germany, China, the Near East and India. Browder used false passports because he had to cover up his trips to highly important secret Comintern conferences which were held in France, and Comintern and GPU missions to European countries, Latin-America and China. With the signing of the Soviet-Nazi Pact, the former open mutual collaboration with the New Deal became impossible, because of the clash of American international policies with the policies of the Soviet Union. The communists got off the Roosevelt bandwagon. They attacked the administration sharply and did everything to sabotage the defense program. The administration took a left-hand wallop at the communists by indicting Browder and Wiener, the Secretary of the International Workers Order, for passport fraud. Both were found guilty and sentenced to serve prison terms. Wiener, however, escaped serving a prison term on the plea that he was dangerously ill, claiming that to incarcerate him would result in his death. Two prominent communist physicians signed affidavits to that effect and Wiener got away with it.

A crisis developed in the top ruling circles of the Party over who was to take Browder's place as acting Secretary of the Communist party during the time Browder was in prison. Minor had ingratiated himself with Browder by becoming the biographer of Browder, the Boswell of Browder, who exaggerated, in pompous rhetoric, the life and sayings of the great oracle of American communism.

Roy Hudson, a lieutenant of George Mink, had by 1941 become one of the outstanding leaders of the Party, serving on its political committee and secretariat. He made a bid for Browder's position and mustered up a majority of the Party's ruling circle for his appointment. Minor also made a bid for the coveted office of acting general secretary. The C.I. Reps were afraid to make a decision in favor of either one before getting definite instructions from Moscow. The matter was taken up with Ambassador Oumansky and then referred to Moscow for a definite decision. In spite of the war and the international crisis, Stalin found time to give the matter his personal consideration and decided in favor of Minor.

Minor functioned as the legal public head of a Party that, following the signing of the Soviet-Nazi Pact, had been thoroughly reorganized on an underground basis. Converting the Party into an underground organization was the work of the conspiratorial genius of the OGPU and two American communists, Charles Dirba, then the head of the National Control Commission, and Jack Stachel, who had perfected the plan for the underground as far back as 1928.

As a result of this plan, which is still in force, the only communists who openly appear before the public as communists are the few high ranking communist leaders of the Party, who cannot hide their identity, and the editors and staff members of the communist newspapers who cannot camouflage their communist affiliations.

Since the adoption of the underground organization plan, the Communist party seldom engages in campaigns under its own banner. It operates almost exclusively through the unions it controls and front organizations. Every day in the week, new organizations around specific issues spring up, which are inspired and financed by the Communist party.

In the unions, the communists no longer disclose their identity as communists. They parade as progressives and liberals. Communist trade union leaders meet secretly with Party leaders and Committees. Before the public, communist trade union officials appear as trade union progressives. They vehemently deny that they are communists.

Communist party records have either been shipped to Moscow or removed to safe hiding places. Party funds are now deposited in the names of individuals and not in the name of the Communist party. Earl Browder's brother, William Browder, had under deposit at one time over a million dollars. The New York state organization of the Communist party deposited, in one year, half a million dollars in two banks, in the name of David Leeds, its treasurer, whose real name is David Amariglio.

Israel Amter, Chairman of the New York state organization, declared under oath, at a Rapp-Coudert Legislative Committee's hearing on subversive activities in New York and in the Public Schools, that the Communist party had destroyed all its records; but he could not explain how the Party could carry out its manifold, complex activities without records.

To determine who is or is not a member of the Communist party is practically impossible, for whatever membership records can be produced have been so cleverly drawn up and padded, as to give an entirely false picture of the organization. The system, instituted in 1939, has not been changed and is still in use.

The Communist party of the United States maintains its membership records through a clever control card system. There are no longer any membership cards in the hands of Party members by which they can certify membership in the Party. A control card is filled out, covering the member, which is sent to a secret address as soon as it is filled out, there to be kept safely hidden for use by the Party. Records of names in Party offices are padded with all kinds of names of prominent public officials, authors, scientists, movie stars, industrialists, heiresses, etc. When such records fall into the hands of the authorities, they are absolutely useless. The Communist party takes no chances. It has developed its own effective methods of controlling and directing its members. An organization of close to 100,000 members keeps the names of its members secret, yet it functions and has every one of the 100,000 members under perfect control. When an order is given, the Party membership reacts like one man—such is the marvel of the communist underground and organizational technique.

The communist underground is prepared for a major attack. It may be wounded but will not be destroyed by the forces which seek to eliminate it from American public life, just so long as the communist world superstructure, resting on Soviet power, continues to exist.

The Campaign Against Jan Valtin

In 1940, a tall, handsome, nervous young man established contact with a small anti-communist circle in New York, who dared to stand against the towering wave of pro-communist and pro-Soviet sentiment in the country. He had a story to tell and wanted their aid and advice. Looking at the hounded, frightened man, no one could foresee that a year later that man, Richard J. Krebs, writing under the pen name of Jan Valtin, would produce a fictionalized autobiography of his experiences as a communist waterfront agent that would sell over 700,000 copies.

The first news of Krebs' arrival in the United States appeared in the *Daily Worker* of May 22, 1938, in an article on the Staten Island spy nest, written by Lowell Wakefield. A true picture of Krebs accompanied the article, which dealt with Nazi spy activities in Staten Island as a backdrop for the case the *Daily Worker* was building up against Krebs. Actual proof of such a tie-up, however, was not presented. The *Daily Worker* presented the case as follows:

"Richard Krebs, ace operative of the Gestapo, the German Secret Service, has been twice seen in St. George and New Brighton, Staten Island, within the past week. Krebs, exposed in Paris as a Nazi spy, escaped from Antwerp and caught an English freighter, signing on as a seaman. The *Daily Worker* revealed that he jumped ship at Norfolk, Va., and for a time disappeared.

"Krebs' appearance in Staten Island adds weight to the charge that it is the clearing house for the Nazi spy ring. The Department of Justice has been notified. He is of medium build, speaks English fluently and is about thirty years old."

The communists and the OGPU were after Krebs' scalp. Krebs, however, succeeded in Europe in slipping out of their clutches and he did so in the United States also. When the OGPU had enticed him into one of its retreats on Staten Island for the purpose of liquidating him, the polite word which the OGPU and the communists use for murder, Valtin had the presence of mind to knock over an oil lamp, start a fire and escape in the resulting confusion. The *Daily Worker* story covered up the OGPU bungling and was printed in order to hide the fact that the OGPU also maintained headquarters on Staten Island and for the identical purposes that the Nazis did: to spy on shipping entering and leaving New York harbor, and to keep in secret radio communication with OGPU transmitting and receiving stations abroad.

Information was passed on to the Department of Justice about Krebs, in the hope that the F.B.I. would apprehend him, since he was illegally in the country and subject to deportation.

But the Krebs story had other and more important angles to it. The OGPU hoped, through Krebs, to get at one of the leading figures in the Hamburg OGPU set-up, Comrade Walter, who had gone over to the Nazis. Walter was the power who dominated the communist Hamburg waterfront set-up and was the leading figure in the international waterfront organization established by the Comintern and the Profintern. When the Nazis took over the communist works in Hamburg, they captured Walter. Disgusted with the failure of Stalin to live up to his promises to support a German uprising, Walter capitulated to a superior force, joined the Nazis and, as a high officer of the Gestapo, served them as he had served Moscow. Through Walter, the Nazis tracked down all OGPU activities in German ports, crushed whatever communist organization and influence remained on the waterfront, and were in a position to keep their eyes on communist and OGPU organization and activities in Germany and other parts of the world.

The orders to OGPU agents everywhere called for tracking down Walter and his agents and killing them on the spot. Valtin, who was merely a German activist and courier working for the OGPU-Profintern section on the waterfront, suddenly assumed stature in the eyes of the OGPU as an important associate of Walter. Valtin, to save his neck and that of his wife and child, had as a prisoner of the Nazis embraced Nazism and served the Gestapo just so he could escape and get out of Germany, but never had he played the role the communists assigned to him.

To get at Walter presented difficulties which even the OGPU could not surmount. To get Krebs was the next best thing. Many former agents of the OGPU, men of Krebs' stature in the organization, had been liquidated in Paris, Antwerp, Copenhagen, Oslo, New York and other cities. Paris and its suburbs accounted for most of the murders, for the Communist party of France, as part of the people's front, had sufficient influence to protect the murderers and to circumvent justice.

The OGPU hoped, after the signing of the Soviet-Nazi Pact, to get their hands on Walter, but their day of reckoning never came, for Walter was just one step ahead of the OGPU. The signing of the pact was a warning to him, for he knew just how the OGPU operated. He took the first opportunity to give himself up to the British. This time Walter got the work he liked in helping British Military and Naval intelligence track down both Nazis and Communists.

For two years after the Staten Island incident, the OGPU tried to track down Valtin. Whenever the trail got hot, Valtin moved, changing his name as he took up new quarters. From 251 W. Fifteenth St., he moved to 569 W. One Hundred Fiftieth St.; from there he took up several other residences and finally, just before his book appeared, he lived under the name of E. Holmberg at 124 W. Eighty-second Street.

Once among friends, fear left the hounded young man. He liked to talk about his adventures and exploits, coloring the dramatic incidents, giving them substance and interest. Listeners often tried to fathom the mind of a young man who boasted about deeds of violence and murder which frightened and disturbed the listener. What most listeners forgot was that Valtin reflected the thoughts and mood of the movement he had just left. Though he wanted to tell the shocking story of the National Socialism of Hitler and the Communism of Stalin, he could not stamp the past out of his mind, nor could he suddenly change and alter the psychological grooves that years of communist association had channeled through the sensitive cells of his brain.

When the book, *Out Of The Night,* was finished, the communists greeted it with a campaign of billingsgate and garbage rhetoric. They moved heaven and earth to kill the book and blacken the reputation of the author. They had influential people bring pressure upon the State Department, the F.B.I. and the Immigration Department to have Valtin arrested as a Nazi spy and for illegal entry into the country.

Valtin feared deportation. He took every legal step possible to prevent it. To prove his loyalty to the United States, he offered his services to Naval intelligence. When the war broke out he enlisted for active duty and saw action in the Pacific. Part of the money he realized from the book, he spent for a country estate, where he has taken every precaution to guard himself against the OGPU.

CHAPTER ELEVEN

LIQUIDATION

THERE is a quiet room on the third floor of the Comintern building. The sun shines through its large windows. The office is clean and sparingly furnished with a few desks, some files and a large steel cabinet closed by two massive steel doors that shut tight with a combination lock. An air of businesslike efficiency and decorum permeates the place. In charge is a short, neatly dressed man, who peers at you from behind thick lenses. He is Abram, head of the Comintern Control department, soft speaking, modest in manner, expressionless. One never knows when he is angry or pleased for, regardless of the circumstances, he always talks and looks the same. The Comintern shakes with long discussions and heated oratory. Abram does not participate, for he is closeted in his room, attending to business. And this little OGPU man, in addition to taking care of the routine matters of his office, such as providing credentials, instructions, money, advice and passports to the hundreds of Comintern agents that pass through his hands, keeps a tab on the army of Comintern renegades and enemies throughout the world. He knows what is going on in their circles in Berlin, Budapest, Rome, London, Canton, Shanghai, Seattle, San Francisco, Rio de Janeiro, Havana, and New York.

A group of Comintern agents were gathered in his office in 1928, waiting for their passports and money. A report came in concerning the treachery of a group of communists who had found themselves in disagreement with the Comintern. He calmly reported the incident to those present.

"Once comrades come in disagreement with the Comintern," he went on to say, "they are bound, if they persist in their opposition, regardless of how honest their motives may have been, to fall into the camp of our enemies. Once they do, they will find out that the Comintern does not forget—that it knows how to deal with traitors." No emotion, no anger, no special emphasis accompanied these words. A cold shudder went through the listeners, for in the monotony of his voice, in the evenness of his matter-of-fact expression, one felt the cold sharp edge of the dagger. His words embodied the realities of liquidation and served as a warning to his listeners, some of whom were outstanding leaders of Communist parties, to watch their steps.

The word liquidate, in communist semantics, embodies much more than its meaning implies. To communists, liquidation is the process of reducing organizations, movements and life itself to the eternal darkness of nothing. Involved is not the normal inevitable end of life in death, but the willed, forceful extermination of tangible living things. The revolutionary psychosis of the communist is embodied in the word, a psychosis which visualizes that beyond a certain stage progress can be achieved and mankind bettered only through violent upheavals and bloodletting on a grandiose scale. The most popular song in the Comintern, that of the German Communist party expressed this communist psychosis. When one thousand or more men and women, Orientals, Negroes, Europeans and Americans, of all colors and nationalities, from all corners of the earth, rose in the crown room of the Kremlin and sang lustily with clenched fists raised high, *"Blut muss giessen"* (blood must flow), one felt the power of world communism, for the Red legions marched hand in hand with death, building their tomorrow on the corpses of today and yesterday.

Liquidation is therefore an important word in the internal history of the communist movement. The record of the Comintern can be traced by a bloody line stretching from the Comintern building and the Kremlin all over the world like veins and arteries throughout the body. The red line indicates, on the chart of the communist world superstructure, the countless number of communists who have, since the day of communism's triumph, been sacrificed by the communist movement on the bloody altar of liquidation. Every method known to the art of premeditated murder—forceful drowning, strangulation, poisoning, slow torture, cremation, submersion in boiling lime and the smashing of brains—has been used in carrying out the edicts of liquidation. Liquidation is not only a European or oriental communist phenomenon, for the bloody red line shows that the communist movement of the United States has also played a part in making up the record.

The Poyntz Mystery

On December 18, 1937, the New York newspapers carried a strange and mysterious story. The personal attorney for Juliet Stuart Poyntz reported that she had been missing for seven months, that he did not know her whereabouts and that all efforts to locate her had failed. But why the story of her disappearance had been kept secret was not explained. The story revealed that seven months before, Juliet Stuart Poyntz left her room in the American Women's Hotel on West Fifty-seventh Street and never returned. Her belongings in the room were said to have been intact and undisturbed, indicating that nothing suspicious happened in the room itself. But why did not the hotel report the matter to the authorities? The answer to that question has also never been forthcoming.

The Communist party, when asked about Miss Poyntz' disappearance, denied that they knew anything about her. Charles Krumbein, the head of the New York district, emphatically told reporters that he knew absolutely no one by that name who ever belonged to the Party, though for years Poyntz had been closely associated with Krumbein in one faction in the Party. She had served for years with him as a member of the District Executive Committee of the Communist party. She had been a delegate to all conventions of the Communist party since 1926, and had also been a member of the Party's powerful Central Executive Committee. Miss Poyntz, up to the year 1934, held the distinction of being the Party's best woman speaker and propagandist. She was featured at important mass meetings and toured the country as a Party speaker and organizer. In addition, she had been nominated by the Communist party over and over again to run for important offices in election campaigns. When confronted with these facts, Krumbein reluctantly admitted that he recalled the Party had such a member, but that she must not have been important because he had failed to recall her or to remember what she did in the Party. For years, he assured his interrogators, she had dropped out of the Party altogether and had done absolutely nothing for the organization.

Krumbein was correct up to a point. Poyntz did drop out of the American Communist party in 1934, under circumstances which Krumbein knew but dared not disclose. She was one of many American communists who dropped out of the Party in that year to work as a spy for the OGPU. Once an American communist is assigned to the OGPU and receives his remuneration from the secret service branch of the Soviet government, he or she is immediately disconnected from the Communist party organization and its affairs. Only those American communists whose OGPU activities are tied in directly with the work of the Communist party and with the Communist International and the Profintern, continue their ties with the Communist party. They are, under pain of the severest consequences, ordered not to attend Communist party meetings and affairs nor to associate with their former friends in the Party.

Poyntz, who was very popular in the Party, suddenly dropped out of the organization, disappeared into the mysterious communist OGPU underworld of spying and counter-spying, plots and counter-plots.

The OGPU wanted her badly. She was typically American in lineage and appearance—attractive, college-bred, cultured, a good mixer, shrewd, alert, and above all, intelligent. She was one who could mingle in the highest circles without arousing suspicions. In addition, OGPU records in Moscow, dealing with her assignment to the most delicate and, in some aspects, very dangerous work, proved that she had been a socialist and trade union organizer before she joined the Party—a sincere, honest and devout Marxist who early broke with the reformist socialists and joined the communist movement. Her record in the communist movement, backed up by an enormous amount of activity and great personal sacrifice, proved her to be a dependable and courageous communist, and suitable for OGPU work.

After preliminary training and work with the OGPU, she received the important assignment to gather scientific information in the United States in the fields of chemistry and physics, which the OGPU considered of great importance to the industrial and military strength of Russia.

But events in Moscow, with which Poyntz had absolutely nothing to do, were destined to play havoc with Poyntz' mental equilibrium. In December, 1934, Stalin's friend, Kirov, boss of Leningrad and member of the powerful Politburo of the Russian Communist party, fell dead from an assassin's bullet. The assassination ushered in the mass purging of communists from Russia and other countries as well; the prominent ones were given trials and executed, the others were just shot and forgotten.

The OGPU also went through a drastic purge and reorganization. Orders were dispatched to all OGPU centers in foreign countries to pack up and proceed at once to Moscow. The American OGPU organization rushed back to Moscow. Miss Poyntz went along. What the American girl saw and experienced in Russia knocked the romance out of communism. She participated in the OGPU inquisitions. She saw how men and women with whom she had worked, men and women she knew were loyal to the Soviet Union and to Stalin, were sent to their doom. She went through a grilling herself, for once you are a member of the OGPU, you are looked upon as a Soviet citizen and not as a citizen of the land of your origin and citizenship. But the Russian communists were still afraid of the Americans. She safely passed the OGPU *smitchka* (cleansing) and returned to the U. S.

She had her orders, but could not carry them out. She spoke guardedly about her disillusionment. Just as soon as a communist of Poyntz' type, essentially honest in her convictions, becomes critical and is beset with doubts about the ultimate justice of the cause she serves, she acts as if the props had been taken from under her, like a lost and bewildered person.

The OGPU assigned selected individuals to contact her for the purpose of setting her straight, which meant putting her in a position where she would be at the mercy of the OGPU. But she procrastinated. She wanted to be let alone for some time—to think herself out of her dilemma before she took on OGPU or Party responsibilities again.

Rumors reached the OGPU that Poyntz was writing about her experiences. But when the OGPU confronted her with questions about what she intended to do, she gave evasive answers. To the question of whether she was going to write about her experiences, she answered in the negative, but intimated that perhaps she might give the matter consideration.

A meeting of the OGPU cell discussed a report on the status of Poyntz. The decision called for her liquidation as speedily as possible.

The decision made, three killers were assigned to carry out the liquidation. The three used another as a decoy, one who, though a member of the OGPU, was not included in the circle who made decisions and shouldered responsibility for the organization. Shachno Epstein, the associate editor of the Jewish daily paper *Freiheit,* was the man, an excellent choice, for he had been Miss Poyntz' lover before she joined the OGPU. Though a coward who cringed in the presence of danger, the OGPU nevertheless used him over and over again in dangerous situations, for his fear of that organization surmounted all other fears. When accosted by the killers, he almost collapsed, and when informed what was expected from him, he wanted to protest, to refuse. He could do neither. Orders were orders. He had to carry them out.

Shachno Epstein called up his former sweetheart saying he wanted to see her in order to talk over old times. They met at Columbus Circle and proceeded to walk through Central Park. Miss Poyntz welcomed the opportunity to talk to an old comrade she had loved.

She was excited, too worried and mixed up about her own affairs to notice the nervous, incoherent talk of her companion. Shachno took her by the arm and led her up a side path, where a large black limousine hugged the edge of the walk. When he reached the car, Shachno suddenly stopped. Two men jumped out, grabbed Miss Poyntz, shoved her into the car and sped away. Shachno stood motionless for a few moments, looking into space. Wiping his brow with his handkerchief, he turned and walked quickly out of the park.

At the next meeting of the OGPU cell, the order of business was a report on the Poyntz case. There was laughter and jubilation in the room, as the killers made their report.

One man reported: "The poor girl, I felt sorry for her. The way she pleaded in the car for her life—the comrades, she said, had her all wrong—she was tired, sick. When I said to her, 'Why are you writing a book—we know, we have pages from the manuscript'—she said it was a lie. 'I want to live. I promise I will not say or write a word against the Party or the OGPU. You can trust me, I have proved that time and again.'"

Then he reported how she cried. "She behaved awful, not at all like a communist. She was so afraid to die."

The other told a gory story—how they had driven her up through Westchester into Dutchess County to some woods not far from the Roosevelt estate—how the pleading, crying, frantic girl was killed and buried in a deep gulley. The body was covered with lime and dirt. On top were placed dead leaves and branches which the three killers trampled down with their feet. He ended his story: "Ah, she was too beautiful, comrades. Too bad we had to kill her."

Lore and Tresca

Ludwig Lore, veteran socialist, one of the founders of the Communist party of the United States, editor of the *Volkszeitung,* columnist for the New York *Post* on foreign affairs, radio commentator, brilliant lecturer and orator, got caught in the mesh of international intrigue and, though he badly wanted to do so, could not free himself. Lore had admired and cherished Poyntz for years; they had been inseparable in their political association in the Communist party until the C.I. called for Lore's expulsion from the Party. Communist loyalty proved stronger than personal feeling and regard for a dear friend. Poyntz denounced Lore and, by breaking with him, confirmed her loyalty to the Communist party and the Communist International. Lore knew all about the Poyntz affair, yet he dared not tell. The man spoke in whispers, as he told the gruesome story, afraid lest someone in his own home, hidden away, should overhear what he had to say.

In his German accent, he concluded: "Yes, comrade, something must be done. We cannot let them get away with it."

But Lore did nothing. His hands were tied for he, too, was a tool of the OGPU he hated.

His status differed from that of the OGPU agent, who served as a paid member of the organization and was under oath to carry out whatever orders were given him. Lore, when a communist, did what was expected of him. He collaborated with the OGPU and served them in whatever capacity possible. His work for the OGPU was a side line, his editorship of the *Volkszeitung,* his main work. He took his leadership in the Communist party seriously, and fought valiantly for his views and policies. He early championed the position of Trotsky against that of Zinoviev and Stalin. For such support, his ouster from the Party was a foregone conclusion. Outstanding leaders of the Party, who backed up Lore before, men like Foster and Browder who owed their rise to the top to Lore's support, denounced him in the most abusive terms and demanded and brought about his expulsion from the Party.

But before the American Communist party was permitted to expel Lore, orders came for Lore to proceed to Moscow to present his case to the Comintern. The OGPU had interceded on his behalf because of the valuable assistance he had given them in the United States. The Moscow leaders hoped that, with Lore in Moscow, they could get him to radically change his views and, in the event he did not, that then they could keep him indefinitely in Moscow, at least long enough to permit the Americans to take the *Volkszeitung* away from Lore and to disperse his following.

But Lore already knew too much about how the OGPU functioned to risk a trip to Moscow. Lore chose to remain in the United States and wisely refused to enter the lion's den.

Lore was the one and only independent communist in the United States. He refused to accept the monolithic concept of the Party. He disagreed with the communist concept of discipline, the strict, rigid, military discipline in which the decisions of the leaders must be obeyed and carried out, regardless of how the members feel about them. In his failure to divorce himself completely from democratic principles and traditions, Lore never quite attained stature as a Bolshevik.

Lore, the split personality, became so involved with the OGPU that in spite of his expulsion from the Communist party and the Comintern, he could not extricate himself from their clutches. The transformation of Lore, who was basically honest in his convictions, did not come on the moment of his expulsion. It took a long time, many years, during which he considered it an honor to serve the Soviet government with the result that, when he wanted to tear himself loose from the OGPU, he could not do so.

He fought the American communists and the German communist refugees in the United States, but never did he unload the information that he had about their tie-up with the OGPU. He understood that he had a moral obligation to do so, but hesitated on the brink of indecision.

Once he attempted suicide by slashing his wrists, in order to blot out a tortured existence based on an inner insoluble conflict tearing his idealistic soul apart between honesty and deceit, truth and falsehood, decision and indecision. To know the man was to know him as an essentially honest, principled person, with a great regard for humanity. Such a man, when he is unable to follow the dictates of his conscience, breaks down in moral fiber and loses his physical stability. To consider one's past a failure, the bloom of youth that scaled the heights of idealism and promised a future of inspirational achievment, dries up the sap of enthusiasm on which the tree of life thrives. The tragedy of Lore was that he got stuck in the midway house. He tried to serve God when he was serving the devil.

The murder of Poyntz, when she was groping her way out of the OGPU domination of her mind and soul, had a tremendous effect upon the harried, impressionable mind of Lore. Lore reached his Calvary. He died suddenly, mysteriously, without any previous premonition of illness.

Carlo Tresca, the Italian anarchist, differed from Lore in all respects except one. He, too, was essentially an idealist. But, unlike Lore, he was never troubled by a conscience. Reflecting in his jovial smile and very bearing the romantic gayety of the Italian, this passionate individualist's journalistic career as editor of *Il Martelle* covered a colorful and adventurous life. Carlo loved good wine, good Italian food, good friendship, fair women, deviltry and humanity. As a fighter, he knew no fear.

Carlo fought injustice from one end of the country to the other. He defied authority and went to jail. Yet he could hate bitterly and fight his enemies unscrupulously. He hated Mussolini, fought him and his attempt to establish a foothold among the Italian-Americans with every weapon at his command. He exposed the Duce and met his agents on the streets of New York in mortal combat.

"Let them dare hold demonstrations in New York. My boys know how to handle them."

His boys did. They were a band of Italian anarchist zealots, whose speed and precision with the stiletto, gun and blackjack baffled antagonists who outnumbered them ten to one.

Carlo Tresca, essentially a man of action, did whatever he did because he thought it was right. He was a sworn enemy of the state, holding that no institution is superior to the individual. He worked on behalf of common causes with every group in the radical movements from communists to socialists to Trotskyites, though he viewed with contempt the theories of the political Marxists. Yet this enemy of totalitarianism, out to destroy the political state, became involved with the ugliest form of the police state, the OGPU.

An affair with a communist sculptress, whose reputation was well established in the art world, brought Tresca in contact with the OGPU. Tresca often spoke about his intimacies with the sculptress with a twinkle in his eye, for he recognized the farcical Rabelaisian circumstances surrounding his life and adventures with a communist sculptress. Imagine a fanatical communist, who believes in everything the Communist party does, falling in love with one who despises the Communist party and sees in Soviet Russia a most brutal and oppressive dictatorship which denies individual liberty and rides roughshod over humanity. That was precisely what happened. But, at the time, Carlo was not the only man in her heart. Her wealthy husband was a communist zealot, who spent his money generously in support of her art and communism. And in addition she was having a love affair with Olgin, one of the top leaders of the Communist party in New York.

When Tresca entered the well-ordered and peaceful sanctuary of the sculptress' studio, he did not come like the gentle bull, Ferdinand, to sniff the odors of perfumed flowers. He came in like a snorting, rip-roaring bull, making life miserable for the diminutive Olgin, who was short, delicate, aesthetic. Tresca was tall, portly, swarthy, with an enticing laugh and a sardonic smile. He was the embodiment of gayety and verve. In the life of the sculptress one supplied the deficiency of the other and the husband supplied the cash. Both lived under the one studio roof with the sculptress. The husband came only on business.

In the morning, the breakfast table was set for three. The sculptress poured the coffee, Olgin stuck his nose into a *Daily Worker* or a *Freiheit,* Carlo gave the sculptress a squeeze and a compliment, shot a glance at Olgin and opened up with a remark: "When will the line change and the American Fuehrer Browder get the hook?" An argument generally started, in which Tresca blasted away at the communists, while Olgin, livid with rage, attempted to answer back. The sculptress tried to maintain a semblance of peace in the family.

The OGPU agents often visited the studio. Carlo met them and became enmeshed in their works. Even after his affair with the sculptress ended, Carlo maintained his OGPU contacts and used them for what he thought was of value to himself.

The outbreak of the Spanish Civil War in the summer of 1936 brought about an unforeseen development between the communists and the anarchists. They found themselves united in a common cause, fighting together against a common enemy.

Tresca worked hand-in-glove with the communists in the United States to bolster up the Republican cause by sending them money, supplies and men.

But before many months were over reports came in of communist attacks against the anarchists, of the arrest, imprisonment and assassination of outstanding anarchist leaders. Among some of those assassinated were Carlo's personal friends, friends of his anarchist days in Italy and in other European countries.

Carlo, incensed, launched into a bitter attack against the communist terror in Spain and the operations of OGPU and Comintern agents. He gathered the facts and publicized them. As I stated in another section, one of the most beloved leaders of the anarchists was slain in cold blood by Sormenti, alias Major Contreras. Tresca vowed to avenge the murder and make Contreras pay for it. Under such conditions, his relations with the OGPU were strained.

The news of Poyntz' disappearance stirred him to action. He personally conducted a wide investigation into the case. He obtained vital facts which indicated that he had clues upon which the authorities could proceed to smash open the case and solve the mystery. He went to the District Attorney's office. The communists noted the incident in their newspapers. They hinted that they would take reprisals against a traitor who went to the police. In communist circles there was open talk that Tresca would pay with his life for his treachery. Tresca steeled his boys for a fight. He let the Communist party know that if anything happened to him, Earl Browder, its General Secretary, would be killed in retaliation. The Party leaders knew enough not to monkey with Carlo's boys. The matter quieted down. The Poyntz case remained unsolved, but Carlo continued to hammer away at the communists, blaming them for her disappearance.

Two years later, the Office of War Information, towards the end of 1942, took steps to organize the Italian-American Victory Council. The Council, to the communists, was of such great importance that orders were transmitted to the Communist party to do everything possible to capture it. But Carlo Tresca stood in their way. The Mazzini Society, the leading organization of Italian anti-fascists, due to Tresca's pressure, had previously, in principle, adopted the policy of excluding all totalitarian and fascist elements from the society. Now Tresca, who successfully had excluded them from the Mazzini Society, took up the fight to exclude both the Italian ex-fascists in America and the communists from the OWI Italian-American Victory Council.

Officials of the Office of War Information fought for their inclusion, but in Tresca's opposition they had an obstacle which they found difficult to overcome, for Tresca hurled damaging accusations, backed up by facts, against the communists and the ex-fascists parading as the champions of democracy.

The communist world superstructure was determined to capture the Italian-American Victory Council, for not only Italy was involved but the European continent, and Stalin's ambitions for world expansion. Moscow rounded up Italian communist agents by the hundreds and shipped them to the United States. The Comintern Rep demanded that the American Communist party settle its score with Tresca on the Poyntz case and on all other matters. The OGPU claimed he had abused their confidence and had treacherously double-crossed them.

Tresca personally told me, shortly before he was murdered, that he knew that the OGPU assassin Sormenti, alias Carlos Contreras, alias Vittorio Vidali, was in New York. He suspected that Sormenti had something to do with the Poyntz case. In this, however, he was mistaken. But he boldly bragged that before Sormenti could get him, his boys would get Sormenti. A few weeks before he was murdered, Tresca confided to friends that he had seen Sormenti in New York and cryptically remarked: "Where he is I smell murder. I wonder who will be the next victim."

On January 11, 1943, Tresca and a friend left his office at ninety-six Fifth Avenue, using the Fifteenth Street door of the corner building, as was his custom. A man stepped up behind them and fired four shots from an automatic pistol. One bullet lodged in Tresca's back, another in his head, and two shots went wild. The assassin jumped into a waiting sedan and escaped in the darkness.

The assassination of Tresca can be attributed to two factors:

He dared to buck the OGPU on the Poyntz case.

He tried to foil the plans of Stalin in Italy by keeping the communists out of the Italian-American Victory Council.

The communists had already stated in regard to Tresca: "It's a work of protection, of elimination from society, of beings who are hateful to themselves and to society."

The time for elimination had come. Charles Pappas bought the murder car. Who was Pappas? The police never found out or did not care to find out. Was he the Pappas, the strong-arm man of the Communist Furrier's Union goon squad? Unsolved murders are a communist technique. The assassins of the Communist world superstructure have committed them on all continents and in all countries. They are masters in the creation of unsolved mysteries.

Murder Across the Border

Stalin feared Trotsky, above all other men in Russia. Trotsky was the one man he wanted out of the way, but he could not summon enough courage to liquidate the one man in Russia who, intellectually, towered above all living Russian communists. The man who organized the military might of Bolshevik Russia out of ragged barefoot men into a disciplined Red Army, Stalin hated and despised for strictly personal reasons. Trotsky had early exposed him as a knave, had upbraided him for violating a military order, which resulted in blunders on the field of battle that proved very costly to the Soviets; he had, in arguments at sessions of the political committee of the Russian Communist party, castigated Stalin and made him look like an ignoramus. But Lenin's loyalty to Stalin saved Stalin for the great historical role he was to play in shaping the destiny of Russia and in a large measure that of all mankind. Trotsky, the towering intellectual giant, brilliant organizer and military genius, suffered from one deficiency, a deficiency that cost him his head—he was a poor politician in the Tammany Hall tradition. Trotsky did not understand how to work with the dirt and manure of politics; Stalin, a master in this field, won out.

Step by step, Stalin reduced Trotsky to impotency, by making powerful alliances against him with the object of ousting him from his positions of power in the government, the Russian Communist party and the Comintern. Then he had Trotsky expelled from the Communist party and exiled from Russia.

The deportation of Trotsky out of Russia involved a sinister plan, the hounding of Trotsky and his death at the hands of an assassin. Every Party in the Comintern had to declare itself on the Trotsky issue and pledge itself to carry out the plan. Trotsky knew about the plan and made desperate efforts to get out of Europe to America, hoping eventually to get into the United States, from where he believed he could carry on his fight against Stalin with some degree of safety.

The American Communist party, following Trotsky's deportation to Turkey in 1929, in secret sessions at the Comintern gave its solemn pledge to do everything in its power to prevent Trotsky from setting foot on the soil of continental America and, in the event he did, to stop him as speedily as possible from carrying on his counter-revolutionary activities against the Soviet Union.

In 1936, Stalin staged the first major purge trials against Zinoviev and others, linking them up to the Trotskyite counter-revolutionary center. This trial initiated a witch hunt against Trotskyites in the Soviet Union and throughout the communist world superstructure, unequalled in the annals of history.

Following the execution of the Trotskyites, the *Pravda,* on February 2, called for a war against Trotsky and Trotskyism all over the world on the grounds that "Trotskyism is the enemy of the whole of mankind."

The campaign against Trotskyism reached such proportions that every section of the movement, including the unions and the front organizations, were drawn into it. Party members, from Browder, the

General Secretary, down to the humblest rank-and-filer had to declare themselves publicly against Trotsky. A joint statement was issued, signed by Browder and Foster, as an answer to Professor Dewey and others who wanted to conduct an impartial and fair hearing at which Trotsky, then living in Mexico, could defend himself, to the effect that: "If Trotsky wants his day in court, let him go to Moscow."

On the twenty-fourth of May, 1940, a band of twenty-five Mexican communist guerrillas, disguised as policemen and led by the famous Mexican painter, David Alfaro Siqueiros, surprised the police assigned to guard Trotsky's house and tied them up. Two squads of gunmen, armed with machine guns, riddled Trotsky's bedroom with cross fire. Trotsky and his wife, who quickly dropped to the floor and crouched in an extreme corner of the room, escaped unhurt. The gang of murderers kidnapped Trotsky's personal guard, the American, Robert Sheldon Harte, and took him to a cabin in the mountains where the two Mexican OGPU killers, the Arenal brothers, killed him.

After this attack, Trotsky's Coyoacan house was converted into a fortress. The guard was increased and heavily armed. Bullet-proof doors and windows were installed. Bullet-proof watchtowers dominated the view of the patio and surrounding territory. Electric switches automatically controlled the double-steel shell doors, which replaced the two wooden entrance doors. A redoubt was built with bomb-proof ceilings and floors. Yet the OGPU finally succeeded in penetrating these defenses of concrete and steel without firing a single shot.

After the first failure of the attempt to assassinate Trotsky, a conference took place in New York between Communist party leaders and the OGPU. Three members of the American party were dispatched to Mexico to see to it that Stalin's vengeance be satisfied with the corpse of Trotsky. The three who went on the mission of death were important communist leaders: Jack Stachel, organization secretary of the Party, Alexander Bittleman, the Party's theoretician, and George Mink.

Mink was Chief of Police for the Communist party's "Cheka" in Barcelona, Spain, in 1937. He organized and executed the assassination of many outstanding anti-communist Spanish Loyalist leaders. In Barcelona, he lived under the name of Alfred Herz at the Continental Hotel.

Stachel is a master of intrigue and experienced in the fine art of bribery. Bittleman, known as *The Rabbi,* can be trusted to give the right explanation for the darkest deeds. Together with Mink, they went, under instructions from the Communist party of the United States, to Mexico City to carry out Stalin's orders that his arch enemy, Trotsky, be silenced.

The assassination of Trotsky, in the late afternoon of August 20, 1940, by Frank Jacson, who plunged a miner's sharp pick into his brain, was no ordinary job. It took months of preparation, the expenditure of lots of money and the collective plotting of the best brains of the OGPU and the Communist parties of the United States and Mexico.

Jacson's part in the Trotsky assassination plot began in 1937, three years before Trotsky was killed. It was decided then that in the event the plan of the Mexican Communist party missed fire, the Jacson plan designed by the Communist party of the United States would be used. The web of intrigue was cleverly spun to satisfy the whims of the best mystery thrillers. A former Trotskyite and friend of Louis Budenz, a girl by the name of Ruby Weill, joined the Communist party at the same time Budenz did. Under specific instructions from Stachel, she was ordered to maintain friendly relations with her former Trotskyite friends. Among her friends was a lonely girl who was much respected and trusted by the Trotskyites, Sylvia Ageloff. Carrying out Communist party instructions, Ruby Weill cultivated Sylvia, and the two became very intimate. What Sylvia did not know was that in the United States the OGPU was receiving elaborate reports on her personal life and character. These were transmitted to Paris where Jacson was stationed, and used by the OGPU to prepare Jacson for meeting Sylvia. The OGPU knew what the girl's ideas were, what she craved, all about her desire for attention and romance and how best to win her confidence. Sylvia was a simple girl, idealistic, extremely honest, and devoted to the Trotsky cause.

The OGPU plans worked out well, for in 1938, Ruby Weill, the OGPU tool in the murder plot, left, together with Sylvia Ageloff, the dupe in the plot, for Paris. In Paris, Ruby met an OGPU agent, and instructions were given to her to introduce Sylvia to the handsome Jacson, who in Paris went under the name of Jacques Mornard.

Ruby built up her friend Jacques Mornard as a wonderful man, just the man for Sylvia to meet. In the early part of July, 1938, Sylvia was introduced to Jacson. Ruby Weill never knew why the Party wanted Sylvia to meet Jacson, and believed all the time that the Party wanted to get some inside information about the Trotsky movement in the United States and Europe.

Jacson swept the poor Sylvia off her feet, and later the two left together for Mexico. Jacson used the passport of a Canadian, Tony Babich, a member of the Communist International Brigade in Spain, who had been shot in the Spanish Civil War. Sylvia Ageloff, trusting the man she loved, happy and no longer lonely, opened the door to the Trotsky home for the OGPU assassin.

In preparing the second attempt, no stone was left unturned to make sure that the deed would be thorough and successful, even to the point of having Jacson make his get-away. But in the event he was apprehended, a story was worked out for him, in which Jacson's past was so constructed as to be most befuddling to the authorities.

There is no need of going into the gruesome details. Trotsky's assassination came at the time it did because Trotsky was preparing to defend himself against the Communist party of Mexico, which had brought libel charges against him. If that trial had ever taken place, it would have astounded the world with its revelations. Trotsky had been gathering material for years and he had in his possession hundreds of affidavits proving conclusively that the OGPU controlled and directed, not only affairs of the Communist party of Mexico, but of all other countries as well. These affidavits were voluntarily supplied to Trotsky by ex-communist leaders. I had supplied Trotsky with such an affidavit, concerning the operations of the OGPU, the Comintern and the Communist party of the United States.

Stalin was afraid of these revelations. In addition, moves were on foot to have Trotsky appear before the Dies Committee. The State Department, however, refused to grant Trotsky a visa for that purpose. Arrangements were being made to have J. B. Mathews, Chief Investigator of the Committee, fly to Mexico to take a deposition from Trotsky. The OGPU knew of these matters. Stalin had too big a stake in the United States to take a chance on Trotsky's jeopardizing it.

Trotsky was also engaged in writing the life of Stalin. Stalin is essentially a vain man with a strong inferiority complex; the cold oriental indifference which he assumes is a pose adopted to hide that fact. Stalin used his power and authority to build up a picture of himself which is not borne out by facts. Workers in biographical research, who were foolish enough to stick to the facts and tell the truth, paid dearly for their foolishness. *Official* Stalin biographies have built up an altogether distorted and highly colored picture of the man. Trotsky knew the facts and was in a position to expose the man Stalin in his proper proportions. Kremlin gossip revealed that

Stalin, when informed that Trotsky was writing his biography, lost his temper and flew into a rage against the American and Mexican Communist parties and the OGPU chiefs in the United States and Mexico. The OGPU chiefs in the room trembled, for they understood one could not trifle with Stalin when he was in such a mood. All these factors made certain that Stalin's final reckoning with Trotsky had to come soon.

Trotsky's assassin, Jacson, feigned insanity when arrested. Confined to a hospital, he beat up his nurses and hurled vulgar curse words at them. He tore the pajamas off his body and ripped the bed sheets and pillow cases to shreds. When the Mexican authorities succeeded in getting a personal history from him, a check-up proved that every detail of his story, his origin, his family, the source of his funds, his political affiliations, everything he said from beginning to end, were false. Jacson, who is still incarcerated in a Mexican prison, remains a man of mystery. But the man of mystery has friends with powerful influence and lots of money. Protected by a pro-Stalinist lawyer, an expensive legal campaign is conducted on his behalf. In prison, Jacson lives like a privileged potentate. His bank account is kept amply supplied with pesos. He enjoys the luxuries which an ordinary murderer cannot hope to enjoy—good food, plenty of wine and the company of charming women in his cell.

The assassination of Trotsky removed from the historical scene the man who, with Lenin, was responsible, above all others, for the Bolshevik revolution and for the organization of the modern world communist movement. The inheritor of their work, a man who had little to do with it, Stalin, remains the undisputed leader of world communism. The ghosts of his victims stalk through Kremlin corridors, but that does not matter to him, for the world recognizes his power and pays tribute to it.

CHAPTER TWELVE

BROWDER, THE PATRIOT

THE Communist party of the United States is many things rolled into one, like a Chinese egg-roll with innumerable fillings.

It is a communist political party, a labor party, a farmer-labor party, a trade union center, an educational institution, a benevolent society, an atheistic society, a religious society, a sports organization, a military organization, a youth organization, a women's organization, about twenty different national societies, a propaganda agency operating on an international scale, an espionage organization, a counterfeiting organization, an agency of a foreign power, an organization of gangsters and assassins, a smugglers' organization, an organization for the distribution of movies, a drama and dance organization, a cooperative organization, a summer camp organization, an organization that runs night clubs and hotels, etc. etc., and finally, a government of revolutionary conspirators within a government, part of a gigantic world organization—the communist world superstructure.

Because the Communist party of the United States is part of a world government, events far removed from the United States vitally affect the destiny of the Party. The signing of the Soviet-Nazi Pact overnight turned the line of the Party in an opposite direction. Little did the American communist leaders dream that the Hess flight to England in 1941, his capture by the British, and his denunciation by the Fuehrer would affect so quickly American communist policy. Uncle Joe was too much engrossed in the ups and downs of the fortunes of war to take a chance on bungling matters by keeping his American contingent informed up to the last minute on the international situation.

It took the American communists a few days to wake up to the reality and formulate the new line. They did not hesitate to call for immediate aid to Russia, but did not know what attitude to take towards Great Britain. Britain was, therefore, ignored. When the National Committee met on June 28, 1941, six days afterwards, the communists, for the first time, knew what their stand should be towards Britain. The Party had its cue from Moscow that the people of Great Britain must be linked up with the people of the Soviet Union. In opening the sessions of the National Committee, which were held in the greatest secrecy, Foster said: "Our central demand, therefore, is that the United States government give all aid to the Soviet and British peoples now fighting against Hitler."

The Party soon got on the right track. The transmission belt organizations, unions and other organizations, which the Communist party controlled, changed in rapid succession from a militant attitude in favor of peace with a victorious Nazi Germany, to one conforming with the new Party line. Like horses in a four-ring circus, they turned when Moscow cracked the whip.

The communists, who had done everything in their power to wreck the defense program and to sabotage the sending of supplies to Great Britain, suddenly found themselves on the side of the "Imperialist War Mongers." The war became a peoples' war. The communists deserted the isolationist camp, abandoned their Nazi and Fascist allies in the North and South American continents, and loudly demanded that Uncle Sam immediately declare war against Germany. The slogan, "The Yanks are not Coming," was turned into the slogan, "The Yanks are Coming." The communists waved American flags. Browder outdid the superpatriots as he paraded his spread-eagle communists up and down the length and breadth of the land, while an army of approving politicians, public servants, and fellow travelers, in low and high places, paid tribute to the Communist party.

The Communist party leadership emerged from the cellar. The communists no longer hid their faces. Only Stachel, the organizer and leader of the communist underground, remained in hiding and made no public appearance.

Stalin played international politics well. He dug up Litvinov once more from the dusty archives of the foreign office, dressed him up in diplomatic robes and, as an expression of goodwill to the President of the United States and to the American people, sent the popular man, as Ambassador, to the United States. The American people were not informed that Litvinov was just window dressing for the man who really ruled the Russian Embassy in Washington—Oumansky, the slick OGPU clerk of the Profintern and Comintern who became a powerful figure in the OGPU apparatus and a personal confidential agent of Stalin. Litvinov made his American debut like a prize angus bull bedecked with ribbons just before he enters the slaughterhouse. He delivered long and scholarly speeches, which had to be approved first by Oumansky. Before many months were up he was given, in addition to his Washington duties, charge of the unimportant Russian Embassy at Havana, Cuba. Litvinov knew when he got that assignment that he was through. The country hailed his farewell speech on the eve of his departure to the Soviet Union and oblivion.

The removal of Litvinov was looked upon by the country as an incident of no importance. Our politicians and diplomats failed to understand that Litvinov's appointment as Ambassador to the United States served to appease the Americans and to lull them into a sense of security concerning the intentions of Soviet foreign policy in the war. Stalin was against trusting his policies to a man with a British-Western orientation and a love for America.

Now that Germany invaded Russia, orders were issued to the Party membership to support the Defense Program. The communists complained that defense production lagged, that it must be speeded up. They called upon the unions to permit the workers to work longer hours and demanded that they adopt no-strike pledges.

Browder sprung the gun by being the first public figure to come out in favor of a fourth term for the President.

John L. Lewis fared badly because he persisted in his isolationist position. The communists marked him as labor's enemy No. 1. Hillman, whom they had criticized for going along with the Roosevelt program before Russia was attacked, became the Big Bertha they used in the C.I.O. campaign against John L. Lewis. With Hillman and New Deal support, the communists tore the C.I.O. wide open and mobilized the forces against Lewis. The mighty Tsar of the coal diggers learned the simple truth of who uses whom and discovered to his amazement that the communists had used him and not he the communists, for they sent him reeling off the lofty pedestal of the C.I.O. and put his associate, Philip Murray, in as president, surrounded by a staff of communist and loyal fellow travelers.

The communists found themselves in an unusual position. They had already tasted the fruits of respectability during the years when they supported the New Deal. The Soviet-Nazi Pact had brought that era to an end. Now they were more than respectable. They were catered to. The days of the leather jackets and the bobbed hair, of demonstrations, hunger marches and riots were things of the past. The communists dressed and played their part. Doors opened that had been shut to them. They were determined to take full advantage of their new opportunities. The attack on Pearl Harbor and the entrance of the United States into the war as an ally of Russia gave the communists opportunities to spread out in all directions.

They were accepted as the representatives of the country's heroic ally, Soviet Russia, and treated accordingly. The communist organization prospered. The Communist party membership rose by leaps and bounds. The organization received and spent close to ten million dollars a year.

An expansive American vista opened up for the Communist party. The "Grand Plan" for the United States, developed with the advice and cooperation of Ambassador Oumansky and an army of communist agents who were sent into the United States, had for its main objectives the following: 1. The glorification of the Soviet Union and support of its war policies and objectives; 2. The demand for the immediate opening up of a second front, which served two different Russian purposes and not the general interests of the war. The communists realized that a hasty, unprepared attack on the Nazis in the European theatre would have the immediate effect of reducing Nazi pressure against the Red Army on the Eastern Front and would involve the United States and Great Britain in a long-drawn-out struggle, during which the Soviet Union would have a respite in which to recuperate and build up her strength—thus the Soviets would become stronger as her allies became weaker. Second, the demand for the second front gave the communists in the United States an opportunity to maintain an independent and critical position on the American government by contrasting the fighting spirit of the Red Army, which they claimed bore the brunt of the struggle against Nazism, to the procrastination of the Americans; 3. The augmenting of espionage activities in the diplomatic, industrial and scientific fields.

Oumansky stressed that, since Russia desired to take advantage of the favorable pro-Soviet sentiment in the United States, it might be necessary for the Communist party of the United States to voluntarily disband itself as a political Party, thus lulling Roosevelt and the country into the belief that the Soviets no longer interfered in the internal affairs of the country. "Now is the time," Oumansky claimed, "to unite all the progressives, the New Dealers. the farmer-laborites, the C.I.O., the communists and communist sympathizers into a political organization, not necessarily a political Party, in order to establish a broad base for communist operations."

As the story is unfolded, the reader will realize that the communists have gone far in realizing the objectives enumerated above. Methodically and according to plan, they worked themselves into the Federal government and into many important local and state government agencies as well.

Leonard Mins, the son of a charter member of the American Communist party, employed by the OGPU, Moscow-educated, wormed his way into the War and State Departments as an expert on Far Eastern affairs and attended highly secret meetings with top-ranking generals at which American strategy on Far Eastern affairs was mapped out. What went on behind closed doors at these meetings became the property of the American Communist party and the OGPU. The advice which Mins gave as an expert was angled to serve the interests of the Soviet Union and the Chinese communists.

Through the Institute for Pacific Relations, headed by E. C. Carter, the communists bored their way into the State Department. Within the walls of the State Department building, a highly successful campaign got under way to shift American Far Eastern policy to a pro-Soviet line. Communists and their agents kept the Party and the OGPU informed about what was going on in the department. Copies were made of important documents, many of which disappeared from the files to find themselves either in the hands of the OGPU, or in those of the communist key man on Far Eastern matters, the prosperous and wealthy Christmas and greeting card manufacturer, Philip J. Jaffe, who supports the communist movement out of his own pocket to the extent of $5,000 a year. To give an idea of the ramifications of Jaffe the communist agent on Far Eastern affairs, a partial list of his activities will suffice. He was a prominent figure in the organization, set up by the communists in 1933, known as the Friends of the Chinese People. Under the alias of J. W. Philips he edited its paper called *China Today* and, also, later acted as its contributing editor under his legitimate name. Jaffe served as a member of the controlling executive committee of the China Aid Council, whose secretary was William E. Dodd Jr., son of the former U. S. Ambassador to Germany. Mrs. James Roosevelt was its honorary chairman. Jaffe served as Managing Editor of *Amerasia*. With Jaffe, on the editorial Board of *Amerasia*, was Vanderbilt Field, a scion of a wealthy family and, at the time, Chairman of the American Institute of Pacific Relations. Jaffe also served as a member of the National Board of the American Committee for non-participation in Japanese aggression. He was one of those prominent in launching the China Aid Information Exchange. He served on the Executive Committee of the American Round Table on India, and held down the position of National Director and member of the National Board of the American Council on Soviet Relations.

During the raids on the offices of *Amerasia,* the agents of the F.B.I. found more than 100 files of highly confidential government documents and a large, well-equipped photo-copying department used in copying valuable documents that had to be returned safely to their files in government departments.

Through *Amerasia,* contacts were established with members of Naval Intelligence, and the State Department was flooded with information and research material to influence American Far Eastern policy.

What happened in the State Department happened in practically every important government department and war agency. The communists and their army of fellow travelers and paid traitors entrenched themselves in the government. They have kept their communist ties a secret. To ferret them out and remove them will not be easy.

The communists applied to the United States their famous Chinese tactic. The communist world superstructure built up its power in China by applying the policy of close collaboration with the Kuomintang and Chiang Kai-shek, while at the same time doing everything in its power to undermine the Kuomintang and bring about the downfall of the Generalissimo. While the communists participated as loyal defenders of the Nationalist Government, they built up their own independent forces, including a large military force, with the support of Soviet money and arms. By collaborating with the Chinese government of Chiang, they were in a position to hamper the government from taking action against the treacherous action of the communists.

Many Chinese liberals, politicians, scholars, business men, and people representing all the social stratas in China, motivated by a desire to build up a united and free China, fell for the tactic of the communists in China. They welcomed the communists as collaborators in a movement for building up a great united Chinese nation. But when the Japanese attacked, the communists had already succeeded in dividing the Chinese nation into two parts, one Kuomintang, the other communists, even though the communists had participated in the affairs of the Nationalist Government and had pledged themselves to build up the Chinese Republic.

The Chinese communist tactic of deceit and duplicity is just another phase of the problem, already discussed, of who uses whom when the communists unite or collaborate with non-communist forces.

The American communists put an American twist to the Chinese tactic. They were in a position to do so because they paraded as super-patriots and the vanguard of the New Deal. The New Deal served as the American Kuomintang for the communists, but with one important exception. The ruling group in the Kuomintang around General-issimo Chiang Kai-shek had back of them years of training in the dark shadows of oriental politics. They understood the crafty maneuvers of the communists. The New Deal crowd were like innocent babes, who had a distorted and altogether wrong conception of communists and communist politics. The pro-Soviet New Deal crowd, from President Roosevelt down to the little bureaucrats holding unimportant desk jobs, accepted the communists as honest idealists who were concerned, primarily, with the interests of the common people. They accepted them as natural allies against the reactionary tories. They underestimated the ties of the American communists with Moscow, and actually believed that in a clash of interests between the United States and the Soviet Union, the American communists would remain loyal to their own country. Communism was to them a progressive philosophy, and the communist economic and political system, with New Deal modifications, far superior to American capitalism and the democratic government of the United States. The communists laughed up their sleeves at such naïveté.

Before the details of the grand plan for a new political realignment were worked out, Stalin surprised the world by announcing, in the summer of 1943, the dissolution of the Comintern. But with Stalin's pronouncement, the Comintern did not cease to function. The communist world superstructure did not evaporate into nothingness. Stalin just hid the fact that the intricate international machinery of the Communist International had been reorganized on a more effective basis to meet the conditions created by the war and the problems that would necessarily follow after the war had been ended. The new conditions confronting Moscow in Western Europe and in the United States, since the crushing of Nazi Germany, prove that Stalin had the foresight to recognize years earlier that changes in the functions and status of the Comintern were imperative. As the communist world superstructure took over one country after another, the open maintenance of the Comintern as an international organization of communist parties became incongruous. Communist heads of European governments, communist members of government cabinets, prime ministers, security, and justice department ministers, ambassadors, etc., could not very well come together publicly at sessions of the Comintern and plot the conquest of the world for communism. In anticipation of such a situation, after Roosevelt and Churchill had agreed to give Stalin wide spheres of influence, other means had to be found by which the affairs of the Comintern could be conducted, clandestinely but, nevertheless, effectively. Right before the outbreak of the war and in the years before the dissolution of the Comintern, Congresses of the Communist International and meetings of the Comintern Executive with communist leaders from all over the world were held secretly and not in Moscow. Communist party leaders went to Moscow for direct conferences with Stalin and other Russians, the nature of which were seldom disclosed. The Comintern conferences and executive meetings were held in France, Belgium, England and Holland, during national conventions of the communist parties of those countries or at a time when International Conferences for peace or other purposes were being held in which the communists participated.

Whenever the Communist party of France held a national convention, the communist parties of all other countries sent delegates to greet the Convention. There they gathered together in secret with the Russian representatives of the Comintern Executive and carried out the business of the Comintern. That procedure was continued after the dissolution of the Comintern. The British Communist party held an Empire Congress of the communist parties of the British Empire in 1947, to which the communist parties of other countries sent fraternal delegates. Some went openly to the British Congress, like William Z. Foster, who represented the Communist party of the United States; others, including a number of American communists, attended the gatherings secretly. Thus, in London took place the first post-war world congress of the dissolved Communist International at which decisions of vital importance to the peace and security of the world were made.

It has already been shown how Russian Ambassador Oumansky conferred with the leaders of the American Communist party on matters which strictly concerned American internal political affairs. Every Soviet Embassy serves as an agency of the so-called dissolved

Communist International. In countries where the communists are in control, the Russian Embassies direct the affairs of the communist puppet rulers and the communist parties. The will of Moscow must be obeyed and the line of the communist world superstructure carried out. The international affairs of the communist world organization are also supervised by special diplomatic missions, by Red Army occupation forces, by agents of the NKVD and by Representatives from Moscow cloaked with plenipotentiary powers, as were the C.I. Reps during the days when the Comintern functioned openly.

The Red Army staff sent to Japan to represent the Soviet government in the occupation of Japan, instead of assisting General MacArthur in solving the difficult problems of occupation, worked overtime in building up and directing the affairs of the communist movement of Japan. With the Red Army staff came an army of trained communist organizers and propagandists. With their assistance and generous grants of money, the Japanese communists made strong inroads in the trade unions and, in a short time, blossomed out into a strong and influential pro-Soviet force that is working to undermine the work of MacArthur and to arouse in the Japanese people hatred of the Americans.

The communist world superstructure, in recent years, has grown to tremendous proportions. A survey of world communism indicates how its organization has expanded into a gigantic international machine, wielding state power in many countries and poised for the capture of power, in the immediate future, in many more. Communists wield state power in the following countries: Poland, Hungary, Czechoslovakia, Rumania, Albania, Yugoslavia, Bulgaria, half of China, Russian-occupied Korea, Russian-occupied Germany and Austria, and the annexed territories of Lithuania, Latvia and Estonia. In all these countries the communists who wield state power have been prominent in the affairs of the Comintern.

As a world trade union power, the communist world superstructure dominates the world's trade union scene. The bulk of the world's organized workers are today in the grip of the communists, in Europe, Asia, Latin-America, Africa, and to a lesser extent in the United States.

Finally—and the significance of this is overlooked—the communist world superstructure represents an imposing force in the United Nations through representatives from Communist Russia, her satellite powers, and those politicians of other countries who have a pro-Soviet orientation. The communists have kept their eyes on the United Nations organization and have seen to it that its technical staff is honeycombed with their people.

Communism, as a world movement, has undergone far-reaching and profound changes. The Soviet Union is an orbit of world power, a pole of attraction, rivaling that of the United States. In an atomic age of conflicting ideologies, a Comintern restricted to the limits of communist parties, representing minorities in their respective countries, could no longer adequately serve as the international organization for the communist world superstructure. It had to be abandoned in its old form for a new clandestine form of international organization, involving new relationships between the communist parties and communist state powers of various countries, necessarily entailing new methods of work and a wide outlook. Behind the dissolution of the Comintern has been built up a new international structure with Moscow still firmly strapped in the saddle as it was in the Comintern. The new world communist structure is more real, more powerful, more effective and infinitely more dangerous. It rests upon a foundation of millions of members. It has absorbed and exercises hegemony over 10,000,000 square miles of the world's territory with a population of over 300,000,000, and it has close to ten million soldiers under arms.

The "dissolved" Comintern's red line stretches clear across Europe, encircles thirteen countries, passes through Moscow into Asia, divides China and Korea into half, and threatens to bleed over the whole of Asia. In Europe the "dissolved" Comintern is poised to seize power in France and Italy in an effort to add more territory and almost 100,000,000 additional people to its rule, and about three million soldiers to its military juggernaut.

The formation of the Cominform—the Communist Information Bureau—following a secret conference held in Poland at an unspecified date during the month of September, 1947, was interpreted as a move to openly re-establish the Comintern. Represented were the communist parties of Yugoslavia, Italy, the Soviet Union, France, Rumania, Czechoslovakia, Bulgaria, Poland and Hungary. The Soviet Union sent Andrei A. Zhdanov, next to Stalin the most powerful figure in the Russian Communist party. Following the conference, the office of the Cominform was opened in Belgrade, the capital of communist Yugoslavia.

The declaration issued by the conference directed its fire against the United States government in support of the Soviet Union. It declared, "On the one side is the policy of the Union of Soviet Social-ist Republics and democratic countries, directed towards the under-mining of imperialism and strengthening democracy, on the other side is the policy of the United States and England, directed towards strengthening imperialism and strangling democracy."

The American communists hailed the formation of the Comin-form as "anti-Wall Street, not anti-U.S." Subsequently, the commu-nist parties of the United States and of the Latin-American countries have officially turned down the invitation of the Italian communist leader Luigi Longo that they adhere to the Belgrade alliance. The European communists look upon the formation of the Cominform as an alliance and not as a revival of the so-called defunct Communist International. Luis Carlos Prestes, on behalf of all the communist parties on the American continent, declared: "We welcome with satisfaction the gigantic work of the European communists, and Warsaw conference. But we do not see at the moment any necessity of taking part in the Belgrade organization."

The organization of the Cominform is a step in the mobilization of the forces on the European continent for a consolidation of com-munist power in the Soviet puppet states, and for the mobilization of both military and mass resistance to the United States. Its immediate purpose is to counteract E.R.P., its ultimate aim the preparation of the European people for a war against the United States.

The new organization did not replace the Comintern. That organ-ization still functions secretly. When the French Communist party's Central Committee displeased Moscow, its leaders traveled to Moscow and not to Belgrade to be reprimanded. Thorez and Duclos got their specific orders at secret meetings of the Comintern in Moscow and the strikes and disorders in France followed. The same thing hap-pened to the leaders of the Italian Communist party, and in Italy, Comintern directives were responsible for the instigation by the communists of nationwide strikes, riots and political disorders.

The formation of the Cominform is a branch of the Comintern. It represents the reconstitution of the Western European Bureau of the Comintern originally functioning from Berlin and, during the Hitler era, from Copenhagen, Denmark.

The "dissolution" of the Comintern, together with the approach-ing presidential elections of 1944, brought about a change in the policy of the Communist party, along the lines laid down by Ambas-sador Oumansky. Earl Browder, pardoned by President Roosevelt, after having served part of his sentence for passport forgery, ushered in the new line and was held personally responsible for it, even though he had little to do in initiating the policy.

In fact, for a brief period following his release from prison, his return to the leadership of the American Communist party remained in doubt. He informed a reporter of the New York *Times* that he did not intend to resume his duties as General Secretary of the Communist party and highly commended the work of Robert Minor, his successor. Browder, much against his wishes, prepared to take on the duties of an OGPU and Comintern agent. But he got the surprise of his life when Moscow, in 1942, recalled him from a brief retirement and reinstated him as the communist figurehead in the United States.

Who is this man, American-born, from Kansas, who held the post of General Secretary of the Party longer than any other man? Browder held the post for fourteen years before he was made the scapegoat of a change in Comintern policy and ousted from his job and expelled from the Party.

Browder's career in the communist movement covered a period of twenty-five years. He induced Foster to join the Communist party and, for many years, acted as his page boy. He worked as an OGPU operative in China and in other countries, and as an agent of the Comintern and the Red International of Trade Unions. His sister, Mary Browder, an expert office technician, became an OGPU agent and held a confidential post in the OGPU bureau for deciphering codes. Stalin saved Browder's neck and his life for the debacle he made in China, where, as an OGPU agent and Comintern representative, his stupidity wrecked the OGPU's headquarters and a Comintern center for revolutionary propaganda and organization, which cost the Russians millions of dollars to promote. Piatnitzky, before the Comintern Executive, demanded that he be punished. Stalin rebuked Piatnitzky and rewarded the quaking Browder by giving him the leadership of the American party. An oriental politician follows strange patterns in building up a machine of faithful, dependent followers.

Browder married, during one of his trips to Russia, a powerful figure in the OGPU organization—a woman who, during the early stages of the revolution, sat as supreme judge of a revolutionary tribunal that meted out death sentences to so-called counter-revolutionists and opponents of the Bolshevik party. When Browder met her, she was assigned by the OGPU to watch over the affairs of the Lenin

University and to ferret out anti-Bolshevik elements that might have crept into the student body. Browder's Russian wife, the narrow, strait-laced communist, imbued with communist objectivity, thought little of taking human life. She traveled to the United States under the assumed name of a communist from Boston who had been deported from the United States, and assumed that name as her own legitimate name upon arrival in the United States. The State Department and Immigration files concerning the case of Edith Berkman have mysteriously disappeared. Due to the apparent disinclination of the New Deal administration to proceed against Mrs. Browder, she has been allowed to remain in the United States, even though she entered the country illegally and, for years, engaged in the most confidential work of the American Communist party among the foreign-born.

Browder cut an unusual figure in the Communist party. In the early years he wielded little influence; whatever standing he enjoyed was by virtue of the fact that he voiced the opinions of Foster. The indefatigable worker and scribe who labored twenty hours out of every twenty-four for the Communist party never developed independent opinions. He always digested and voiced the opinions of the Russian Comintern leaders, copying their line of reasoning, their modes of expression and the phrases they used. He typified the bigoted, fanatical zealot, loyal to the Comintern and to his chief, William Z. Foster. During a factional fight in the Party, he plotted the assassination of Jay Lovestone. Only the presence of Lovestone's personal spies in the Foster group prevented the murder plot from materializing.

Upon Browder's shoulders fell the task of carrying out the orders of the "dissolved" Comintern, to engineer the fake dissolution of the Communist party of the United States. On January 11, 1944, the National Committee of the Communist party unanimously recommended (as Browder expressed it): "In the interest of national unity and to enable the communists to function most effectively in the changed political conditions and to make still greater contribution towards winning the war and securing a durable peace, that the American communists should renounce the aim of partisan advancement and the Party form of organization."

The proposal to "dissolve" the Communist party was, in turn, unanimously adopted by delegates to State and District Conventions, which elected delegates to a national convention of the Communist party, held on May 20-22, which also unanimously adopted the resolution.

Such unanimity in the American Communist party over such a vital decision is impossible without a mandate to the Party from the Comintern or Stalin.

When Browder rose at the convention and jubilantly declared: "I hereby move that the Communist party of America be and hereby is dissolved," he carried in his pocket the "pochat" of the Comintern to introduce such a motion which Gerhart Eisler and a special representative of the Comintern had worked out with him, including details on how the dissolution was to be carried out. More important, Browder, in spite of his assumed air of honest sincerity, knew at the time that only the name of the Party would be changed, that the communist superstructure in the United States, an organization representing much more than a political Party engaging in election campaigns, would be kept intact and even strengthened.

The convention came at a time when Stalin gathered in the fruits of Roosevelt's appeasement policy. Roosevelt gave Stalin much more than he hoped for. In return, Stalin gave Roosevelt nothing but a worthless declaration that the Comintern had been dissolved. Stalin was interested in bolstering up Roosevelt's appeasement policy by organizing around the appeasement policy a political force which would resist any attempt on the part of the United States to end the Roosevelt policy.

The Teheran Conference, at which Roosevelt agreed to a partition of the world, extremely favorable to communist aggression and, in utter disregard of the principles laid down in the Atlantic Charter, opened up new vistas for the communist world superstructure. The communists geared themselves to capture the world, preferably without a violent struggle, by tieing the United States to communist destiny in maintaining and expanding the policy of Teheran.

Browder set the tone when, speaking for the liquidation of the American Communist party, he declared:

"Everyone in America who wants to exclude one or another group or category from such national unity, on any grounds not entirely based on the consideration of winning the war, is an enemy of Teheran. . . . We must fight against and defeat all the enemies of Teheran; we must unite all who support Teheran by word and deed."

The communists sought to pull the wool over the eyes of the

American people by promising, through their new political coalition, to end the outbreak of great class struggles within the nation, following the termination of the war. They declared: "We shall already now begin to lay the foundations for post-war national unity, so that the disturbing influence may be checked and, if possible, eliminated."

The communists, to accomplish their insidious purposes, repudiated socialism, became the proponents of class peace, advocates of law and order and the champions of the free enterprise system of capitalism.

The communists, with such a program backed up by Russian support and millions of dollars, hoped to so corrupt the political channels of American life that the country would fall an easy victim to their machinations, thereby helping them to use American prestige and power on behalf of the aggressive ambitions of Red Imperialism.

The Communist party proved, when it was a small revolutionary organization which refused to compromise its communist program, that it could organize farmer labor parties, united fronts, and draw many influential Americans into its orbit. During the days when the Communist party did not hide its program, it had in its employ a United States Senator from the State of Minnesota, Ernest Lundeen. An airplane accident terminated his services on the Military Affairs Committee of the United States Senate at a time when the United States was building up its military potential in preparation for the war against Nazi Germany. From 1926 until the time of his death, he was a secret agent of the Communist party. In 1926, 1927 and 1928, then still a Congressman, he met often with the General Secretary of the Communist party and with its Secretariat at Communist party headquarters to plot out his political and other activities, and to get his orders and directions from the Party. Under the new set-up the communists, no longer appearing as communists, hoped to outdo themselves in drawing into their nefarious plots men high in political, business and cultural affairs.

The Communist party had, as a Communist party, traveled far in the United States. In October, 1942, Mr. Sumner Welles, Under Secretary of State, gave Browder, the head of the Communist party, a statement on American policy towards China, which urged that the unity of the communist and nationalist forces in China should be achieved by conciliation. The Under Secretary of State of the world's most powerful state had to show consideration to a minority fifth column political Party, because that Party had tremendous influence in Washington and powerful, influential friends, agents and followers of the Party line right in the State Department. With the new policy, the communists knew they could go much further, that they could infiltrate every department of our government and, from the inside, so tear down the foundations of American institutions that actual seizure of the government would become an easy matter.

During the convention, in May, 1944, at which the communists were supposed to commit hara-kiri, there took place a secret underground continental conference of the American sections of the "dissolved Comintern." Delegates were present from the communist parties of Canada, Mexico and the Central and South American countries, to work out a hemisphere program. At its "death-bed" the United States communist war horse was very much alive, and the existence of the communist world superstructure very much in evidence. At the convention, addressing the visitors of the Latin-American countries, Browder, speaking about the blind and greedy and short-sighted imperialist forces of the United States, gave the keynote to the secret deliberations that were to follow when he shouted: "Their day is finished, although they will not depart from the historical scene until they are licked and removed."

The convention dissolving the Communist party adopted all resolutions unanimously. All the present leaders of the American Communist party participated in the fraud, together with Browder, and the representatives of the "dissolved" Communist International. Out of the convention, the communist organization emerged under a new name—"The Communist Political Association." The Communist party members switched to the Communist Political Association. The headquarters of the Communist party on Thirteenth Street became the headquarters of the new organization. The newspapers, magazines, subsidiary organizations, all followed suit—a typographical change in the mast-head, a new sign on the door, and the transformation was completed. Uncle Sam Browder and his Spread Eagle Communists were set to whoop it up for American capitalism, as vociferously as they had been set up to denounce the American system and call for its destruction.

The insidious work of the communists did not change. They carried on as before in the government, in the unions, in the churches, in the schools and in the armed forces. When the war ended, the communists were so well entrenched in the armed forces, had their men so strategically placed in the public relations set-up of the Army and to a lesser extent in the Navy, and had so many of their people in key positions on the Army's publications serving the G.I.'s, that they set the tune for the G.I.'s. But the hand of fate intervened.

In February, 1945, a sick American president conferred at Yalta with Marshal Stalin, who pressed him for more and more concessions. In April Roosevelt died. In May, the war in Europe ended. Stalin realized that the policy of appeasement died when Roosevelt died.

Communist policy suddenly changed from friendship for America to hostility. Browder, caught in the change, was forced much against his will to become the victim in the Communist party whc had to shoulder the blame for the liquidation of the Communist party, in order to dramatize the reversal in policy towards America.

An agreement reached with Browder, to which he consented, called for his elimination from the Communist party. In return he was permitted to visit the Soviet Union, where he obtained a contract for the printing and distribution of Soviet books in the United States and for the translation and sale of American books in the Soviet Union. Through this pro-Soviet business activity, Browder assumes the air of objectivity on Soviet-American issues, writing, lecturing and speaking over the radio in defense of the Party line and policies of the Soviet Union. But it is interesting to note that he recently registered with the State Department as a foreign agent representing the Soviet Union.

Those elements of the communist movement who influence public opinion found themselves under terrific pressure to conform to the new line. Strict adherence to the communist philosophy and the Party line was demanded from writers, actors, lecturers and fellow travelers in this category. When the communist writer, Albert Maltz, insisted that a writer must follow his art and conscientiously depict the truth and the reality as he sees it, regardless of the Party line, that a writer cannot be forced to write as the decisions of the Party direct him to, he was pounced upon by the leaders of the Party and denounced in the *Daily Worker* and in the *New Masses*. Communist writers and the wielders of the left pen were forced to declare themselves one by one on the Maltz issue. In the end Maltz, in tears, retracted his words and condemned himself for his failure to understand the duties and obligations of a communist writer and artist.

The Maltz incident showed how a witch hunt is carried out against followers who refuse to follow the Party line. The campaign against Browder subjected every leader of the Communist party to severe inquisition to test his loyalty to the Party and the international line of the communist world superstructure. The meeting of the National Committee of the Party held on June 18-20, 1945, brought together a frightened, panicky group of men and women who had to be careful of each word they uttered.

Browder, the man who pictured himself as the coming Stalin of America, found the pedestal on which he stood kicked from under him by the man who put him there. Two men took his place, one old in the Party organization, the other new. Foster, who wanted the job of General Secretary of the Party, did not get it. Stalin used him once more to serve his purposes, but refused to give him the place that he coveted. Instead, Eugene Dennis, a young man relatively new in the upper circles of the Party, got the post.

Who is Dennis? In 1905, in the city of Seattle, a son was born to Francis Xavier Waldron and Nora C. Vieg, who were married in April, 1904. Dennis' mother died when he was quite young and his father died when Dennis was twenty-four years old, at the North State Hospital for the Insane at Sedro Woolley, Washington.

The young man Waldron first made his appearance as a communist in the Young Communist League of Seattle in the year 1928, where he was noted for his high-strung explosive temperament, his incessant bickering, his fanatical intolerance and an uncontrollable ambition for communist leadership.

Dennis graduated from high school in Seattle in 1923, and attended the University of Washington for a period of five months, from September, 1925, to February, 1926.

When he registered for selective service, Dennis claimed he was born in August, 1904, four months after the marriage of his parents. He refrained from registering for selective service until February 16, 1942, for it was not until February, 1942, that persons born in August, 1904, were exempt from military service. In his selective service records, Dennis claimed that he had married Regina Karasick in 1928, a Communist party member and the former wife of William Schneiderman, the District Organizer of the California section of the Communist party. The divorce suits of William vs. Regina Schneiderman were not filed until November, 1936. Whether Dennis actually married Regina Schneiderman in 1928 or in 1936 is not disclosed.

In 1928, Dennis claimed he was a seaman. He disappeared from the Seattle organization and, in 1929, showed up as an obstreperous trouble-maker in California in the Los Angeles city organization of the Communist party. 1930 finds Waldron active in the riots of California's unemployed. Arrested on a charge of inciting to riot and released on $500 bail, he jumped his bail by failing to appear in court.

In December, 1930, Eugene Dennis, under the name of Paul Walsh, made application for a passport, claiming he was born in Austin, Pa., but the birth records in Austin proved that no individual by the name of Paul Walsh was born in the town in the year stated.

Dennis, attached to the OGPU and assigned to take up special studies in the Lenin University, obtained the passport by perjury and forgery in order to visit Germany, France, Italy and England. He spent most of his time, however, in the Soviet Union, where he received training as an OGPU operative and Comintern agent. His education in the Soviet Union completed, Dennis next showed up, in December, 1932, at the American consulate in Johannesburg, South Africa, to have his passport renewed. In 1934 Dennis was in Shanghai, China, carrying on confidential work for the OGPU.

1935 found Dennis back in Moscow, where on January the 8 of that year he received a service passport permitting him to return to the United States, from Elbridge Dubrow, the American Vice Consul at Moscow.

Upon his return to the United States, Dennis was given the position of State Secretary of the Communist party of Wisconsin, a position he held from 1935 to 1937. During that period he helped to wreck the Socialist party in Milwaukee; enrolled the ablest socialist organizers into the ranks of the Communist party and won over to communism the widow of Victor L. Berger, the first socialist congressman in the United States and a bitter opponent of communism. Meta Berger became a secret member of the Party. The fortune her late husband built up was lavishly spent to support the Communist party and its activities. Dennis' good work in Wisconsin, the fact that he was trained in the Lenin University and had worked as an agent of the OGPU, brought him into the top leadership of the Communist party. In 1940 Dennis' name assumed importance in the communist press and the Party membership recognized him as one of the powerful figures in the Party's inner circle.

The OGPU agent, born Francis Eugene Waldron, who secured

false passports and operated under the aliases of Gene Dennis, Paul Eugene Walsh, Francis Xavier Waldron Jr., and Milton, a communist globe traveler and spy, now heads the Communist party of the United States. In his selection for the top honors of American communism is seen the pattern of the leadership in the communist world superstructure. In Europe, China, Latin America, wherever communist parties are at work, the Party machine is entrusted to men and women who have been tried and tested in the field of OGPU espionage and Comintern revolutionary conspiracy. The Eugene Dennis of today may become the saber-rattling Moscow gauleiter acting as the President-dictator of a Communist America tomorrow.

INDEX